TOO STRONG FOR FANTASY

MARCIA DAVENPORT

TOO
STRONG
FOR
FANTASY

UNIVERSITY OF PITTSBURGH PRESS
Pittsburgh and London

Published by the University of Pittsburgh Press, Pittsburgh, Pa. 15260
Copyright © 1967, Marcia Davenport
Published by arrangement with Charles Scribner's Sons, New York
All rights reserved
Manufactured in the United States of America

Library of Congress Cataloging-in-Publication Data

Davenport, Marcia, 1903-
    Too strong for fantasy / Marcia Davenport.
        p.   cm.
    Originally published: New York : Scribner, 1967.
    Includes index.
    ISBN 0-8229-3834-0 (cl). — ISBN 0-8229-5907-0 (pb)
    1. Davenport, Marcia, 1903- —Biography. 2. Novelists,
American—20th century—Biography. I. Title.
PS3507.A66515Z47   1992
813' . 52—dc20
    [B]   92-53723
                                                                                      CIP

J. M.

IN MEMORIAM

List of Illustrations

TOO STRONG FOR FANTASY

. . . It was a theme

For reason, much too strong for fantasy . . .

DONNE—*The Dream*

☙[C H A P T E R O N E]❧

A BOOK of the kind I am about to complete—much of it has been written in fragments for years past—can only take form in the late span of one's life, when detachment and a sense of humor temper an undue preoccupation with oneself, and give a point of view unobscured by illusions and passions which belonged to an earlier time. It is too late to change anything, but never too late to weigh and to learn. My life has comprised relationships, interests, associations, and occupations almost impossible to synthesize in a single personality. I was born in June. People I know who ascribe to the zodiac anything more than fortuity say with complacency, "A typical Gemini." Very well, if they wish it so. I have not believed this the reason for the plurality, far beyond duality, of elements in my character and my life.

When I contemplate these elements: persons, activities, places, tastes, events, I am quite bewildered at their divergency. I am a metropolitan person, born on Manhattan Island and rooted in it, who nonetheless has lived as much in Europe as here and catlike, am no sooner out than I want to be in. I am dependent for well-being upon the beauty of ancient architecture in its natural setting of the European continent, but I live in the increasing hideousness of New York, loathing every change and resisting surrender to the ugly present, but unable to pull up stakes and move away. My attachments have always been as much to places as to persons, though the men and women who have been the central forces of my life are of permanent stature and identity, which I know from having been destined to survive them.

I always meant to be a writer from my earliest recall, and like all such people I lived from infancy in the world of stories and books, most of them fantasy. When I began to outgrow fantasy history seized me by the throat and has held on ever since. History is inseparable from place and politics and political men and so this has proved in my experience. I was born into music through my mother, Alma Gluck, and while fortunately I had no talent as a potential performer, the soundest part of my education was saturation in music so thorough as to give me professional relation to it. New York, they say, is not America, but with my husband I was active at the core of a history-making Presidential campaign. As an American I had no innate tie to Central Europe but I was immersed in the life and fate of Czechoslovakia for many years and only left my second home there in the cataclysmic days of March, 1948. I am not a countrywoman but I have run a working farm in Vermont, and owned for fifteen years a place in Italy where I grew extraordinary roses, fruit, vegetables, and other garden delights about which I cared intensely. Yet one day I gave it up. I cannot live contentedly without a cat or away from a large body of water which I must be able to see from my windows. I am miserable if I have to remain more than six months at a time in the same country, but I have lived for nearly forty years in the same apartment in New York and written all of my too few books in it. I am not gregarious but I like to entertain, and this continues when my circle has narrowed to a few good friends whose interests I share and they mine—different interests unrelated each to the others. Mostly I am alone. I do not like it but it is the inevitable consequence of a life based on the writing of books—the redundant lonely art— no matter how far at times I have diverged from that art to do other things or, alas, to do nothing at all. I am charged with nervous energy and I am also bone-lazy.

[4]

The latter might be the reason why this book has remained so long unfinished and also a certain work of fiction which I began years ago. There is some truth in this and some virtue in facing the truth. But it is even truer that I was obstructed by political circumstances from access to what I needed to know, perhaps more exactly to see and to feel, before I could approach what Somerset Maugham termed the summing-up, in my own experience or in fiction. The barrier was finally raised when in the spring of 1965 I returned to Prague for the only time since I had left it in shattering circumstances seventeen years before. The return was harrowing, as I had expected, and in general I learned little that I did not already know. But nothing can substitute for primary personal experience. I went back to a major source of my life's motivation and thus of much of the work that has flowed from it; and finding the source dry, the magic gone, the invocation silenced, I shut the door for the last time and came away. But not to futility or frustration.

Now I can assemble this book, in a mood and from a point of view and by a plan different from anything I have written before. I say 'assemble' because much of its content has long been written. I expected when I came to finish the manuscript that I would put the segments and fragments in chronological sequence, inserting in their apposite places additions and transitions and excerpts from notes, letters, diaries, and other material. Basically that is my plan. But I feel the plan will be improved if it is flexible, if I step out of it if I wish, to pause and look about and give to the whole a sense of place equal to the senses of time and of persons. Place has always been of primary importance to me. My most productive associations as a writer have been fundamentally with places. Each such place has entered early into my attachments and necessities, has remained for major spans of my life an increasing force, and has been the medium in which my books had their origins and their growth, after which I returned to New York to write them. At the last, each place has come full circle, its function fulfilled and its hold on me slackened so that there has been a termination to my dependence and my attachment. There have been relatively few such places because nobody could live long enough to go through very many saturation-cycles of place such as I have described. The only one which has not come to the end of its cycle is New York. I am still here. I do not know how long I shall remain here. My reasons for remaining are neither sentimental nor mundane. New York is now a moloch about which nobody could be sentimental, and the life of a metropolis neither asks nor gives much to a solitary woman of my age except the company of her surviving friends. I suppose I am reluctant to cut the tie because I have done all my work in New York and I still know it to be the best place in the world to work. I hope I have a few books left in me and I would not risk the mistake of thinking I could write them anywhere else.

Disposing thus of place and its importance to me I look back across the years and know of course that the real substance of my life, of all lives, is the men and women with and through whom I have lived. It is said that a novelist should have no personal history to write because his life's story is already in his novels. If that is true, then I have left a number of novels unwritten. I have never deliberately written an autobiographical novel. I wrote one novel which traced certain figments of my own life but otherwise I have peopled my books with creatures of my imagination, draping their acts and their characters on rudiments of reality and setting them in actuality of time and place. Just as I have sought never to repeat the scheme or scope or locale of any book, but to make each one a total departure from its predecessors, so I have also never felt impelled to make myself a fictive character in a novel. This has its limitations as my much-beloved editor and friend Maxwell Perkins used to point out to me. I believe it was his aim to guide me towards overcoming my deep-laid resistance to writing autobiographical fiction, knowing that

I was cutting myself off from the richest vein of material mined by all major novelists. But Max died in 1947, when I was forty-four years old, and though I have wished to fulfill the aims of which he believed me capable I have remained unable or unwilling to weave fiction out of my own identity. I have said that if I should ever come to such writing it would not be fiction, and apparently the time is now.

But I have not come to this conclusion easily or even voluntarily. It has forced itself upon me. I have been writing novels for over thirty years, never without toil and trouble, but with a measure of accomplishment. I have been reading novels all my life. I suppose there is not much I do not know about novels and novelists, their lives, and their problems. I read the work of contemporary novelists who are decades younger than me and I am aware of the forces which shape the fiction of what is drearily and redundantly called our time. Yet I too am a contemporary person because I am alive and active in my way in the world which I still inhabit. But I cannot and will not shuck off the values and tenets of my generation, born at the beginning of this century. One of these tenets is a suitable reticence about oneself and the men and women who are and have been the complement of one's life. This reticence of course brings a writer into conflict with the basic law of literature—to write about what he knows best. All good novels are about believable people who are the creatures of the author's imagination which in turn has used for its raw material every man, woman, and child the author ever knew; also many he never knew or only imagined he knew. His fictitious creatures grow from composites of prototypes whose design more or less intentionally mingles real traits of character and personality with imaginary ones and should result in the creatures' developing identities and wills and motives and acts of their own. Sometimes, though, the novelist uses real prototypes admittedly and recognizably and if he is a genius like Tolstoy or Balzac he may write a classic. It does not follow thereafter that he is not a problem to himself and to those with whom his life is involved. I am afraid the novelist can't win.

But rather than concede defeat in a combat with myself I have for a long time been judging the two opponents—the reticence and the novelist's necessity—from the position of the referee who has to resolve the fight and declare one party the winner if only by the other's default. I have not asked for anything so dramatic as a knockout. I was prepared to be satisfied if I could get a decision. And the decision appears to be that the necessity is about to win over the reticence—but not in the form of fiction. For the first time I find that I cannot bend the men and women I have known to the shapes and purposes of my imagination. They are too strong. Their fibre is inviolable. They will not consent to be fragmented or illusively reproduced for use in montages, their characters dismembered and redistributed among my creations, their acts changed in motive and timing to fit my designs. They want their own way. They keep their identities intact, though most of them are dead. So I am going to give the people of my lifetime their heads, writing what I have to write about them; and since the result will not be fiction, I shall be among the characters.

But even though it must be my place in the schema as the one fixed element which all the meteoric ones touched in their sweep, I do not think of myself as the centre of this account. In my mind that is not my place or my function in relation to those with and through whom I have lived. Rather theirs is the generative and the motive power, I the artifact that they wrought. I am not fatuously disclaiming whatever I myself have been able to accomplish by a combination of aptitude, incentive, and hard work; but those would have availed me nothing had I not been placed where I was, and when, and in the relations I bore to those who gave my life its form, its range, its color, and its meaning. When novelists turn to personal reminiscence they often risk failure. I believe this is because a novelist is, or ought to be, a kind of sieve through which the raw materials—persons, emotions, scenes, events—of his experience are pressed to become the basis of a soufflé whose seasoning and leavening are supplied by his imagination and his invention, his gift for story-telling. Autobiography has little relation to this and therefore the personal writings of novelists are apt to be dull. I do not want to write an uninteresting book, which I might do if I considered myself the central character.

So I begin with my mother, Alma Gluck. She was and she has remained since her death twenty-nine years ago the strongest and most permanent force in my life. The world I first knew is still vivid to me in the reflection of her personality. It was a small, slow-paced world and it seems more real to me than many of the changes which have taken place since. Horse-cars in New York are not beyond my memory, nor hansom cabs, nor motor taxicabs when they were a novelty, their passengers apprehensive or thrilled by the adventure. My first memory of a taxicab is one in which I rode away from Mendelssohn Hall with my mother after she had sung a recital there—and today, almost sixty years later, I still encounter people who remember that recital or its counterparts vividly, though naturally not in the same way I do.

I always sat in the front of the centre box when my mother sang and whether legitimately or not, I felt suspended as though in a special pocket of air apart from the rest of the audience, enthralled with worship and pride. Afterwards there was the greenroom reception upon whose fringe I waited impatient to have my mother to myself again, and finally that magic-carpet ride in the taxicab, or presently her own motor, filled to bursting with flowers and my beautiful mother in the midst of them, her face bent over a pink rose. Her favorite rose was the Killarney, which seems to have vanished in the evolution of some hybrid; but my mother was scarcely known to the public before her preference for Killarney roses caused them to fill the spaces—to me, enchanted—which she occupied.

What a radiant creature she was! My earliest memories are of a simpler, less dazzling person, and my later ones follow the emergence of a character which attained stoic magnificence at the end. But her first triumphs have so authentic a romance and are so integral in my mind with the due rewards of the hard work which was her ideal that my tangible reminders of those days are inexpressibly dear. Her clothes when she sang; the daring, sparkling style for which she was known; her coronet of brown braids; her invariable long white kid gloves and the fans she carried and held unopened in her hands; these are all widely remembered. But only I have an old-fashioned yellowed white satin box full of French kid gloves, brittle with age and still faintly fragrant, and another pretty box containing battered and splintered fans. And only I know the reasons for those elegances which became her cachet. She had the great, heavy hands of the artist, especially the musician; and in her youth (for she was little more than a girl at the time of which I write) she thought her hands ugly and was ashamed of them. She wore the gloves to hide them and carried the fans to teach herself to hold her hands gracefully and still.

But when she was singing, intent on the perfection she exacted of herself, she forgot vanity and its accoutrements and those strong gloved hands clenched and twisted the closed fan, crushing like matchwood its sticks of ivory or sandalwood or tortoiseshell. She never knew she was doing that, she was the least destructive of people, and afterwards she would look ruefully at the fan with eyes full of consternation. Admirers sent her all sorts of fans, and Althea Jewell, her dearest friend and constant companion, used to slip the finest ones away to safety, putting plain paper ones with wooden sticks in their places.

Our clearest early memories as we grope through time and

space are the tactile impressions made upon our senses—the caressing parent, the purring cat, the taste of the fruit we loved or the egg we loathed, the scent of our mother's hair, the sight of a Christmas tree. Some remember only stringency, but that too takes the form of a harsh voice, shivering cold, dry bread, broken shoes which hurt the feet. In the light of deliberate intention to go as far back as I can and trace my earliest sensory impressions I find that they revolve entirely around my mother. Their tangible form, in which they are still real to me, is not primarily of myself as a young child, centre of my own consciousness; but of my mother, warm, demonstratively loving; delicious to touch, to smell, to look at and above all, to listen to; and on the periphery of this myself, distinctly an accessory to her, the central identity, but nevertheless included and present in a way that few children would be. I loved the role, I was (I realize now) intensely proud of it and my possessiveness about it is a living emotion to this day.

The facts behind it are simple: my mother took her first singing-lesson when I was two years old, when she had never had a servant in whose charge to leave me, and so she kept me with her. Thus I remember a couch in a corner of Maestro Buzzi-Peccia's studio where I was propped with a doll while my mother took her lessons. And so I remember the speed with which she must have learned Italian, for in one infantile moment I had never heard a word of it and in the next it seemed as if I had never heard anything else. I was in Como with my mother because her teacher had gone there for the summer, and she followed in order not to interrupt her lessons, and was speaking Italian as if it were the only language she knew.

It was the same wherever we went, and when I was five years old we had been in Switzerland and Paris and Germany and my mother was speaking French and German too without hesitation. That seemed perfectly natural to me and to the extent of a small child's vocabulary I followed suit. From the retrospective view we sum up such impressions and memories and make conclusions about them; but I smile now at the difference between the evolved fact that my mother's linguistic gifts equalled her musical ones, and the interior, personal facts that she was lovely and gay and cosy and young; that she worked hard at the fundamentals of making herself into a serious, very distinguished artist, the while she made all my clothes and pasted our handkerchiefs on the looking-glass to dry overnight, and counted her sous and centimes anxiously before ordering our food. I remember, therefore, the sound of her lessons, the sound of her laugh, the sound of her exquisite speaking voice in a relaxed flow of many languages; the excursion-boats and funiculars that we rode upon, the terrifying Simplon Tunnel (just opened at the time of which I am writing), the chicken—greatest of treats—that she bought for me to eat after renouncing something else in order that I might have it. And all this, before her transformation into the personality whom the world knew, is the stuff of which my mind and my instincts were formed, impalpably in infancy and probably too rigidly in later life: the concept of life as work, the compulsion to pursue that work at all costs or without counting the cost which when the accounts are rendered must be paid unprotestingly and in full. But my rigidity, as my mother herself warned me, has proved a grave limitation while she, more flexible, warmer, wittier, wiser, remains the better model of the example she set me. Yet she too acknowledged defeat in some instances where life challenged her. So though I think her disappointments and defeats in no way her fault, I cannot claim for her a perfection that she did not possess, although much of what she was seemed to me at the time to be perfection, and in the expression of her art, it really was.

Her origins and her early life are variations on a familiar theme, so often re-told, so much the flesh and blood of New York, that it has become an American legend. Both my parents were part of the tidal wave of emigration from the Russian Pale and Eastern Europe which in a generation swept a million people, fleeing persecutions, pogroms, and conscriptions, onto the shores of Manhattan Island. My father's parents came early; they were married in New York and he was born there in 1872. But my mother was born in Rumania in 1884, during the long toll of years which marked the slow hegira of her family from southern Russia across the Prut through Bessarabia, on towards the Promised Land. Her mother was old when my mother was born, a woman of about forty-nine, who had had six much older children and buried three of them; a fantastic woman about whom there was something forbidding and mysterious which nobody knows to this day. Nobody can ever know now.

My grandmother was a hunchback, bent so double that when I was a child of eleven I stood taller than she. She died at about that time, already very old, and as she never learned a word of English nor spoke any other language in common with me, I had no way of communicating with her. She was born about 1835, where and in what circumstances I do not know. More than any closed book in the whole span of my imagination, I should like to have been able to read that one. There were stories—more probably legends—about her which suggest her having believed herself to be a person of unaccountable importance. It seems strange that her family found a husband for her, crippled from birth according to one tale, or in infancy according to another. Certainly the husband was no catch, but what man could have been in the exigencies of that miserable life? All I know about this grandfather, all anybody knows, is that he started the move to America which he never lived to see; that he got as far as Iasi (or Jassy) in Rumania, where he earned a precarious living as a trader owning a horse and cart; that he was obsessed with music and singing and opera; and that that obsession was all his surviving daughters remembered about him.

His work, I deduce, consisted of collecting farm produce from peasants who lived far outside the town and themselves were too poor to own the means to get their goods to market. My grandfather took their produce for them and I suppose sold it on commission. All I ever knew about him were the tales of his passion for music, and his attendance at the theatre which must have been the only one in such a drab Balkan town as Iasi. But travelling troupes of opera-players visited it from time to time, and my grandfather was their ardent patron. He could have afforded only the cheapest place in the house, but when he had not arrived home late on the night of a market-day, his family knew he was at the opera. At such times he left his horse and cart in charge of an urchin whom he paid to sleep in the wagon. Afterwards my grandfather had a long drive home, for the lot of such people in Rumania was the same as in the rest of Eastern Europe and they were required to live in remote delimited districts.

So he arrived home very late to find his wife and daughters waiting to be told what he had heard. What was the opera? But first he must eat; and from the pot hanging over the smoky hearth-fire they ladled him out the food that was the staple diet both of the Rumanian peasants and the poor Jews: a mess of yellow cornmeal boiled in water, called *mamaliga*. The Italian peasant's polenta is the same thing. It can be very good if butter and cheese or the makings of a sauce are within one's means, but the only sauce known to my mother's first home was the classic one: hunger.

It was not my mother but her eldest sister who reminisced that while my grandfather ate his supper his family clustered about him, asking a stream of questions about the opera. He would answer after he had eaten. Then, with his five eager females gathered like an audience before him, this bearded, black-coated and, I was told, very handsome man would begin at the overture and finish at the finale of the opera he had heard, singing it through from memory, himself impersonating the orchestra and the singers, acting out the drama and improvising in his own language a text in place of the original he did not know. No doubt he took the wildest liberties, but my aunt declared that when he was through they had heard that opera.

My mother was a very young child at this time, for she was only about two years old when her father died—of pleurisy or pneumonia, they said, but no doubt of hardship too. He left my grandmother, an ageing woman, in dire poverty, with four daughters the eldest of whom was then twenty years old. This extraordinary woman, my Auntie Cecile, took upon herself not only the support of her family but her father's pathetic unrealized ambition to move them all to America, "a golden land" as the old-world song had it, to which then as now the wretched of the earth wanted to go.

My aunt's trade was her needle, the only one possible for a woman in those days and circumstances. She had been apprenticed as a little girl to a seamstress who trained the child by the cruel device of tying her thimble-finger in place to accustom it quickly to its work. At her father's death my aunt stepped forward to become not only the breadwinner and head of the family, but the mother as well, for she ran the whole show, leaving my grandmother to her mysterious self-appointed function of disdainful leisure.

My memories of my grandmother, vivid in view of the fact that I did not love her as a child ordinarily would, are curiously dramatic. I never knew her to convey a warm feeling about anything except her supreme pride in my mother, with whose upbringing she had had almost nothing to do. I have heard that she gave the voice to the family, as her husband must have given the musical temperament; the old woman claimed that as a girl she had had a better voice than any of her daughters. They all had good ones, but were outshone by the youngest who, as the fairy-tale used to have it, was the fairest and most gifted of all. But I have always believed that to have been less a matter of luck or chance than of the determined, courageous devotion and the tough discipline of my Auntie Cecile. Whilst she carried the whole load, my grandmother spent her days sitting in a high-backed armchair, her snow-white hair falling like a cloak around her, covering her hump; and from her wrinkled nut-brown face with its glittering eyes there issued a shrill angry voice in a cascade of screams. She had as I remember it a terrible temper, and since I could not understand a word of her language I never understood what she was screaming about.

Legends about her wander through my mind. I cannot claim any of them as incontrovertible for I suspect that some of their color is the embellishment of time and distance. But they contain some seed of the probable, else why would I ever have heard them?—I cannot remember from whom. My grandmother appeared to consider herself entitled to the best of everything (which she had never had) by what prerogative nobody knew. And this, combined with the lacunae which fire, panic, and dispersion have left in the records of all such families, gave rise to the notion of a mystery about her origin. At any rate, her situation in Rumania was desperate and my aunt undertook the formidable project of moving her mother and sisters to America.

Here there emerges the naïve but glorious thread of faith in the great free country across the sea, with its streets paved in gold. The familiar procedure was followed: the breadwinner must go ahead alone, to work and save enough money to bring the family afterwards. My aunt first painfully saved the money to go to America, and then slaved in New York at sweatshop labor to earn enough, starving herself meanwhile, to pay her family's passage. I have always wondered how they lived and who took care of them while they were waiting in Iasi. Certainly my grandmother did no work, and furthermore she occupied her leisure by going out from her poverty-stricken home to walk on the single fine avenue of the town.

There among the shops was one where china and glassware were sold. In the window of this shop stood a complete service,

I suppose for twelve persons, of Bohemian ruby glass, which comprised goblets of every size, from tiny liqueur glasses up through the whole panoply of wines. The set must have been a showpiece for the shop which could not have had much of a clientele for such wares in such a town. My grandmother conceived a perverse passion for this set of glass, whilst she was living in penury; and for months, for years, she haunted that street, gazing at the service of ruby glass which was never removed from the shop window. Meanwhile, down on the East Side in New York, my aunt was sewing from dawn until late in the night, saving in bitter self-denial the hundred dollars or so which would bring her family in the steerage to America. After about two years she scraped the last of the fare together and sent it to her mother. And my grandmother went out and bought the set of ruby glass.

This story would seem to me barely believable—except that both my mother and I have had streaks of comparable improvidence. It may be in the blood. The tale ought to be left as it stands here, but I have never given it one of its rare airings that I was not asked how the family got to America in the end. My aunt started all over again and again saved the same sum of money by the same bitter toil. But this time she bought the steamship tickets and sent them to her mother instead of the cash. And in 1890, when my mother was six years old, they arrived in New York.

My aunt ruled the family like a martinet. She was exceedingly strict with my mother, who was a bright, beautiful, mischievous child with enormous brown eyes and the vivid charm which was remembered all their lives by people who were her schoolmates. The charm never put her in danger of being spoilt by her family—she used to say in later years that she was eighteen years old before she knew that a chicken had anything but a neck. My aunt's earnings had to be spread paper-thin and my mother remembered always the thrill of the very occasional penny she was given if her sister could squeeze it from the budget.

[17]

First the child had to earn the penny by good behavior or good marks at school; the latter were easier for her. The actual possession of the penny was a vast excitement heightened by the tantalization of deciding how to spend it. One could buy, she used to tell me, a piece of watermelon for a penny, or a few "shoestrings", the rubbery strips of liquorice which children so strangely like; or many other kinds of cheap candy, or St. John's bread, or a hunk of coconut. Days sometimes passed in the throes of choosing. She would take all afternoon to make up her mind, only to change it when she stood staring at the shop-window or the vendor's cart. By then it would be supper-time and the decision far too serious to be hastily closed, so the question stood open for tomorrow or a series of tomorrows.

"And what did you usually buy in the end?" I asked her.

"A piece of coconut," she answered. "I hated the taste of it, that was why I went through so much torment, because I was turning down the things I really liked."

"But why?"

She laughed. "The coconut was hard to swallow. You chewed it and chewed it like a cow her cud, so it lasted longer than anything else and seemed like more for your penny."

Such reasoning explained many of her ways as a child and all the rest of her life too. Her approach was direct and her methods drastic. One day, she told me, she came out to the stoop of the tenement to find one of her playmates crying there because another little girl had broken off one of the legs of her toy tin stove. The stove would not stand any longer and the child was inconsolable.

"I'll fix it for you," said my mother, and at once neatly broke off the other three legs. The little girl howled and tried to stop her, but my mother planked the stove down on the step and walked away saying, "It stands up now, doesn't it? What more do you want?"

Not only was the neighborhood public school the only one

imaginable to such a family, it was beyond the utmost they could have dreamed of in Europe. It was the beginning of life in the promised land. My mother was sent to school immediately she arrived in New York. Then and there was laid the foundation of her passionate love for America which was inspiring in its un-affected, articulate sincerity. The first words in English that my mother learned were those of the Pledge to the Flag, which the class of infant immigrants were taught to repeat at the opening of school every morning, standing at attention before the flag. And too the children were taught the meaning of those words by some forgotten, harassed drudge of a teacher who instilled into one child an indelible belief which all the diversions of success and the great world never altered, that this republic was dedicated to the ideal of liberty and justice for all.

My mother kept all her life her unabashed reverence for the ceremonies and sentiments of American tradition. She taught me, and later my much younger half-sister and brother, the Pledge to the Flag and the rules for honoring it, which were never mentioned in the select private schools where we were educated. She herself taught us the texts of the great national documents and made us memorize them. Every Fourth of July the flag flew on our lawn and after luncheon my mother gathered together every member of her family and household and read aloud to us the Declaration of Independence, with such sincerity that no eye was dry when she finished, herself in tears. We were taught to stand whenever we heard the National Anthem, and taught so young that I at least have never sensed the sheepish self-consciousness which blocks this simple expression in many people. The habit is so dyed in me that I keep to it even when I am alone and hear the anthem by chance, as when it is played to close a day's broad-casting on a radio station. I love the observance and I love the sense that it is a legacy from my mother.

For her, as for thousands of New York men and women, the tenement stoop was the backdrop of childhood memory. There the little girls used to gather to play with cheap dolls, to swap decalcomania transfers and prizes from penny candy, to whisper their secrets against the shrill chanting of other girls' hop-scotch and rope-skipping on the sidewalk, whilst the boys roared at shinny or ball in the middle of the street, alert for fighting invasions by rival gangs from neighboring blocks. When the fights turned rough and the brickbats began to fly the little girls fled into the hallway to hide until it was safe to come out on the stoop again. And there my mother ruled unbeatable at the girls' favorite game, jacks. How could she help but win, with her deft, enormous hands? Tournaments were organized among the public grade-schools and at the age of eleven, my mother emerged as the champion jacks-player of the city. Her own memories of those days were sparse but sharp. If she talked about them at all it was to admit herself a ringleader of mischief and to contradict the legend that she never sang a note until she burst miraculously upon a delighted world. She made short work of that.

"I didn't mean to try to be a singer," she said, though my aunt used to look down her nose at that; "but sing? Of course I sang. We all sang. The tenement was bursting with us singing."

And so it was. The warmth of song and laughter lifted the family of women above the rigors of their bitter, crowded poverty. My aunt was the moving spirit, a blending of austerity, tenderness, good sense, and good taste. It is astonishing and touching to realize what she accomplished out of character, wisdom, her two hands and fortitude. She was aware that the baby of the family was very gifted, but her way of meeting that was to supply the best education she could, a strict old-fashioned upbringing, and leave the rest to nature. She never forced or hung over the child in pride, ambition, or suspense. In her own words she believed that "if it's there it will come out in good time, and you cannot get something out if nothing was put in."

The years of desperate stringency could actually not have continued for very long, because during the first decade in America the two middle sisters, much nearer my aunt's age than my mother's, were married. Then my Auntie Cecile had the courage and the enterprise to leave off her piecework sewing and open a custom dressmaking establishment of her own. This quickly became a success, for I remember the flourishing, busy place from my earliest childhood. It was in the centre of the fashionable shopping district, on Forty-fifth Street just west of Fifth Avenue. A little way down Fifth Avenue was the ladies' tailoring establishment of Bergdorf & Goodman, two young men who had come up, like their neighbors, from 'downtown', bringing their skill and their fine taste with them.

All such people knew one another well, and all my life I have heard their reminiscences of my Auntie Cecile whose establishment was called "Madame Cecile." Her reputation was based on her cutting, for upon that depends the success of the modiste. Her clientele were a group of solid, well-to-do, mostly Jewish women, a few of whose descendants to this day touch the links of a chain which runs back to the turn of the century. Auntie Cecile made the trousseau and the wedding-gown for Aline Frankau, famed in the theatre as Aline Bernstein the scenic and costume designer, and in literature as the great romance in the life of Thomas Wolfe. Aline's sister Ethel Frankau is and has been for a lifetime the fashion arbiter of Bergdorf Goodman's. My friendship with Ethel is the comfortable, laconic relation of people who know everything about what has made them who they are, and eliminates the interjacence of repetitive small-talk.

In *East Side, West Side* I drew a portrait of my Auntie Cecile, calling her "Auntie Esther", which I believe does justice to that unforgettable woman. I drew too on my own memories of "The Place" as she used to call her dressmaking establishment, and of the time I spent there as a small child. It was, of course, time when my mother was occupied with rehearsals and coaching in the beginning of her career. I was never left with anybody else. A day at The Place was a wonderful day for me, highlighted by lunch with Auntie Cecile at Maillard's, and full of sights, sounds, and smells which are vivid even now. They are all recorded in the memory of Jessie Bourne, which took shape for me almost as a letter written to Max Perkins.

Only from the perspective of age is it possible to see the real design in the network of lives which, interwoven with our own, make us the individuals we are. This is equally true of time and place, as our fates have scattered us about in them, sometimes without apparent reason or sequence. In age, spans of time are measured in their true rather than their seeming lengths; reasons become apparent for all that happened to us and for where it happened; individuals emerge from long-closed chambers of memory, sometimes to an importance which we did not understand whilst our relation to them was immediate. A decade, one sees when one has completed six of them, is a very short span of life. It only seems long in youth and in the processes of young lives. I think of this in relation to the first ten years of my mother's life in this country, which carried her from the bewildered mass of human raw material dumped from the steerage and Castle Garden into the cauldron of the lower East Side, to the brilliant girl who was just finishing high school ten years later. Another ten years was to find her launched—at the top—in the art she was born to serve, and that was not so much miraculous as the consequence of the austere influences which formed her and which in her own hands became the instrument not only of her own accomplishment but of what she moulded from the clay that was myself.

One of the mysteries of my mother's personality that has always challenged my imagination is the shining thread of natural good taste which ran through every impression of her that I have ever gleaned, as far back as anybody could remember her. Where did she learn the beautiful English that she spoke, with an inflection of great delicacy and a polish that was neither regional nor national? This was no adult accomplishment like the many other languages she spoke and used as naturally as the beautiful clothes and jewels which success brought her. She spoke the same English from my very earliest memory; and since I was born only three years after the end of her New York schooling, she had had no time or opportunity for such refinements of education as beautiful English diction. Her speech, then, was a spontaneous expression of personality and must have been self-taught —but how, without precept? Nothing is more familiar in New York than the accents of its pot-melted people eloquent of the racial and social huddles in which they grew. My mother never bore a trace of that. She was in truth a thing apart; but nobody let her think so. All girls in her circumstances expected to work for a time before they married, and when they did marry, their families chose their husbands and arranged their marriages by inflexible ancient rules.

So my mother took a training-course in stenography and typing and went to work in an office. It may have been there that my father first saw her, though he was acquainted with her family. It seems banal to write that she was spectacularly beautiful. Her special quality beyond Grecian beauty of head and face was a glowing warmth which then, when she was seventeen, and for years afterwards, illumined every motion and sound that she made. My father, twelve years older than she, began to besiege her eldest sister with repeated, urgent proposals to marry the young girl. He was modestly established in the insurance business and well-known downtown where he had once been an alderman. He seemed to everybody concerned except, as she told me long afterwards, herself, a suitable husband for the girl. Marriage was indicated not only by tradition and her family's wishes; at seventeen or eighteen years it is a mirage which promises to a strictly brought-up girl much that has been beyond her reach. The marriage took place in the spring of 1902, and I was born in June of the following year, in the flat where my father had taken his bride to live, a new flat on St. Nicholas Avenue, a district long since swallowed up by the tragic slums of Harlem.

In those days this was a pleasant part of town for people of moderate means, who lived in substantial new apartment-houses which were breaking up the solid blocks of old-fashioned, high-stooped family brownstones. I cannot remember St. Nicholas Avenue—presently we moved to West Ninety-third Street at Riverside Drive—but I do remember clearly the bustling growth of the whole upper West Side. It was still changing from a craggy, goat-populated sprawl of shantytown hills to the preferred residential district it had become at the turn of the century. I know now that there was a race among the forces of real-estate promotion, the New York Central Railroad, and millions of newly prospering, restless citizens, as to which of the two halves of upper Manhattan should become the more desirable one after the pressure of money and numbers had burst the quiet old cocoons of lower Fifth Avenue and Murray Hill. It seems extraordinary today that such apartment-houses as we lived in should have been new and comfortable while upper Park Avenue remained a double row of bleak coldwater tenements for years until the New York Central tracks went entirely underground about 1913.

But much harder to imagine is the brief span of time before destiny, hitherto veiled by the commonplace, stepped softly into that Harlem flat and touched my young mother with its fingers. My father, gregarious and acquainted with all sorts of people, had a friend who was passionately addicted to opera, one of those everyday business men who outside his work, really lives in the opera house among its habitués. This man never missed a performance, like the standees you may always see and recognize there. Since this was about 1905, and very much the Golden Age of Song, the man was well rewarded for his devotion. It seems that one evening my father invited this man home to dinner with him. As they entered the flat the man stopped, transfixed at the sound of singing somewhere inside. My father replied to his friend's astonished question that yes, it was his wife who was singing. Presently she appeared and was introduced. The next moments passed in excited inquiries on the guest's part and mild surprise on my mother's. No, nobody had ever told her what a voice she had, nor suggested that she study singing. But I have gathered that it did not need much urging on the part of a stranger to make the idea of singing-lessons appeal to her. If it is true that up to that time the thought had not occurred to her, and I am sceptical, it is also true that as long as she lived she was eager and receptive to the idea of learning anything which she believed herself capable of doing well.

The opera-loving business man was a providential instrument, for his acquaintances around the opera house led him in his inquiries about singing-teachers straight to the best one in New York—Maestro Arturo Buzzi-Peccia. This was a warm, smiling man with a black spade beard (dyed, about which my innocence one day horribly mortified my mother) and not a word of English at his command. He had been a figure in musical circles in Milan, well-known at La Scala, in whose tradition singing for him began and ended. He came to New York on the musical waves which brought Caruso and Scotti before 1904, and Maestro Toscanini with Gatti-Casazza in 1908. Arrangements for my mother's lessons almost made themselves. Part of these were that Buzzi gave my mother her lessons at less than his usual fees, and thus often at odd hours when he was not occupied with his regular pupils.

There was not money enough to underwrite the singing-lessons and the necessary peripheral expenses—Europe in the summers, and how different a Europe from the one my mother had left fifteen years before! Lessons in Italian, music and scores and a piano and I suppose an occasional seat at the opera, though that must have been lagnappe, the connections being what they were. I have never been told the details, but I am certain that my mother was determined to finance her own study and all it involved without dependence on her husband; and he could not have afforded the expense anyway. I do not know from whom, but I am quite sure that my mother borrowed the money she needed and surer still that she paid it back with interest in full out of her first earnings. The total could not have been very much. She told me that she managed her first summers in Europe with me, steamship fare and everything else, on about four hundred dollars for the two of us; and I remember vividly the humble pensions in which we lived and her ingenious devices for saving money. She managed on about ten dollars a week.

She used to say, laughing, that she took me along as a chaperone, which was true insofar as she was too shrewd to underestimate her own beauty. Later in her life there was plenty of scope for gaiety, mischief, and flirtation, but at this time, in her early twenties, she was very serious. She told me she knew that men would not pursue her if she deliberately encumbered herself with a small child. But she never treated me like an encumbrance, and not much like a small child either. She wanted to see the great sights of Europe, and without attempting to explain or expound them beyond my comprehension, she took me along and I saw them too. Tombs and crypts must have fascinated her, which may be why I remember so clearly my first sight of Les Invalides; and also, in Milan I remember the ghastly cadaver of Saint Ambrogio in its glass coffin, richly vested and crusted with jewels, and the climb up the stairs from that crypt, my short legs aching. When we came in sight of the rose window Madonna, I asked my mother if that was that gentleman's wife and child?

It was in towns like Como and in Swiss villages that my mother sought the cheap pensions, but she had quite a different idea about Paris. She wanted no part of its student life or its bohemian adventures. She was in Paris to perfect her French and polish her style and her presence. We lived, accordingly, in the Hotel Régina, then a first-class hotel on the Place des Pyramides with its gilded equestrian statue of Jeanne d'Arc facing the Tuileries. Later, when I could understand, my mother told me how she had arranged this. Holding me by the hand as usual she went in and asked to speak to the manager. She told him that she was a music student, very poor, planning to spend so much time in Paris and able to afford only so many francs for a room. She was unwilling to live in dirt or disorder or without the protection of the conventions. Could he advise her?

He gave her a servant's room under the mansard in the hotel, which we reached by climbing the garret stairs after the lift stopped at the top floor. We ate at the Restaurant Duval across the Place, Duval in those days being a chain of cheap, clean eating-places comparable to Childs. All my life since, whenever I have crossed the Pont Royal and the Tuileries to come upon Jeanne d'Arc and the Régina—now with a clean façade like its neighbors—I have had a longing to recapture those beloved distant days. But until 1965 I never entered the hotel. Then I did, to walk once through its gloomy halls and glance into its mournful salons, deserted except for a glum tourist or two. Despite its face-lifting it looked as though it had not had a new curtain or piece of furniture in all the years since we had lived there. But I did recapture a glimmer of my beautiful mother in her long, sweeping skirts, short padded jacket, and enormous hat; and of myself in a sailor-suit, black stockings, and high buttoned shoes, with long corkscrew curls, hugging a doll and asking my mother as we stepped across to the Duval if we were to have chicken that day?

Once, walking in the Tuileries, we saw a balloon-vendor whose balloons were shaped like animals. I begged for one and my mother bought me a pig. It was bright pink. She did not buy anything without careful examination of her purse and in those days sous and centimes were worth something. I am hazy about the details, but I do remember the pink pig in our cramped room, floating out of my reach on the end of its string. Somehow I failed to realize that the way to get hold of the pig was to draw in the string. The effort I did make involved climbing onto a piece of furniture, one of my mother's long hatpins, and of course, the end of the pig. I was scolded and I understood why. Destructive-ness was naughty and so was the failure to be careful of a toy that she had bought me when she could ill afford it. But I got the message even more clearly in the ensuing days when there was no chicken for my dinner.

Such peaks of early memory are all I can discern through the blur of vaguer impressions. Only my mother's identity is clear amidst factors that I was too young to grasp in the short space of time before her career began. The charming story is true, that her engagement by the Metropolitan was the result of her singing in the presence of Maestro Toscanini when she did not realize she was giving an audition. Buzzi had told her to come for her lesson on a certain evening, and on her arrival at his door, he clapped his hand to his forehead, dramatically excusing himself for having confused his engagements: he had friends there for supper. (It is known that I borrowed elements of this episode, like almost no others in my mother's life, for my novel, *Of Lena Geyer*.) Buzzi's beautiful pupil stood in the doorway saying she would come another time, but by then his friends, old cronies from Milan, had become curious. They turned from the supper-table to peer at the girl and tease Buzzi with obvious insinuations. He rebuked them, saying they quite misunderstood, this was his most promising pupil. In that case, said Toscanini and Gatti-Casazza, go right ahead with her lesson, we will sit here and listen while we finish our wine.

I not only do not believe this was the accident it was claimed to be; I also do not believe that my mother was naïve about the supper-guests. Obviously she knew who they were and was thrilled —also not the least disconcerted. I only think that Buzzi sprang the confrontation on her and on them with consummate craft. He went to the piano and the lesson began as usual with scales and vocalizing—during which Maestro Toscanini told me years later, he was enjoying Buzzi's joke. But when Buzzi began the accom-paniment to an aria, Maestro jumped up and pushed him from the piano and sat down himself to play what he wanted to hear my mother sing. I do not know what else the 'lesson' comprised, but it included "Regnava nel silenzio" from *Lucia*. Gatti then asked her to come to the Metropolitan next morning for an audition, which she sang for him and Andreas Dippel in the dark, empty house. She had never been on a stage in her life and had had no dramatic training at all. Gatti nonetheless gave her a contract to sign and a repertoire to learn in the months before the opening of the 1909–1910 season. She told him her misgivings about her lack of stage experience but he brushed them aside. She could pick up stage business, he shrugged, as she went along.

This seems an incredible attitude for Gatti-Casazza. The Metropolitan comprised the greatest roster of luminaries of that fabled Golden Age. Gatti was a cold-blooded realist if ever there was one. What could have prompted such an impresario to take a chance on a grass-green beginner who had never sung in public, never been on a stage? I suspect it was a showman's instinct. He was engaging a young lyric soprano for the minor roles of little sisters, confidantes, and sprites which are scattered throughout the operatic repertoire. In her first season she sang eleven such parts in three languages. Her voice was very beautiful and her technique superlative, in that respect she was a polished artist. But he must have been betting on her personality, the radiance and wit, the come-hither, the indefinable tinder which sparks the instantaneous link between performer and public; it can be called charm or magnetism but in truth it has no name. It is wholly personal.

Gatti's instinct—prodded by Maestro Toscanini—was not wrong. From the night of her début Alma Gluck captivated New York, and other audiences as soon as they heard her. Until very recently I have never read the reviews of those appearances. For more than twenty-five years I have kept my mother's scrap-books put away with her letters and papers, and only now when this necessity commands it have I opened those crumbling pages, to try to separate fact from legend and the embellishments of memory. I see it is true that she was an immediate sensation, more surprising because of the small roles she first sang; and I see something else in the writings of those be-laurelled critics, Krehbiel and Aldrich and Henderson and their contemporaries, which I would never have supposed.

To me, then when I first saw and heard him, and until the day he died forty-eight years later, Maestro Toscanini was a supreme being—the supreme being after my mother. As a small child I was overawed by him, and when I was older he became not only the god and the arbiter of music for me, but the dearest friend I have ever had. His eminence now what it is and musically was as long ago as 1908 when he first came to New York, it appears incredible that some reviews of his early performances dwelt upon the singers, made some mention of the generalities of the performance, and wound up with a sentence such as, "The conductor was Maestro Toscanini." I can only add that those celebrated critics did not lounge in such complacency very long. Maestro jolted them. He conducted the music of Verdi and Puccini as they had never heard it before, though their writings reflect that they came rather slowly to the realization that the motive-power of a unique performance emanated from the tyrant in the pit rather than from the idols on the stage.

Then he gave them Wagner—*Götterdämmerung* and *Tristan* (which I first heard with Fremstad and Burrian, a tough standard of comparison for the generation-later Flagstad and Melchior); and *Die Meistersinger* which the critics were so myopic as to pronounce "too Italianized." My musical experience has spanned the epoch when critics wrestled with the language to find words and phrases—a futile effort, since I slaved at it myself—to describe a Toscanini performance as it really was. To turn back today and read the well-written opinions of the Messrs. Aldrich, Krehbiel, and Henderson is like listening to the post-prandial pomposities of gentlemen who have taken three hours to consume

twelve courses with all the proper wines, and can no longer see
the room for the cigar-smoke. Yet in erudition, authority, and intrinsic importance they excelled any of their successors since
Lawrence Gilman.

They show up fustily in their reactions to the Toscanini in-
novations and departures from the standard repertoire. To be
perfectly fair, time has since justified their indifference to works
by composers like Catalani, Franchetti, and other contemporary
colleagues of Maestro's whose music he insisted on playing. But
when he went to the opposite extreme and revived the immortal
works of Gluck, fountainhead of all operatic composition thereafter, he was thought to be indulging a peculiar affinity of his own
and dispensing opera that was very much caviar to the general.
The first of his two historical Gluck revivals was the production
of *Orfeo* in 1909. This is one of the most beautiful scores in all
music and one which Maestro loved and served with a special
dedication. It has never been a popular opera, which made it the
more surprising that my mother's first appearance with Maestro
in the single-aria role of The Happy Shade should have been so
noticed then and so remembered since. I was six years old at
the time. Infancy is reason enough why the whole association
should have made so deep an impression; but retrospect shows me
that *Orfeo* colored my life and my mind; that it was germinal to
the processes which made me a reader and a writer of books.

I T was the afternoon of Wednesday, the twenty-second of December, 1909. I had been brought to the dress rehearsal of *Orfeo* (I cannot remember by whom) and seated on some folded coats to raise me high enough to see. The enormous dark spaces around me did not seem strange, nor did the enacting of the Greek myth on the stage, since my mother had already read me the story of Orpheus and Eurydice from a book which was to become the passion of my solitary childhood—Bulfinch's *The Age of Fable*. I believed the legend implicitly, for I did not know the difference between belief and illusion. Before my eyes in the fearful cavern of Hades were a gaggle of writhing Furies, the devils and damned souls who inhabited what I had been able to grasp of the concept of Hell. My mother had told me not to be frightened, that this was only make-believe; but I was frightened, really because I wanted to be. I was immersed in the realization of a story—stories, apart from my mother, being the core of my awareness.

Now there was added the new and third element which at this perspective I know to be substance of my whole life and mind; then, of course, only an overwhelming impression: music in totality. Hitherto, music had been my mother's voice. In one afternoon it became all that it is in its maximum force. I did not suddenly and with comprehension beyond my years grasp the nature of an orchestra nor realize that those Furies roaring "No!" to Orpheus's pleas were the members of a chorus. But I was sitting directly behind and close to the source of this raging sound. I saw him driving the demons with his flailing right arm, saw the incantatory motions of his left hand, saw his face—now contorted and fanatical, now a masque of austere absorption—in the dim lights from the pit; above all, heard his voice, the curious muffled croak which could and did that day shout above his own fortissimi; and sing in lyric passages unknowing that he was singing or how strange his cracked tones were. He was Maestro. I know now how much of all this I was too young to apprehend. I know that my intimate knowledge of *Orfeo* as music, as melody, as orchestration, as chorale, as all that it is beyond my primary impression, is the sum total of a lifetime. But on that day more than fifty-five years ago the child perched on the folded coats perceived what it was that he made happen.

The second act of *Orfeo* is where its impact lies—the passage of the heartbroken singer, son of Apollo the god of Music, through Hades and into Elysium in search of his dead wife. It is as well known and repeatedly used in art as any classic legend can be, root and seed of poetry and music in hundreds if not thousands of versions. The two scenes can be evocations of everything that Hell and Heaven strike in emotion and imagination; and they were on the day I am remembering. For all I know, the settings as they were then might be preposterous to present-day eyes which would expect them to be impressionistic and non-literal. Long ago that was not the case. Hades was a dark jagged cavern licked by tongues of fire and filled with a mob of fanged, crippled fiends crawling and writhing about the stage, dragging themselves up to block the way of Orpheus with his lyre as he begged them to let him pass. The part was sung by the great contralto Louise Homer, but for me at least there was no dearth of illusion that Orpheus was a man. When, finally, with the beauty of his song he subdued the Furies they slunk down, and the depths of Hell erupted in a terrifying sight, another mob of the damned who were, of course, the ballet. The Dance of the Furies was exactly what the words imply: rage, hate, violence, a seething boil of motion at a frenzied tempo.

The music is extraordinary. I have never heard its breathless horror fully evoked by anyone other than Maestro. He whipped the strings into a shrill snarl, the whole orchestra into a diabolical chopping beat, the climax a terrible crash from a great bass gong, the knell of doom which I have always thought of as the pagan parallel to the awful hammered drum in the *Dies Irae* of the Verdi *Requiem*. That was my first encounter with Maestro's evocation of Hell—and I believed every particle of it.

Then the devils subsided, Hades melted away, scrims and gauzes moved and shifted, the scene was bathed in silvery light; here were the Elysian Fields. Here seated at a harp was a Blessed Spirit, singing music that I knew already, a vision of comforting loveliness which belonged to me, my mother: an angel in Heaven. Only through the mind of a six-year-old child can such emotion be conceived. From any other view it would be sentimentality and its purity of credence vitiated.

I have no memory of the last act. Was I taken out before it to join my mother in her dressing-room? I remember the room but not which of those on the women's side of the house it was; I have wondered since. What I see vividly is Maestro coming through the doorway, smiling and pleased with my mother. I cannot remember their words, only the sound of their voices speaking in Italian which of course I understood. My mother was tall, and this was the measure of my surprise that she was taller than he. She was still in costume, a classic fall of Grecian draperies of pale chiffon, with her hair bound in a double fillet, and she was radiant at his approval. He was all motion and expression. His step was almost dancing. His hands were lifted and moving lightly from side to side as they used to do, for instance, in a passage of the Third Leonore when he wanted delicacy and animation from the strings. He smiled at me with the warmth he always showed to children; I remember his cracked voice repeating *la bambina* as my mother had just said it. But I was still overawed by what I had seen and heard as he was conducting, and his face is what is etched on my memory of that moment. I see the strong black eyebrows, the black moustache which ended in two needle-points sharply up-turned; most clearly of all, his eyes. He bent down to me and I have kept ever since that first impression of his eyes. They were soft deep brown seemingly filmed with a milky lustre, eyes I have never seen resembled in any person else. At that moment they appeared piercing in their glance; and in truth, they were always more acute than their expression or than Maestro's reputation for near-sightedness suggested. He saw what he wanted to see, like deaf persons who are sure to hear what has been whispered.

There my memories of that day evaporate. But plainly, as I place them now in a long sequence of forces and happenings which formed my imagination, my tastes, my sense of purpose, my char-acter, my faults and deficiencies, what I eventually accomplished, and wherein I failed, those memories are the quiddity of me.

However, though *Orfeo* was so tremendous and indelible in impact upon me, it was not in fact the occasion of my mother's début with the Metropolitan. That had taken place five weeks earlier at the New Theatre, at Sixty-second Street and Central Park West. For a brief time the Metropolitan ran there a short-lived venture, presenting lyric and comic operas lighter than the mainstays at the big house. At this writing the matter suggests a startling and coincidental prevision of the Metropolitan's move to Lincoln Center, which some sixty years ago nobody could have conceived. There was nothing secondary about the casts and productions at the New Theatre. Its season opened on the 16th of November, 1909, with Massenet's *Werther*. The cast included Edmond Clément and Dinh Gilly, celebrated tenor and baritone from the Opéra-Comique, both in their débuts; Geraldine Farrar as Charlotte, and Alma Gluck as Sophie, her younger sister. I remember little about this. I was taken to a dress rehearsal or an afternoon performance of every opera in which my mother sang, since I was much too young to stay up at night; and whether the performances I heard were rehearsals or repetitions I do not know.

The *Werther* has always shone in my mind with a retrospective glow from the lovely personality of Geraldine Farrar—not as she sang Charlotte, which I cannot remember as I do other roles of hers—but for my mother's account of Miss Farrar's kindness and generosity to a bewildered beginner. Originally the Massenet opera was to have included a French soprano called Christine Héliane, making her début with her colleagues from Paris in the part of Sophie. She could not be on hand for the rehearsals and Alma Gluck was assigned as rehearsal substitute. Mme. Héliane arrived during the weekend prior to the Tuesday opening, and I do not know the details of the happenings which resulted in the summoning of my mother to sing the dress rehearsal on the Sunday. Only the next day did she realize that she was to sing the performance. After the charming air, *Du gai soleil* at the end of the second act, she said she started for her dressing-room hearing "a funny noise in the distance like rain on a tin roof." Miss Farrar stopped her in the wings and said, "You little idiot, don't you know what that is?" and herself led the new young singer out for the ovation which established her overnight.

The very next afternoon Alma Gluck sang another small part which she had rehearsed expecting it to be her début role, Esmeralda, the dancer with the travelling circus, in *The Bartered Bride*. The Smetana opera in that distant time was an ornament of the august Hofoper in Vienna, sung in German and unknown in its original tongue outside its native ground in the 'Austrian' provincial town of Prague. The Metropolitan's performance at the New Theatre was conducted by Alfred Hertz of the company's German wing. It bore the authenticity of its 1908 production under the direction of the Bohemian-born Gustav Mahler. It was again sung by Emmy Destinn, the superb Czech soprano, as Marie; and the Polka and Furiant were staged by the company's Bohemian ballet-master Ottokar Bartik and danced by a corps of Bohemian dancers who were imported from Vienna together with the scenery and the costumes. I have the programme in my mother's scrap-book. I remember her in her short ballet-skirt, tripping along a tight-wire (she explained to calm my fears that it was only a board laid across a couple of supports) twirling a parasol and singing in German the little air which I would one day know as *Milostne zviřatko*. Someone else remembered her in that and other roles—an immigrant who was working in a brass foundry in Bridgeport, Connecticut, and sometimes saved up the price of a trip to New York and a seat in the top gallery at the opera. His name was Jan Masaryk.

The first home I remember was the apartment in West Ninety-third Street, and that only in streaks alternating with blanks and silences. I remember a long hall through the flat, with my room at one end of it. I remember how bitterly cold the winters were, with the wind howling up from Riverside Drive a few steps away. I do not think it is my imagination that winters were much colder then in New York than they are now. I remember the misery of being taken out of doors by Anna Czerny, the maid who had been my mother's first necessity in the beginning of her career. I hated to be told to play out of doors, I resisted all efforts to make me jump and run and exercise, as I have resisted them ever since. I knew no children with whom to play. I do not know where I would have met any, for I had never been to school. I never mastered the physical skills which children take for granted; I was ten years learning to ride a bicycle and I never did learn to roller-skate in spite of tears and scenes.

I liked to stay in the house with my dolls, my cat—even then I had one—something like weaving or toy knitting in my hands, and my mother practising nearby. These are my memories of how my time was filled until books magically and suddenly, it seems now, made all other occupations unnecessary. My mother used to say I had been born a little old woman and I am afraid she was right. For I feel that not only was I born old, but born looking back over my shoulder at the past.

My dread of 'outdoors' was simply fear of the cold. I can

remember crying from the pain of frostbitten toes and fingers as no modern child would do, and they wear little clothing compared with what my mother loaded on me. She dressed me in warm underwear with long drawers, over which long stockings —black for everyday and white for 'dressed-up'—were pulled and held up by garters attached to a garment called a ferris-waist. To this was buttoned a pair of fancy nainsook drawers. A one-piece flannel petticoat with armholes hung from my shoulders, over it a second petticoat of embroidered nainsook; and finally, my dress.

My mother still made all my clothes. She was an extraordinary needlewoman, the product of Auntie Cecile's training; and all her life she was never at leisure without some piece of sewing or, later, of needlepoint embroidery in her soft, heavy hands. She had no other domestic gifts whatever. I never saw her in a kitchen and she always maintained that she did not know how to boil an egg. I have never attempted a synthesis between that and what must have been the routine of her early married life. I have still a dress that she made for me when I was eight or nine years old, the sort of party-dress that was worn over a pink china-silk slip, with a broad pink silk sash tied at a non-existent waistline somewhere about the hips. The dress is a succession of bands of white organdie, minutely hand tucked and hemstitched, put together with fine rows of hand-tatted beading and finished with tatted edging, to which is whipped real Valenciennes lace. Perhaps it was in this dress that I was taken to hear her sing, for those were the great occasions. Certainly I remember no children's parties and, as I have noted, no children or playmates at all. I never missed them.

Those early years were in essence the walls of a benign stockade in which I lived wholly concentrated on my mother—I suppose, too, on myself though I do not see it so in retrospect— inside which no other identity belonged, not even my father whom I almost do not remember at all. I do not know the sequence or the time or the reasons for his elimination from my mother's life and thus from mine. There are no patterns of memory in which he appears. I know that my mother meant this to be so. I do not know exactly in what year she was divorced nor any details of the matter. I was never aware of a break in the ground beneath my feet. My mother was my world and she deliberately made that a world in which I had her and her alone. I was never a witness to the ignominies of a broken marriage and I believe that, apart from my mother's shielding me from such impressions, her marriage was not sufficiently intrinsic to her real life for its termination to have been traumatic. She was gay, she was warm, she was both excited by her success and very serious about her work, she was swept in a single year from total obscurity to national identity; and she lost neither her head nor her footing. She kept me with her and took me about with her on occasions when I should have thought, from this view, it would have been nerve-racking to be encumbered by a small child. In a word, she loved me: she gave herself to me. In the process she gave me everything that has been my measure of aspiration and beauty and character and courage ever since.

She did even more. Having built this groundwork she realized, and made it possible for me to realize without too much suffering (there was some) that her work—she never called it her career and I never heard her use the word except scathingly— would necessarily take her away for long stretches of time and that I would have to go away to school since it was out of the question to leave me alone in New York with a governess or a maid. Time would change the basis of her life and mine, which could only have remained so enclosed whilst she was first trying her wings and I was very small.

Perhaps it is difficult for present-day people hardened to the usages of modern press-agentry, with its apparatus for the explosive inflation of new celebrities in sound, television, print, photography and publicity of every kind, to realize what really happened in the case of my mother's meteoric success. She had no press-agent.

She had no person or agency paid to put her into public notice. There were no electronic media of communication with their 'shows' featuring the names of the moment. There were no news-magazines with colorful reportage and cover-stories. All the notice Alma Gluck received was the comments of the music critics and the ovations of the audiences every time she sang. Repeatedly the comments stress her intelligence, her personality, her presence, her charm—beyond the beauty of her voice and her superlative technique. The voice was a pure lyric soprano, delicate, but pointed and brilliant so as to fill the farthest reaches of the biggest house. The technique was flawless. It would be recalled in a later time when such vocal discipline had vanished, as a real coloratura. In a musical world still inhabited by Lilli Lehmann, Melba, and Sembrich, then in the closing years of their careers, mastery of every vocal exaction from the longest *sostenuto* to the most dazzling fireworks was the basis of a singer's art. A singer, said my mother, is a singer—or should be; she should sing well any and all music that lies in the range and size of her voice.

Now two facts quickly became self-evident to my mother, who whether judging herself or someone else, saw with the accuracy of the schoolroom ruler for which she found so many uses. The first was that she felt handicapped by her lack of stage experience; she even had real distaste for the theatrical side of opera-singing. She said in so many words that she was no actress. In her time at the Metropolitan there were presented no works by Mozart, Donizetti, or Rossini, where she would have been ideal. Only to have heard her sing the music of Susanna and Zerlina as she did for me alone, would have been musical history. In the general repertoire there are not many major roles for a pure lyric voice; she perceived this promptly. The second discovery came less than a year after her Metropolitan début when she sang her first song-recital, in Mendelssohn Hall. I have the reviews before me, and it is the case that the recital was a sensation. Most of the leading musical personalities of New York were there, in a hall packed to ranks of standees. She sang fifteen songs in English—their texts translated from the originals of Rimsky-Korsakoff, Moussorgsky, Rachmaninoff, and Smetana; ten songs in German—Beethoven, Mendelssohn, Schumann, and Strauss; a Tuscan folk-song; and nobody knows how many encores. Not one operatic aria. Her programme was distinguished, unhackneyed, thoughtful, and difficult. She knew then and there where she belonged in music.

So did the critics; their writings all say it. So did the audience, taking to their hearts the personality who was already the favorite soprano in the Sunday night concerts of that era at the Metropolitan, when its artists appeared in mufti and sang arias and ensembles from the repertoire. But those were not song-recitals; and when she turned to them she became the singer who was remembered—and still is to this day by survivors of those times—in every state in this country, in Elks and Shriners meeting-halls, in the 'opery-houses' of dusty little Western towns as well as in the concert halls of every city in the land. They saw her with great dark eyes glowing and her chestnut-brown braids in a coronet around her head, in a draped white satin gown (made by her sister), wearing her long white gloves and carrying her small fan, coming out on the stage in the swift, light trot, almost a run, which was her hallmark. I think they never could have known the origin of that charming gait. It lay in her feet, large (by that day's standards!) and to her mind, ugly like her hands which I so loved. She deliberately disciplined those feet to short, light, graceful steps, and with her magnificent erect carriage, she was a thrill to look at before she had sung a note. I may as well append here that one of the uses of that overworked school ruler of hers was to whack me across the shoulders if I slouched or dragged my feet when she was teaching me to stand and to walk properly.

Thus on the one hand she had a contract with the Metropolitan which had until 1915 to run, and on the other she much preferred to sing concerts. By the spring of 1911 she was in great demand for song-recitals and for appearances as soloist with symphony orchestras and in performances of the great oratorios which were then much more widely heard all over the United States than they are now. In those days, at a time when small American communities are thought to have been benighted in their ignorance of the arts, there flourished local music festivals whose spirit and quality were superior to much that is heard today. In Cincinnati, Louisville, and Richmond; in Portland and Bangor, Maine; in Norfolk, Connecticut and then as now in Bethlehem, Pennsylvania and many other places, there were amateur singing-societies and choral clubs who in spring or summer, under the patronage of one or more wealthy music-loving citizens, held annual festivals at which they sang *The Creation, The Seasons, The Messiah, Elijah,* and the great choral works of Bach and the other composers. The orchestra came from the nearest city which had a symphony orchestra, the conductor and chorus-master were first-rank, and the soloists the best to be had. Alma Gluck was the soprano most in demand for these festivals. She loved such engagements and sometimes she took me with her for the several days she spent at them.

Best of all was the Norfolk Festival in Connecticut, which was the personal creation of Mr. and Mrs. Carl Stoeckel, patrons of the Litchfield Country Choral Society, who lived in a white clapboard mansion called The White House, surrounded by gardens as renowned today in gardening lore as they were for their beauty then. The festival concerts took place in a former barn which they had converted into a rustic auditorium called The Music Shed. There was a special house on their place which they turned over for the festival week to the artists who came to perform, and even from my memory it was a wonderful house-party, the members all musicians at the height of their powers, full of gaiety and hilarious ideas for impromptu parties. Maud Powell, the violinist, and her husband were there, Mr. and Mrs. George Hamlin, Sidney and Louise Homer, Reinald Werrenrath, Clarence Whitehill, and many others. I was of course too small to be witness of the parties, my own memories are of rides with Mrs. Stoeckel in a basket-gig through the gardens and woods. But I have some snapshots of a burlesque of *Madama Butterfly,* with my mother dressed in her own Japanese kimono, her hair stuck full of knitting-needles, singing on the porch steps to a group of her colleagues who were laughing their heads off.

And at Norfolk I had my first lesson in the usages of the tact which children indigenously lack. When we were leaving, Mrs. Stoeckel drove us in her carriage to the railway station where as she kissed my mother good-bye she gave her an enormous bouquet—it must have been more than two feet across—of the lilies-of-the-valley for which the White House gardens were famous. A gardener had brought it in a special cart to the train. My mother buried her face in the flowers, expressing delight and thanking Mrs. Stoeckel effusively—sincerely, too. At which I said, "But Mother doesn't like lilies-of-the-valley, she says their perfume makes her sick."

For days after, I bore the bruise on my arm where my mother's heavy fingers had pinched me slowly, deliberately, and with searching intent.

I see now how fast and how far my mother's world widened even in the first two years after she began to sing. New experiences and new acquaintances both professional and personal crowded in on her. In my own retrospect they did not crowd me out and I think this remarkable. I realize how our early intense intimacy was necessarily diluted, but when she spent time with me and put her attention on me she was always the same—warm above all; overflowing with tenderness; gay and full of play, also very strict and exacting. Modern parents might be surprised, in fact, at how strict she was, but I loved that. I was in a certain way afraid of her when she was cross with me, but I knew that if there was a scolding or a punishment or a spanking—I got plenty of them—it was sure to be followed by immediate reassurances of demonstrative love. It was natural to her to be demanding and quick-tempered (not so much the case when she was older); and equally natural to be loving and to sparkle with laughter, jokes, games, and innumerable little songs which she kept always for me alone.

I cannot remember what she did, if anything, about my education before the autumn when I was eight years old. Up to then I did not go to school. But I learned to read so early that I have very little recollection of when I could not read. This is a commonplace in the childhood of all bookish people, and in comment about the reminiscences of such persons one often finds boredom or irritation because—cliché—a writer was in childhood a bookworm, a loner, a dreamer, a weaver of fantasies, and something of a prodigy in his ability to read at a very early age. I do not see why this is not as much to be expected as that an embryonic musician should show precocious musical aptitude, which they do. It may be of no interest to the world in general that Edith Wharton was writing stories on brown-paper bags with stubs of pencil when she was a small child, but it is of urgent interest to writers, since many of them have done something similar on their way out of infancy.

Tell me a story! When I was a child that was the natural demand of most children, and two generations ago they loved stories more than they do, or are supposed to do, today. Contemporary parents and teachers hold theories which in my opinion do not form or discipline the minds of children on the one hand, and on the other, they reject fantasy and tales of wonder and magic, since those might be construed as flight from reality and we all know what that means. I feel this the place to state that native writing talent, disciplined to the production of communicable literature, is very often flight from reality; and if that is another way of saying that writers tend to be what used to be termed crazy before the word got lost in a wilderness of technical euphemisms, then I have said it.

So to me reading became very early what a family, playmates, and play are to most children. If I ought to have been unhappy because I was so much alone, I did not know it; all I needed was books. I liked best of all the very books on which modern child psychology frowns—fairy-tales, myths, legends of magic and the fantastic. I believed them all. I peopled a whole imaginary world with a crowd that ranged from the Greek and Roman gods to the characters in Grimm, the Andrew Lang "Color" books of fairy-tales, the Lane (expurgated, I did not get to Burton until later) version of the Arabian Nights, and even the Land of Oz. It strikes me now that only the last were stories with an American setting, and for the first time I wonder whether that was an influence which was to draw me all my life to the Old World. Two exceptions among classic stories remain vivid to this day. I did not like the tales of Hans Christian Andersen, because the people were too folksy and humble and things did not happen by magic; and I disliked the Wagnerian gods and the saga of the Nibelungen. I heard my first *Ring* at the age of nine and was given a book about it to read beforehand, but I never knew until the rise of Hitler why I had always detested the whole crew.

My mother sang the few lyric soprano parts that there are in Wagner. She sang Freia in *Das Rheingold*, where she was called "a vision of youth and springtime, sounding even lovelier than she looked." She sang Venus in the Paris version of *Tannhäuser* which was the one then used. But her favorite part, she used to say, was the Forest Bird in *Siegfried*. "That's my idea of opera-singing," she said. "I go down to the opera house in a street dress, stand on a ladder backstage, sing on my cue, collect my money, and go home."

She bought the first house she ever owned with her first earnings after she began to sing at the Metropolitan, the first of a lifelong succession of houses. She had what we called the Builder's Itch, and I have inherited it. From then until now my life has been lived against an obbligato of sawing and hammering, the seductive slap of plaster onto walls, the swoosh of paintbrushes, and the sense of purposeful commotion which means building (alteration) in progress. Neither ruinous plaster-dust, nor the smell of paint and varnish, nor workmen flinging their lunch-leavings and cigarette-butts around, nor any mess they precipitate can disconcert me, otherwise as fussily neat as a cat. Unless the roof is actually off a house I like nothing better than living right in it while a major operation is under way. And I got this, of course, from my mother.

The curious thing is that neither Mother nor I ever built a house from scratch. This might be accident, but I believe the truth is that neither of us would ever have yielded the real power to an architect, and we both had sense enough to know that we lacked the knowledge to make original plans for a projected house. But our kind of house! Nothing could touch us. My mother was very precise about all kinds of measures and figures, and she kept always within reach the two-foot schoolroom ruler I have mentioned. And, in any house occupied by herself or me or in the houses of friends, after sitting quietly with her needlework for a time, or when dummy at bridge, she would rise from her chair, reach for her ruler, and start a slow, apparently aimless promenade around the room. With the ruler in her right hand she beat a soft tattoo on the palm of her left hand. Her face was inscrutable. Nobody paid attention to her, nor she to them. In a little while her gait would quicken, and much like a dowser following his forked stick, she would hurry from a window to a door, from a corner to the fireplace, measuring as she went. Finally she would turn around and casually, as if continuing a conversation, she would say, "After you knock down that partition beyond the bookshelves, you will have fourteen extra feet in which to turn the room around, break open a couple of decent windows, and get rid of that arch that looks like a face with the front teeth missing."

The first house was a plain, small white salt-box, not old or picturesque in the least, at Lake George, New York. It was not on the lake shore but up on the edge of a splendid forest which

clothed the slope of the Adirondacks beyond the village of Lake
George. I have not seen the region in fifty years and I understand
it is now a disastrous summer-resort monstrosity, but in our time
it was remote and lovely. That forest beyond our house was the
first I had ever roamed in, and there I had the first playmates I
had ever known. They were the daughters—typically he had a
large family of daughters and no sons—of the rector of the small
Episcopal church in the village. Their name was Parrott, and my
two friends were Edith and Martha. I remember something of
the games we played, all invented by ourselves, and the clearing
in the woods with the inevitable hollow tree where we put letters
and stories which we later 'found' as if by magic. I suppose this is
banal, but children in their curious way are banal in their tena-
cious repetitions and reflections of what interests them. My appetite for reading gave rise to an endless game which we called
Gods and Goddesses, taking the characters of course straight from
The Age of Fable. Sometimes we acted out the myths as Bulfinch
related them and sometimes we improvised variations of our own.
We loved dressing up in anything we dared or were permitted to
borrow from home, and I always insisted on being Athena, with
the cover of the wash-boiler for my shield and various articles
from the kitchen cupboards in the guise of helmets and spears.

I suppose my mother tried to turn me from my reading-fever
to something more usual for a little girl. But perhaps that would
have entailed her becoming something she was not and taking a
view of life that was not hers. By the time she was wondering how
to make me more like other children I was not only too book-
bound to change but I had acquired my first cat. The two fixations
are inseparable. I cannot remember the cat's name but it was a
nice, round-faced grey kitten and I loved it with the special love
which only cat-people can understand. It was with me every moment of the day and night. I hugged it and kissed it and did all
the things which are variously stated as bad either for cats or for
people; but if kissing cats could kill, I should have been dead

decades ago. I made a doll of the kitten, I dressed it in doll's clothes and pushed it round in the doll's pram, and the kitten co-operated, purring patiently all the while. I also have a strange, naughty memory of sitting under a cherry-tree with a book, my kitten, and the ennui of a terribly hot summer day. For some reason I began to feed cherries to the kitten who, most uncatlike, had not the sense to refuse them. My mother was very angry when the kitten was sick later on my bed.

She was angry, as a matter of fact, freely and for reasons which now seem wholly justifiable, since they derived from her own strict upbringing and the standards of perfection which she was able to exact of herself as an artist, but not of me, or indeed, of anyone else. She was keenly conscious of the gaps in her own education most of which she later filled, and stubbornly determined that there be no similar omissions in mine. She had, for instance, never studied the piano, which annoyed and mortified her and became symbolically something never to be allowed to repeat itself in a child of hers. So at the age of seven I was started on piano lessons. My mother's aim was not to make a pianist of me (I had no talent), but to drill me in a discipline which would instill rigid habits of work, and also insure that I be as literate musically as otherwise. I daresay present-day parents and teachers would be appalled at my mother's methods, but the important thing to me is not what I suffered at the piano, but that I loved my mother then with unwavering adoration and I love her now even more in retrospect. So the long hours of supervised practice, the twenty and thirty repetitions of single measures and phrases, the fanatical exactions of counting, the smacks across the knuckles if my hands lagged, and the real spankings when I was altogether bad, do not matter a bit today. I only think it deplorable that I am not a reasonably good pianist. It is the case, however, that with one glaring exception when I was nineteen, my drilling at the piano was the only part of my mother's discipline from which I rebelled. The time I first jumped the traces, when I was about eight years old, I sneaked out to the woods on the edge of which there was a thick blackberry-cane and there I hid, lost in my world of make-believe and eating blackberries, until Anna, our maid-of-all-work, came and found me.

"You catching it sure," I remember her saying in her flat Czech voice. "You catching it licking, sure."

So I went back to the house to my fate. The house was, as usual, in the midst of a building alteration, and lumber lay strewn all around it. My mother, after telling me to sit down on the piano-stool and wait, went outside and chose a piece of split shingle. Never before had she spanked me with anything but the flat of her bare hand, but Mother's hand was no negligible weapon. This time evidently she felt the need of something more and the spanking was memorable. When it was over and I was convulsed with sobs, she sent me upstairs to stay in my room until she came for me—which I knew from past experience would be soon, and with enough love and comforting tenderness to balance the spanking. So I climbed the steep boxed-in stairs, with my mother standing at the bottom watching me. "You've got to learn to work!" I heard her saying. "You'll never amount to anything if you don't learn to work."

"Oh, yes I will," I said. I reached the top step and turned and looked down at her, angry and beautiful, with her great eyes widened by temper. I was afraid when I saw her eyes like that, and I cried, "Oh, please, don't make your eyes big, Mother! Don't have big eyes any more!"

"How can I help it?" she said. "What am I to do with you? If you don't learn how to work you'll never amount to anything."

"Yes I will!" I said again.

"Not if you don't learn what work is."

I was still frightened but at least the spanking was past. And I felt the need to say something, it was the first time I remember having an answer to her challenge of hard work for its own sake.

"I *will* work," I cried. "I know just what I'm going to do!"

"And what will you do?"

"I'm going to write books, so there!" I said.

My mother laughed, God bless her.

My first piano teacher was a charming, lively, laughing woman who came to accompany my mother's practising and give me piano lessons, and remained to become my mother's closest friend and for many years her travelling companion. Her name was Althea Grant Jewell. She was tall and handsome, with prematurely white hair and a dimpled face that seemed full of light, always smiling. She was a spinster, the last survivor of an old Brooklyn family; a woman of rare character. She was not at all the person one would expect to be a piano-teacher and accompanist, but there she was. I think she must have been the finest influence in those emerging years of my mother's life. She had too a gaiety and sense of play like my mother's; it seems to me the two were constantly in peals and shrieks of laughter. My mother called her Alfy, I Aunt Alfy. She never accompanied my mother in concert, but she was with her throughout every tour and much of the time between tours she lived with us.

Together those two women barnstormed the United States at a time when any town other than the largest cities was a primitive, provincial horror in respect of hotels, conveniences, and above all, of food. Alfy's sense of humor and wild resourcefulness, together with my mother's flair for the ridiculous and her hard-headed way of getting things done enabled the two to turn their touring hardships into a series of hilarious adventures. A few of these, with fictitious variations, appear as elements in *Of Lena Geyer*.

Althea Jewell married late in life, after my mother had retired, and she outlived my mother by many years, the last of which were passed in terrible suffering and helpless invalidism. It was implicit in her character that she remained smiling and gracious as sunlight to the end of her life.

Another person who entered our circle in the same way was

Samuel Chotzinoff, "Chotzie" to the musical world and numerous friends outside it, for a long lifetime until his recent death. He did not come, like Alfy, for my mother's sake but as an appendage to Efrem Zimbalist whose accompanist he became when Zimbalist arrived from Russia to make his American début in 1911. It was Chotzie's first job. As the devotion of Efrem Zimbalist to my mother quickly became spectacular in its romantic persistence, Chotzie was incidentally very much in our house. For a time he was my mother's accompanist also, and for some years my piano teacher. Chotzie was folksy, companionable, widely read; he had a wild and original sense of humor and a gift for thinking up clowning parties which I remember scattered through a span of fifty years and innumerable places. He was also lazy, thoughtless, and selfish. But I think nobody else, except myself, had so acute and perceptive an appreciation of my mother's voice and art.

When one comes to set small chips of the past into the nearly completed mosaic of a life, one sees that time and events which seemed a long span in a child's mind were actually comprised in a very brief period. One discovers, looking back in perspective, how identities and associations came to have their permanent influence and stature. It is natural that Maestro Toscanini should have remained the central force that he was in my life, given the first impressions I have described. The next fundamental was my mother's concern that I hear all the performances of music it was possible to arrange. Between 1909 and 1911 when I went away to school, I was taken to afternoon performances or dress rehearsals of the principal operas in the repertoire, all but the German— and some of those, too—conducted by Maestro. They were sung by artists who are musical history. Self-evidently, the men were Caruso, Scotti, Amato, Didur, Leo Slezak, Otto Goritz, and a remarkable character-tenor named Albert Reiss whom I remember best because he sang The Witch in *Hänsel und Gretel*. I suppose the women were diminished by my concentration on my mother, but the sopranos I heard oftenest and remember best were Emmy Destinn, Geraldine Farrar, and Olive Fremstad. In sum, the first performance of each Verdi and each Puccini opera that I heard was conducted by Maestro and sung by the artists I have mentioned. I heard my mother as Mimi, as Marguerite, as Nedda, and in many smaller parts.

I may be mistaken in ascribing to those first impressions the reason why my standards and my taste are what they are, but I do not think so. There is corroboration in early phonograph records for the convictions of those of us who hold that most of those singers, technically and in the magnitude of their personalities and powers, sang as none have done since. (It is also true that some of them were less good musicians than some of their successors down to the present day; but that is a matter to come to in its own sequence.) Here, I am reaching back only to touch the force which influenced my whole later life—music in totality; and, from the first, music in story. These were stamped into the malleable substance of a child like footprints which harden after they have been impressed in soft cement. My idea of *Aïda* is and always has been what Maestro conducted, with Destinn and Caruso; the same is true of *Tosca* and *Butterfly* with Geraldine Farrar, and indeed of all that I heard. Nobody told me that Caruso was a tenor or even that he was Caruso; all I knew of him was a laughing fat man I saw once or twice in my mother's dressing-room, who drew funny pictures of himself and other artists. But his singing was my introduction, I now see, my indoctrination, into how all his roles ought to sound, and nothing has changed those concepts since.

I found years later, and now retrace with some surprise, that other personalities of whom at that time I was unaware, were also rudiments of later account in my work, if not in my life. One of these was Gustav Mahler. In 1910 he was a conductor of the greatest eminence; he is more recognized as a composer today. A series of quarrels had ended his tenure as musical director and chief conductor of the Court Opera in Vienna, after which he came to New York in 1907 to conduct opera at the Metropolitan and later, concerts at the Philharmonic Society. I do not remember ever meeting him, though I must have seen and heard him, since he conducted *Pique Dame* in which my mother sang the "Mozartiana" aria of Chloe. He was a moody, irascible man in failing health at that time—he died in 1911—but his prestige was enormous and the musical world held him in awe only exceeded by Maestro Toscanini after Mahler's death.

I have no personal memories by which to say anything of Gustav Mahler as a musician or a personality. But a time came when I needed him, to take his real place in the Vienna Opera and the Metropolitan, in my novel, *Of Lena Geyer*. It was possible by then to reconstruct Mahler from all that had been written about him, but I based the reconstruction on my mother's actual memories of him. Apparently he latched on to her as soon as she began to sing, for in November, 1910, she was soloist with him and the Philharmonic. She sang among others, two new songs composed by Mahler, *A Tale of the Rhine,* and *Morning in the Fields.* The latter has a difficult, syncopated rhythm and she worked hard to perfect it. (In passing, I never heard her mention Maestro Toscanini's celebrated temper which in fact did not frighten good artists; he gave them confidence. But she did find Mahler snappish and sarcastic.) During her first rehearsal with him, she told me shamefaced—for such a thing is impermissible—she was trying so hard to please him that she was unconsciously marking time with the tip of her shoe. Mahler stopped the orchestra and said, "You need not beat time, thank you, Madame Gluck. I am here to do that."

"I could have died," she said.

In those last years before the First World War (and the onset of the income tax) one feature of New York life was very much what Edith Wharton in 1905 had depicted in *The House of Mirth*: Society in its immense town houses and country estates, entrenched in multiple millions, some of old vintage and some of the buccaneer era. The entertainments of the day were formidable, great sumptuous dinners and receptions planned and executed with cold magnificence and ostentatiousness such as few living people have seen or can remember. The preferred entertainment was the private musicale after dinner, in the ballroom with its ranks of little gilt chairs, where the greatest artists of the Metropolitan and the concert world sang or played for perhaps half an hour each, for a fee possibly as high as $2500. Two artists were usually engaged for the programme. Musicians have always had their own jokes about these relatively ghastly occasions, some taking the view that this was easy money for the trouble, others that nothing would induce them to touch it. The decision was sometimes taken in reaction to the personalities of the hosts and hostesses. Some were respected and liked as serious patrons of music, others detested for their arrogance.

My mother immediately became a favorite for such musicales. I suspect she accepted the first engagements because of the very high pay for the very short performance. But her high spirits, her beauty, and her sparkling personality won her as much favor as her singing. She did not continue to sing at private musicales for very long, but they produced acquaintanceships of varying degree, some friendships, and her first meeting with Efrem Zimbalist. It has always been a family joke that he picked her up on a ferry-boat; but the fact is that he did. He had arrived in New York in the autumn of 1911, already the violin sensation of London and Berlin. He made his New York début playing the Glazounov Concerto with the Philharmonic, and some weeks later was engaged, like my mother, to perform at a musicale at the house of General Edward P. Meany near Morristown, New Jersey. My mother on her way there was sitting at one end of the passengers' lounge on the ferry-boat, with her accompanist Arthur Rosenstein, and Althea Jewell; and Efrem Zimbalist was at the other end, with his brand-new accompanist, Samuel Chotzinoff.

My mother told me years later that of course Efrem Zimbalist knew who she was; their mutual manager, "Pop" Adams, had in fact coached him. But Chotzie's version of the story described his companion as transfixed when he looked at the beautiful young woman. He sat there dumbstruck. Finally he whispered to Chotzie, "What do I do?" And Chotzie gave him a push. There was a general rearrangement of seating for the rest of the trip and the return, with the accompanists as far away from the artists as possible.

My own first memory of Efrem Zimbalist is vague as to date, but he appeared at our house loaded with toys, some of which terrified me. He was and is to this day gentle, warm, dear to me as only a living link with my mother could be. He has been angelic to me all our lives. In the beginning, it takes no imagination to see, he wanted to win the little girl's affection as part of the supreme emotion of courting her mother. So toys and gifts rained down. When they were dolls or pets or books I was ecstatic. But he also gave me a bicycle, roller-skates, and ice-skates. I remember those with utter horror.

Until I went away to school I was with my mother as constantly as her work allowed, and sometimes I wonder at the patience with which she took me along with her as much as she did. It is tension enough to sing and be at one's best in public appearances without the presence of a child who may, indeed, will do the maddening things that children do. Once my mother was to sing an afternoon recital at one of a series of stuffy, elegant subscription musicales. It was at the Plaza, and she took me along. That morning there had come to the house a large box from a fashionable furrier, and I was in fits when I saw what was inside.

"Pussies!" I shrieked, embracing a long stole and a large flat muff of real chinchillas (a great rarity then.) "Oh, pussies! How wonderful!"

But Mother was cross. She had been solicited to buy the furs, had told the furrier she was not interested, and he had nevertheless sent the box to the house, asking Madame as a favor to him to wear the furs to her concert, and afterwards, if she still did not want to buy them, he would call and take them away.

I began to tease and beg to carry the muff to the concert.

"Certainly not," said my mother. "It doesn't belong to me, I told them not to send it here, and it's going straight back to the shop. Put it back in the box."

"Oh, please," I cried, and thereafter made such a nuisance of myself that my mother, no doubt to save her nerves from further bedevilling, suddenly gave in.

"Very well," she said. "Carry the muff. You look like a fool with it and—" she bent on me her great brown eyes, already a little wide with ruffled temper—"remember that that thing is worth thousands and thousands of dollars and doesn't belong to me. If you lose it, God help you."

I lost it. I remember the concert, I remember every note, every line of her face, as my mother sang *With Verdure Clad*; I remember the gown she wore and the crowd in the green-room afterwards; and I remember the moment when we were alone in the motor and Mother looked at me and asked, "Where's the muff?"

The strangest thing is that I cannot remember what happened after that.

I HAVE always been fascinated by retrospection in measures of time. One decade seems to have been endless, another very short, another lifted almost wholly out of the context of previous and subsequent existence. Perhaps I sense this keenly because of the disparities between different phases and epochs of my life. The experiences crowded into my first eight years were overly dramatic for a child, and they were the reason for my mother's subsequent efforts to redress the balance and put me more into step with the normal pace of schooling and the associations and occupations of a little girl. This did not work very well.

Two solid plinths had taken form in my emotions and my mind: my mother and my intensity about her and all that she was; and my passion for books, to which the essence of solitariness is intrinsic. Between these plinths there had to be strung the realities of education and the lessons of learning to live with people. I was better at the former than the latter, probably because incentive was more attractive in the first instance than the second. The decade between 1911 and 1921 seems interminable as the span between the two poles, tinged with memories of homesickness and unhappiness, but illuminated by the joy of reunion with my mother at vacations and the consistency with which she saw to it that I heard her sing at every possible opportunity, and heard other music regularly and constantly. The same ten years—and I have not dwelt much upon them in memory until now when I am fitting the elements of *fait-accompli* into place—comprised influences apart from my mother, some clear and some rather amorphous, which I recognize for the long-range forces they were, for good or for harm to myself and to others.

In the autumn of 1911 my mother was beginning her third season at the Metropolitan, which proved to be her last because she wanted to devote herself entirely to recitals and concerts. Her contract with Gatti had two more years to run and he was reluctant to release her. However, she had a friend at court, the same generous and far-seeing Chairman of the Board who backed Maestro Toscanini to the hilt in his stipulations about rehearsal-time and all-star casts—though Maestro never spoke or thought of singers as stars. This was the late Otto H. Kahn, the last of the great underwriting patrons of opera's grandest age. His taste and judgement were equal to his munificence, and he was a very good friend to my mother. (He also saw that she was well advised about the investment of her earnings.) I conclude he was convinced through a combination of his own discernment and my mother's charm. The result was that he interceded with Gatti to release her from her contract at the end of that season. She remained a devoted friend of his and years after she had ceased to sing at musicales in rich people's houses, she delighted to go to parties at the Otto Kahns' and sing there because she wanted to.

When she saw that she would be away more than half of every year, touring the length and breadth of the United States, she had to decide on a school for me, a decision that would be difficult in the case of any young child. I find it strange in this instance as in others to which I have never given much retrospective thought that I never later asked my mother what was the sequence and who might have been influential in choosing the school to which I was sent. I have tried to reach behind the veil of time and my memories of persons long dead to see if I could touch the connection. I reason that it must have been Althea Jewell who introduced my mother to a lady called Mrs. Robinson, about whom I remember nothing but her name and an affectionate personality.

She was old and she wore a widow's bonnet something like those in pictures of Queen Victoria. She was fond of my mother and as I remember it, she took a particular interest in me. So I believe she must have been a factor in deciding that I was sent to St. Mary's School at Peekskill, which is run by the Community of St. Mary, an order of nuns in the Episcopal Church, closely aligned with the Anglican High Church. As I try to recall my feelings about it at the age of eight, and so passionately attached to my mother, I find it strange that I was not irreconcilable to the idea of going away to school; in fact I have little memory of any emotion about it. So my mother must have succeeded in reassuring me that I was not being painfully separated from her. And I had already felt the dreariness of her absences from home, necessarily leaving me alone with a governess.

I had been accustomed to a great deal of demonstrative affection and I see from this perspective that there must have been concern for the risk of so young a child having to go without it, had I met that at school. I was by far the youngest pupil at St. Mary's and the Sisters were very good to me. They were tender and kind and, I see now what I could not have known then, patient with a child who was probably difficult and certainly in many ways a freak. I was fond of the head of the school, a small wry woman called Sister Mary Maud, because she owned an enormous Maltese cat which I was allowed to have with me much of the time. And I loved Sister Mary Christine, whom I saw more than anyone else, and who became my godmother when presently I was baptized. She died long ago and I had not seen her for many years before, but her warm laugh, her pink-cheeked face in its starched, winged white coif, her gentle voice, and her tenderness endeared her vividly to me.

These are not the impressions commonly drawn from memories of life in convent schools. I remember nothing of grimness, austerity, punishments, bad food, or a forbidding atmosphere such as has been so often described in French and much other literature. I was homesick, I missed my mother, and I had always been too much alone to fall easily into a pattern of communal living.

But my mother came to see me as often as possible, she endeared herself to the people around me, and she did all she could to bridge the gap between my previous existence and that at school. She gave the school a box for a Saturday matinée subscription at the Metropolitan, to which a party went by train for each performance. I was the only child who went to all of them and for all I know, the only one who really cared to go. I have a remembered sense of my own importance in this connection, which is not very pleasing; and I remember too the time my mother came to sing a recital for the school. I was very proud of her and of my place in the centre of the front row, where I would probably not otherwise have been. She looked her loveliest. She wore a white satin gown with a long train which she swirled with grace around her feet as she took her place in the bend of the piano and began her first group of songs. At that point Sister Mary Maud's cat made a stately entrance onto the platform, padded across it, examined my mother's train, and proceeded to arrange himself comfortably on it. The girls of course began to break up with giggles and I remember my agony, torn between the indignity to my mother and my attachment to the cat. She sensed at once that she had lost her audience and looked down from their convulsed faces to see the cat asleep on her train. She stopped singing and began to laugh while someone took the cat away, and then she started over again.

I never knew until after her death that my mother was sentimental in a way that has largely vanished in the compressed spaces and abrupt rhythms of present-day life. Today it is considered undesirable, mawkish—the vernacular would say 'corny' or 'square' —to keep old letters, pressed flowers, locks of hair, or other tangible tokens that will make a clutter, take up space, or invoke what some opinions consider sentimentality. But that is what my mother did, and did almost secretly. When she died I brought to my house her files, photograph albums, scrap-books, boxes of correspondence, and other papers. I have already noted that until I needed them for this book I had never read her press-notices; but more personally, I had never been able to bring myself to go through the letters. Only very recently have I done so. The record begins with my own infancy and continues to the end of her life. There are wide and scattered gaps; she did not keep every letter I ever wrote her and I have not got every one that she wrote to me. I have none, to my great regret, spanning the principal years of my education, which suggests that somebody in the process of teaching me neatness encouraged or even required me to destroy letters when they had been answered.

But what I have got beside me are many letters that I wrote to my mother when I was first away at school, addressing them all over the United States when she was on tour. They remind me of the itineraries she used to leave with me, with notations when to mail the letters to catch her on the way. There is nothing worth quoting in the short, carefully-written, and correctly spelt letters of a child but they corroborate my sense that I cannot remember having to learn to write or spell. These became part of me as early and as unconsciously as reading did, and I still wonder just how this happened long before I went to school. What I am grateful for is the proof that memory has not confused me, in emotion, in chronology, or through wishful thinking.

Through the screen of fifty years and more these letters bring back the reality of a child's joys such as they were, and griefs—"I cried for you today and missed you very much"—but they cannot tell me the reasons for decisions that were taken about me. Perhaps it is as well. I know my mother felt that I had been too precociously involved in the excitements and splendors of her success and that somehow she ought to separate me from her public identity, at the same time keeping the intense relation between us what it had always been. From this distance I realize how difficult that was, and also how strong a force in her comments on her own life and the lives of women in general. Constantly she stated that she believed it impossible for a woman to be an artist or pursue any career and also be a good wife and mother. And between the two, she insisted, the second was the right and the better choice. Again and again she said this, wrote it to me in letters, declared it publicly and privately, and from the bottom of her heart believed it.

Of course she was struggling with a massive dilemma. Only dimly and by very gradual degrees did I come to realize this, and not at all while I was still a child. She was in point of fact involved in a dichotomy which inwardly I know she never fully resolved. She sang not primarily at the behest of a driving ambition but because she was born to sing and could not otherwise have fulfilled herself. Once committed to singing it was her nature to serve her art by the highest standards, whose aim was, in a word, perfection. Nothing but the hardest work achieves this, if it can be achieved at all. I have already noted how young I was when she began to indoctrinate me with this concept of work. But I was too young then and for years afterwards to understand that at the same time that she was living by such doctrine, she was also dealing with herself as a woman impelled by the deepest emotions.

Much more can be understood of this by a bit of chronology than by words. She met Efrem Zimbalist in 1911 but she did not marry him until 1914. Neither he who is dear to me, nor she if she could speak, nor I who feel that reticence is more telling than revelation in this instance, would have me reiterate how deeply they were in love. From the first he besought her to marry him; from very early on, she wanted to. But for three years she would not consent. Her reluctance was rooted in the conviction that she could not create a real marriage whilst she was at the height of her career—that dislikable word which she abjured and for which I can find no functional synonym—or on the way to the height. And she wanted no less than a real marriage. She had other motives for long hesitation. Efrem Zimbalist was five years younger than she. Though new to the United States he was one of three violinists who were considered the world's foremost (Jascha Heifetz had not yet emerged from Russia.) As an artist he was her peer and she believed, her superior. But no violinist is the public idol that a young, beautiful, and superlative soprano can be, nor do his earnings and his celebrity compare with hers. All of this held her back. Within a year of leaving the Metropolitan she was more in demand than any concert artist in this country, and only John McCormack drew audiences and commanded fees as large as hers. Also by then she had begun to make records for the Victor Talking Machine Company, and this both increased her audiences and cemented her hold on a nation-wide public. It also greatly increased her income.

Who of my age does not remember the old hand-cranked Victor machine with the convolvulus-shaped horn, and the slightly newer Victrola without the horn which presently succeeded it? Families sat around these machines in small-town 'front rooms' and farmhouse parlors all over this country, and played on them the records they loved, almost entirely those of singers, since orchestral and instrumental recordings of music longer than a song or an aria lay a generation ahead in the future. They loved the voices of Schumann-Heink and Caruso, John McCormack, and perhaps best of all, Alma Gluck. I think the basis of this was the quality of intimacy in her voice, which in concert made each member of the audience feel she was singing directly to him or to her; and which came through on her records in a way that made people consider them personal treasures. The testimony of this is the letters she received all her life and which I still receive to this day, telling how the writers grew up with *Come, Beloved*; with *Ave Maria* (Bach-Gounod); with *My Laddie, The Land of the Sky-Blue Water, Carry Me Back to Ole Virginny,* or whichever of her records were their favorites. A great many of these were simple ballads and folk-songs and old-fashioned hymns. My mother learned that American people liked what was genuine, whether it be a classic of Handel or Bach, or a sincerely and beautifully sung version of *Old Black Joe*. She sang what her audiences loved to hear, and the key to her art and her character was that she gave the same degree of scrupulous musicianship to everything she sang, and condescended to none of it. Musical snobs sometimes remonstrated with her for singing stuff like *My Little Grey Home in the West*. She paid no attention to them. (Incidentally, her own name for that song was "Little Grey Hole in My Vest".) She had her reasons for what she did, in the faces of farmers and their families who drove fifty miles on dirt roads in model T Fords to hear her annual concert in the nearest town; and in letters from women who saved their egg-money and pin-money to buy her records.

I shall have more to say about the records and what they have meant to me all my life. At the moment I am negotiating the stream of memory. It is a devious stream, sometimes deflected by tricky currents. My intention is to float, inert as one must be when floating. I begin to feel the motion of the slow stream, I respond to it; but suddenly I am jolted. A sharp, chopping wave jars me, rolls me over, forces me to swim rather than float, demanding exertion. This is the other sort of remembering, not easy floating on the water of time but positive effort, cleaving the water with direction and drive. This is stress, and it yields memories from other sides of my life, sides apart from my mother and in fact largely hidden from her by motives I cannot explain. I know that I was sometimes desolate away from her—sometimes quite contented, if I was sufficiently occupied and interested—but I cannot give a reason why after the earliest childish griefs, I refrained from complaining when I felt unhappy or lonely, exiled or misunderstood. I know she never told me it was my duty to be brave about it for her sake. And I know that neither I nor probably any other child could have had the fortitude or the reasoning-power consciously to be self-sacrificing. I think more probably that children accept their lot simply because they are children. Or else my mother had so securely assured me of her love by the time I was seven or eight that I never feared that separation from her meant any dimunition of my importance to her or her devotion to me.

School was sometimes painful because it was so difficult for me to adapt myself to life with other children. The girls teased me, I have forgotten just how, but clearly because I was different from the rest, a freak, with my inability to play games, my precocious love of music and books, and even the fact that I was put in a French class with much older girls because I spoke French already. But some things there I loved. I loved the Sisters, I loved the animals and the garden where each girl had a little plot of her own in which to grow what she wanted, and I loved Chapel and the religion that was taught us there. My first impressions were awe and appreciation of the beauty and the sense of mystery, before I had any concept of their significance. Like all convent schools St. Mary's instructed all pupils alike and expected them and the lay teachers to share the ritual and the observances of the Community. Since I do not know why it was decided to send me to a Church school, I have never thought personally in terms of religious conversion, for I never knew or had any previous grounding in a religion from which to be converted. The only prayers my mother had taught me were the Lord's Prayer and "Now I lay me down to sleep." When the Sisters at school began to instruct me in prayer and then in the meaning of what they taught; when I was baptized and in due course confirmed, and when my godmother was the readiest recipient for the affection which it was my nature to give, I responded. We have all heard cynical comments about religion or religious institutions getting their hooks into children before the age of fourteen, after which the effects cannot be undone. Bigotry and narrow sectarianism aside, I have no quarrel with such indoctrination. I also have no quarrel with people of metropolitan worlds and articulate professions who are generally agnostic, who consider intellect incompatible with faith, and faith impossible or preposterous in this century which may well see the end of Western civilization or of this planet. In later passages of childhood I encountered people who were more didactic, more intolerant, and more intrusive than the Sisters who instructed me in religion. The Sisters were gentle and serene and simple of heart. I value these qualities the more highly as they are abraded in the present day.

In summers the little white house at Lake George rocked with the laughter of my mother and Alfy and their friends. Sidney and Louise Homer with their large family lived at Bolton Landing up the lake, to which we used to go in a motor launch for picnics. I still loved Edith and Martha and the magic games we played. But some niches of memory are curiously bare. In New York I was much aware of Efrem Zimbalist, smiling, speaking little English, with curly fair hair, always bringing me presents; but I do not remember him at Lake George, which must mean he was abroad, playing in London and on the Continent. In fact, he once travelled all the way from Petrograd to spend one day with my mother in New York and returned immediately to Russia for concerts there. Sometimes my mother was in Europe too— she went to study with Jean deReszke, who was the chief source of her wide and beautiful repertoire of French songs. She also studied with Marcella Sembrich who had then retired, and whose Queen Mary-like style and manner my mother used to mimic outrageously.

There are some three years which run together indistinguishably. I knew later of my mother's romance, but I did not realize it then, evidence of a careful plan of hers to weave the threads of her life together to make a strong fabric, and to do that gradually enough to give it depth and thickness. She succeeded extraordinarily. I was a jealous and possessive child and she had been my whole world. When she finally told me in the spring of 1914 that she was going to be married, I was perfectly thrilled, as though I had come to the proverbial happy ending of one of the fairy-tales I knew by heart. Many years later I realized that she must have been apprehensive, and planned the dénouement in fear of how I might react. By then we were all so devoted and Efrem Zimbalist so wholly my father in my mind and affections that I never told her she need not have worried.

I remember dancing round and round her dressing-table where she was braiding her hair, asking her what she was going to wear, not even grieved when she said I could not be present because she was going to London where she would sing for the first time, and where she would be married. I was to spend the summer at Lake George with I cannot remember whom, to look after me, and the friends and occupations I was happy with. But I had been ill that spring and had been taken out of school. There was a great deal of doctoring and special care. I had always been a difficult child to feed because I would not eat the things suitable for children, and the fight had been given up to force me to eat them. Oh, the slimy boiled egg or the cup custard or the milk that my mother ordered to be served me, meal upon meal, until I should break down and swallow it! But I never could, the agonies always ended in vomiting and tears, and my torments were at last remitted. But apart from meat and rice and fruit I do not know what I ate, and I suppose somebody told my mother that I was turning into a problem.

She was already worried about that. Boarding-school, no matter how fond I might be of one or two adults there, was not the answer. I was too young for it. My mother had been unsuccessful in her first attempt to find the solution for me during three long winters of her absences on tour and now she would be away more than ever before. The whole question, as I have noted, was one that wracked her and became progressively more difficult when she had a husband and eventually two more children to intensify her conviction that they must have precedence over her career. But in those years she was at the height of that career, singing between eighty and one hundred recitals a season, which is an average of three to four a week in about six months; a gruelling schedule especially when it meant unintermittent travelling between appearances.

When her two younger children were infants it was possible to leave them in New York with a Nanny (who, they told me years later, was a monster instead of the paragon my mother believed her to be). But I was in the midst of my schooling, and at an age when my mother was convinced I must somehow become adjusted to living with other children. She or somebody she knew and trusted conceived an idea that I must have something too easily put in a phrase that can be a travesty and a delusion. That phrase is family life. From my experience I think family life can only really exist for those born into a family or linked to it by close blood ties. Arrangements intended to make of an outsider 'a member of the family' except in instances of definite temporary duration, are fraught with sorrow, fears, uneasy dislikes, and the most ominous forces which shape us—the hatreds, resentments, and disappointments which as children we instinctively bury. Those seeds can bear bitter fruit. I know because I have reaped it.

At the age of eleven I was a spoilt brat. There was in me none of the natural give-and-take, share-alike, live-and-let-live which several children in a family supply to one another. I had had more discipline in application, perseverance, and concentration than the average child but circumstances had made me turn some of that on the attainment of my own wants. I had no idea how to live or play with children unless like Edith and Martha they chanced to enjoy sharing my queer world of fantasy; but no children except those two ever had. Solitude, with books, with a cat, with a doll, was my instinctive norm. My mother was worried about it. I have always been grateful that she did not try for my sake, as she did later with her youngest child, to burden her art by herself trying to fill the deficiencies which an artist-mother imposes on a child's life. I have always taken to myself the right to choose what I wanted of my mother, and her art has been my greatest satisfaction and inspiration. As a child my pride in her and my adoration of her were so absolute that they separated themselves altogether from my own troubles. It did not occur to me to wish to be with her when her work made that impossible; and it also never occurred to me that my unhappiness for seven years in alien surroundings was one of the prices of her success. Later in her life she said something about this, regretful and conscience-stricken. I said, "Forget it. It was worth it." And it was.

Everything about the plan, from its first broaching to me, was wrong. Somehow it had to fall in 1914, that doomful year which for so many individuals of my generation was as shattering a break with the past and as black an augury for the future as it was for the world itself. The First World War retains for me an immediacy in some ways sharper than much that followed it. I am surprised to realize that I was eleven years old when that war began, and fifteen when it ended. I think of myself as having been much older; in comprehension and concern I was older. Our noses had not been so savagely and repetitively rubbed in war as they have been since. Perhaps my insatiable reading during that war—of newspapers and journals, of the writing it precipitated—H. G. Wells, Henri Barbusse, Arnold Zweig, the fallen poets Brooke and Kilmer, the cartoons of Raemakers—all of it shaped my mind and personality, keeping their recollections of that time indelible. And I wonder if it can be true that the farther one peers back down the halls of memory the sharper the early impressions appear.

In June of that year my mother and Efrem Zimbalist were married in London. Just before, she had sung her first recital there and enchanted the British public. The ultimate plan to return there for more concerts and also on the Continent was of course obliterated by the war and that was how it happened that her whole career was confined to the United States. She never had a regret about it. Althea Jewell had gone with her as usual when she went to London, and after the wedding went along, in her own words, to chaperone the honeymoon. I never quite saw the reason for that but my mother enjoyed her jokes about it. The party were in Chamonix when France declared war—I have my panicky letter to my mother of August 6th, 1914, begging her to come home—and there my mother did something which makes me lean to believing the story about my grandmother and the Bohemian glass.

Immediately war was declared, currency restrictions were clamped on tourists. Gold became the only valid money. It was impossible to cash drafts on banks or to draw gold from any source, so people had to make do with what gold they had on hand, if any. My mother and her honeymoon party were caught with very little gold and were obliged to wait in Chamonix until arrangements could be made by consulates to supply travellers with funds and transportation—in this case, to Genoa, from which they eventually crossed the Atlantic in what my mother described as a cattle boat.

While her bridegroom spent his time struggling with financial and travel problems my mother and her friend Alfy went out daily for their usual long walk through the pretty streets of Chamonix. There in the window of a souvenir shop was a small red leather bag, a sort of reticule, embroidered with beads, its drawstrings knotted with tiny grey shells. My mother wanted to buy it for me. The shopkeeper asked a shameful price and would accept no money but gold. Alfy dragged my mother away. The days passed and the party's small store of gold had to be used for urgent expenses. They were uncertain how long this would go on and it continued until my mother was down to her last gold-piece. Every day she and Alfy passed the shop and every day Alfy dragged her away. There is no explaining why my mother had taken such a fancy for that little bag. The day came when she gave Alfy the slip, hurried to the shop, and spent her last gold-piece for the little red bag, which I have to this day, crumbled almost to dust.

When she returned to New York she told me about the plan

that had been made for me, and in the telling she made her first serious mistake with me. As if this were a matter for happy anticipation she said that I was to go to Philadelphia, to stay with friends of hers and be a member of their family while she was away all winter. I had never heard of these people until then and I know that my mother had met them only a short time before. They were friends of some London friends of Efrem Zimbalist's —and everything my mother knew of them convinced her that they could supply what she so much wanted for me: simple family life, intellectual and scholarly associations, education in a good day-school, and the company of four children. She told me they would be like brothers and a sister (a fatal thing to have said.) I remember no reaction of the least interest or enthusiasm about any of this; I felt doubtful, uneasy, and suspicious. Something was being put over on me. But I did not say that to my mother.

Though it is obvious that the arrangement had been made and could rightly only have been made on a basis of mutual responsibility, with my mother paying Mrs. G, as I will call her, for her care of me, the matter was distinctly not presented to me in that light. I was somehow expected to believe that the G family were taking me in as a member out of—what? It could not be affection for a child they had never seen; it could not be devotion to my mother whom they scarcely knew. I think it must have been a mistaken idea of taste which created the confused fiction that Mrs. G was doing something unprecedentedly hospitable and kind; yet it was also made plain to me that I was not to consider myself a guest in her family, exempt from the obligations and burdens, the punishments too, of her own children. Perhaps, because I was so proud of my mother and so convinced she was the most wonderful person alive, it was feared that if I knew she paid Mrs. G, I might act in bad moments with want of tact. I know now when it cannot matter, that a frank explanation of the arrangement would have been wiser, with the admonition and the continuous lesson to me that I had an obligation of good manners which could only be discharged through an understanding of the very point about which I was never enlightened.

The G family were unusual. At their best they were intelligent, but pretentiously intellectual. At their worst they were brusque, ungentle, hypocritical, and totally controlled by the most domineering woman I have ever known. Collectively they possessed, I think, the opposite of that carelessly-flung term, the inferiority complex. Mrs. G imparted to her family the conviction of a superiority whose nature was never apparent to me or to many others who nevertheless made the feint of accepting it. This superiority had nothing to do with mundane or material or social matters; it was a thing of the intellect and of a word which Mrs. G used beyond any realistic interpretation: 'character'. Exactly what she meant by that I do not know to this day, for she never defined it by word or example as the combination of elements that it is or can be. She used and stressed other words to exhaustion: 'loyalty', 'home', 'family'. These served as tenets of a dogma apparently created by the G family as if in place of a religion which they did not, as was their right if they chose, profess. (I said my prayers secretly.) But no connection was made between the words and the real elements out of which their meaning should grow. Loyalty cannot be exacted; people do not necessarily love a home; a family is only a living tissue of close ties when all its members are mutually impelled to make it so.

But a formidable legend had grown around Mrs. G and her family. She was considered a remarkable woman, an exemplary mother, a creator of ideal family life. I was supposed to accept this and in a great flowering of loyalty, character, and group feeling, conform to her rules of what The Home should be. Of course I did no such thing. I was at first bewildered, later repelled, and always frightened. At this distance of more than fifty years since the impressions which a child could not analyze, I know what the defects of the G family were. Taking their tone from the domineering mother, they all lacked tenderness and humor; and by humor I do not mean the capacity to be funny. I mean that breadth and tolerance, that warmth and ease, that gleam of cynicism without which an understanding of human nature is impossible, and without which we are devoid of the power to see ourselves even in fleeting glimpses as other see us. Perhaps more than humor I am defining humanness. The G family also lacked modesty and graciousness of spirit. As for me—I lacked everything. I was, as my mother told me long afterwards, a prig and a brat.

Mrs. G took herself with deadly seriousness and imposed that acceptance on any person she held so privileged as to enter her circle. What in the name of Heaven was my beautiful, gay, warm, witty, worldly mother doing amongst such people? I can only explain it as a wistful and conscience-stricken idea that this was the sort of home and family life a child should have. My mother was trying to find it for me since she had been unable to create it herself (thank God.) By the end of her life I was able to laugh with her about the G's, and to comment about them in our own way, with a twitching eyebrow, a foreign monosyllable, or a charade about life in their midst which made us howl with laughter. But an eleven-year-old child on first confrontation with that life had no such defences, and any natural reactions to its strictures (most of them absurdities) were considered 'arrogance,' 'insolence,' or 'superficiality.'

On an autumn day I arrived alone at the West Philadelphia railway station, where I had been told to leave the New York train. Mrs. G, or Aunt G, as I was to call her, would meet me there. I had been put on the train in the usual way that anyone puts a child travelling alone, with an aside to the Pullman porter to look after her. I had been alone on a train before; that did not trouble me. When I had left the car and was standing on the platform beside my luggage I saw nobody who might be the Aunt G I had never seen. But almost at once there came hurrying towards me from the other end of the platform where the daycoach passengers were emerging from the train a very stout woman dressed in a coat-and-skirt of an odd bright but dark blue. She spoke to me. I do not remember what she said, but I remember bitterly the mood and tenor of her welcome. It was sharp annoyance that I had been sent to Philadelphia in a Pullman car; I should have travelled by coach.

It was not only a necessity of the G family, whose means were limited—but what of it?—never to travel in first-class accommodations; it was an affectation militantly to despise people who did, except on very long journeys. Mrs. G lost no time in telling me that I had been sent to her to learn how 'real' people lived, and to unlearn some of my spoilt and splurging notions absorbed in the few years (though a child has no such perspective) since my mother had come into fortune. She was so irritated by the Pullman car episode that I do not know how many days it was before I felt in her anything but the censorious chill of the first moment. Perhaps she disliked me from the first but if so, I thought for years afterwards, should she not have withdrawn from the arrangement and sent me back to New York? However, my mother had said all too frankly, in her typical way of sheathing a barb in warm-hearted chaffing, that I was to be "made into a child instead of a fussy little old woman"; and I suppose Mrs. G considered that a challenge to her widely discussed merits as woman and mother. Probably she thought of me as raw material upon which she had been engaged to exercise these talents, and many human aspects of the situation were ignored. I had had from my own mother discipline as severe as anything I ever saw Mrs. G mete out to her children, but it was dispensed in quick temper which was immediately dispelled in loving and demonstrative tenderness. I never saw Mrs. G tender or affectionate, by my measure, with her own children, and even less had she any such impulses towards me.

The disillusionments came fast. One of the worst, a real shock, was the first. I knew nothing about the daughter of the G's, a little older than myself, and when I saw her on that first

day, and saw that she had a conspicuous physical handicap, I
asked her if she had hurt herself. I meant it as concern, but I
was answered with a glare, the seed of mutual loathing which
lasted for years. In my ignorance I had been horribly cruel, but
nobody had forewarned me that the girl was a cripple.

I had to share a room with her, not only because I was to
be initiated into such ordinary arrangements of family life, but
because the G's already filled every room of their good-sized
house. Never before or since has it happened that I have had to
share a bedroom with anybody. Some people are born really
unable to do so. The inability to adjust to such an arrangement is
not necessarily selfishness or stubbornness, though it may be;
there is a temperament which requires at times to be alone as im-
peratively as bodies to perform their physical functions. I have
often thought with horrified sympathy of those who have the
physically solitary nature, forced by poverty or other necessity to
share bedrooms with other people. I have heard men describe it
who had their first trial of it in the army. Such people agree that
the most miserable hole alone is better for them than the most
comfortable room imaginable, shared with another person.

I remember with most distress the seven interminable years
(with blessed respites in the summer when I was at home) of
breakfasts in the G family. Here was family breakfast at its most
horrible. The G house was dark, one of the ugly brown sandstone
dwellings built by thousands in American cities about the end of
the last century; hideous outside but more hideous inside, with
fumed-oak dadoes, dark embossed wallpapers, tortuously carved
stair-rails, and leaded windows with occasional bits of stained
glass, to shut out more light when little enough came in. There
was a dark breakfast-room between the kitchen and the dining-
room, and it was here that five uneasy children had to take their
places punctually on icy winter mornings, with Mrs. G scowling
at the head of the table. Mr. G was almost always away, his learned
profession requiring constant travel, so his rare presence when he

was there became an occasion. He was a genial person and I have a distant sense that his wife was on her good behavior when he was present.

Mrs. G was always sullen in the mornings, with or without comprehensible reason. Any child who in recent days had incurred her wrath remained in a state of disgrace for an indefinite time —sometimes for weeks. And for that child breakfast-time was hell, its reverberations feared by all the others. I grew used to hearing Mrs. G praised as a wonderful mother, commended for never failing to breakfast with her children 'even when she had one of her headaches' and see them off to school. It would have been better for the children had she stayed shut up in her room in the mornings, since she almost never greeted them with warmth or sent them off with a smile. We used to come down to find her glowering in her place, and go to her to kiss or be kissed good morning. She would turn her head away, her mouth pinched, and offer the angle of her chin to be kissed. She treated her own children no differently from me in this respect. And the legacy of those dreadful breakfasts fixed for the rest of my life my habit of breakfasting alone in my room, which has nothing to do with whether there is anybody to wait on me. At times I have had no one, and if so have been happy to go and prepare my breakfast and carry it to my room myself.

Mrs. G also had the rule that a mother should always be at home to greet her children when they arrived from school. How good was that for the children when they were met by scowls or sullen silence, the result of some disgrace into which they had got themselves any day, or many days, before? I have known a number of people who bore the affliction of harboring resentment, but I have never known anyone so dyed in that fault as Mrs. G; and to this day I shrink from the memory of its effect upon defenceless children.

Of course her children and I did do many of the reprehensible things for which we were punished and kept thereafter in disgrace—'ostracized' was her word. And I have no doubt that I was exasperating to the G family. How do I know that the children did not loathe me and resent my presence? I was not particularly popular either at the Quaker school we attended. I can dismiss my standing as a student by admission to very good marks—but only in subjects which interested me or in which, like languages, I had natural talent and previous proficiency; but I was conceited. And when I was incapable or uninterested—most so in mathematics—I was incorrigible. Nobody short of a congenital idiot could do as badly as I did wilfully, once past the memorizing of the multiplication-tables. Like all avid readers I could memorize nearly anything and I used that trick to get me through what I hated too much for honest application. On the other hand, my early childhood of omnivorous reading had given me real grounding in literature, so that I suffered torments over the mauling and butchering of the classics that was done in school. When my English class were studying *The Merchant of Venice* and *Paradise Lost* (I think of both because of the trouble I got into) the procedure was the cannibalism which keeps their magic from touching children introduced to them in American schools. Teaching may be different today, but it was not as recently as a dozen years ago. Grammar, allusion, the language as technicality were stressed, evoking apathy or contemptuous impatience in the few and leaving the many stumbling in a wilderness where their grunts and barks were a mockery of the poetry and the dreaming it invoked.

While my English class were reciting, each girl required to stand and read off a few lines which she or others would then tear to shreds in the pursuit of grammar and allusion, I would be lost, pages or chapters ahead, in the enchantment which overcame me on opening any book. If called on to recite I would raise my head, startled and bat-eyed behind my glasses, and gape at the teacher, for I had not heard a word of what was going on. This deviation from conformity of course meant trouble.

Also my passion for books got me into trouble with Aunt G, despite the pride of the G's in their intellectual life and their house—The Home—full of books. Once when Mr. G was due home early in the morning from a tour away at work, the family breakfast was to be a special festivity, with all his favorite dishes (no burnt porridge!) and everybody on his best behavior. But the day before, I had started to read *Jane Eyre*—for the first time, curiously. I had had to put it down at bedtime and from the moment I woke in the morning I could think of nothing else. I got up and dressed and took my book to a corner intending to read just for the few minutes until we were to be down to greet Uncle G on his arrival. Hours later I heard the heavy tread of Aunt G shaking the last flight of stairs to the top floor, and marching to my door to throw it open furiously. I had never before received such a tongue-lashing as the one I then caught. "Disloyal!" was the burden of her tirade, together with all its synonymous viciousnesses of character. From this distance I wonder what was the root of the woman's obsession. Had she merely chastised me for rudeness she would have been right and the incident not have rankled forever after.

Another time, after I had been allowed to have a membership in the Mercantile Library in Philadelphia, I went there one afternoon after school and sat down in the reading-room with a novel of Zola. As usual, time evaporated and I came back mentally from Paris just in time to see that I must hurry not to be late for supper. When I ran into the house, already terrified of the impending storm, it broke much worse than I had expected. This time I was accused of deceitfulness. I could not understand what I had done, except again forget the clock because I was lost in a book. No, I was lying. Aunt G had proved it for herself. I was in despair, strangled with tears and protest. I really believe I have a native incapacity, probably a form of timidity, and functional beyond my volition, for deceitful action. Mrs. G knew this perfectly well. Yet she accused me of a monstrous deceit. She told me she knew I had gone to the movies instead of to the library as I claimed. And this was a double crime because we were forbidden ever to go to movies at all. Disobedience, beyond deceit.

In vain I insisted I had been right there in the library all afternoon. No, she said; she had gone to the Mercantile Library herself to check up on me, and she had not seen me in the Members' reading-room. It was only after the intervention of her husband and their eldest son, who also used the library, that it was realized I had been sitting in the outer of two reading-rooms; I had not known I was supposed to be in the inner one. She had walked twice right past the room where I was but had not thought to look for me there. I cannot remember whether she ever apologized for her unjustness. But I do remember that it was weeks before she spoke a civil word to me, or looked at me with anything but rancor.

If I had had no recourse from the G aegis, and nothing during those years to give me joy and laughter, fun, and sheer happiness I shudder to think what the results might have been. I turned out to be too much of an oddity as it was. I grew used to hated Philadelphia—who would not? But somehow I understood that it was an ordeal to be endured not only for my mother's sake but because she believed it necessary for me. She enabled me to understand this without her putting it in words. There were no drab 'little talks', no hovering evidences of ultimate concern. She believed from the roots of her own life and personality that hardship, stringency, are essential to human stature. Material poverty was not a hardship to which I might realistically be subjected; something had to be substituted. What had to be, had to be. She held that life is fundamentally hard; its happinesses are to be earned, not handed out as rights receivable. This is a tough philosophy, not much encountered in the current Freudian view of human fate and behavior; and while it inflicts suffering, I would still rather live by it than by certain more contemporary approaches to life.

I was only in Philadelphia during the school year. In summer I was at home, and summers were paradise except for hours of daily slavery at the piano. A whole summer vacation with no work to do was alien to my mother's ken. At Christmas and Easter vacations and various weekends I went home to New York. I can still feel the sheer bliss which made my nose, ears, and eyes tingle as the car that had met me emerged from Pennsylvania Station and started home in a cacophony of honks and blats from taxis and trucks. I would keep the window down and drink in the sharp air of New York, unknowing and uncaring whether it was loaded with the pollutants about which some of us recently have been agitating. How I loved it! It was alive. Everything about New York was alive to me and everything about Philadelphia dead or deadly. There is a sheer what-the-hell about the roaring swagger of New York which is in the marrow of my bones and which all the jeremiads about urban degeneration cannot drain away.

My mother and Efrem Zimbalist were an enchanting couple, and their circle widened fast and far. He was more than good to me; indulgent, generous, patient if I ever got on his nerves which I must have done. He taught me to call him "Papuchka", the Russian diminutive which amounts to "Daddy", and Papuchka he has remained. All my life the subtle balance of time and age has held him in this paternal niche but not long ago I pointed out, with a groan of protest at time's beastliness, that he is only fourteen years older than me and now we are old alike, the gap between us filled by tribulation and grey hair. "Oh my God," he said, "it's im-*poss*-eeble!"

He used to keep my mother in fits of amused apprehension and all of us in howls of laughter with his passion (long outlived) for gambling, for bargains, for collecting things, and for going to auctions. In 1931 I wrote a Profile of him for *The New Yorker* which detailed many of these antics and acquisitions, and which at the time he did not much like; but he was mollified by my mother's delight and everybody's approbation. When he and my mother were married they bought a house on the West Side, which was followed in a few years by a brownstone on Park Avenue, the home of my girlhood. Summers became the essence of happiness for all of us with the move in 1916 to Fishers Island, where my mother bought a vast 1908-ish 'summer cottage' of stone and weathered shingle, which crowned the low hill above Hay Harbor, and I think held more joy and high spirits, good parties, and hospitality than any house I have ever known.

Perhaps it was the spaciousness of those houses, part and parcel of the dear dead days, which incited Efrem Zimbalist to allay his boredom while on tour by dropping into auction-rooms and bidding in everything he saw. In this way there came to the entrance-hall in New York the eagle, supposedly of ivory, with a wing-spread of about six feet, which stood on a pedestal in a corner and shed its clattering feathers on the marble floor. When we were moving into the Fishers Island house, a big empty place to be sure, an unannounced van arrived from somewhere to deliver a job-lot of stuff that Efrem Zimbalist had bid in at an auction. I can still see my mother standing on the stair-landing, her eyes as big as cart-wheels, speechless, her expression slowly changing from rage to convulsed mirth as the moving-men lugged in a fourteen-piece set of Victorian horsehair furniture, a glass-doored bookcase eighteen feet long, gargantuan rolls of Brussels carpet, a gingerbread curio cabinet complete with contents, a number of odd sofas, and half a dozen oil paintings, one of which Papuchka insisted was a Rubens.

Looking back on the extreme contrast between the gloom of Philadelphia and the felicity of home, echoing with music and laughter, I realize that my mother was more aware of my sufferings than she admitted. To have said anything would have been to deny her purpose. To do something was more like her. At home both in New York and at Fishers Island mine was the largest and prettiest room in the house but for her own. Except for unrelenting hours of piano practice, with my teacher living right in the house, my summer days were filled with boats and swimming, friends and freedom. My room had a big balcony—what used to be called an upstairs porch—and there, when I was not otherwise occupied, I could settle with my book and my cat and the vista of water and boats before me, to dig into what have become the prerequisites for contentment ever since.

But there was little need for flight into solitude in the summer. Fishers Island was heaven for the young just because it was an island, in those days a tiny, remote community where everybody knew everybody else and we all did the same things together. I and my friends had the run of the house and freedom to raid the enormous ice-box, really a cold-room chilled by blocks of ice heaved in daily through an outside hatch. Our cook Hannah left us cold chickens and turkeys, hams, and ribs of beef. My mother never minded how many of us trooped in after the early movie on the Post, the Coast-Artillery station named Fort Wright, which was dismantled and abandoned years ago. When there was target practice for the big guns, the 16-inchers generally shattered someone's windows but nobody protested.

Nearly all my memories of those summers are wildly hilarious. It suited my mother when her concert season was over to lay aside Alma Gluck and all that part of her life, and be the person the other part of her commanded. Our house was full of guests, musicians among others, but there was a great deal in my mother and her husband which appealed to people who had no relation to them as musicians and, in fact, never knew them as such. In New York my mother made for herself and her husband a place at the confluence of the streams of society, the great world, and the arts; in her time more a classic blending in the tradition of old-world capitals than anything resembling the celebrity-studded gatherings in public places, over-inflated by press agents and reportage, which are part of the scene today. Parties took place in houses, her house, her friends' houses. The friends were real friends and the houses real houses. The parties were memorable.

I remember two in particular, the year I was eighteen. My mother gave a dance for me in the summer at Fishers Island and another the following winter at home in New York, but on both occasions her own friends outnumbered the gawky young like me, and I wound up watching Nicholas Longworth, Frank Crowninshield, Walter Damrosch, Paul Cravath, and Cornelius Bliss among many others, giving a beautiful time to a lot of beautiful women few of whom knew I was there.

This was indeed Cinderella at the ball. Reality was seldom gilded over for me. My mother's strictness, her austere aims for me which like so much else, she never stated in words, were what I was up against; but not until I could see from the vantage-point of maturity did I grasp the extent of her own dichotomy and of the transference of that in certain ways to me.

Those were the years when she was at the height of her career and also, in 1915 and 1918, bore two children, my sister Maria and my brother Efrem. Purposely I omit the qualifying 'half' in my relation to them. I feel and so do they that our lifetime of mutual devotion and harmony is our mother's legacy, the family feeling that she strove to create but did not live long enough to see in permanence, since I am so much older than they. Each of us has had our own disruptive and tempestuous encounters with life but among ourselves there has been only the serenest affection, and never a single disagreement. Efrem Zimbalist too has been integral in this. I have seen too much of life not to appreciate how unusual this is. I think of it sometimes when I go back in memory to the winter of 1918–19, when because of my brother's birth in November my mother undertook a self-imposed ordeal which was to undermine her health and with it her voice. She was ardent, I would say almost fanatical, in her concept of motherhood; part of this was her insistence that a mother should nurse her baby. My sister had been born in the summer, and it had been possible in advance for my mother to arrange six months thereafter free from concert engagements. But when she told her manager in the spring of 1918 that she was to have another child, and therefore wanted to cancel the concert engagements already booked for the next season, he protested violently. She had been booked solidly all over the country at her usual maximum guarantee, and she could not cancel any concert without paying a forfeit to the local management, nearly equivalent to the amount of the guarantee. The total in forfeits had she cancelled the season would have been astronomical—to be blunt, over two hundred thousand dollars. Pop Adams asked why she could not leave her baby at home to be bottle-fed, and go ahead with her commitments like any other artist?

Not she. First came her inflexible concept of her duty as a mother. In later years she never spoke about that gruelling winter, except occasionally to remember some minor bit of comic relief in it. She decided to go on tour in January, only six weeks after the birth of her son. She would take him along so that she could nurse him. In order to do that and have enough rest and privacy and good food to make the undertaking possible at all, she hired a private railroad car and turned it into a travelling home and nursery. It was called the Pioneer. In addition to the staff of cook and two other Pullman employes who ran the car there were the baby and his nurse, the accompanist, the piano tuner, my mother's companion, her maid, and a man from her managers, the Wolfsohn Musical Bureau. Once or twice I was there briefly when the car was near Philadelphia. Three-year-old Maria was in New York with Nanny Staunton, Efrem Zimbalist himself away on tour. It was exactly the broken-up pattern of life which my mother disapproved and dreaded, the crux of her conviction that there can be no synthesis between an artist and a materfamilias, that any attempt to give precedence to one will do irreparable harm to the other. Other women's experiences have not necessarily borne her out; what I learned of this from life, and what I practised, are threads in the fabric of this book.

She was a delicate human being—not so delicate of stature,

for she was tall and strongly boned—but delicate in nerves, in tastes, in her proneness to fatigue and, of course, in voice. So finely-spun and pure and lyric a soprano voice is a fragile thing. To keep it perfect a woman would have to spend her life taking care of it and giving nothing of her life-force to anything else. This was what my mother would not do, what she had not done in my own infancy when she was never deflected by ambition, excitement, or thrilling new experiences from her care of and devotion to me. She was the same woman a dozen years later, when the visible burden of proof was the Pioneer and its prohibitive equipage instead of the garret bedroom in Paris. I do not know how she came through that winter even as well as she did. It was a crushing, depleting experience. She never said so. On the contrary, she was outwardly amusing and gay about it. She sang recitals two and three times a week, living on the car, usually in transit, nursing her baby at the stipulated regular intervals. She did tell me that she lived in terror not only of catching cold, the nightmare of every singer; but also of fatigue or tension that would upset her and, in turn, the baby. She had no hotels and their deadly cold-storage food to struggle with, no trains to catch; but in every city the Pioneer was shunted out to the freight-yards for the length of its stay, and she had to learn to sleep in the pandemonium and dirt of hissing engines, clanging cars being moved and coupled, shrieking whistles, shouting railroadmen and all the rest of it. Also the undertaking cost a fortune. She told me that she paid out much more than she earned that season. But that was also the year in which her newly-issued record of *Carry Me Back to Ole Virginny* sold over one million copies, by far the largest sale that any phonograph record had ever had.

Money was not her problem. The income tax, initiated in 1913, had grown with the war but was still nominal by today's fearful comparison, and my mother was a good business woman. Like all people who have made fortunes by their own powers she had her quirks. She dressed beautifully, she dressed the babies smartly and me as well as one can dress a *Backfisch*—the German word (fried fish) which is more eloquent than any synonym or epithet for a teen-aged girl. But if I wanted anything prettier or more grown-up than she thought suitable I had to earn it by working for it—if I were allowed to hope for it at all. I remember when I was about fifteen I longed for a black silk bathing-suit. Those were still the days of tights, long black stockings, and sailor-collared bathing costumes; a girl's or a child's was made of wool or alpaca. I begged for silk taffeta. She said I could have it if I hemstitched a tablecloth for her, for of course she taught me to sew. She drew the threads. The cloth was of fine linen, about five feet square, the threads drawn all across it in twelve-inch squares, and it took me until the following summer to finish the cloth. My mother used it all her life and I have it still.

The time was to come when she lost interest in the material possessions which had once amused her, but she had great style and she did everything with flair. She had a Rolls-Royce landaulet when those were rarities, and a chauffeur called George who was a dragon-guardian to me. But she thought George and the Rolls too showy for the simple life (in some thirty-five rooms) at Fishers Island, so they were left in town. This created a problem in transportation. Efrem Zimbalist could drive the car that was kept at Fishers, but he could not be called away from his practising or his own leisure to chauffeur my mother—and she did not drive or wish to learn. She decided to solve the question by keeping a horse and trap; we had a stable and plenty of grazing for a horse. Moreto, the Italian gardener, could groom and harness it.

So she went to New London, the mainland town that is the island's trading-place, and bought a horse. The horse was a roan mare, a draught animal built like a Percheron, with feet as big as barrel-heads. Her name was Lizzie. She cost, said my mother smugly, thirty-five dollars, a most appropriate economy. Lizzie arrived before her equipage, which would follow 'presently.' All my life I had loathed that word, it was my mother's way of putting off a definite answer to some question or request of mine. And presently there arrived a spanking yellow gig and a fine new harness studded with what looked suspiciously like silver. Mother became the sight of Fishers Island. She was pregnant at the time, and wore what she called a pink gingham tent. Nobody who saw it will ever forget her driving that cart-horse on the dusty roads in her dainty gig, clop clop clop.

Years later when my mother asked me by long-distance telephone to find a document she needed among the papers in her desk, I found the receipted bill for Lizzie's cart and harness. They had been made to order for three hundred and fifty dollars.

I do not remember what became of Lizzie but she was soon succeeded by the decision that I had to be taught to drive a car, not for my own pleasure but to run my mother about. George was imported from town to teach me to drive, and bringing the Rolls, he taught me. I was fifteen years old and as Fishers Island was a private enclave, drivers' licenses were not necessary as I remember it. George taught me first on the Rolls because he said if I handled that well I could thereafter drive anything. He was right. That was the last summer of the war, and all of us were busy with 'war work'—child's play in the light of the fates we have lived since. I do not know whether we girls and women were of real use, with our Red Cross bandage-rolling and our trainees' canteen for the men from the big base to which Fort Wright had been expanded. I know that I drove a supply-truck between the Army dock and the mess depot, and I still wonder who put me up to it, because dozens of other young people were equally capable and must have envied me the job.

❧[C H A P T E R   F O U R]❧

BY contrast with life at home it seems incredible that I was still grinding out the winters in Philadelphia. I believe I must have reached a defensive indifference to much that I had hated when I first went there. And it would be untruthful— possibly overdramatic and self-pitying—to say that I cannot re- member a single mitigation. There were some. Mr. G was a his- torian, a former university professor, and he fostered my taste for every aspect of historical study, from the daily newspaper battle-front despatches to the techniques of organizing chronologi- cal and geopolitical material, and the use of reference works and maps. In the light of much that happened later, I see that he imparted a real sense of the war as world war, at a time when attention and emotion were preponderantly concentrated on the Western Front. Everybody of course thought of the German as the Hun, the beast of the apocalypse; at the same time I had an awareness of the Austro-Hungarian problem, its origins, its complexity, its ramifications, and its consequences, which may have prepared my mind for much that was to impress and color it permanently, and only about ten years later. I was also sharply aware of the Bolshevik revolution in 1917. My Russian stepfather and many related associations made this real and urgent. I have never had to strain backwards to recapture a sense of immediacy about the major historical convulsions of this violent century; I was handed them to ingest when they were, so to speak, fresh and hot and raw.

Through the same years the fine hand of my mother guided

me into saturation in music. All the years I was in Philadelphia my mother subscribed to four seats for the Friday afternoon concerts of the Philadelphia Orchestra, her stipulation being that I must always attend—I never wanted not to—and whichever of the G's as chose. Those were the best years of Leopold Stokowski's tenure as conductor. The programmes were sound, solid meat and bread-and-butter, against which he eventually rebelled. That was the time of his orchestra-building, when he developed and burnished the incomparable tone and sonority of the Philadelphia Orchestra which it has incredibly retained through the decades since he left it. He departed excoriating the stuffy Philadelphia audiences for their stony indifference to his rare ventures into the contemporary, and away from the standard repertoire. It must indeed have been galling to him, but it was the ideal way for a young person to learn and to keep forever the great main body of musical creation. His programmes were predictable in form and content. An opening work of classic music, loveliest of all Handel or Haydn or Mozart; nearly always a soloist to play one of the great concertos, and what soloists!—Hofmann, Rachmaninoff, Stokowski's then wife Olga Samaroff, Gabrilowitsch, Bauer among pianists. Kreisler, Heifetz or my Papuchka the violinists. Every season my mother—naturally perhaps, I remember few other singers on his programmes except when he played a choral work and he often did. Then the symphony, one of the titans—too much Tschaikowsky of course, it was that epoch—but I received a salting-down in Beethoven, Brahms, Schubert, Mendelssohn, Schumann, as fundamental as the rudiments of language. The concert always ended with what I called a Big Noise—the *1812 Overture* or the *Marche Slave, Scheherazade* or *La Grande Pâques Russe, Finlandia,* a Wagner excerpt, or one of Stokowski's own stunning transcriptions of Bach.

This was as remote as possible from my introduction to opera, bound tightly to my emotions about my mother and integrally to Maestro Toscanini. But Maestro had left the Metro-

politan in 1915 and vanished into wartime Italy. For years we had
no contact with him and also none with the Metropolitan; after I
went to Philadelphia I heard little opera. But those Friday afternoon symphony concerts, with their acres of grey heads belonging
to ladies who had correctly removed their hats, who put the hats
on again and rose and clambered out during the Big Noise in
order to catch the Main Line or the Chestnut Hill train; those concerts were schooling in the basic sense of the word. It was not
inspiration, it was learning. By the time Maestro returned to this
country and was conducting the Philharmonic, it was as though I
had done my home-work. With the body of music committed to
ear and to memory I was ready for him to put it where he has
put it, permanently in the frame of his authority. Forever alive
in his records and in my brain and heart, music to me is what he
played. It is his precision, his tempi, his accents, his phrasing, his
fanatical clarity, his unbelievable dynamic gradations, the pianis-
simi like the famous handkerchief he let fall at a rehearsal to illustrate his wishes, the fortissimi that made us literally sweat and
feel the tops of our skulls rattle, the crescendi that scared the
living lights out of us, the diminuendi that put us in tears. I have
said already in this text and I suppose I shall say again that words
are not the medium to communicate experiences in music; but
words are good enough for the statement that music had never
sounded before, according to any reliable account, as it did when
Arturo Toscanini conducted it, and there are legions of us today
who are witness that it has never sounded the same since.

So much runs together in the collective memory of school
years and the sameness of routine in youth that it is difficult to
isolate this or that experience unless it was a primary one, remembered without effort and incised in a certain part of the
brain. Such is my memory of the first symphony concert I heard
Maestro conduct, which was anyway a historic event. In December
of 1920 he brought the orchestra of La Scala on a concert tour of
the United States. The first concert of the tour took place in

Christmas week when I was at home, and of all places, in the Metropolitan Opera House. For Maestro, when he left in a rage in 1915, had departed swearing he would never again set foot in that house, certainly not conduct in it!—and for what reason I do not know, it was precisely there that he reappeared, on the 28th of December. It was a very great occasion. Every personality in the musical and social life of New York was there. My mother had one of the centre boxes; she was beautiful in a white gown and carrying a great ostrich-feather fan. I sat just behind her and I even remember the dress I wore, which she herself had made the previous summer, of tucked nile green chiffon with a velvet sash of the same color. I was seventeen years old and I think as gawky a seventeen as there could be, with bands on my teeth and my stiff, curly hair skinned back from my forehead. At least I had good skin, I think the only agony of youth I was spared was spots and pimples.

But the concert! What I remember is the Fifth Symphony, as sharply and with the same shivering startlement as if an icy key had been dropped down my back. I had heard an awful lot of the Fifth Symphony in years of weekly concert-going, so the notes were all in my head; but what happened to them then was total transmutation. The rest of the programme had less impact on me. Walter Toscanini tells me it included Vivaldi, Respighi, Debussy and Wagner—typical of Maestro, and the last two no joy for me in the long later view.

Afterwards we went back to see Maestro. I remember his delight at seeing my mother, his croaking voice as he called her "Alma! *Cara!*" When she drew me forward to shake his hand he might have been looking into space. I recollect no recognition on his part. I of course was dumb, not shy exactly, simply aware that it was not my place to speak. I see the moment from his point of view. He loved little children and was always demonstrative with them, which had been his first way with me. And of course he loved pretty women. But an in-between creature like a seventeen-year-old girl? I do not think he ever had a responsive reaction to one of those except his own granddaughters. He simply looked through me. I did not mind. He was God and I had been given a glimpse of Heaven. I was not to hear and see him again until 1926 when he was conductor of the Philharmonic. Thereafter began the long main span of my life in music, the twenty-eight years when I heard him week in, week out, here and abroad, with many orchestras, in many places; and of the friendship which was like a cutting from old roots that grew slowly into a separate vine through which all the threads of my later life were twined, to last until his death—and indeed, beyond. It is not his name which gives him immortality but the legacy he left and was; the music the incorruptible treasure; the man whose will and mind and force and warmth stay blazingly alive.

But how clumsy I was in those girlhood years. Now I want to see them if I can, from my mother's view; then I did not and could not. Through most of the time from about 1920 on I was foreshortened in capacity to understand her and to realize what was happening to her by preoccupation with myself, struggling into the initial phases of an identity of my own, most of it clumsy and confused. Now if I take a long view backwards and weigh both my mother's life and my own in the balance, I am astonished and chagrined that I did not fully realize that she was going through a tragic trial of fate; and while I rightly ascribe my incognizance of this to my own selfish myopia, it is also true that she kept her sorrows to herself with gallant, wordless pride. For the ordeal of 1919 had taken a heavy toll.

In summary, about myself, I finished my seven Jacobean years in Philadelphia in 1921, and in the autumn of that year went, most unwillingly, to Wellesley College. There had been no question about my going to college; my mother's most determined fixation was that I have a degree. And I was eager for it—but not at Wellesley or at any comparable women's college. In those days they all had nice-nelly overtones, and all of them had required courses for freshmen which were either mathematics or something even ghastlier, like the physics at Bryn Mawr. To me mathematics meant imprisonment in a den of snakes. I wanted to go to some good university where all my courses would be elective and I would never hear of mathematics again. My mother flatly refused. A university meant coeducation, that in turn meant to her unchaperoned association with boys, arbitrarily ruled out as unthinkable. (If she could see the world today!) A women's college it had to be and so, for just what reason I cannot remember, the decision was Wellesley.

I was not there long. The mathematics bugbear made my life intolerable. Ungregarious as I was, and indifferent to sports, the only college activities that might have made a human being of me were barred because I had a perpetual condition in the two required courses of freshman mathematics. No student could join in any extracurricular activity, which could have been music or dramatics in my case, who had a condition in a required course. So I was mostly in Boston. I went there regularly anyway for my piano lessons—trust my mother to force me to go to Wellesley and then decide I must have my music lessons elsewhere. The Boston Public Library was just around the corner from my teacher's studio. Between that and the Boston Symphony I was well insulated from college, though I did get very high marks in history and English. And I received a self-taught lesson in personal finance which I will never forget.

I had never previously had an allowance of anything larger than minimal pocket-money. I do not think I had ever had more than four dollars in my possession at one time. When I went to college my mother put me on an allowance of a hundred dollars a month—and a bank account!—out of which I was supposed to buy my clothes and pay all my expenses except my tuition and board at college. In the first days of the new régime I went to a bookshop in Boston and paid seventy-five dollars for a complete, unexpurgated edition of the Burton translation of *The Thousand Nights and a Night,* in seventeen volumes. It is a limited, numbered edition, and a good one. I was thrilled with it then and I still am today. It took up all the space in my small room, and it left me in a dizzying financial snarl whose details I have long since forgotten; but inevitably I could never fill up the hole I had blown in what should have been a budget. All I remember is that there remained a persistent deficit of some two hundred dollars which kept me scrabbling and robbing Peter to pay Paul. Matters came to a crisis, and I was so terrified my mother would learn about the mess that I finally made a tearful clean breast of it to Papuchka. The angel gave me two hundred dollars and swore me to secrecy, for we would equally have caught hell had my mother ever found out; and this is the only time I have ever referred to the matter since.

In the summer of 1922 my mother let me go to France to study at the University of Grenoble, in a party of American girl students. There was vastly less supervision of our activities and our time than she would have approved, and we found there young men from several American universities. My mother would not have let me go if she had realized who all the students would be. I did not know beforehand, myself; imagine my surprise. Actually it was very good for us, and our behavior, by comparison with present-day undergraduate mores, was positively puritanical. Before we arrived in Grenoble we paused briefly in Paris and from there went to see the battlefields of the Western Front. The war had ended three years before. I do not know what I expected but what I saw was illimitable spaces of blighted bone-colored land, shorn of trees and all vegetation, dotted by the bleached rubble of shattered villages and ridged by undulating streaks where the trenches had been filled in. Nothing grew; not a blade of wheat, not a wild poppy, not a weed. Dry, dusty, xanthous earth, a wind soughing over the desolation without a tree or a hedgerow to break its passage, the bright summer sky glaring over whitened nothingness. In following years I crossed those fields of France more times than I know, lush and fat with grain and sugar-beet and fodder for the magnificent Percherons which drew the laden farm-wagons on the straight tree-lined roads that never curved as far as the eye could reach. I watched those trees grow from tiny saplings which, that post-war summer were the only plants in sight, the first venture towards restoring the terrible blighted country-side.

In many places shell-craters still stood gaping, vast whitish clay bowls with muddy slop in them, in which could still be seen the flotsam of battlefields, pieces of artillery, wheels, a helmet, a rusted bayonet, even a high German field boot: why had it not disintegrated in that time? Along the roadsides were vast tangled masses, high, like nightmare hedges, of rusty barbed wire. Many a gun-emplacement still remained, a mound of ugly crumbling concrete pounded by shellfire. I have had my nose rubbed in much of Europe's share of this frightful century's mania, I have seen the saturation-bombings of the second war while they were still smoking, and much else of man's insane drive to perdition. But probably because I was young, because it was etched on a pristine surface, because I had been reading about it for years, soaking up everything from war correspondence to poetry and fiction, the impact of the Western Front was smashing. Sharpest of all remains the bleached clay of every vista the eye could see, total blight.

We spent the nights—two, I think, at Verdun. I have never forgotten it. We lodged at the ancient Hostellerie du Coq Hardi which still, like everything French, exists, and is listed in Michelin as an 'hôtel très confortable.' A large part of the structure, perhaps half, had been blasted away by artillery fire. A few yards from our bedroom doors a large sheet of some material like black tarpaulin had been tacked across the passage, held in place by crossed boards; and on the other side of it was nothing. The wind blew through it with an eerie whine. They gave us the inevitable beautiful food for dinner and afterwards I went upstairs and stood at the window of my dark room, looking out. The moon was full. Across the street the houses had been pounded by shellfire, high shells evidently, like the fire-bombs of the second war which hit the roofs and pulverized the interiors, leaving the façades standing. That was what I stood and stared at, crumbling housefronts, skull-faces of houses with holes that had been windows, like eye-sockets and nostrils, ghastly in the moonlight. I looked for a long time. Then the good dinner I had eaten rose up and smote me; I fled to the lavabo in the passage to nowhere and was sick.

In Grenoble I had a glimpse of French character which twisted my view for years to follow. I lived with the other girls in a pension for young ladies, the house of a Monsieur and Madame Josse. They could have come straight from the pages of Balzac, perfect pen-portraits of French provincials. They were parsimonious, suspicious, stingy, avaricious—and dirty. The only bath was in a locked shed in the garden; baths had to be ordered from the single brutally overworked servant and paid for—one franc for a cold bath, five francs for a hot. The food was served out at meals by Mon*sieur* Josse, his wife so pronounced his name and therefore everyone else did; good food, of course, but in tiny portions. We were young and hungry, and as university students were free to come and go; accordingly, I went—to the nearest charcuterie and the neighboring baker's. Those matters are trifles. But I shall never forget the day when Mon*sieur* Josse informed us, "Mesdemoiselles, tomorrow the house will be closed. Everyone will remain inside and all the doors and windows will be locked." They were. The iron roll-shutters were not raised and from outside the house gave the impression that it was deserted. Why? Because the tax-collector was to make his rounds that day. This was at a time when all of France was plastered with propaganda posters pleading with Frenchmen to pay their taxes; Marianne amidst the ruins, in rags, ravished, with one breast exposed, one arm outstretched and the hand begging. "Français!", the caption read, "Payez Vos Taxes!"

I do not know that I learned much at the University except the roots of an absorption in French history and literature. Perhaps modern students abroad on exchange-study programmes attend lectures more consistently than we did. I acquitted myself well enough and the short summer interval, the first time in my life that I was shed of the minute supervision under which I had always lived, was a necessary part of coming to terms with oneself. I wish I had done it better. Certainly we American students did not run wild with the freedom which was new to most of us. Inevitably there was a lot of pairing-off, the natural concomitant of propinquity; but nothing of the cool experimentation which modern permissiveness appears to expect of the young. We were shy, hidebound by parental traditions which were not, contrary to much that has been said, wildly jettisoned by those of our age at the onset of that decade. We were—the word takes groping for —decent, in a touching way. There was a strong overtone of simple romanticism in our relations. Anything of more scope or duration than a dancing acquaintance somehow had to be circumscribed within a definition of 'love'—and none of us, aged between about eighteen and twenty, had the least notion of what love is. Often our delusion moved on in sequence to something termed an 'engagement', which was a matter for feeling thrilled and partaking of the same experience as most of one's friends. As for the serious implications of an engagement or beyond that, of marriage, we were so immature that I wonder now how any of us struggled through eventually to reality. As long as it remained unreality, I suppose there was little harm in thinking oneself 'in love' and 'engaged'—which happened to me as it did to most girls I knew.

But in September I had to go back to Wellesley and those required freshman courses in solid geometry and trigonometry, the examinations in which I had flunked at the end of every previous term. It was intolerable to a good student to realize that if by the end of her sophomore year she had not passed the final examinations in freshman mathematics, she would automatically be flunked out. This was my imminent fate, which I realized in

March. I was terrified of my mother. There is no exaggeration too strong to describe what would have been her rage had I actually flunked out of college. I floundered and struggled with tutoring and the help of my few friends to prepare once again for the math examinations but I remained totally incapable of grasping even what trigonometry was about, much less comprehending what one was supposed to do about it.

One day I had a stomach-ache, I do not remember how severe, but certainly not disabling; and it caused a sort of explosion in my brain and my will which until then had been really docile and incapable of rebellion against any decree of my mother's. I walked to the railway station, without plan or luggage, and got on the first train for Back Bay where I changed to the train for New York. I was wearing a plaid skirt with a round-collared blouse and a sweater, and saddle oxfords. In my right mind I would not have dreamt of wearing such clothes off the college campus or, more to the point, of doing what I did at all. I arrived home to find (which I had overlooked) that my mother was in South Carolina on a spring visit with the Prettymans. So I sent for our family doctor and told him I felt sick and he sent me to the Roosevelt Hospital to have my appendix removed. The first time I saw my mother was when she was holding my head while I was retching my way out of the ether.

It was not said, and perhaps not understood, that I had run away from college, but when I was recuperating from the appendectomy it became plain that my mother expected me to return to Wellesley and my torments there. I panicked. I had no idea what to do and I was ready to do anything without thought of consequences or of any relation of the situation to reality. I telephoned the young man at Yale to whom I had become engaged in the childish sense I have described, and he, himself fed up with college and ready for any escape, came to New York. We ran away to Port Chester and were married. I was nineteen years old.

Of course it was a catastrophe. I suppose in my addled and panic-stricken state I was momentarily deluded by feelings which cannot be comprised in any serious concept of real life, and momentarily confused into thinking that a little house with white curtains and my own furniture and beautiful Belgian linens (typical of my mother) was my manifest destiny. My bridegroom's uncle in Pittsburgh provided him with a job there, so to Pittsburgh we went. We lived there eighteen months, by which time I had a child and had taught myself the rudiments of housekeeping. What I did not know was that that brief detour into illusion was the sharp turn which was to precipitate me into my real grapplings with life and the beginnings of my real identity. In a way whose meaning only later became clear, I was in process of learning that any or every experience however unconnected with others, and seemingly remote from the main stream of one's interests, can emerge long years later as an element in the whole design of one's destiny. I was then too young and too confused to establish any relation to Pittsburgh except that of sheer marvelling at the spectacle that it was.

The situation with my mother was tenuous. She had been heartbroken by what I did, but she took the position of trying to make the best of it. She stopped my allowance, rightly I feel, for the one great lesson she was sure I still had to learn was the law of cause and effect. But she did not propose to punish me with an edict of banishment; had she done so I am sure the loss would have been very much mine and hers almost not at all, for it grieves me to realize how little in those years I gave her anything more than blind affection.

Then my husband's job changed and to my utter despair, required a move to Philadelphia, the one place I loathed and held in bitter memory. But we moved there; and one morning a few weeks later, when I was twenty-one years old and had a five-months-old baby, I woke to find the young man gone, and gone for good. I never saw him again. This was towards the end of a week, probably a Thursday. I had almost no money and nothing would have made me turn to my mother, either to inform her or to ask for help. The G family with whom I had passed those seven dreary years had left Philadelphia or were in process of leaving it, but I was not in touch with them anyway. I had to get a job and get it then and there.

I telephoned to one of my friends who had also left Wellesley and asked her to come from her home in upstate New York to stay with the baby and me until I got a job. She arrived that evening. Meanwhile I learned that there was a job open as copy-writer in the advertising department of a Philadelphia specialty-shop, then a branch of a Fifth Avenue store in New York. I applied for the job, lying like Alcibiades as to my capability to write copy and prepare advertisements for the daily newspapers. I got the job. My salary was to be thirty-five dollars a week, and I was to begin work the following Monday.

Then I went to a good employment agency and among other girls, saw a young German about eighteen years old, who had just arrived in this country. She had no English and I had never properly learnt German but we could communicate. I told her my situation. I said, "I will pay you half of my thirty-five dollars a week. Out of the other half I will keep fifty cents a day. Can you take care of my baby and my flat and feed the three of us on fifteen dollars a week?" She would try, she said; and she succeeded.

So I began the life of hard work which is the only life I was really fitted for, by destiny or by circumstance. I cannot remember just how and when I told my mother what had happened, but I do remember with towering admiration how she took it. She said calmly, "This is the consequence of what you did. You have made your bed and now you must lie in it." Not only did she not offer to help me; I would not have taken money had she offered it. The only cushion between me and pennilessness was a tiny income of less than sixty dollars a month, which came from a trust she had established in my infancy, by whose terms the income had been payable to me since my twenty-first birthday. It just paid my rent. So the only part of existence and survival which I did not earn was the roof over my head. My mother also said, or did I say, I cannot remember, that it would be as well if we did not see each other for a time. She was so bitterly disappointed in me, and I so humiliated by the mess I had made, that there was a wall between us. It was better for me to work out my solution in isolation, and a cruel irony that I had to do it in Philadelphia. But it was necessary to proceed on the basis of grounds for an eventual divorce, and in Pennsylvania there was a residence requirement for divorce of two years following desertion. I had most certainly been deserted, and my mother said that two enforced years in Philadelphia was a just dispensation of fate.

I was clumsy at my copy-writing in the beginning, and necessarily full of bluff. I learned by studying what others had done in this specialty. I pored over scrap books full of advertising, and read the copy in the fashion magazines—and I may say, I have scarcely ever looked at one since. This sort of work is a knack. The best part of it is the discipline of working to deadlines, and I picked up quite a bit about type faces, layout, halftone and line-drawing illustration, newspaper format, and a lot of technical stuff that I have long since forgotten. My salary was soon raised a few dollars and I also became a moonlighter. At home at night I wrote advertising copy for a chain of hat-shops which paid me something like thirty dollars a week. So within six months from my desperate start I was earning seventy-five dollars a week, and I suppose upwards of forty years ago that was the equivalent of more than two hundred today. It was not much then, but it was as much as my fleeting husband had earned, and it was the basis of my permanent orientation to the whole rest of life: independence.

Summer came, and with it a letter from my mother asking me to come to Fishers Island with the baby for my two weeks' vacation. It was heaven, but in a way radically different from

what I had known before. I had removed myself from the circle
of my old friends most of whom were still enjoying the pleasures
we had shared. I was too old for playmates and too young to par-
ticipate entirely in my mother's life, a gay one, the house full of
guests, with lots of golf and swimming and bridge. One of her
closest friends was Frank Crowninshield, the editor of *Vanity Fair*.
He was a witty and charming bachelor, full of kindliness and I
think the most polished perfectionist in the art of friendship that
I have ever known. He had a quality of grace and gentleness
which one might not expect in the glittering circle of which he
was the hub. Many of the dazzling lights of the theatre, music,
literature, painting—everybody who was anybody and thus nominated for his memorable *Hall of Fame*—were capable of being
mean, envious, devious, or vain, except in their relations with
Frank. He brought out the best in people. I loved him, we all
loved him. Conversely, I think of another friend of my mother's,
now a legend as Frank Crowninshield is, whom I bitterly hated,
Alexander Woollcott. He and his circle, Alice Duer Miller, Harpo
Marx, F. P. A(dams), Heywood Broun and the rest, were all
friends of my mother's. Woollcott had been a games-playing
companion of hers for years. When I was still at school and home
for vacations, I used to come in on winter afternoons to find my
mother and Woollcott playing backgammon. I was gauche and
timid and loaded with every disadvantage of my age including
bands on my teeth and corrective spectacles. My mother would
look up and greet me lovingly and say to Woollcott, "You know
my daughter Marcia . . ." And Woollcott, who had been through
this time and again, would glance at me without recognition and
say, "Disaster, isn't it . . ."

I learned years later that one of the special aberrations of his
twisted personality was hatred of the children of his friends. I
never understood why my mother let him get away with it, I
wished she would order him out of the house and if she had
realized how I felt, she would have put him out, instead of think-

ing the brute funny. But now I understand the reasons, which she may not clearly have sensed herself, why she leant on congenial friends and surrounded herself with their games and laughter and the occupations with which they filled her time. It was to take up the slack in her life that came with the end of her singing. This was veiled by her own valour of spirit, possibly by her managing to believe what she insisted was her own choice when in fact it was not. That summer when I went back to Fishers I began to grasp much that before I had been too purblind to perceive. She and I were both gingerly in avoiding sore spots and I believe it was then that we began to evolve a *modus communicandi* which was to serve us for the rest of her life. It came very close to conversation without words; sometimes by the use of mere monosyllables, or by one of us stating the beginning of something and then falling silent, leaving the other to fill in the implied content for herself. But this was not always the case.

Even when she was ill, or prostrated by fatigue, which from then on she was increasingly, her natural verve and sense of play kept the mischief in her speech, the beautiful clear sheen in her speaking voice, and the *enfant terrible* always ready to pop out from behind the least threat of stuffiness or boredom. To the end of her life she kept the quality of incandescence. Her light was natural, not the artifice of forethought or planned illumination. Perhaps there is no verbal art visual enough to reflect the glow of a truly radiant personality, and my mother was one. I think the best one can do is suggest that it was as though light shone from her and around her. When she was present everyone knew she was there, though she might not have made a sound or moved from one place in a room to another. Like the sun or the moon, I suppose; and this is no sentimentalizing because she was my mother. Everybody who knew her remembered radiance as the essence of Alma.

She was also fortified by a backbone of iron pride in the best sense of the word. I know now how cruel youth can be in its selfishness and self-absorption, and how far I had gone in those worth-less directions through a passage of time when my mother must have needed understanding, tenderness, and consolation as never before. The years when I was the most fractious and the worst disappointment to her were the very years in which she had to face the one great tragedy of her life (she did not live long enough to suffer the deaths of those she loved.) That was the loss of her voice. She would not have put it in this way. It was her insistence that she stopped singing because she wanted to, because she wanted to devote herself entirely to her husband and family. God knows she did so. But I know, and in an obfuscated way I knew then, that she was suffering and too proud to admit it. I have never talked about this with Efrem Zimbalist and he is manifestly the only other person who knew what was happening. My brother and sister were small children; they never heard her sing, nor knew her as what I consider her real self. I doubt if she allowed her husband to know the whole force of her will to transform neces-sity into choice. She did it with apparent joy and grace and ab-solute sincerity. She was relieved to be free of the rigors of touring and the long winters away from home. She made herself and her house the centre of a life that was sparkling, interesting, gay, full of music and musical parties—gambling ones, too—in the mid-1920's which today seem to fascinate memoirists and social his-torians. New York was both gayer and quieter than now, its articulate life a whirl of concentric circles in which my mother moved and sometimes brought together at her house in various groupings; occasionally all together. An evening would begin with chamber-music or, if they were in the mood, perhaps a spon-taneous performance of the Bach Double Concerto by my step-father and Jascha Heifetz accompanied by Chotzie who had been everybody's accompanist in turn and was then courting Jascha's sister Pauline; go on to a buffet supper for ten or twenty or a hundred, and wind up with a table-stakes poker game that lasted until dawn.

One summer there was a house-party which included Jascha and the Fritz Kreislers, and most of the time was passed in musical games and improvisations, including the airing of light music that all three violinists had composed. Whether it was a bet or a compact I have forgotten, but the result was that they all undertook to write the scores for musical comedies. I forget what happened to Jascha's, but Kreisler's was *Apple Blossoms* and Efrem Zimbalist's *Honeydew*: both had long Broadway runs and tunes that are played by dance-bands to this day.

Some time after I had returned to Philadelphia from my vacation my mother appeared one Sunday at my door with Frank Crowninshield just as I was coming home from church. They had come, they said, to take me out to lunch. Crownie was cosy and sweet, and only much later had I the sense to realize that he had undertaken to keep an eye on me in terms of where my obviously temporary job would lead. But at the time I had my nose so glued to the grindstone that I did not feel the pat of a knowing hand on my back.

As they were leaving, my mother asked me, for the first time since I had struck out on my own if there was anything she could do for me. By the grace of God I uttered the one word which was galvanic to her: house. I had been living in a dreary, dark, very cramped flat converted from one floor of a former private house. My piano took up so much space that there was no place to sit down in the room with it. During my lunch hours, or when walking to work, I had seen the narrow streets, back alleys actually, threaded between the main residential streets of Philadelphia. They were lined with tiny Federal-period brick houses, originally mews and servants' quarters, which people were now reclaiming from the slum condition to which they had degenerated. Panama Street was the first and prettiest of these, and there were several others only waiting to be tackled. A rundown house in one of them could be bought for a couple of thousand dollars and completely renovated and restored for about twice as much more. Instantly my mother's eyes shone with a fanatic gleam. In all her life I never knew her to turn down the possibility of buying, renovating, or altering a house.

The money arrived at once. The little house took shape quickly, one room to a floor, with a pocket-sized back yard garden. Presently I moved in. My life was becoming less grim, my salary was raised from time to time, and somehow I made friends with a group of women much older than myself, widows all, Philadelphia ladies of classic definition, most curious company for me. We used to dine and play bridge. One of them was Mrs. Russell Davenport, a large, handsome woman with a peculiar hooting voice, very much a personality. She had wide-spaced eyes whose color was that real rarity, green. Her friends called her Nellie. She was the mother of two sons, both away, the elder in Paris and the younger at Yale. She and her friends were kind to me, I have no idea why, for Philadelphia is notoriously inhospitable to strangers and most so to people from my milieu in New York. But the ladies were gracious, and I still remember what that cost them one Saturday evening when my mother had come down to spend the weekend with me and, of course, to put in her oar about the house. After dinner my mother looked up suddenly from her needlework and said, "What does one do on a Saturday night in Philadelphia?"

What, indeed, I thought; but I fetched the evening paper and we looked at the entertainment page, usually a desert. But my mother cried, "Look! The Marx Brothers!"

They were trying out *The Cocoanuts*. We rushed to the theatre and bought seats which turned out to be in the middle of the front row. It could only happen in Philadelphia. In the lobby amongst the incoming crowd were several of my grande dame friends who were plainly very pleased to meet my mother. Some of them sat in the row behind us and we chatted until the show began. It was a riot—and Philadelphia sat on its hands. We were fuming. The boys worked hard. The audience was a dud. Groucho in desperation came down to the footlights and began a wild, zany soliloquy which elsewhere would have had the audience howling. Nothing here. He scanned the house, looking for something, anything, to which he could pin a gag. Suddenly his face lit up, he went down on one knee like Al Jolson, arms outstretched, and shouted, "*Oy!* Alma Gluck!"

We could feel the freeze from the ladies behind us.

My mother by that time was not singing any longer. She sang her last recital in 1924, frail in health and so taut with self-discipline that I remember it with pain. She had in fact sung very little since 1921. Her career therefore was very short, little more than ten years, which makes it the more extraordinary that she remained so much loved and so well remembered by the American public. Her gramophone records were of course the reason for her permanence in American music. Few people today realize how short a time she was actually before the public, but it was long enough to make her a legend in this country. She was about thirty-seven years old when the pearl-like lustre of her voice began to cloud with the fragility of her health. I first noticed in the early 1920's that she was frail because I so often found her flat with exhaustion, lying on the couch in her room in the afternoon, trying to sleep. The fresh and glowing beauty that she presented to her friends and the world was not a façade, nor was her gaiety; they did not fade for many years but they were sustained from within by grace and wisdom and will-power. She suffered horribly from insomnia and from disturbances of a digestion which had always been extremely delicate: all her life she ate from preference the food of a child. Now, long after the fact and with full knowledge of the circumstances, the reasons for her failing health are all too plain to me. At the time it was imperative to take one's cue from her: head up, gallant, undefeated, smiling.

From the first years when I was away from her as a small child, she built up for me the precious legacy that I have treasured all my life, her records. She made about one hundred and forty altogether, including some that were never issued for sale because she would not release them. Making those acoustical recordings, decades before the electronic tapings, patchings, splicings, blendings, and doctorings of the present day, was a nerve-racking ordeal. It meant a trip to Camden, New Jersey, to the recording laboratory of the Victor Talking Machine Company, whose chief, Calvin Childs, was a dear and stalwart friend. A matrix was made from which the records were pressed, and the matrix had to be flawless. This in turn meant that there might be two or four or any number of trials before the perfect matrix was achieved. Even an audible breath from someone present would spoil a matrix. She used to say that a day in Camden, singing into that little black box, was more exhausting than a week of concerts. Each time she made a new record she added it to the collection that she was keeping at home for me. Then and ever since I have had beside me the row of albums full of fragile 12-inch and 10-inch records which presently are to go to the Library of Congress.

People in the present day have had little chance to hear my mother's singing. Her records are almost unobtainable and those in existence are more than likely to be badly worn. They were recorded forty to fifty years ago, when recording was primitive and orchestral accompaniments, by comparison with today, laughable. The piano sounded better, and there are many too with violin obbligatos beautifully played by Efrem Zimbalist. If, however, a record of Alma Gluck's in reasonably good surface condition is played on a modern phonograph, adjusted to no greater dynamic amplification than the volume of a normal voice, it may be understood why for me and for others like me, there is no present-day *singing* of the same definition. By *singing* I mean exactly that; not a question of beauty or quality of voice which is anyway a matter of personal taste and emotion for the listener, and not quite the same for any two or more listeners. I mean the execution of an exacting specialty of musical art, the result of a combination of natural equipment with the self-application of standards of technique which no longer exist. It was learned by precept and arduous practice. Students and musical bystanders have always assumed that to study with this teacher or that, by this or that method, is the way to vocal mastery. That is nonsense. Maestro Toscanini used to go further; he said that singers are born and not made.

Nobody can teach taste to an individual, it must be innate; and nobody today can exact of singers such precision of technique as the immortals had, which all modern singers lack—good musicians though many be, and beautiful voices though some of them have. They cannot impeccably sing a scale (especially chromatic) or a run; they cannot turn the voice cleanly in florid embellishments at any tempo; they lack accuracy of attack; they cannot trill; they cannot sustain the formidable legatos of Handel or make a faultless glissando; they cannot sing staccato; most of them do not even know what portamento sounds like; they cannot sing pianissimo and effortlessly expand their voices through gradual crescendo to piena voce or reverse themselves in equally controlled diminuendo. Some of them can do some of those things but all of them cannot do all of them; and all of it and a great deal more was the normal foundation of my mother's singing and that of her foremost contemporaries and predecessors.

I have often been asked for advice by young singers and students. Not only have I no advice to give about teachers or methods; I cannot tell them where to go to learn by example, for there is nothing today which they may take as a standard of perfect singing at which to aim. But I have often thought, and never gone beyond mere thinking, that I should like to give a young soprano with a beautiful well-placed voice a number of my mother's records, each chosen as a special facet of a multiple technical perfection, and say, "Study these; and if you can, do likewise."

The list would include: *Come, Beloved,* which for many years was called by musicians the finest piece of singing ever recorded, because of the perfect mastery of Handel's classic legato line, and the phenomenal control of the voice. *O Sleep, Why Dost Thou Leave Me?* is in the same class, with the addition of an adagio trill that could stand the application of a thousand-power magnifying glass. *Rossignols Amoureux* of Rameau is even more exacting and displays the command of a palette of technique which in a word, demands everything. At the other extreme of the artist's versatility there is *Lo, Here the Gentle Lark,* hackneyed and draggled by students; but my mother's remark about it and about all coloratura singing was a scornful shrug that anyone should think her fioritura extraordinary. "A singer should be a singer," she said. "She should be able to sing everything, by any composer, that lies in the range and size of her voice. Otherwise she is an amateur."

She used to say also that what one learned, mastered absolutely, and then possibly laid aside, was more valuable than learning new tricks as one went along. She only sang coloratura fireworks in the early years of her career, considering them to be a relatively meretricious way of bedazzling one's audience when one could be giving them solider fare, something more sincere in its human appeal.

I would next include in my list Thomas Arne's *Lass with the Delicate Air* and *Have You Seen But a Whyte Lily Grow?* Their lesson lies in my mother's English diction. This is a matter shamefully bad in most Americans and not always good amongst the English themselves. Americans slur and swallow their consonants and grind their R's; the English pinch and distort their vowels. My mother loved the English language and sang it with relish and diamond clarity, thereby heaping contempt on the snobs who used to say more than they do now that English is an unsingable tongue. My mother did prefer to sing all music in its original language, feeling that no translation can approach the synthesis of music with its native speech. The peak of her concert career fell, however, during the four years of the first war, when to its shame and its own loss the American public wallowed in ignorant hysteria

and refused for the most part to allow German music to be performed. Or, if the composers had been long and safely enough
dead not to be held enemy propagandists their songs must be sung
in English. For this reason my mother sang and recorded few
German Lieder since she felt that few of them could stand translation.

For the same reason she had a very large repertoire of French
songs and recorded the loveliest of them. I cannot pretend to much
liking for French music and I used to feel frustrated when so
much of her art went into it. I have an inexplicable antipathy to
the music of Debussy, which is irrational because it goes back to
a time when I could not (except for Mozart) have known the
work of one composer from another. But when I was very small
and she was practising *Aquarelles* with Althea Jewell, I remember
clapping my hands to my ears and wailing, "Please, Mother! Please
don't sing that any more!" But I would tell my hypothetical student to listen most carefully to *Le Bonheur est Chose Legère* of
Saint-Saëns, lyricism at its ideal and phrasing that is superlative
art; and to Reynaldo Hahn's *L'Heure Exquise,* which was my
mother's own favorite of all her records—meaning that it met
her own standards and best expressed what she herself cared most
to do.

And yet some of my dearest favorites she never recorded, I
have no idea why. At every recital the first group on the programme was classic music of the epoch I love best, that of Bach,
Handel, Haydn, and Mozart. She used to sing *Jauchzet Gott,* the
opening of the Bach Cantata No. 51, in a style so unbelievable
that the memory makes me tingle all over, fifty years later; and I
can only humbly beg that nobody else ever attempt it again, for
those I have been so unfortunate as to hear have been swamped.
Haydn's *Mermaid* rippled like the water she lived in. As for
Mozart—he was, curiously, little sung and played in my childhood
but every note of his music that my mother sang was like a min-
iscule bead of quicksilver which eventually coalesced to make a

force in me that became a life propellent. *L'amerò, sarò costante* from *Il Re Pastore* was an aria that my mother often sang in concert; others she kept as a private treasure for me. An unpretentious song that I loved to the point of weeping when I heard it was *Star vicino* by Salvatore Rosa; and another, Charpentier's enchanting *Chevaux de Bois*. None of these were recorded; how I wish I had been old enough to ask for them in time. My fictitious student, though, can listen to *Depuis le Jour*; and bow down and pray.

My mother sang more beautiful Russian songs than anybody, all taught her of course by her husband and many arranged by him. At first she learned their words phonetically and sang them as he told her to, but she improved on that by learning Russian and making it the eighth language in which she was fluent. At the opposite extreme, she learned most of the American songs for which she was beloved from friends of hers in Virginia. She used to go every spring to stay with Helen Stevens, the daughter of the president of the Chesapeake and Ohio Railroad, who lived on what had been an antebellum plantation near Clifton Forge, and had a group of Richmond friends who came to make up hilarious house-parties in which as a child I was included at my Easter vacations. All the Virginians, including of course the Negroes on the place, used to sing spirituals and folk-songs, every one of which my mother adopted; and that was the origin of *Carry Me Back*, for which she was probably better loved and known than for any other single song. (I have received a letter about it on the day I am writing this, from someone who heard her sing it over fifty years ago, and even remembers what she wore.) When the First World War was over, some men brought my mother a battered record of *Carry Me Back to Ole Virginny*, framed like a picture, with a letter stating where the record had been carried and played, and what it had survived, during their unit's service in the trenches.

She sang many concerts for soldiers in the training camps

after the United States entered the war in 1917. One of the largest was Camp Lewis in the State of Washington, where she sang out of doors to some forty thousand men—and in those days there were no microphones and amplifiers. My old friend Paul Hoffman, now of the U.N., told me that he was a rookie at Camp Lewis at that time, and would never forget her concert or how beautiful she was. I was present at only a few of those camp concerts, but she sang one wherever there was a base near a city where she stopped on tour. Nearly always there was the moment like the one I witnessed at Fort Wright, when before the concert the Commandant asked my mother if she would like to have a copy of the words of the National Anthem—most singers did. I can see her still as she raised her head with a proud smile and said, "General, I have known all three verses of The Star-Spangled Banner since I was six years old, and I am going to sing them now."

CHAPTER FIVE

ONE evening in 1926 I dined with Mrs. Davenport and met her son Russell, who had just returned from a year in Paris. He looked very like his mother, with the same wide green eyes, bowed eyebrows, and broad, strongly-boned face with a cleft chin. He was four years older than me, twenty-seven at that time; and he was like the proverbial young romantic who, when asked by a friend of the family what he intends to be, replies, "A poet." Russell Davenport was a poet. If a man could have come to terms with the real and the kinetic life of this country and this century by being a poet, and thereby earning enough to have the best of everything, Russell would have had few problems.

He was a most peculiar young man. I had never seen anybody like him and, for all I know, he nobody like me. In Paris he had been moving on the fringes of the galère who were the protegés and habitués of Sylvia Beach and her bookshop, the expatriates who have given the place and the epoch the fame and the flavor caught by Hemingway in his posthumous *A Moveable Feast*. Russell had known them all—slightly; Hemingway himself, Scott Fitzgerald, Gertrude Stein, Harry and Caresse Crosby, the Gerald Murphys, Janet Flanner and her circle, Margaret Anderson and Jane Heap. But he had been absent a good deal from the inner circles at the Dôme, the Rotonde, and the Deux Magots, following in the train of a startling young woman whose name was a firebrand in the 1920's and quite forgotten today. She was Dorothy Speare and had written a novel then thought lurid, called *Dancers in the Dark*. Today it would probably seem like *Peter Rabbit*. But when Russell in the early stages of our acquaintance told me that Dorothy Speare had a voice, and was really concerned to become an operatic soprano; that she had been singing at small theatres in Italy and would one day certainly arrive at the Metropolitan, I was sceptical. I thought I had reason later to be jealous but by the time I finally met her and once heard her sing, it was not jealousy that prompted me to tell Russell, "As a singer she is a complete phony and will get nowhere; what happens to her as a writer I couldn't predict."

He was furious and we had a hot argument. I capped it by saying, "The day you tell me about sopranos will be the day the roof falls in!"

Though he hardly ever lived there, Russell Davenport was a Philadelphian through his mother, who was related to a complex of old families. Among his innumerable relations was the colorful matriarch "Auntie Gaga", Mrs. George C. Thayer, whose son Charles Thayer has recently written a delightful memoir of her. Russell Davenport's father, who died in 1904, was a descendant of the John Davenport who emigrated from Coventry in the seventeenth century to found the Colony of New Haven, and the institution of learning which evolved into Yale, whose Davenport College is named for him. Most of the Davenports had been clergymen, nonconformists originally, later in the Episcopal Church, in Connecticut and New York. Russell's maternal great-grandfather was the noted missionary Bishop of Minnesota, the Bishop Whipple whose name is a kind of legend the threads of which I never wanted to unravel, since something was said about a strain of American Indian blood, and I so hoped it was true that I did not want to find it might be only a story.

The senior Russell Davenport had been a well-known metallurgist when, late in the nineteenth century, Britain and Germany were far ahead of this country in that science. It was he who at the Bethlehem Steel Company first produced heavy armor plate and gun-forgings for the United States Navy—a matter to which I was one day to give close and grateful attention. After his death Mrs. Davenport took her sons to California because Russell, following a childhood illness, was left with defective hearing in one ear and it was thought the benign climate would be helpful. He was educated at the Thacher School at Ojai, possibly the source of much that was fresh and original in him, compared to what he might have been as the product of a conventional Eastern school. When he finished school at seventeen, the United States had just entered the war and he was too young to enlist. He joined the American Field Service and went to drive an ambulance on the Western Front, where he was assigned to a French division. He was awarded the Croix de Guerre with two citations for bravery under fire.

We made an unforgettable journey in 1937, retracing the routes he had driven in his tinny Ford ambulance which held four *blessés,* whom he loaded into it in the thick of the fighting, and drove to hospital under gas attack and shellfire; often, he said, they died on the way. By the time we were there Nature had restored the land and the verdant countryside, but not so much as to erase my own memories of blight and blast, which were childish impressions alongside Russell's experiences of seventeen months. He amazed me. He would steer the car off the road, over a ditch, and heading as it seemed, nowhere, would crawl and bump along saying, "Around that next hump there will be a dip in the land and after I go along at the bottom of it we will come to a culvert and beyond that a brook which used to be such bottomless mud that it swallowed up the wheels . . ." and go on to describe the battles against time and the lives of the wounded in the ambulance, usually in the pitch dark, agonizing about the duckboards which might have been blasted away since he had crossed them the last time.

After the war he went to Yale and graduated in the class of 1923, a famous class like that of 1920, which produced Harry Luce and Briton Hadden, who thereafter founded *Time.* Russell's first

job was a brief run on the new magazine—for the rest of his life
he was to be on and off the editorial staffs of the Luce papers—
which he left to go West again because of the great romance of
his youth. He had long been in love with a beautiful girl for
whose father he went to work as a newspaperman in Spokane. But
Russell was too restless and too talented to remain subject to a
tyrannical person like his boss and prospective father-in-law.
There were other obstacles to the fulfillment of his hopes and the
engagement was finally broken off, leaving Russell with the material and the powers to write a magnificent long poem called *The
California Spring,* on which he worked for years. It was published
in 1931. He started it in Paris in 1925, but most of his time there
went into the externals of acting like a 'genius', looking like an
artist, and cultivating habits and mannerisms which were con-
spicuously modelled on what we know of Balzac. He went in for
all-night sessions of impassioned scribbling, kept awake by excessive doses of black coffee; and for infrequent haircuts, a black
slouch hat, and a flowing black cape which he wore for years afterwards. He never did attempt, though, the white monk's robe in
which Balzac dressed for work.

But Russell Davenport with the probable exception of E. B.
White was the finest natural writer I have known. His talent was
not for fiction, though why the poet's art of imagery is distant
from the novelist's imagination is a mystery. Like most young
writers Russell supposed he was going to be a novelist, but he
was wrong. His gifts lay elsewhere. He had no idea of starving in
a garret for art's sake; but that which was piquant about a poet
in a garret or its equivalent, without starvation and without
squalid anonymity, appealed to him. He liked luxury and he
wanted what we all want: everything. Our friendship grew gradually. He was the first person with whom I could share my passion
for literature and I was able to contribute to the growth of his
taste for music.

My exile in Philadelphia was resolved by the termination of

my necessity to stay there. The little house had served its purpose, as all houses for me successively have except the one I have never left. I let it in 1927 and with groans of relief and prayers of thanksgiving, returned to New York. I consulted Frank Crowninshield as he had told me to do. *Vanity Fair* was not the place for me, I was anxious for meatier work and was not interested in the dragonfly world which it so memorably mirrored. I wanted to be a journalist and Crownie thought the place for me to try was *The New Yorker*, then less than three years old. Curiously, the letter of introduction he gave me was not to Harold Ross or some member of the editorial staff, but to the business manager whose office was not even in the same building as the original *New Yorker* offices in West 45th Street. This must have been because the only work I had to show was advertising copy that I had written in Philadelphia. The business manager, John Hanrahan, put in a word for me with Ross and I was told to write one column on trial. It was to report on the construction and layout of an apartment house then going up, that being the boom era of the finest apartment houses ever built. I have always had a passion for architecture and a worm's-eye relation to its practical applications. The assignment was like handing a porterhouse steak to a hungry hound. I was hired immediately as a general staff writer. My basic work was as reporter for *The Talk of the Town*, then written by E. B. White, James Thurber, and Wolcott Gibbs. My job was leg-work, gathering at its sources the material which the rewrite geniuses turned into the front-of-the-book.

An assignment could be anything, from interviewing a newsworthy person or perhaps a crackpot that Ross was curious about, to working up a long series of stories on the food supply of New York City and its distribution. This was fascinating. For weeks I got up at two or three o'clock in the morning to be at the opening of one of the great wholesale markets—Fulton Fish Market, Washington Street for the fruit auction, The Bronx Terminal, or the freight terminals in Jersey City, to see how the produce came in and how the various purchasing elements bought it and got it to retail stores, hotels, restaurants, and all its final destinations. One story on the Police Department made me a friend I long cultivated, Christy Bohnsack, who must have been the press representative of the Department—if there was such an office. The first time I went there they fingerprinted me, to my delight.

Then there were the columns in the back of the book. I wrote the apartments column and enjoyed it more than anything else, combing through half-built buildings (they *built* them in those days!); pussyfooting along exposed joists, whizzing up and down on the open hoist in which the bricks and mortar flew up to the masons on the high floors, poring over blueprints and floor plans. Then it was *Out of Town,* a column about places to go for weekends and rustic dining. Then Lois Long, at that time married to Peter Arno, had to take six months off to have a baby, so I did her fashion page, *On and Off the Avenue*—which to my amazement she has continued to this day—and her restaurant column. Before the Christmas season we had masses of extra shopping pages and coverage for *This and That.* In short, at various times and sometimes all at once, I wrote five different back-of-the-book columns all under different pseudonyms, and did leg-work for *The Talk of the Town* besides. We all worked as hard. We thought nothing of working from early morning until nine or ten at night, with a sandwich for lunch at our desks. Then after a dinner break the proofs would start coming in. They had to be corrected and rewritten in whole or in part after Ross got his hooks into them, so it was the rule rather than the exception to work from eleven or twelve at night until dawn. Three or four hours' sleep and we were at it again.

It was priceless experience and training which I see most clearly now on looking back at it across a lifetime's work. I knew that Katharine White (then Angell) was a superlative editor, with a discriminating mind and a laconic, understated way of putting her ideas. I knew that Andy (E. B.) White was a genius—it was enough to see him make three limpid sentences out of a page crammed with raw material. But when I stood in the messy shoe-box of an office he shared with Thurber, ankle deep in crumpled scrap-papers which were the doodles that Thurber threw away, the same doodled dogs and subhuman creatures who were soon to make him immortal, I had no idea that I was touching literary history and neither did anybody else.

None of us were very well paid. *The New Yorker,* while clearly a success, was by no means the gold mine it thereafter became, and our paychecks were modest. I did well enough because I wrote so many columns and was paid for them by the piece on top of my salary as a reporter. I averaged about two hundred dollars a week in earnings and was happy as a clam.

I was also beginning the time of my happiest relations with my mother, which deepened and intensified for the rest of her life. Tutelage and authority were behind us. Her indoctrination in the values of hard work and standing on one's own feet had taken hold. We had in fact everything in common, there was barely nineteen years' difference between us in age, and she sometimes remarked that I was the only tie in her life which went all the way back to its roots, and long antedated her present family and her public identity.

In 1926 she had sold the big house on Park Avenue, holding out like the realist she was for her own price from the syndicate who were assembling the land for an apartment house. She bought a pair of adjoining brownstones in Fast Forty-ninth Street across from Turtle Bay, and tore them down, replacing them with a charming double town house, now converted into flats, which has a Tudor-style brick façade and above the entrance Grosvenor At-terbury's plaque depicting a singing angel and a violin, woven round the five opening notes of *O, Rest in the Lord* from Mendels-sohn's *Elijah,* which she had so often sung and loved so much. Passersby today can have no idea of the significance of this plaque but it is eloquent of my mother's feeling for her home. She

bought the two houses chiefly in order to make one huge room
for music forty feet long, across the back of both houses on the
second floor, overlooking a garden of the same width. She designed the right-hand house around the remaining space for herself and her family, and made of the other half a smaller house
which she planned should some day be for me, but that was not
how things turned out. When I first returned to New York I
could not have used so much space or afforded to live in such a
house, so she rented it to Henry Luce who lived in it with his
first wife and their two sons. I had a flat around the corner in
Fiftieth Street, where I lived with my little girl and our nurse-
housekeeper, who saw more of my mother than they did of me,
working nearly the clock around.

Those years were the height of the Prohibition era, and the
whole subject bored and annoyed my mother to distraction. Of
course she thought Prohibition barbarous, but as she had never
in her life liked to drink anything but mineral water or hot milk
with a little coffee in it, she was irritated by the nuisance involved
in obtaining and serving drink. Yet she entertained a great deal.
Efrem Zimbalist had a nice taste for wines and saw to the buying
of them. He insisted there be a good wine-cellar in the new house,
with a door that was built by the York Safe people and furnished
with a combination lock. While he was about it he also had them
build a safe for her jewels in my mother's dressing-room.

But my mother had the bizarre obsession of refusing either to
lock anything up or to insure it. She had an irrational loathing of
insurance. She called insurance companies grafters, usurers, and
similar names, insisting that she could manage her property without paying huge insurance premiums which would only go to re-
imburse slobs who were so careless as to get burgled or let their
property burn up. She was furious about the two safes. Both had
doors which locked automatically when shut and could only be
reopened by somebody who knew the combination. In scorn, with
her great brown eyes flashing, and me standing by, she listened,

tapping her foot in a way which I had learned to dread as a child while the man from the York Company tried to tell her how to dial the combinations of the safes. When he had gone she wrote out the combination of the jewel-safe and pasted it on the door.

She did not do that to the wine-cellar, probably thinking it might be an invitation to bibulous servants, but she also refused to learn how to open the door. Efrem Zimbalist was away much of the time on tour. So whenever she had a dinner-party she would telephone me beforehand at *The New Yorker,* telling me to come to the house and open the wine-vault. Sometimes I was out on a story—it could be anywhere from the Bronx Zoo to the roof of an unfinished building—and the office would relay a message that my mother was trying to reach me in an emergency. Even worse was the confusion about gin. Neither my mother nor I had ever touched the stuff when it was drinkable, and now everybody was driven to making at home a vomitorious concoction of grain alcohol, distilled water, glycerine, and juniper extract. I had to make it for my mother's parties; she would have no part of it. From some bootlegger we had a regular supply of grain alcohol, which came in gallon jugs that were kept in the wine-cellar. Once when my mother had asked me to make some gin for an imminent dinner-party, there was a reason, which I have forgotten, why beside the bottle with the 'gin' in it I had also left a jug of alcohol standing in the pantry. My mother had some new servants who came with the best references and were declared to be expert. She put the dinner menu in the pantry and thought no more about it. The first course was Crabmeat Cocktails. While the guests were gathering in the drawing-room the new butler appeared with a tray of glasses of pure grain alcohol with bits of crabmeat floating in it.

I do not know how I found or stole the time, but I was in my mother's box every Friday afternoon for Maestro's concert with the Philharmonic. Sometimes I had heard the same programme the evening before at the first of the week's concerts, and often I went again on Sunday afternoon. A few years later when I was a music critic I spent nearly as much time in Carnegie Hall as the orchestra did; but working on *The New Yorker* did not give me such leeway and as I remember it, my absorption in Maestro's symphonic conducting was a gradual growth like my own relation with him. But it was growth from the main root of all that I indigenously was and felt. At that time I was an in-between creature, neither the clumsy girl he had not recognized six years before, nor a person who had anything to say to him different from what everybody said. . . "Oh, Maestro, the concert was wonderful!" . . . "Oh, Maestro, thank you!" If I found myself at the dinner table with him, always in my mother's company and proudly aware of her beauty and wit and the laughter that sparkled around her, of course I was dumb. Not unhappily dumb, not at all the daughter the psychologists like to take apart, who suffers from inferiority, overt or suppressed, in the shadow of her brilliant mother. I simply knew she was more beautiful and amusing than any other woman, and I thought myself damned lucky to be there at all. Maestro would say a few words to me in Italian and if I answered, it was in English. I had not spoken Italian since childhood and though I understood it perfectly I had some diffidence about speaking it.

Now that I think of it, I am surprised that he accepted me as he did, for Maestro claimed it one of his violent prejudices that he would have nothing to do with anyone who was divorced. But as in the instances of some other notable animadversions, he cut the suit to fit the particular piece of cloth; of course he made exceptions to many dreaded strictures. And also he probably had no idea at that time what really had been happening to me. I was simply Alma's *bambina* who like his own daughters was no longer a *bambina,* but by no means yet an identity in her own right.

At that time he was exactly sixty years old. And it is accurate to say that he had the intellectual and physical powers of a man twenty years younger. He also looked it. In the twelve years since he had left the Metropolitan, he had gone first to the Italian fighting fronts, conducting military bands at the firing-lines along the Isonzo. Then he undertook to reestablish the disorganized and demoralized Scala; the first step was the tour on which he brought its orchestra to this country in 1920–21. Thereafter he spent nine years as musical director and head conductor and autocrat of the great theatre, where he made history which belongs in the record of his art and his time and himself, not in a personal memoir which should and will confine itself to one person's knowledge of a man who was unique. But sometimes I have to cite an artistic act or decision of his because it so wholly illuminates his character—like the time at La Scala when he prepared a new production of Bellini's *Norma,* and after some sixty rehearsals, arrived for the dress rehearsal, began it, and then cancelled the whole production. "The music is too great," he said. "It is beyond human powers."

Though La Scala would probably have acceded to any imaginable wish of his—and they did not have American union scales and other staggering obstructions to unlimited rehearsals—he had a growing desire to devote himself to symphonic music, which he paraphrased in the claim that he was getting too old for the rigors of opera. (Ten and twenty years later he was not too old for it when he wanted to conduct it.) So he went to New York as guest conductor of the Philharmonic for a limited number of concerts, which blew the roof off the musical life of the town. Until that time New York had had two major orchestras, the Philharmonic and the New York Symphony, whose conductor was my mother's dear friend Walter Damrosch. Neither orchestra was viable economically and in 1928 it was decided to merge the two into the Philharmonic-Symphony and make Maestro its permanent conductor.

He was in New York every year from autumn until spring, and he lived with Signora Carla in the Astor Hotel, which was run by Fred Muschenheim, a German-born gentleman of the old school, whose gentle wife was called Elsa. Their hospitality was lavish. The Muschenheims' house was a narrow brownstone, the last survivor of its epoch, squeezed between the Astor with which it connected, and Shubert Alley in West Forty-fifth Street. When I was invited to supper with Maestro after a concert in the early Philharmonic days it was usually at the Muschenheims', occasionally at Maestro's own apartment in the hotel. I was oftener at the latter later on when I was less an appendage of my mother. Very occasionally the Toscaninis came to my mother's house. My mother was never a member of the group which came to be called the Toscanini Cult, whose high priest and priestess were Chotzie and Pauline, whose crazy antics and practical jokes Maestro hugely enjoyed, and who were fanatical about him musically and otherwise. My mother had known him intimately years before the Toscanini Cult came into existence—in fact, it was she who had introduced Chotzie to him. She was less emotional or possibly, hysterical, about him and his music than the Chotzinoffs and their relations and friends. At that time I was somewhere between the two extremes, insatiable in my appetite for the music, but too diffident—if that is the right word; anyway, too introvert, not un-inhibited and prankish enough to play in the league with the cult who were also jealous and possessive and desirous of keeping their fun and games with Maestro to themselves. Later I moved in and out of that circle depending on place and circumstance, and later still I had my own friendship with him which lasted to the end of his life.

When I met Russell Davenport he was only staying briefly in Philadelphia to be with his mother and he soon left, as talent will, to go to New York. He rented a flat in a cold-water tenement on the East River. This seemed eccentric at that time, though it would not be today if such quarters could still be found. Most of us who had spent our lives on the central spine of Manhattan scarcely knew the East River existed. Its shore was a tangle of warehouses, slaughter-houses, and cold-water tenements, and of course there was no East River Drive. The exceptions were at the corners of Fifty-seventh Street where Mrs. Vanderbilt and Elisabeth Marbury had daringly built the first of the beautiful town houses that are still there, and a group of imaginative aesthetes had put up the fine cooperative apartment house at 1 Sutton Place. Down the street the Phipps estate owned the rows of unimproved five-story cold-water walk-ups, tenements, but not in the sense of the filth and overcrowding of the lower East Side or Harlem. These were just plain flats in which ordinary working-people lived, called railroad flats because the rooms stood end to end in the constricted space like the cars of a train. Russell rented one in the house on the corner of Fifty-fourth Street and the river. Most of the rooms were dark and so cramped that they held little beyond one basic piece of furniture. But the kitchen at the back was the room that overlooked the river, a room the full width of the house with rattling windows commanding the view, a coal range, and a primitive sink with cold water only, in fact. There was a large table where Russell wrote and entertained his friends and we ate many a good meal that I cooked. Such houses had no central heating, so the warmth of the kitchen range was essential.

Here Russell set about being a writer. Since a novel that he wrote there is unremembered, and the poetry beautiful if nowhere to be seen, that interval has no relation to the work for which he was known in the most effective years of his life. He was still full of the panache that he had brought back from Paris, and he lived by practising his own peculiar system of finance, which less imaginative or daring people would not have had the nerve to attempt. He had inherited a very small amount of money, so small that conventional investment of it would not have yielded income enough for him to live on for as much as eight weeks out of a year. Instead, he played the money in the stock market, turning round and round on it and picking up enough profits to enable him to live as he liked. He was clever at that and clever enough too not to lose his nest-egg in the crash of 1929 when it came. This peculiarity of his was the reason why he was always able to quit his well-paid editorial jobs at the intervals he did, when he wanted to do something else; somehow he could always manage. And he was not rich, though he lived as well as he liked to do and later encouraged me to do the same. He was indeed the poet living in picturesque disorder in his metaphorical garret, but we dined all the time at Twenty-one (then a speakeasy, bless its heart), went to the theatre in the best seats—Russell's deafness dictated those—and his time was wholly his own while mine was mostly *The New Yorker's*.

My mother liked Russell well enough but had her reservations about him; however, he was often at her house with me. She was obviously aware of the nature of my relation with him and I realized how it appeared to her. On the one hand she had brought me up with inflexible strictness, and she clung to a residual notion that I should continue to toe the line in respect of conventional behavior. On the other hand she knew perfectly well that I had been badly burnt by my ignominious démarche into matrimony. Plainly I would never again rush blindfold into anything—nor would any young woman who had got beyond childhood and was groping her way towards realistic life. At that time I was not really thinking of marriage, though I probably wanted it more than Russell did; it was not part of his scheme of things at all. Like any other young man in his situation he was having the best of several worlds, and I was not inclined to force matters. I knew that my mother not only would have done the same in my place but that she had done the same in her own place. And yet, the time came when she simply could not keep hands off. I believe her motive was that she wanted to see me married and settled; she was doubtful about Russell because she was afraid of his creative and eccentric side. It is a very curious sidelight on my mother that, herself an artist and married to one, wholly the creature of talent and wholly cognizant of what it meant and what its forces were, she held all her life a wistful regard for people who were everyday people, for men who worked with their hands or were occupied with functional matters, for women who were simply women, good wives and mothers. Of course that was at variance with her own regard for achievement, her basic obsession with work for its own sake which she had dinned into me since earliest childhood. But this is one of the mysteries of personality.

One day she seemed in less than her usual serene good humor and I knew she was going to work up to something. She did. In a few words she came around to the subject of my private life and vehemently expressed her disapproval of it. She talked like a Victorian, stuffy and scandalized. "This can't go on," she said. "It won't do." She grew more agitated and soon began to have what I used to call in childish fear, 'big eyes.' "I won't have it!" she said finally.

"You won't?" I said. We stood looking at each other across her dressing-table. She was regal. I was calm. "Just what can you do about it?" I said.

I was completely self-supporting; independent. She knew it. Suddenly she burst into a peal of laughter.

"Thank God!" she said. The indoctrination had won.

But she still wanted me to be married and in her oblique way she precipitated that result some time later. Like many of the combinations of elements which make life the involuted and contradictory thing that it is instead of an orderly progression from point to point or end to end, there was a force working in me which had nothing to do either with my enthusiasm for my job or my relation with Russell. This was my growing and compelling preoccupation with Mozart; with the music, and with the personality and life of the composer. I cannot even remember when the music of Mozart had first gripped me so peculiarly that it was always a thing apart. When I was so young that I could not know there was such a thing as a composer I had a primary reaction to the music of Mozart. My feeling for all eighteenth-century music is not separate from this and its root may well be Maestro's *Orfeo* which had had such tremendous impact on me at the age of six. Ever since I can remember, a phrase or a melody or a characteristic ornamentation or resolution of Mozart's has struck something in me like a shiver of recognition. It may seem flippant to cite the following, but that is not my intention; I do it to show how physical such a thing might be. I once had a dog, the only time I have ever had a dog instead of my essential cat; and that dog, like any creature in my house, heard music around it all the time. What is music to a dog? But if I played a record of the Fifth Brandenburg Concerto, the dog would come running from wherever he was and plant himself in front of the gramophone. Incredible? A possibility that a flute and a cembalo in the key of D major made an agreeable vibration on the dog's ear-drums? There is lots of other music in the same key with similar scoring, and it was played all the time. Can a dog recognize a melody? I do not know. But my first reactions to any music of Mozart's were like those of that dog.

Also, to quote my own words from another book, "my childish reactions were component with my adoration of my mother. With rare exceptions I loved whatever she sang because she sang it. But the music of Mozart stands apart in retrospect from this childlike readiness of acceptance. It had magic of its own, beauty separate from my mother's beauty of voice and face, tenderness different from but matched only by hers, identification with Mozart's name at a time when I was too young to know other composers' names or music of themselves."

Another childhood experience intensified this. I must have been nine or ten years old. My mother was a disciple of Marcella Sembrich and used to study repertoire with her. One day she took me along. Madame Stengel, as Sembrich was in private life, sat at the piano and played, and my mother stood behind her, one hand on her shoulder. They sang the Letter Duet, Sembrich the Contessa's voice and my mother Susanna's. I stood in a corner, nobody else in the room, spellbound, bewitched. I had never heard of *Le Nozze di Figaro,* I had no idea of the meaning of what they were singing or its context. But there they were, the old voice frail and reedy, my mother's fresh and radiant, in a dialogue whose style and charm personified a whole world, a world in which I wanted to live. I knew that then. I never forgot it.

With all those years of concert-going in Philadelphia, and now with Maestro at the Philharmonic, there had never been enough Mozart for me. The music of Mozart was not played much in this country in the first quarter of this century. Symphony conductors and their audiences leant heavily to the nineteenth-century composers; the great piano virtuosi were partial to Liszt, Rachmaninoff, Tschaikowsky and, thank God, Beethoven and Brahms. A Mozart concerto was a comparative rarity. Maestro sometimes played the overture to *Die Zauberflöte;* he played the G minor and the Jupiter Symphonies and he had a special predilection for the Haffner, all of which was manna to me; but he played much less Mozart with the Philharmonic than he was later to play with the N B C Symphony.

None of the operas were to be heard at all. The last *Don Giovanni* at the Metropolitan had been in 1907, the last *Figaro* in 1916. My mother sang their arias for me, but I had heard neither opera in performance, nor *Die Zauberflöte* either. As for the lesser ones, even *Così Fan Tutte* was almost unknown in this country. I knew the scores as best one can from playing piano transcriptions, and I had such records of arias and brief scenes as existed at that time, some years before the first experiments in recording anything longer than the content of a single 12-inch 78-rpm record.

So I was tormented by frustration in not having access to the body of Mozart's music. Then by degrees I thought increasingly about the man himself. I sought out such biographies as existed, and after noting that all the definitive material was in German, I read what there was in English. There was very little indeed, and that of the thinnest texture. The preposterous nineteenth-century concept of Mozart as a gay little man, dancing minuets in a white wig and a dandy's clothes, a spun-sugar animated doll, had come to some terms with reality, but insufficiently. No American had ever written a biography of Mozart, and in England nobody had written a modern biographical study, modern in the sense of the author's intent to recreate if he can his subject as a living personality of flesh and blood in full dimensions, faults and all.

This type of biography was then having great success at the hands of Lytton Strachey. Francis Hackett's portrait of Henry VIII was a work of this kind. So was the brilliant *François Villon* by D. B. Wyndham Lewis. These and other books of similar definition had been published in the years before I resolved to write a book about Mozart, and I was influenced by them. Curiously, my preoccupation with contemporary biographical writing had not extended to that about composers. The first volume of Ernest Newman's stupendous, definitive work on Wagner did not appear until 1933. But my attitude towards Wagner can wait for another point of reference than this.

It was the winter of 1929, January or February. I went with Russell Davenport to stay outside Boston with his closest friend, Maxwell Foster, a brilliant, contentious lawyer and literary scholar, and his wife Elizabeth. The weather was bad and we spent most of the time indoors, sitting over log fires and listening (Elizabeth and I) while the two men engaged in violent intellectual argument and much reading aloud of poetry in dramatic, chanting strophes. I do not remember until then having said much to Russell about my intensifying obsession—for it was that—with Mozart, but at a certain moment we were standing by ourselves in the bay window of the Fosters' dining-room, a bay of old small-paned sashes full of potted plants. How curious that one remembers such details when much else, so much more necessary to total recall, has gone beyond one's reach. I was talking about Mozart and I think that was the first time I said that there was no good biography of him in English and none at all written by an American.

"Well?" said Russell.

That was it. I felt inside me, I think I can say, in my head, that sensation like the click of an electric switch, which is the signal that an idea has become a book. This is a mysterious thing and one that cannot be simulated or synthetically contrived. It has marked the beginning of every book I have written, more exactly it has marked the fact that the book *was there to be written.* I would not dare undertake a book unless the thing had happened, genuinely and spontaneously. I cannot reach for it or go to it. It must happen to me. Several times I have experienced it and thereafter found myself unable to write the book that it signalled. But each book that I have finished and published has had its initiation in that experience, and in each instance I can remember exactly where and when and how and in relation to whom, if anybody, the click, as I call it, took place. Always it has come long after the fact of deep interest in or knowledge of, or involvement with, the subject and the material; it is I think a kind of small explosion like spontaneous combustion of materials tightly packed and long stored, sometimes under pressure.

The decision was made and I had to figure out how to implement it. I would have to go to Europe, to pursue my plan of re-living Mozart's life in sequence and geography as closely as possible, of seeing every house and palace and theatre, every church, every structure still existing, in which he was known to have been. I would have to work in libraries, in museums, in the archives of music publishers, theatres, and other entities. I would have to assemble a library of all available Mozart material and buy it because I needed to own it and be able to mark and annotate and cross-check the sources. Almost all of it was in German: I would have to learn German. That did not faze me, I plunged into it like a spaniel into water, not caring whether I spoke it correctly so long as I functioned in it and read it effortlessly. And of course I would hear the music unlimitedly in Austria and Germany, where it was basic to every instrumental and operatic repertoire.

I calculated what this would cost, not a small sum because I was not preparing to do my task in a small way. I could not be hampered by petty economies like being unable to purchase expensive books or restrict the amount of travelling I had to do. Also I had to finance myself through time to work. Curiously, I cannot remember just what I planned to do about *The New Yorker* other than obtain an indefinite leave of absence without pay, but I suppose I was counting on doing part-time work there after I returned from Europe, first to study and organize my material and then to start writing my book. I reckoned that I would need twenty-five hundred dollars.

I went to my mother one day in March and told her about my plan and asked her to lend me or give me or advance me on any basis she would, twenty-five hundred dollars. She refused.

This appears so shocking that I hesitate for her sake to relate it, but her motives were not at all what they would seem to one who did not know her or understand her. Her refusal had nothing to do with money. I know why she refused. It was what I call the second half of her who did so, the half that insisted on a woman's being a woman, the half that had dragged herself and a nursing infant all over the United States, the half that held simple human values high above the rewards of ambition and talent, all the while the first half was dinning into me the exhortation to work, the compulsion to achievement. She admitted none of this and I have come to comprehend it only after many years and much reflection. She gave me no concrete reason for her refusal, she simply implied that I was overreaching myself and why did I think myself capable of writing such a book? What she was really hoping was that I would never take off into the deep seas and dangerous wildernesses of an artist's life; she knew its hazards and so now do I, but I would not forego them if I had it all to do over again. She thought by discouraging me to check my impulse towards such a life and keep me, for the sake of my own happiness, on safe, circumscribed ground.

I was very upset. I went over to Russell who was waiting in his flat to hear my news, for he was keen on my project and it had become a vital part of our common interests. He listened to what I had to say. I remember so well that tenement kitchen, the table at which we were sitting, the battered coffee-pot and the cup with its saucer full of his cigarette-butts. He shook his head slowly and said, "Well, I guess we'll have to get married and then we can spell each other through things like this."

So my mother had her wish, which was of course my own but not the only aim of my emotions and my mind. Nor was it Russell's. My mother could not know, nobody has ever known, the real nature of that marriage which was embarked upon as a working partnership, not a marriage to fit anybody else's definitions or necessities. Of course we loved each other and had a passionate attachment; but each of us was a person of extreme duality of character and temperament. He was the most total example of two-persons-in-one that I have ever known; supremely admirable at his best, a devil at his worst. My own qualities were less excessive but equally disparate. I was feminine, sentimental, domestic, a creature of the hearth who had to use her hands to cook and sew and make things; and also one who had to walk out to stay alone abroad for months on end in pursuit of the knowledge and experiences and the absolute necessity for Europe out of which came the books I had to write and which he desired and expected me to write. In community of interests, in congeniality of intellectual and many other tastes, in a euphoria of crackling excitement when we worked on something together, it was magnificent. But when it was wrong, it was torment. How could two such characters not make a life of irreconcilable extremes out of the contradictions that both innately were?

We were married in May, 1929. His mother and mine both had their misgivings as to the daughter of the one and the son of the other. But they got together and each gave us a like amount of money, which bought the apartment on the East River where I still live (I had been longingly watching it under construction) and some means on which to turn around. Neither sum was a great deal of money as basic property, certainly not by present-day values; and all this happened six months before the stock market crash which affected so many lives and led to the depression which formed a generation, generated revolutions and philosophies, and permanently changed the political and social face of the United States and the world.

Russell did not give up his bohemian bachelorhood without qualms. In fact he was so appalled when he realized what he had done that he did not speak to me the first twenty-four hours after we were married. We used to roar with laughter about that later. We spent that summer mostly with my family at Fishers Island, and moved into our less-than-finished new apartment in the autumn, during the week of the stock market crash. I was such a fool about finance that I had little idea what was happening, and it was a benevolence of fate that none of us were severely battered in the débacle. This was probably because neither my mother nor his had been living in extravagance that could not have been maintained after the bottom fell out; also there had been no speculation on margin that would have wiped anybody out. But everybody was a lot poorer on paper and in fact. Russell had salvaged his little hoard in time and we pooled that with our wedding presents. Thereafter for years we turned round and round on that tiny capital—Russell's curious manoeuvre; tiny in the sense that it could not yield enough income to live on. But there was money for me to go to Europe when I needed to, for Russell to resign from his job or take a leave of absence when he wanted to do something else.

I have often thought how ironical it was that while my

mother did attain her wish to see me married, she also turned me over, with just enough money to push me in that direction, to the one man who wanted of me exactly what my mother was afraid for me to be. And in the long run both were right. He saw the positive side of such a woman, my mother the negative. At first he and I expected that we would both write books primarily. I saw no further ahead than the Mozart book for myself, and he published his only novel. Thereafter it was the sobering atmosphere of 1930, combined with the realities of an established ménage, which decided him to go to work at Time, Inc. An experimental project was under way there, shaping up the idea that was to emerge as *Fortune,* and Russell was one of the group who evolved the new magazine. One of them was the dearest friend we ever had, Parker Lloyd-Smith, who became an intimate of both of ours and of our house, a man of charming, whimsical mind. I was still on *The New Yorker* and I ran our apartment with the help of a zany individual named Charlotte, who cooked by the light of nature (wonderfully) and was a natural clown. Russell and I both had our sights set on Mozart, and eventually on the books each would write, abetted by the other. As it turned out through the years, I had more books in me than he did. But we could not know that originally, nor could we foresee that he would realize his powers as an articulator of opinion in this country, as an idealistic and a realistic force in its politics and its national and international life.

By the early winter of 1930 my mental teeth were set much harder in Mozart than in *The New Yorker,* and though I still had the whole bulk of the research ahead of me, not to mention the writing, I felt I had to get some kind of opinion or reaction from a publisher before proceeding with the work. This may be because I have never been satisfied with dusty answers; I have always preferred certainties even when they were unfavorable or even catastrophic. At whose suggestion I cannot remember, but I think someone on *The New Yorker,* I went to see the late Eugene Saxton, the well-known editor at Harpers. I described to him the book

I wanted to write and he said, predictably, that if I wrote the book he would as soon look at the manuscript, but could give me no assurance that it would be something Harpers would want to publish.

This should not have discouraged me; if I had not been so green I would have expected nothing else. But I was discouraged. Before I undertook that book I needed some assurance (which no beginner should dare expect) that somebody was going to publish it. Russell Davenport's friend Phelps Putnam, the poet, was staying with us, and I told the two men about my interview with Saxton. Putnam protested that an idea like this deserved more encouragement, and he was sure I would get it from Max Perkins at Scribners. The year before, Scribners had published Putnam's first brief book of poems and Put had become one of the writers who worshipped Max Perkins. He asked Max to see me and next day I found myself in the famous, cluttered, dusty office sitting beside the shabby oak desk with the slithering piles of books and the rough-rider-hat ashtray on it; and behind it the reserved, laconic man with the sensitive face and the extraordinary eyes. Max said little. His essential quality was always to say little, but by powerful empathy for writers and for books to draw out of them what they had it in them to say and to write. He listened to my description of the book I wanted to write. I may add that no editor in New York could have had less interest in Mozart or in music generally than Maxwell Perkins. It was fiction that he was interested in, and he was regarded with devotion and awe by established and would-be novelists. But he drew from me my reasons for wanting to write my book. Then he said, "Go ahead and write it. We will publish it."

To this day I recall that moment as one of the heights of my life. He had never seen a word I had written, and those that existed were journalism. He suggested I write a few pages of the proposed manuscript and let him see them. When I did so, he took the folder and looked it through from back to front, something which thrilled me for a special reason. He nodded and told me to keep right on. I never knew his thoughts about this until, three years after his death, Scribners published a volume of his letters. In one written to the critic, Alice Dixon Bond, he said:

> "You ask about Marcia Davenport—we immediately accepted her first book, 'Mozart,' even though not a very great deal of it was written. One could tell from what we saw of the manuscript that she had skill, and from what we saw of her that she was unconquerable and would do what she undertook."

I cannot read those words without extreme emotion. They came to me in 1950 in a remote retreat where I had been struggling to rise from defeat on every front where life can engage one. If Max had been so sentimental as to leave me some personal legacy for my help and guidance, this would have been it. The 'we' in his letter was the most editorial 'we' ever used. After every other motive for trying to get back to work (or to life—in me the two must be synonymous) had proved too weak to stir me, Max's belief in me was and still is the challenge I must measure up to, the compact in which I will not let him down.

I never had the talent or, as in some of Max's authors, the genius to come through with writing which made literary history. The excesses in character and personality, the wild unruly drives in Fitzgerald and Hemingway and Wolfe, were left out of me and out of my capacity to write. I never had a quality like Marjorie Rawlings's feeling for the simple materials with which she worked, or the natural lustre of Nancy Hale's prose. I had what I had—authentic knowledge of certain large elements of life and the world. I had vigor and I could work on big canvas; I preferred to. I was driven more by the need to write what I knew than what I was. In youth I had an overpowering appetite to extend and engorge that knowledge and Max came into my life at the right time to spur me ahead. Nothing like fiction was mentioned until well after the publication of *Mozart*, but the ferment was implicit. Max lived to see me through three novels, and only in the third had he begun to guide me towards writing from within the self rather than from outside it. I cannot tell where the difference might have led had he lived longer, but I do know that when I set off in pursuit of Mozart I found myself in the atavistic home of a large part of my life and my mind, the source of elementary experience and emotion, the wellspring of much that I have written and of much that I have still not written. But that which cannot be transmuted into fiction will be recorded before the end of this book.

I FIRST saw Prague in the raw grey dawn of a day in March, 1930. My research on Mozart was taking me on a literal re-tracing across Europe of every step of his travels, though not necessarily in the exact sequence of his journeys. I had first to assemble source material, so I had been in Berlin buying books from the great musical antiquarian Leo Liepmannssohn, and paying homage to the manuscripts in the Prussian State Library. My first major destination was of course Salzburg, but I decided to stop on the way in Prague for the reason that a few months before in New York, Mr. Gatti had finally broken the sound barrier and mounted, for the first time in twenty-eight years and the first in my experience, *Don Giovanni.* This was because he had the cast for it—the historical cast of Ponselle, Rethberg, Fleischer, Pinza and Gigli. But the artists were not my primary concern, the score was; and I nearly went mad. I was saturated in everything I had learnt about *Don Giovanni,* and Prague was the basis of it. Some of the richest material lay there, not only about *Don Giovanni* but *Figaro* too, for Prague had been the place of its first success, the reason for Mozart's love of Prague and his great popularity there. He was the idol of all its people, the commonalty as well as the nobility, acclaimed and feted as he never was otherwise. This happy treatment in Prague was in extreme contrast to his bitter struggle for recognition and for a bare living in Vienna. I was already so possessed by Mozart, and my emotions so identified with his, for his letters are almost the equivalent of knowing the man in person, that it may be I reacted to Prague from the first with the love that Mozart felt for it, the only community which gave him the affection and the recognition for which he was starved elsewhere.

But when I stepped from a wagon-lit into the Wilson Station at six o'clock that morning, I knew nothing whatever about the contemporary city and the country to which I had come. I knew not a soul in Czechoslovakia. I had a letter to the Librarian-Archivist of the State Conservatory of Music, and that was all. I knew only the barest outlines of the history of the small new republic, the residue of reading the tangled and prejudiced accounts of the Versailles Peace Conference. I was utterly confounded by my first confrontation with the language. I stood in the middle of the station looking at a pair of doors marked VCHOD and VÝCHOD (entrance and exit); and I thought this must indeed be a wilderness of unpronounceable tweedledums and tweedledees.

Presently I found myself in a taxi careening down the left-hand side of a street slippery with sleet and rain. There was nothing much to see between the station and the Esplanade Hotel, which are in fact a moment's walk across a small park from one another. My room at the hotel was small and dark, no particular augury of cosiness or comfort. But I sent for some breakfast and had my first taste of Czech coffee and Czech rolls and butter as they used to be in a good gone world. I ate everything on the tray and sent at once for another. Then I had a bath and a rest. It was still early morning, and by nine o'clock the rain had stopped but the sky remained grey. I put on my hat and coat and went out on foot.

Usually in a strange city I first study, and always carry, a map. That morning I set out without one. I do not know why. I could have picked one up at the hotel, but I decided not to do so, and I walked without plan, wherever instinct should lead me. The hotel is in the modern, commonplace part of Prague, at some distance from the old quarters with their beauty and charm. I walked straight on, turned a corner, and started down Václavské

Náměstí, which is spectacular only because of its width; it is said to be the widest and proportionately the shortest boulevard in Europe. I followed my nose as though going by a trail of pebbles, walking slowly and gazing at the prosperous shops, the stolid, heavy-looking men, always carrying brief-cases; the plump, blond-ined women; the abundance of eating-places and of tempting things to eat. The smells were extraordinary. I seem like a dog to measure much sensory impression by smell, and in those days the Prague smell was a rich compound of coal smoke, roasting coffee, beer, smoked pork, and frying onions. I liked it; I liked the frank animal well-being of it; and I walked on, full of a rising sense of contentment that was altogether new in my experience of strange places. Without hesitation at the bottom of the boulevard I crossed Na Příkopě, the broad modern avenue that meets it, passed through the arcade of a nearby building and emerged, as I had sensed I would, in the eighteenth century, standing in Ovocný Trh (The Fruit Market) and looking at Stávovské Divadlo, the theatre which was the central landmark that I had come to see, where *Don Giovanni* had had its first performance.

To this moment I can recapture the surge of delighted recognition with which I felt myself transported back into the world where my mind for so long had been living. My imagination rushed to people the scene with the faces, the pigtails, the knee-breeches, the leather aprons of the eighteenth-century market porters who would have been working around this square. And when I stood listening to the gabble of peasant women at their stands, presiding over their baskets of scrubbed potatoes and jolly cabbages, there was little enough difference between reality and the picture in my mind's eye. I walked slowly all round the theatre, a charming small house of neoclassic design, and came out upon the street it actually faces; I had seen first its rear elevation. This short street leads into another market square called Uhelný Trh (The Coal Market), lined like the Fruit Market with ancient arcaded houses. That day was goose-market day and Uhelný Trh was full of geese, both dressed and very much alive. A pandemonium of honks and hisses added the final touch to a living scene as if by Breughel, and I felt as though I would never come down to earth again.

I picked my way through flocks of geese, market-women, housewives, ladies accompanied by cooks or chauffeurs, restaurant buyers, small boys ducking and whipping through the melée as they seem to do in all such crowds; and I wandered out the farther end of the market square towards the tiny twelfth-century church of St. Martin, passing in the narrow curving street the house where Mozart lodged when he first came to Prague; and I walked on, feeling my way by instinct until I found myself in Staroměstké Náměstí, the Old Town Square, with its glorious Gothic Town Hall (destroyed in 1945 by the Germans); its world-famous Orloj, the mechanical clock with the Apostles marching round when the hour struck, which was hit in the same explosion; and the needle spires of the Tyn Church soaring behind the soft yellow arcades which line the great open square.

That part of Prague is poignant to me beyond expression. To it I returned in 1945, full of hope and ingenuous joy, to weep unashamed at the ruins of the Town Hall. Every day I went to the old market squares not only to buy food but to chat and joke with my friends among the market-women. By the changes in less than three years I saw what was happening, first for better, then for worse. Today Staroměstké Náměstí is blank, dull, empty except when its great expanse is filled with mobs at rallies. Then they hide its noble architecture with a tribune draped in red banners, surrounded by streamers of lying slogans and bloated lithographs of party satraps; then it is raucous with drilled robots shouting as Hitler's pigs used to do. The Jan Hus monument is shamed, the Tyn spires brood mournfully over a jungle of braying loud-speakers, and the loveliness I first met half my lifetime ago is gone forever.

I could not know that then; in the wildest of nightmares I

could not have dreamt it. Not after I came to know the country well, not after long study of its history and deep sharing of its fate, could I have believed what was to happen to it. That first day is a truer measure of my bond with it than much that has happened since. It was a rich experience to find the joy of personal identification with a realm that I had first learned to know and love in imagination. But I did not realize then that after Prague should have given me the delight of re-living its attraction for Mozart there would lie a whole new world of fascination and of lasting attachment beyond. The city and the country for twenty years thereafter held for me that fertile mystery which we call inspiration. A very large part of that has been unconscious. I drew from a natural well within my mind Czech nationality for the singer I named Lena Geyer. Bohemians and Moravians and Slovaks have moved in and out of most of my work, more it seems by their intent than by mine. Some of this may be atavism. Some may be romanticism. All of it is truth and therefore much of it is tragedy.

But that, as it should be, is balanced by joy. Once I had discovered that source of good life for myself I returned to it again and again, more times than I can count, but at least once every year and sometimes oftener, until the first curtain of darkness came down. I used to wander through the countryside all alone, driving my car wherever my fancy led me, stopping at village inns and sometimes at farmhouses where, in my ignorance of the language, I communicated mostly by signs with smiling peasant women who fed me delicious food and put me to sleep in featherbeds—down from their own geese and linen of their own weaving —and once took me along to such a village festival as the Czech wedding in *The Valley of Decision*. In this way I saw at one time or another every part of Czechoslovakia except the extreme eastern tip of Slovakia, and Ruthenia. And my feeling for the country grew until I settled with the knowledge that here I had found my second motherland, the need for which has been an elemental hunger in many a writer through the ages.

So I stood for a long hour in Staroměstké Náměstí that first morning; and finally I walked on, still following my nose, burrowing through the labyrinth of twisting mediaeval streets, none of which then had any plan for me. But my instinct for water always carries me towards it, and one cannot go far in any case in the Old Town without emerging on the right bank of the river Vltava. I came to the river through the ancient street called Karlová Ulice, and so ahead of me saw the eastern arch of Karlův Most, the Charles Bridge, so famed and fabled a landmark that no possible words can serve it now which have not often served before. Many persons have written before me, many who felt no personal emotion at all, that this lyric poem in stone and sculpture spanning the brooding waters of the river, and forming the foreground to the rising green heights of the opposite shore, where Hradčany with its buttressed walls, its towers and spires, its soaring cathedral, the glorious wealth of Gothic and baroque creation at its apogee, is the most beautiful sight in Europe and as cities go, in all the world.

To write of the successive moments of that day, the unique day, I suppose, of my whole life, is to be faced with conveying the most moving possible experience, only to try still harder to express the feelings evoked by each new impression. To say that I was breathless, or awestruck, or many times moved to tears seems like exaggeration too easy to write and too hard to believe; but it is the truth. Most compelling of all was the probing, haunting sense of recognition. I knew all this that lay around me. I knew it from some distant realm long antedating my measurable life. This was buried knowledge and buried instinct, rising from something too intangible to be given a name, to claim a home such as my mind and my nativity had never known before.

I walked slowly across the Bridge and ever since have been glad that I did first cross it on foot. I touched with delight the grey stone coping, heavily carved and faintly pitted but smooth with age. I studied the statues which line the span at even intervals, Gothic saints with great billowing stone robes and haloes of the gilded iron lacework which graces so much of the soaring beauty of Prague. Thus I passed under the western arch of the Bridge, and eyeing the wonders before and above me, I kept on walking, not only as far as the fortress Hradčany, but as far as my strength and the daylight could take me. I cannot say how far I roamed, or into precisely which of the steep streets and squares and courts of the lovely quarter called Malá Strana, the Little Side, which was first the seat of the Bohemian Kings, then of the nobility of the Habsburg Empire, then of the Government and the diplomatic missions when the Republic was created in 1919. I know that I walked all day long; that I saw for the first time the beautiful street called Loretanská with its butter-yellow baroque houses in one of which I was to live out the extreme crisis of my life; and towards evening, when I stood exhausted, leaning on the parapet of Hradní Příkop, gazing from the great height at the ancient roofs of the huddled houses below, at the needle spires and onion domes of the churches, at the sweeping gardens and tender yellow façades of the palaces; raising my eyes to the curving majesty of the river, with more beauty beyond and the misty countryside in the farthest distance, I felt nothing else so strongly as that this was where I belonged. I said aloud, "This is where I mean to spend the end of my life."

So much for the mind and the spirit. The body is important too. Evening had come. I got into a taxi and went back to my hotel, startled at the bustling, neon-lighted Václavské, which prided itself on being modern no matter at what aesthetic price. I was extremely hungry. My lunch had consisted of hot *parky* (a couple of sausages, *ein Paar Würsterl* in Austria, but these were better) bought from a smiling peasant woman at her street-corner charcoal brazier and eaten from my hand with a hunk of black bread as I wandered about. Nobody appeared to think that bizarre, but nobody would in Central Europe. For dinner I had the best Czech cooking and all cooking is vastly interesting to me. There

was foie gras from Slovakia, the equal of any I ever had in Stras-
bourg; there was sublime mushroom soup; there was crisp and suc-
culent roast little pig served with the first Czech dumpling
(knedlík) I ever ate; and a prodigious sweet which I did not want
but which only proved what I had always heard—that the famous
pastry-cooks of Vienna were and always had been Czechs. I drank
a good many glasses of the beer which has never been the same
since Hitler slammed the gates shut on Bohemia, real Plzeň
draught beer as it used to be drawn from the keg, pale straw-
colored, delicate as good Chablis, with a firm snowy crest. It was
always served in thin, tall, tapered flutes, which could be ordered
in measures up to a litre, the outside of the glass faintly frosted
with the perfectly tempered chill. There was no other such beer
on earth, and there has been none since Czechoslovakia has been
dragged down its long *via crucis.*

I went up to my room to bed. It was not a particularly well-
sprung bed, and it had the maddening three-piece Central European mattress which is a torment to bodies not born to this oddity.
But the sheets were of polished linen almost as thick as doeskin,
and a cloud from heaven, enclosed in a snowy damask case, floated
over the surface of the bed. This was the *peřina*—pronounced
per-zhina, and untranslatable; the oblong bag filled with the finest
goose-down, which is never quilted or stitched. It is shaken up to
a great fluff and lightly dropped upon the bed, so delicious and
teasing to the touch that I can only describe the sensation as
putting one's fingers into a bowl of whipped cream which somehow is not wet. Beneath this I slept blissfully and next morning
woke in great content to begin my work.

My first problem was language. I knew of the fierce pride of
its citizens in this new succession state, which prompted one to
apologize for speaking German if one had to resort to it. Few
ordinary Czechs at that time spoke English. Occasionally one encountered linguists, like a physician who attended me once when I
had influenza in Prague, who spoke nine languages, none of which

was English, French, or Italian. But everybody knew German. Everybody educated sooner than a decade before this had learnt German in school and grown up in the Habsburg world where German was the official tongue. But the hatred of the Czechs for any reminder of the old days was so strong that most of them if spoken to in German, clumsily pretended not to understand it.

On the other hand, they had vociferous affection for the United States and next to their own adored President Masaryk, regarded Woodrow Wilson as the creator of their country. I kept this in mind as I groped for a means of communication with anybody I wanted to talk to.

"Excuse me," I would say in German to a scowling, sullen, or indifferent face. "I am an American."

The scowl or the look of suspicion would vanish to be replaced by a beaming smile, usually embellished with gold teeth. (Today the teeth would be steel.) "I should like to ask you something," I would continue, "but unless you happen to speak English, do you think you could consent to talk German with me?"

Of course they could. I spoke German like Sam Behrman's Jacobowsky—wrong but fluently. The Czechs did not care how I mangled the language, if anything I think they rather enjoyed it. Thereafter I had no difficulty. Research in that atmosphere, fraught with vivid memories and tangible associations with Mozart, was a delight. I soon met Dr. Vlastimil Blazek, the Archivist of the State Conservatory of Music, who was living at that time in the Villa Bertramka, the small eighteenth-century country house where Mozart and his wife lived as guests of Franz and Josefa Duschek during the final weeks of Mozart's work on the score and the rehearsals of *Don Giovanni*. The Bertramka is an enchanted place, still rustic and surrounded by gardens and vineyards although it is in the heart of Prague. That is one of the endearing beauties of the city—the prevalence of gardens, greensward, trees, and open spaces amidst the glorious baroque architecture. Behind the graceful yellow house the Bertramka garden rises up the hillside, its lowest level adjoining the house and forming the balustraded terrace where Mozart's beloved game of bowls was played whilst he sat at a little table overlooking the Duschek farmyard, writing down the score of *Don Giovanni* which stood entire and perfect in his head. Nothing disturbed him, he delighted in the rowdy jokes and laughter of his friends, who saw to it that the glass of punch at his elbow was kept full, and shouted to him when it was his turn to play in the game.

Here Dr. Blazek gave me all his particular and authoritative knowledge of Mozart in Prague, together with generous advice and fruitful suggestions. He engaged a university student to make for me translations into English of all the material on Mozart in Czech. He bore benevolently with my sketchy scholarship and my probably over-romantic enthusiasm. And he had the sensitive hospitality to invite me to come to the Bertramka garden and use it for my working-place whenever I chose. So for the time of my first stay in Prague and the next year too, I spent part of every fair day sitting at a table placed where I liked to think Mozart's writing-table had been, working on the notes and bibliography and eventually the manuscript of my book. I did not have to strive to recapture the atmosphere of Mozart's happiest experience; I was saturated in it myself. For years afterwards I used to go back to the Bertramka whenever I was in Prague, to gaze from that dark green garden at the view spreading out below the hillside, the river with its garlands of bridges, the Gothic needle-pointed spires, and to my left, Hradčany on its height beyond the hill called Petřín, a different view of which I was one day to live with, framed in my own windows.

And on my first Sunday in Prague I went to the National Theatre to hear *Prodaná Nevěsta*, Smetana's *Bartered Bride,* which is the Czech national opera. I had heard it only once before, when my mother sang Esmeralda in Mahler's fine Metropolitan production, but I remembered little of that. My only familiarity with the music came from years of hearing the overture as a concert piece. The Metropolitan had done the opera in German but it is a work which genuinely requires its native language, too deeply rooted in the folk-song indigenous to Czech character to transplant (translate) successfully. Since almost no foreigner can have a reason to know Czech it is notable that this incomprehensible language is no barrier to complete enjoyment of *The Bartered Bride.* It is a simple tale of peasant life, verisimilar even to the village idiot, its plot so artless that verbal comprehension is not necessary. Its glory lies in Smetana's orchestral and choral enrichment of a stream of folk music; and in the national dances, particularly the polka, which that day I saw performed as though each member of the ballet had learnt it as a child in his native village—which they all probably had.

The sets and costumes were beautiful and they were authentic. Since 1870 this opera had been the keynote and the touchstone of the Czech national revival which culminated in the postwar republic. It was the pride of a peasant people. The costumes did not look theatrical, but like real national folk dress which varies from province to province and even village to village. It was worn only on Sundays and festival occasions. The clothes were rich with hand embroidery, the men's shirts and waistcoats, the women's multiple petticoats and skirts, and especially the beautiful silk aprons handed down from mother to daughter. The women's white blouses with fantastic sleeves were the special marks, like the headdresses, of each village. The sleeves were of fine lawn, minutely pleated by fancy ironing and puffed into balloon or lantern shapes. And everybody wore high kid boots, the men's black, the women's often red, which were also family treasures. All this was reflected on the stage and in the delighted audience which packed the house. The solo voices were not very good; like most Slavic voices the women's were too meaty and the men's too hard, especially the sopranos and tenors. But the chorus was superlative, the best I had ever heard, and the orchestra excellent. The conductor was Otakar Ostrčil, who made the old 78-rpm recording before the Second World War, which is unexcelled. I could not have written parts of *The Valley of Decision* without it.

So from the very first there was more for me in Prague and in that country than the pursuit of Mozart who had, so to speak, sent me there. In the same sense, he sent me to other places and scenes, experiences and associations, to good ground and bad, into the basic medium which became one half of my life and my mind and thus of my work, while the United States remained the other. From that time on my life has been double-based, rooted in parts of Europe as strongly as in my own country. If I am cut off from one root or the other I am frustrated and disoriented both in my work and in myself. I am not and do not feel like a traveller in Central Europe and in Italy; they have put marks and hooks into me, they are what I had to write about, equally with the substance I have drawn from my own country. Now that the distance factor has been almost eliminated; now that the acceleration of communication, exchanges of tastes and outlooks, economic and industrial internationalism, even the frivolities and too frequently the cheapest and worst aspects of both worlds, have all been shaken up together, I am not always certain just where I need or want most to be, but I expect to die a chameleon.

More than thirty-five years ago I had the chance to work in Germany for a fine and valid reason, before pestilential vice had worked its way to the surface and touched off the degenerative chain of events whose ultimate results we cannot yet know. I had been there previously only once, as a small child with my mother, so young that my only memory is of a trip up the Rhine in an excursion boat and of my mother ingenuously singing *Die Lorelei* as we passed the famous rock, to the delight of the other passengers.

When I went to Berlin to begin my research on Mozart, I found a counsellor in Leo Liepmannssohn, the leading dealer in Europe in musical books and manuscripts. And a more remarkable man came to my help in a way and for reasons which I have never really understood. He was Dr. Johannes Wolf, the Curator of the Music Division of the Prussian State Library. Today I marvel at my brashness in having set forth on my project with so little scholarship and preparation. My only qualifications were my love of Mozart and his music, general musical literacy, and a youthful enthusiasm which must have been the extenuation for my deficiencies. I knew that the music manuscript collection in the Prussian State Library was then the greatest in the world. Our Library of Congress has now succeeded it. In Berlin were two-thirds of all the Mozart manuscripts extant, and a proportionate number of those of the other titans. I can scarcely believe that I had not thought before leaving New York to arm myself with suitable letters of introduction. I could easily enough have had them; the late Carl Engel, one of the world's foremost musicologists, was an intimate friend of my mother's and of our house. At that time he was the head of Schirmer's, and later of the Music Division of the Library of Congress. Letters from him would have bridged the gap in my identity so far as European libraries and musical institutions were concerned. I never thought of it!

Instead, the morning after I arrived in Berlin, I went to the State Library and handed an ordinary visiting-card to the guard at the Music Division, with a request to speak to the Curator. I was shown at once into the office of a slight, white-haired man with near-sighted eyes. He placed a chair for me and listened while I explained in my appalling German why I had come. His English was even less good. It is extraordinary how people can communicate when they want to. It was not difficult for me to identify myself in terms of my family and its place in music, but I did feel such a fool. Dr. Wolf did not seem to think it strange that I proposed to write an American biography of Mozart, though some people in New York had thought so; and after we had chatted for a few minutes he said, "So. Of course you have come to study the manuscripts."

I nodded timidly; I supposed this must be a privilege difficult to obtain.

"Good," he said. He rose and took from his desk a massive bunch of keys. "Come with me."

He led the way from his old-fashioned office, agreeably cluttered with books and scores, with the inevitable row of plaster busts of the immortals all round a high dado, into a passage at the end of which there was a steel door, much like one in a bank vault. A guard opened this and shut the door again behind us. We were in a long, alley-like chamber, without windows, but excellently lighted overhead. The walls of the passage, almost as long as one's range of vision, consisted of steel doors. Dr. Wolf unlocked a long row of these on our right, and opened the doors. Inside, on indexed shelves, lay the great bulk of Mozart's manuscripts and a large number of his letters as well. Dr. Wolf lifted a heavy case from its shelf and laid it on a table. There was a row of tables down the length of the vault, with a chair at each.

"I think you would like to see this first?" he said. Carefully he opened the protecting covers. Inside lay the manuscript of *Le Nozze di Figaro*. I was afraid to touch it, but I was so moved that I dropped into the chair and sat holding my head up so that the tears would run down my face and not onto the autograph title-page. I think Dr. Wolf pretended not to notice. Presently he said, "There is only one rule here in the Library. You will use no ink in taking notes?"

I shook my head, wiping my eyes; ink! Dr. Wolf had his watch in his hand. He said, "It is now ten o'clock. You will be ready to go out for dinner at half-past twelve? Good. I shall come back for you. You understand," he added, smiling, "you are locked up in here."

I had no words to thank him or to say anything else. He went away, leaving me, a total stranger with no verifiable identification of any kind, entirely alone with one of the world's greatest treasures. I have never heard of such a thing before or since. Obviously it was his responsibility to judge the reliability of individuals, but a scholar is not a detective, and in Berlin of all cities, I should have expected the formalities for accreditation to such a library to be extreme in their rigidity. His introduction to the world I had come to explore was a major inspiration. I sat in that vault day after day, studying the manuscripts and making notes; and sometimes Dr. Wolf would come by to see how I was getting on, and sometimes he would bow me into his office where he would give me advice and, I fear, discover the real depths of my inadequacies. I remember the twinkle in his eyes when I was about to leave Berlin and he gave me letters of introduction to colleagues of his in Leipzig, Prague, Salzburg, and Vienna. Neither of us thought at the moment of Paris, and that was the one place I had trouble; at the Conservatoire they flatly refused to let me see the manuscript of *Don Giovanni*. I forget what contortion I had to execute before I could see it.

The sequel to my Berlin experiences is a strand of the nightmare in which our century is damned. Leo Liepmannssohn was able to escape to London from Hitler and his *Judenrein* Reich, somehow keeping together enough of his collection to reestablish himself there, where his successor firm still exists. The saintly Dr. Wolf was summarily dismissed from his post when the gangsters seized Germany, and for years thereafter my efforts to learn what became of him ended in a blind alley which I rightly feared was a concentration camp. His daughter, who escaped to this country, eventually told me that her father survived imprisonment and died after the Second World War. He was one of the rarest souls I ever knew.

I went on to Salzburg. I have so many associations with the place, which will appear in their sequence, that my first stay there remains memorable chiefly by contrast with all the rest. The weather was dreadful, the clammy chill of late March, the mountains shrouded in clouds, streaming rain most of the time and drizzle the rest. The town appealed to me for two reasons, Mozart, and the baroque architecture which I adore. But Mozart loathed Salzburg as anyone can see who reads his letters. Its Archbishop, whose servant he was, treated him like a dog, and except for the happiness of his family life in the house where he was born in the Getreidegasse, he had no attachment to anything or anybody there. But I was moved and excited by proximity to so much that had been part of his life, and my imagination had free rein in recreating the epoch and the scenes of his childhood and youth. I had understanding help from Dr. Alfred Heidl at the Mozarteum, where I spent my time, or else exploring every part of the town that had any association with Mozart; palaces, churches, streets, the houses he frequented, every spot where he was known to have been.

It was horribly cold and I went every day for my midday dinner to the Peterskeller, an ancient wine-cellar and common people's eating-place underneath the monastery of St. Peter. I liked its low vaulted ceilings, the small rooms each with its big green tile stove and bare, scrubbed, long wooden tables where one took any empty chair, exchanging a greeting with the people already there. The place was steamy from the damp loden capes and Alpine hats with *Gamsbart* brushes hanging on pegs along the walls. A big plate of good hot soup, a dish of boiled beef or *Kalbsgulyasch mit Nockerl,* a glass or two of their own white wine, while a monk wandered through the place absent-mindedly blessing the customers, was a cosy and restful interlude. It is the way I like to be and to work when I am deep in something, especially in Europe —alone, and without thought of company or occupation apart from my main concern. I have always felt pleased that I first knew Salzburg in that way, rather than in its crowded international guise when it mounts its Festival at midsummer.

Finally I arrived in Vienna. And this is the time to remind the reader that this book is really about the people who have been my life rather than about me. I had so much to absorb in Vienna that I was at it day and night, in and out of doors, a sponge soaking up the juices of all that I cared most about. I am much less enchanted with Vienna now than I was then, a disillusionment initiated by Hitler. At first sight I fell for it completely. I could not get enough of its architecture. I have worn out more shoes there than anywhere except Prague. I still like to look at it even when much of its spirit is gone or changed or vitiated. I kept encountering people who told me it was no longer the real Vienna, who complained or whined nostalgically about the old days, whose clothes were shabby and whose outlook hopeless. The city swarmed with beggars. I was too uninformed politically and in economics to comprehend the real effect of the breakup of the Empire, the fragmentation that left Central Europe open first to Hitler and then to Communism, as Otto Bauer, the Austrian Social Democrat, had predicted in 1919. Neither Woodrow Wilson nor Franklin Roosevelt was correct in his insistences about the reorganization of Europe after both the wars, and the end is not yet. But this is not the place for hindsight. In 1930 and for years thereafter I could see only from the view of Czechoslovakia. In Vienna I was not even aware of the reverberations of the world financial crisis which were to culminate the next year in the crash of the Creditanstalt and prepare the ground for Austria's eager acceptance of Anschluss and its heiling monsters.

What I did in Vienna was pursue Mozart all day long and go to the opera every night, or every night that I was not at some concert. For the first time I could hear as much Mozart music as I could keep up with. Symphonies, chamber music, masses, serenades and divertimenti, concertos for his own pianoforte and an amazing variety of other instruments which he composed usually because some player he knew begged for one in a hurry for a special engagement; big concerts, small concerts, professional, amateur, in-between. It was a royal binge for me. And, with unemployment rampant, the country reeling, the city moribund, the Staatsoper was rich and proud and glorious, the very beggars in the streets insisting that the government, as it always had, spend whatever was necessary to keep this the foremost opera house in Europe and the Vienna Philharmonic, in its pit, one of the world's leading orchestras. And so I first heard Lotte Lehmann.

I do not know why I went to *Die Walküre* at all, for I do not gravitate to Wagner unless there are artists, or an artist, that I particularly want to hear. I had not yet that special motive about Lotte Lehmann, but I was respectful and impressed by the Staatsoper though tempted as I have always been to snicker at Wagner's pretentiousness and pomposity. The door of Hunding's house flew open, the orchestra stormed, and Sieglinde came in with a single phrase which as closely as I can describe it, knocked the breath out of me. I came up rigid on the edge of my seat and remained transfixed throughout the act. No voice had ever hit me in that way, not my mother's because the emotions and the associations were wholly different, not any other singer's ever. The voice, the artist, the personality were all of a piece. I did not weigh how she sang or what was her command of her resources or judge her by any of the reflexive measures drawn from lifetime indoctrination in the art. She was both feminine humanity and total dramatic illusion through the beauty of her voice and the immense sincerity of her fusion with the character. Her German was a blessing to the ear.

Franz Schalk was the conductor and all I remember of him is the reflection of his eminence as I knew it later through Lotte's reverence for him; he died the following year. But in that same period I heard him conduct, and Lotte sing, the first *Fidelio* I ever heard; and *Der Rosenkavalier*. If the Sieglinde, to whose creator I cannot surrender my mind except for *Die Meistersinger,* had almost taken me apart, the Fidelio put me together again and was of course one of the structural steel beams in the eventual creation of Lena Geyer. The Marschallin I regarded then, and after uncountable further experiences of Lotte's portrayal of it, I per-

manently consider, the finest dramatic impersonation I have ever
known in opera. And *Der Rosenkavalier* is a long way from being
among my favorites as a work.

Lest it be thought I was a romantic pushover who had taken
leave of her senses, I can add that I also heard the standard
Staatsoper versions of *Butterfly* and *Tosca*—in German. Lotte
sang the roles, but she was neither Lotte nor Butterfly nor Tosca.

I went away possessed by her voice. I was not to meet her
for several years, nor have any idea that she would become one of
my most beloved friends. What had happened to me in Vienna
was the rare experience of primary personal emotion in response
to a voice. It is intangible, inexplicable like any matter of human
chemistry. Its physical attributes incline one to say it is analogous
to falling in love. The ecstasy and the total satisfaction evoked by
a voice are personal and may not have the same effect on any two
people. My meat may be, if not your poison, at least unpalatable
or indifferent to you; or vice-versa. Nobody argues the validity
of a great voice; when you hear one, you know it. But it may
never be a personal thing to you, and in my lifetime, very few
have been that to me. The first was my mother's, of course. The
second was Rosa Ponselle's—for its sheer incomparable beauty.
The third was Lotte's. To me she had the most moving voice in
the world. It had splendor but it was not forbidding like those of
other Wagnerian sopranos. Lotte was warm and she was an artist
beyond any comparison in her power to color her voice with dramatic and poetic feeling. She did the same when she sang Lieder;
but first and foremost, she was the theatre, she had the magic of
illusion in her throat. Off the stage she was (will she forgive me?)
fat; she looked like a Hausfrau which she never was; her face,
while I thought it beautiful because I loved her, had none of my
mother's classic beauty or the striking Latin grandeur of Rosa
Ponselle. Lotte was Lotte. By her own avowal she could not properly sing a scale. She had resisted her teachers' efforts to drill her
in technique. If called upon to sing Bach or Mozart she would

say, *"Ach, Gott! Ich hasse das!"* because of the rigid technical exactions. She hated the part of the Contessa in *Figaro*—die Gräfin
in Vienna—because it lay in the break of the voice in the key of
C and demanded a commanding classical technique. But she
opened her mouth and tones came out of it that have never been
equalled for me in beauty and emotional power. Of course she
was a good musician, how could she not be with her enormous
repertoire and her command of music like *Fidelio* and all the
works of Strauss? But she did not approach her art so much from
the musician's view as from sheer innate instinct. She thought and
felt like and became the creatures she depicted; she sang what was
written for their paper souls and turned them into flesh and blood.

When I returned home, raving about Lotte Lehmann on top
of everything else I had been drinking in, my mother reacted with
less interest and enthusiasm than my husband did. Vaguely it occurred to me to wonder if she could have been jealous, but ra-
tionally I knew that was not so. She was concerned about me personally and what kind of life I was going to make, judging me by
this long account of my first working journey in Europe, which
may seem strange for a bride. In truth, I was a strange bride. But
I was the woman my husband wanted me to be, which is better
than being the woman one wanted to be oneself. I was embarking
on life with just the opposite sense and purpose from what my
mother had done, and she could not understand that this was
what Russell Davenport and I both wanted. It is self-evident that
we were not a match made in heaven, nor have I ever seen one.
Those which mature to permanence and serenity are works of
long, forbearing, mutual unselfishness and masterpieces of patient
human art. We did not have those qualities. We did have one
great mutual strength, our work, the attitude of each to the other's
work, the support and stimulation we gave each other. For this I
am eternally grateful to Russell Davenport, and he was equally
grateful to me. We were at our best when jointly pursuing these
interests, largely in our own house; he was a good host and I liked

to run a house and have it full of our friends; but he did not confuse that with an idea that I be primarily, and surely not exclusively, a wife. There were times when I verged on such confusion and got hurt in the process. We were both at our best when our work stood ahead of all other elements. Few outsiders understood this, nor was there any reason why they should.

My mother sometimes hinted her misgivings to me, but she could hardly tell my husband to make me stay at home and be a model wife when that was the last thing he wanted either of me or in his life. So she stood in happily for me with my daughters, the second born in 1934, and kept them with her in the country whenever I loaded my car with typewriter and books and scores and files and lumbered off to Europe, indifferent to those who thought me selfish or restless or ambitious or spoilt. I had as much of those faults as any person, but they were not my primary motivations. I had to make a life of my own apart from my husband; he had made that plain from the very first. And I had to write books, I had always known I had to write them; the straw to make the building-bricks could only be garnered in the old world. I had warnings, some impersonal, some straight from my mother's shoulder, that those bundles of straw might turn into crushing burdens, which the greatest of them surely did. But I have never been able to plump for the cautious or the prudent choice. I have made the impelling, the fermentative, the reckless one when my necessities bade me; and of course I have had to pay the price.

萌[C H A P T E R S E V E N]醾

NOBODY in the early 1930's existed without appalled awareness of the times. Some of us who were then at the peak of our youthful energies and are now in the last third of our lives are mildly surprised that the generations younger than ourselves regard the period as a mystique. It engages historians and political economists and sociologists; it appears to be a favorite field for graduate theses and documentary expositions. In the view of many who were children or not even born at the time, it suggests that we were all ground down by the paralyzing Great Depression, from whose eternal night we were reprieved by Franklin Roosevelt and the New Deal. This is a free, probably a mischievous oversimplification of the case and the epoch. Obviously we all knew what was happening to our country and the world, and obviously we cared, each in his own way and for reasons vital to himself and to others. Those of us who did not leap eagerly into the baptismal river of the New Deal were not necessarily reactionaries, die-hards, economic royalists, the sheltered and privileged, or even black Republicans. Many were men of brilliant, probing, articulate open mind like Russell Davenport and his co-editors and colleagues who produced *Fortune* at a time when business and industry were reeling with catastrophe and the idea of the world's most expensive periodical, to be devoted to that business and industry, appeared madness. The overt and dramatic aspects of world-shaking events and forces—wars, depression, revolutions, any of what this century has comprised—tend to make the later observer overlook that the vast majority of people during those cataclysms had to live their lives, put one foot before the other, do their work, pursue their interests, make their mistakes—and laugh. We had laughter and gaiety, while achingly aware of Okies and Arkies, Hoovervilles and apple-sellers, such as all to-day's affluence with its sour undertone of psychotic obsessiveness, cannot command. We had George and Ira Gershwin, Irving Berlin, Jerome Kern and the young Dick Rodgers to write our songs; Eugene O'Neill, Bob Sherwood, Sidney Howard, George Kaufman and Moss Hart to write our plays; Maestro at the Philharmonic, titans at the opera; and the immortals of this century to write our books—only the broad sketch-lines of a picture of depth and fullness.

Our lives had shape and purposefulness and nobody had heard of a search for identity. We knew, as perceptive men and women knew in 1914, that we were living on the edge of a great divide; but we were not clairvoyants and could not foresee the vast levelling process which has changed the face of most Western countries today. For my husband and me life and the world were not a matter of rich or poor, privilege or deprivation. We were not rich, but we were not poor. We were reasonably established in the wake of our parents, who had not had great wealth or the views that go with it, and therefore had not undergone bruising experiences in coming to terms with a changed world. We also both worked hard. It happens to be the case that writing, editing, and the variants of our profession require talent. If we had needed jobs in some field of work where talent was not the prerequisite we might very well not have found the jobs; and we would have suffered the face-grinding which dyed an epoch, fermented a continuing social revolution, created a psychology and a terminology and a literature, and with Marx and Freud is said to have conditioned the articulate world of the ensuing decades. For my own part, I was so fortunate as to have work to do which publishers wanted to publish and people wanted to read. I was untouched by Freud, which makes me the Square I am today, quite an old

woman, with her feet planted in reality and the world framed in
a vigorous sense of humor. Through the depth and strength of my
roots in Europe I had my raw confrontations with the essence of
this century in Hitler (have I read lately that he is now considered
old hat?) and the successors to Marx. Let it not be thought that
any of us were granted remission from the primary agonies of our
time.

My mother was forty-seven years old in 1931. She had never
been scholarly, but she was intelligent, with a quick and questioning mind that urged her towards new ideas and concepts and
gave her a profound reverence for scholars, scientists, and learning. She was completely unpretentious. She was too witty and
too much a realist to think of conversing with Albert Einstein or Abraham Flexner in the range of their activities at
the Institute for Advanced Study, of which Dr. Flexner was
the Director; but Abe Flexner was one of her dearest friends
and he brought his colleagues to her house for the fun they had
there, the music, the congeniality, the nonsense. About that time
two brilliant young musicians, Sascha Jacobsen the violinist and
Marie Roemaet Rosanoff, a magnificent 'cellist, became friends of
my mother's and with friends of their own, violinists and viola
players, came regularly to her house to play chamber music. We
called these Quartet Parties, and quartets primarily were played, a
feast of Haydn, Mozart, Beethoven, and Brahms. Sometimes Chotzie was dragooned into playing the divine Brahms piano quintet,
kicking and screaming because it is so difficult and he was out of
practice, but Mother would sniff, "You lazy so-and-so, shut up
and play!" Sometimes Papuchka sat in, or Jascha Heifetz if he was
there; and sometimes on the other hand, the Quartet were confronted by Professor Einstein, timidly pleading to be allowed to
play second fiddle. He was a ghastly violinist but they stood in
awe of his eminence and were honored to be in his company. But
their sidelong glances of agony as he scratched and squealed along
with them, beaming under his halo of fuzzy white hair! He seldom

counted correctly, which confounded them in the world's greatest mathematical physicist.

Sascha and Marie and their colleagues presently formed the Musical Art Quartet under the aegis of my mother and several other friends, and for some years played an annual series of concerts at the Town Hall, to which we all joyfully subscribed. But we loved better the Quartet Parties in the big music room in Forty-ninth Street. It would not serve my purpose to drop here a string of names of the friends who came to the parties; they are nearly all dead, and they were a cross-section of the theatre, the literary and musical worlds, brains and beauty and talent, lightly sprinkled with social figures who loved music, and dear old friends who loved my mother. The parties were impromptu. She would ring me up on the telephone and say, "Marcella?"—her name for me when she was up to something—"will you come on Friday and decorate my party?" What this meant was that I should see the cook and attend to the buffet supper and the drink, all of which bored her and which in fact she had not the strength to bother with. She always spent the afternoon lying down, but when the guests began to gather she would be at the top of the stairs, gay and bantering and beautiful and chic, the inspired kind of hostess who seems to be the most popular guest at her own party. We spread ourselves around the big room, leaving the sofas and chairs for the oldest and most eminent, curling ourselves up on the floor. One of the most enthusiastic of us was George Gershwin, a treasured friend of mine, whom I knew in this frame of classic music rather than as a Broadway figure. At that time he was studying composition with Rubin Goldmark, another old friend of my mother's. It seems incredible that when George wrote his earliest and some of his most glorious songs he had almost no knowledge of theory and composition. He was a genius of melody and a natural pianist, but he never really confronted music as music until he was already famous. It was fascinating to see him listening to music. His long, ovoid face was immobile, as if turned to marble;

I remember how fantastic was that transported face with the cigar sticking out of it. When the quartets were over and the relaxing had begun, the supper eaten downstairs—George always plaintive about his indigestion—and the older guests departed, we dragged George most willingly back to the music room where he sat and played his songs, sometimes singing with his cigar clenched in his teeth, sometimes all of us singing as we leaned in a gaggle over the piano, clamoring for what we loved.

"*My One and Only*, George!" "George, please! *Someone to Watch Over Me!*" "*I Got Rhythm!*" "My turn now—*Strike Up the Band!*" " *'Swonderful!*"

I think he always played that without being asked. He would stay and play as late as anyone could stay and listen, hours past midnight. And one day, not imagining that this was out of the ordinary, I invited him to our box at the Philharmonic the next afternoon. Maestro played the Pastorale, and I still cannot believe what George told me, that he had never heard Maestro conduct before. George as he sat there looking, I see now, into eternity, for he was dead in about five years, was not the same man as the enchanting tunester his friends knew at parties. He was a genius staring into the crucible of genius, and it was frightening.

In the last years before he died in 1937 I used to see him occasionally alone; he would ring up, it seems to me on a Sunday night, and ask me to come over to his apartment in Seventy-second Street. He had music on his mind, ideas for music which he did not live to work out, and he would sit at the piano and play and talk at the same time, about works he hoped to compose, about the same yawning question that confronts every operatic composer, the libretto, the endless search for the right libretto or the right book or play to furnish the right libretto. I never believed myself capable of writing one, I have never attempted anything in the scope of the theatre, but he was groping and I had a sense of groping with him, towards an idea growing out of the melting-pot of New York at the turn of the century, with the opening scene set in the steerage of a ship full of immigrants. He was one of the loneliest people I have ever known, and in that loneliness beneath the panoply of success and the clamoring crowd, I knew him best.

I never thought of my mother as ageing or realized early enough that she was really ill. She did nothing to let me realize it. In some ways she never changed. When I came to her house on returning from weeks or months in Europe it was nearly always to find the kitchen range out on the pavement or half the windows gone because she was 'turning the house around.' She had got bored with it the way it was and was turning the rooms back to front. Perhaps initially to have a toy to play with, but also because she was losing the taste for summer-resort life she bought a small house in Connecticut in Litchfield County, which at first she used in the spring and the autumn when she wanted neither New York nor the sea. Later she spent much of her time there. It had once been the usual hill farmhouse which imaginative people bought for a song and converted into something picturesque. This one was a little too picturesque. My mother bought it from Charles Rann Kennedy, a mystic playwright who wore a toga and chaplet and made a small outdoor Greek theatre (a dandy croquet-ground) where he and his wife Edith Wynne Matthison, the actress, used to mount his plays in the spirit of what my mother and her husband called the inner-innerness. The house had been reamed out to make a draughty-arty two-story studio with a balcony (fine for charades) along one side that led to some uncomfortable bedrooms. The whole thing was such a mess that restoring it to a cosy house gave Mother and the village carpenter all the occupation that the one craved and the other needed for years thereafter. In the vicinity there was a scattering of kindred souls, amongst them the G's from Philadelphia, at whom I could now poke all the fun I wanted since I was no longer their victim. My mother devilishly encouraged me, calling them the Serious Group of Little Thinkers. "Disloyal!" I would intone in mock self-reproof, and we would howl with laughter.

I spent part of one summer with my family in that house while my mother accompanied Efrem Zimbalist on a concert tour of the Far East. He was one of the first Western musicians to play in Japan, China, Korea, and what was then the Dutch East Indies. He made many such tours and it is an interesting sequel that in recent years there have come to the Curtis Institute of Music, whose director he has long been, students of great talent from Japan and Korea, whose parents and their generation were introduced to Western music by him. During that journey my mother went to Australia to visit Madame Melba who died the next year, and who gave my mother a tiny black-and-tan toy terrier, I think a Manchester; anyway, it was the smallest dog we had ever seen. Mother called it So-So. When she brought it back to New York people were naturally curious about such a rarity and usually asked her if she had brought along its pedigree.

"Oh, I looked at it," she would reply, "but it was so much better than my own that I tore it up."

Fortune first appeared in 1930, the beginning of a span of crowded and hard-working years for Russell Davenport and me. I had stopped working on *The New Yorker* to put my full time on Mozart, which kept me locked up all day. But I heard music constantly at night, it was the fuel that stoked the boiler, and I do not remember who it was that suggested I might as well keep my reporting hand in and make a little money on the side by writing the music criticism for a small magazine which the Theatre Guild, then at the height of its success, distributed to its members. I do not remember whether it reached a wider public. This did not take as much of my time as a newspaper or a big weekly would have done but it required me to go to concert and opera performances that I might have skipped. I usually made my choices, provided the artists were good, on the basis of the programmes; any Mozart that was played I was sure to hear.

But there was time also to make a revolving door of our house for the group of men who were the original editor-writers of *Fortune.* We were specially fond of Archie MacLeish and his wife Ada. Archie's prose was beautiful as only a poet's can be, even when he wrote about business and industry. He was not very pleased to be forced by the realities of the day to earn money even by the highest class of journalism. And out of *Fortune* came a rich bonanza for me—T. M. Cleland, the great typographer, illustrator, and book designer. He designed the original format and typography of *Fortune,* I suppose the handsomest magazine ever published up to then. By sheer chance, his avocation and greatest enthusiasm was the music and the personality of Mozart. He heard from Russell that I was writing a biography and came to look the situation over. He liked what he found; he was constantly at our house, bringing his own Mozart records to share with me and borrowing mine, and presently he told me—he did not ask or suggest as though there might be any question—that he intended to design the book I was writing, do the typography, the binding, and the jacket. I do not know what this beautiful work must have cost Scribners; they may have been appalled but they never told me.

The shining thread that ran through life was our dearest friend, Parker Lloyd-Smith. It is difficult to evoke the memory of a man who died so young, so long ago that I can remember how we loved him but not exactly why. He was a little younger than Russell. I do not remember what he had been doing before he joined the brilliant group who shaped up *Fortune* in the year before it was first published. He had a wonderful gift of laughter like my mother. With a gnat-bite, a barb as light as dandelion fluff, he would despatch anything or anybody that was pompous or took itself solemnly. He was a popular bachelor and we really knew little of his personal life; at the same time he was such an intimate friend of ours that our house was his second home. He was in some degree a rebel from a rich and ultra-conservative family whom we knew slightly. We thought them heavy going. Perhaps that was why he took to us and our house; he felt free. He liked our wacky Charlotte who called him Mr. Loyschmidt (she spelt it Leuschmidt) and always laid a place for him at our dinner-table whether he had said he was coming or not. He did come nearly every day. He went to Fishers Island with us at weekends, he enchanted my family, he fitted into every group and every game. We loved him very much, both of us alike. He and Russell and I enjoyed things more together than any of us separately or paired in two.

On a September morning in 1931, I was getting dressed when Russell came into my room with a look of fearful distress on his face. He tried to speak and seemed to choke on the words. Then he said, "It's Parker. Parker is dead. Suicide."

I was sitting on a stool putting on my stockings. I said, "No. No, that's not so."

I do not know how long it was before the fact penetrated. I kept saying "That's not so. I don't believe it."

But it was so, and nobody ever knew why. Parker had leapt from a window of his twenty-third-floor apartment. I suppose today, with everyone his own psychiatrist, I would be plagued by people volunteering to analyze Parker's neuroses and explain the suicide of a brilliant, witty, poetic, sardonic, sentimental man who brought light-heartedness into every house he entered and a quality of joy into ours which it never had again. He died on a Wednesday. On the previous Sunday evening after dinner by ourselves we had sung songs and hymns until two o'clock in the morning. I wonder why. All I remember is playing the hymns and all of us singing, but not how it came about. We had never done it before. Parker had a feeling for religious expression, like me, which few of our contemporaries shared; it was a silent understanding. He left no messages when he died, but he made a few bequests of small personal possessions. To me he left his German Evangelical prayer book, hand printed in Nürnberg in 1740. Its flyleaf bears Parker's book-plate with this motto, perhaps after all the explanation that we sought and could not fathom: Scientia Dementia Est.

This was the first time anyone dear to me had died, the first rent in the long, torn fabric of life, the first person I had ever seen dead. I wonder why it was we who were asked to go to the 67th Street police station to identify him. I have never since passed through that street without thinking of him. I learned something there that I was to remember seventeen years later, and by it grope to cast light on the most dire, unfathomable darkness I have known.

The weeks following Parker's death were the first such time I had ever lived through; the lost spaces when one cannot realize what has happened, the vacuum in which one wakes each morning with a sense that the day is over before it has begun. This is intensified by the telephone. One is torn apart each time the voice one hears is not that of the person one loved; worse are the moments when one picks up the telephone from habit to call someone to whom one can never speak again. Russell suffered the same way. We were both working hard, the only way to get through such a passage, but we were stunned. I never wept, an unusual reaction for me. I cannot remember feeling anything for weeks.

Early in November my daughter reminded me that I had promised to take her to the annual Empire Cat Club show, which then used to be in Madison Square Garden. I had forgotten about it. We walked slowly through the aisles lined with cages occupied by glorious cats. Normally I would have been in ecstasies but as it was, I felt no pleasure. We were ready to leave and were passing the last cage in the last aisle, when something caught my skirt and I stopped to disentangle it. I looked down into the face of a very young red Persian kitten, who had thrust his paw through the bars of his cage and caught my skirt with his claws. The little face entreated me; I heard the kitten purring as I bent down. It rubbed itself against my fingers as I put them through the bars. I found myself in tears. The ice fell away from where it was lodged inside me.

"Is this kitten for sale?" I asked the woman who was sitting there.

It was, she said; the price was ten dollars. I ought to have been suspicious, either that the kitten was not a good one or that the woman had some discreditable reason for wanting to get rid of it. Ten dollars was a ridiculous price for a good long-haired kitten. But none of that mattered, then or later. The kitten had elected me. That is the way real cat-human relationships are formed. I found a shoe-box in back of the cages somewhere, we punched holes in it, I paid the woman and took the kitten home. Not until I was in the taxi did I remember that Russell for two years had refused to have a cat in the house, my first attempt—to induce a country cat to live with propriety in the city—having been a failure. I took the kitten in its box to Russell's room where he was in bed with one of the recurrent stomach ailments that were more often an escape-hatch than an affliction. Without a word I put the box on the bed, loosening the lid. The kitten sprang out. Visibly Russell fell apart, as I had done. Nobody could have resisted that kitten. It was Russell who named him Tamerlane the King of Persia. And Tam for sixteen years thereafter was the companion of every instant of my life except when I was in Europe.

I soon learned why the woman had asked only ten dollars. Tam had every ailment that a kitten can have. He had fleas. He had worms. He had ringworm which of course I caught, and which cost ten times the price I had paid for Tam, to cure. He had dreadful intestinal troubles requiring care such as one would give an infant. He had rickets so badly that at one time he could not stand up at all. Two veterinarians advised me to put him down, saying that such a kitten was not worth raising, but all I did was weep and look for someone who would understand why I had to keep him. That someone was Dr. Raymond Garbutt, who understood cats and the aberrations of what I call cat-people, with intuition only explained by the fact that he was a cat-person himself, a gentle, deliberate man who did not need the language of words in which to communicate with animals.

We won the battle, after months of the most difficult nursing. When he was a year old Tam began to bloom. He was spectacularly beautiful, a big sixteen-pound cat with wonderful eyes of deep topaz and a coral-colored nose. If it is ever claimed that a cat does not feel, nor in his eyes show emotion, that person can never have known a Tam. He had a glorious coat and great thick plodding forepaws on which he used to proceed into a room with the self-assurance of royalty. Like most beautiful animals he had a keen sense of vanity and of his own importance and knew exactly how to show himself off to best advantage, taking a pose in the centre medallion of a Persian rug, or choosing a piece of furniture upholstered in soft blue or green, the colors most flattering to him. But all that was like the vanity of a pretty woman. It was his character for which I loved him. He was attached to me as people mistakenly think only a dog can be attached. They can never have known the devotion of a cat. Dr. Garbutt used to say that Tam's extraordinary devotion was developed through the struggle to save his life, which he sensed he owed to me. I do not know.

About that time, my husband began to pine for a farm. I have never had the least wish to live anywhere in the country that was not directly on a large natural body of water. I was unable to persuade Russell of this. The only waterfront places were in Connecticut or Long Island, which he spurned as suburban and banal. Nearly all our friends had houses in just those areas, mostly in Fairfield County which was accessible to town. Not for Russell. He wanted a real farm, not that he proposed to become a farmer, but for the principle of the thing. Archie MacLeish had and still has such a farm at Conway, Massachusetts, where we went several times to look the region over. It was not quite right; not, God forbid, remote enough. But Max Perkins, of whom I had seen a lot prior to the publication of *Mozart* in the spring of 1932, had a branch of his family living in Windsor, Vermont; and by a process deriving from Max we found ourselves in Windsor looking at farms which his brother Louis had hunted up for us.

So we bought an abandoned hill farm, two hundred and fifty acres of meadow and fallow fields and woods, with a tumbledown salt-box house and a falling-down red New England barn. It cost less than three thousand dollars. In those days I think ten thousand dollars could have bought any piece of property on the Atlantic seaboard. This was at the utmost depth of the depression, and I cannot reconstruct the reasoning by which Russell thought it made sense to be two hundred and fifty miles from New York, an eight hours' drive at that time (and no direct rail service) years before there were any thruways. This was no retreat for weekends. It took a whole weekend just to go and come. In reality the time we spent there was time that Russell took in leaves of absence from *Fortune,* intending to write poetry and books. He actually spent it digging ditches for water pipes and digging us into a morass which was at first an adventure of wild hilarity.

The house had no plumbing or running water, no electric light, telephone, or any convenience or improvements installed since its building about a hundred years before. It was in such a state of dilapidation that if one stepped on one end of a floor-board the other end flew up and cracked one on the head. The roof had leaked so badly and long that the upstairs rooms were holes full of plaster crumbled from the walls and ceilings. We did not attempt to use them at first. The barn was a death-trap because the whole floor was rotted, but we had no need of it anyway and Tam found it the happiest hunting-ground in catdom. Russell promised me that we would do nothing to the house except make it basically habitable, largely with our own hands. We had to hire a plumber to lay on the water which fortunately flowed by gravity from springs, and install the plumbing-fixtures which we bought second-hand from a house-wrecking concern in First Avenue. We did not attempt electricity, we used oil lamps and candles, and the kitchen range was an ancient black monster that burned wood. It was ugly, smoky, and ornery, but it cooked the best roast meat I have ever eaten, and Charlotte and I were unfazed by it even on the hottest summer days. Vermont by the way can be hotter than Greece, a statement based on thorough experience with both.

Something about that place invited a cheerful madness. Friends flocked to see us there. Its remoteness, as well as our natural hospitality, made it necessary to put them up, but I cannot remember how we managed, for we had almost no furniture. The idea was to spend no money except for imperative necessities. There were beds, a table to eat at, kitchen chairs around it, and a lot of packing-cases and crates to put things in. Of course there was a piano, to me a fundamental necessity like a bathtub or a kitchen stove. Dudi Irion, the head of Steinway's, had roared with laughter when I asked him where I could buy a piano for less than a hundred dollars, and sent me to some piano-graveyard where I got an ancient whining upright.

My doctor Connie Traeger, the brilliant Cornelius Horace Traeger, now so eminent that I wish the President, the Senate, the national health agencies, and the whole medical profession would leave him alone so there could be time to enjoy life as we used to do, came to Windsor all the time and amused himself shooting woodchucks and nailing their skins to the barn door. My agent Carol Hill had just been married to the more celebrated literary agent Carl Brandt, who was also an authority on American antique furniture and glass. They spent their free time motoring and antiquing in New England, constantly dropping in on us. How they reconciled our madhouse with their taste for fine old furniture, beautiful old houses, and stately elegance, I do not know, but to this day Carol, my beloved friend of nearly forty years, and I can make ourselves hysterical by remembering that place in Vermont and above all, my mother who simply could not keep away.

"Russell digging ditches," Carol says, "Charlotte prancing in and out of that hellish kitchen, you in tears because you couldn't find Tam—" (he was under the floorboards hunting mice), "Connie shooting, those damned pancakes for breakfast"—they were good but she fights calories—"your mother walking around in a trance with her measuring-stick, and the Gilmore dressing-case!" —at which we shriek. The dressing-case was the outcome of a nice cheque that my mother-in-law had given me for my birthday, and I had spent it on a pigskin dressing-case made to my order and fitted with just the toilet articles and necessities I liked. It was lined with blue morocco leather, had an outer cover to protect it, and weighed over forty pounds—the last piece of fine luggage I owned before flying made all such things obsolete. There was no furniture in my bedroom at Windsor except the bed; clothes such as they were hung on a row of pegs on the wall; and the Gilmore dressing-case stood on a crate to serve as a dressing-table.

We spent the first summer in our madhouse and when we went to town we simply locked the place up and forgot it, driving down those narrow, twisting, high-centred Vermont roads with Tam crouched against the back window howling his head off. We left behind in the care of our nearest neighbor, a dour dairy-farmer who thought us crazy, Russell's surreptitious acquisition which should have warned me what lay ahead. It was a pig he had bought which we named Max. In a letter to Ernest Hemingway that summer, Max Perkins wrote, "These Davenports (I have seen a lot of them on account of her book) have moved to Windsor and taken a farm there, and their only real farming item is one pig, and they named him Max. But I am in hopes it was after Max Foster."

It was, but Max Foster rejected the compliment and tried to pin it on Max Perkins.

I had extracted a promise from Russell after the appearance of Max the pig that there would be no more démarches of this kind, which could turn the place into a burden instead of a joke. But during the winter he kept seeing visions of what he thought was essential there and he set his mind on a light pick-up truck. My mother was at dinner with us one evening, listening to this kind of talk about station-wagons and trucks, or a convertible combination of both. Suddenly her face lit up.

"I know!" she said. "I'll take the Rolls-Royce out of dead storage, sell the body, and have a station-wagon truck put on the chassis. Just the thing."

I had forgotten all about the Rolls-Royce. When she began, in tune with the times and her own changing outlook, to turn against everything typified by Rolls-Royce motor cars, she had sent hers to dead storage, where it ate her up in storage charges for years. She always refused to sell the car because no Rolls-Royce had ever been known to wear out; therefore one must count it a permanent asset. Now she saw a way to justify its existence. Horrified, we pointed out that the Rolls had never done better than six miles to the gallon, and even without the staggering cost of maintenance, the spectacle of a Rolls-Royce convertible truck would finish us with the suspicious hill farmers who were our neighbors. All we wanted was a second-hand Ford or Chevrolet that could be turned in for a newer one when necessary. Mother was furious.

"You don't understand anything about economics!" she said to Russell. (*Fortune* would have been encouraged to hear that.) "Rolls-Royces never wear out. It is sheer waste to leave that thing stored out at Brewster's." It was, but not in the sense she meant, which was contrary to the very hard sense she really had.

In the end Russell bought a used Ford pick-up truck from the disposal yard of Borden's Milk Company. He spent a lot of time driving around the countryside in it and one day he was gone until long after dark. In town I was used to his habitual latenesses and absences, but here there was neither *Fortune* nor diverse company to swallow him up. I was afraid he had had an accident in the truck; he was a reckless driver.

Late at night I heard the truck come clanking in from the road, and with it another noise: MOO-OO-OO. My blood froze. I rushed outside to see Russell untying two cows from their perch in the truck. I blew my stack, reminding him of his promise not to encumber us with animals. Russell said coldly that a farm was not a farm which was not farmed. From there on each thing led inexorably to the next. We had to hire a man to stay on the place year round and look after the cows. His name was Jimmy. He had a fat slattern of a wife who could not cook or do anything a working countrywoman would know how to do. She used to send Jimmy six miles to Windsor and back innumerable times a day, to buy a loaf of store bread and a can of beans—on our gasoline; or butter when our cream was spoiling because she was too lazy to churn. Jimmy was no farmer, he was simply one of the thousands of drifters whom the times had turned loose to take any job they could get. Once he was there it meant he had to have a house to live in. I flatly refused to let him and his devil of a wife live in ours.

Now I am sure it is already clear that the operative noun in my mother's brain was "house." In all her life I never knew her to baulk at a demand that money be spent at the behest of this compulsion, when she was capable of refusing to come up with money for any other reason, or without reason. I remember once asking her for three hundred dollars to buy a modest fur coat that I badly needed, and being told I could earn it or go without. But when Russell said he had to build a cottage for Jimmy, Mother instantly shelled out the money.

The farm proliferated, more animals appeared, and a vast flock of Rhode Island Reds materialized in the hen-houses it had been necessary to build because it was false economy to employ Jimmy without giving him enough to do. We raised seventy dozen eggs a week, proceeding by what I learned from Department of

Agriculture pamphlets and dinned into Jimmy. We sold them to
a distributor in Boston, except for the metal cases of them which
came to us in town. If I served a huge soufflé or some other spectacular egg dish at a party, the guests would say, "Imagine, all
those lovely eggs from one's own farm for nothing."

"Not exactly," I would say with bitterness. "The eggs cost
about five dollars a dozen, so enjoy them."

Russell bought a pair of oxen—Holstein oxen. He had to buy
farm machinery for the oxen to haul, all of it second-hand and
ready to be junked. Instead we were constantly paying to have it
repaired. He bought a hay-wagon. The barn hayloft had not been
used for fifty years, but there had to be somewhere to put the hay,
so the barn had to be rebuilt. At least it served as a garage.

And all the while we were there less and less. We were both
working very hard in New York, and earning enough for our
normal needs but not for that bottomless pit at Windsor. Russell,
in contradistinction to much else, had carefully worked out our
budget. It was based on our pooled earnings, it made sense, and I
was the one who executed it, kept the accounts, and paid the bills.
And on the first of each month the bills would arrive from Windsor, not one penny of which we had personally incurred or au-
thorized. $579 owed the hardware store. $622 owed the grain and
feed store. $237 owed the service station and repair shop. Our
budget and our whole financial structure were regularly shot to
hell.

As long as the farmhouse itself remained a crazy-patch of
makeshifts done by our own hands I did not rebel. Then my
mother stepped in. She could no longer endure the challenge of
a whole house, falling down, with sagging sills, flapping floors and
doors, chopped-up rooms, lean-to kitchen, rattling windows, *a
house to be remodelled*—in her sight like a bottle of whisky to an
alcoholic. She took fourteen thousand dollars and rammed them
down my throat, ordering me to renovate and remodel the house,
reinforce the foundation, put in electricity, add a big wing, put on

a new roof, finish the house inside and out, and paint it properly. I said I'd rather not, thanks; couldn't she just leave the money in my eventual inheritance, since that was what it was coming out of? No. For a wonder she did refrain from drawing the plans and doing the supervising; I do not know how she controlled herself. So I had the fun of doing over the house. I did forget the stairs until almost too late to get them in; but as the old wreck took form and turned into a big white clapboard country house, I froze on it completely.

Other pressures made me hate the thought of living there. Russell was preempted by concerns of his own which are irrelevant here. I refused to stay alone in Vermont and fled to Salzburg. Nobody could do anything about the jackass Jimmy, who was visited at intervals by me with strict injunctions against piling up any more costs and debts. I might as well have exhorted him in Arabic. One autumn day in 1936 I got into my car early in the morning to drive to Vermont alone. I stopped to lunch with my mother in Connecticut and told her what I was about to do. She shrugged and said, "Why didn't you do it long ago?"

By telephone I arranged with a wholesale poultry dealer in Boston to meet me at the farm next morning and take away all the chickens and ducks in one job lot. With another telephone call I disposed of the cows and the oxen. Then I drove on to the farm and fired Jimmy. His horrible wife whined that they wanted anyway to go and do factory work in Maine so I packed them off with severance pay and their fare. Inside of twenty-four hours I had dumped the whole incubus and when I returned to town and told Russell he could not have cared less.

Then a dear gentleman called Mr. Beal came out of the blue and asked to rent the farm by the year as an experiment to see whether he might like to live there permanently. I would have let him have it rent-free but that was not necessary. I never saw the place again. Life became increasingly active and diffused through many interests and travels, my mother's health failed altogether, and after her death I was first paralyzed by grief, then plunged into the vortex of the Willkie campaign. At its very height, when we were living on the campaign train and working twenty hours out of twenty-four, I received a telegram from Mr. Beal with an offer to buy the farm. His offer must be accepted or refused immediately because he was holding open an alternative, contingent on our reply. Russell was at breakfast in the dining-car, surrounded by the day's speeches for release and drafts of speeches in preparation. I hated to interrupt him but I had to telegraph Mr. Beal.

"Wha'h?" asked Russell, his nose in his coffee-cup and his green eyes on his papers. I said I was obliged to answer Mr. Beal and what did Russell think I should say?

Say anything, said Russell, waving his hands; couldn't I see he was busy? Say what I liked. So I sold the farm. Russell never realized it until months later. He might then have accused me of taking advantage of the situation, but the vacuum, if any, had been filled by the delightful waterfront place we had rented in Connecticut, and by the sailing yacht, the good ship Cindy III, which Russell and his brother John bought together. She gave us all the best times we ever had and confirmed me forever in my refusal to live away from water.

The beginning of my own identity was the publication of *Mozart* in 1932. Hitherto I had been an appendage of my mother. In her view and in mine I could only be other than that through effort and accomplishment of my own. The crux of her fixation— I think obsession not too strong a word—on work and the importance of work was that every person should stand on his own feet and make his own name. She spoke quite fanatically about this. Nobody should attempt to make his way on the strength of somebody else's name, most particularly not on that of a parent.

"If a child of mine," she said many times, "should ever attempt to be a musician and use my name, I will come back from my grave and haunt him all the way to hell."

This made as deep an impression on me as anything she ever said. My brother, who is a very good actor despite the meretricious medium of television, must have heard this as much as I did, because he wanted to be an actor from the time he was a boy, and my mother reacted with anguish and protest. Here again was the duality which made her seem inconsistent. Everybody must work; but the kind of work she most respected and hoped her son would do was something solid and functional. Had he wanted to be an engineer, a lawyer, or a professor of economics, she would have been ecstatic. But an artist, any kind of artist, she resisted passionately. She was a realist, she dealt with persons and situations according to facts; but the one fact she refused to face was that talent was inherent in all of us. My sister is the most talented of the three. She could have been a musician, a writer, an illustrator, an actress, and she has my mother's fantastic gifts as a linguist. She is the only one who had no wish to put any of this to use in a profession, and so she never did.

From my present long view—I am already ten years older than my mother was when she died—I weigh these matters with considerable understanding; at least they make me ask myself questions that did not occur to me when I was young. What was at the root of my mother's views? How well did I really know her? —not as my mother, not in the emotional intimacy of our relation, but objectively in the light of her own experiences? She had a stubborn gallantry about herself which nothing was permitted to breach, and had it been possible in some symbolic court of inquiry to ask her what she really felt about herself and her fate, she would never have admitted defeat. Her proud courage made it inadmissible to doubt that she was doing what she chose when she risked and then sacrificed her voice as she did. But I believe that for her to have to stop singing was in certain ways to stop living, and that the secret frustration and sorrow of that fate were more responsible than anything else for her early death. By whatever name a disease is called, there are some mortal diseases that have their roots in the heart and the spirit before they attack the flesh.

There was a day when I dropped in at her house, years after she had retired, and went through the rooms where she would ordinarily be, calling her. I could not find her, but the maids told me that she had not gone out. I went on up to the isolated top floor of the house, the children's former nursery. As I was climbing the last flight of stairs I heard music beyond the closed door at the top; so I stopped calling her and quietly opened the door. She was alone, sitting on the floor beside an old-fashioned hand-cranked Victrola, with open albums of her records all about her. She was playing her record of Reynaldo Hahn's *L'Heure Exquise* and she was weeping bitterly, tragically, as she had never in her life allowed anybody to think she could weep. I shut the door and got away. After that I knew a different woman; but she did not know that I knew.

After my mother's initial scepticism, which is a gentle under-statement, about my Mozart project, she resigned herself to the fact that I meant it and always had when I said I wanted to write books. But it was her nature to demand that any form of accomplishment prove itself the hard way. So when the book was published and the reviews were laudatory; when the book received the serious commendation and recognition that the first American biography of Mozart deserved (provided it was good and regardless of who had written it) she was astonished. I think she even doubted at first whether the book reviewers and music writers knew their business. All of a sudden she found she was proud of it. She gave a big party for me, naturally attended by all the prestigious people of music; and by Mr. and Mrs. Arthur Scribner, of whom I stood in awe; also with a good deal of protest, by Max Perkins and his wife Louise. Louise was delighted to come but Max detested anything of the kind and I wonder how she prevailed on him. It was no literary cocktail party, it was a big dinner, with toasts by Carl Engel, Frank Crowninshield, Walter Damrosch, and I forget who else; and in the midst of it I had the feeling that the only people in the room who did not belong there were Max and I. I had no notion then that the next step would be fiction, though Max had. I was very fortunate that my first book was not a novel; in that sense, I never wrote a first novel at all. By the grace of God I was lifted over a field-full of pitfalls and carried along on the current of writing realistically about what I knew deeply and well.

When I brought Max the finished manuscript—though not the final one, completed after his editing—of each book I wrote, he always did the same thing. He looked at the last page first. I am sure he did not know in the beginning what this meant to me, but the fact is that when I am ready to write a book, I write the ending first. I did it with *Mozart* and I have done it with every book since, including this, whose end has been written for many years. When long spans of time intervene, innumerable revisions of my final paragraph or page inevitably have to be made; but the idea must remain strong enough to stand up in its original form and confront me with its rightness. Only then can I begin at the beginning and write the book, not necessarily with facility or speed, and usually with tortuous difficulty. But I know to what conclusion I am working. Without that there is no book in my mind. There is only a mass of material. I did not draw this idea from Mary Queen of Scots or from the words of Edith Wharton: "My last page is always latent in my first." I got it from my mother.

When I was a small child undergoing her remorseless drill at the piano, she would make me begin each new thing the same way. When it was a 'piece' I had to learn the last line first. When it was something longer, a partita or a sonata or whatever, she would take the music and put it on the rack with the back of the closed book facing us. Then she would open it at the last page and make me begin there. I was required to perfect that, which might take a week or more, and then we began at the beginning. After a long time I asked her why.

She said, "Because whatever it is you do, the last impression is what people remember. Do your work as well as you can throughout. Begin well, with attack and accuracy. Drive it through. But whatever else, make the end the best. Know exactly what you are aiming for and finish with a bang."

Of course there is no relation between musical or any other performance and the writing of books. My mother could have had no idea what effect her teaching would have on me. The aim of a book is not to wow an audience. But a book which builds from the first page to the last, carrying the reader to a right and inevitable conclusion, can only come from a writer who knows where he is going before he sets out. It does not matter whether the book is fiction or non-fiction. Everything must come to an end; but the writer's advantage is that he can know the end when the victim of circumstance, which we all are in this our life, cannot.

A copy of the Mozart book had been sent to Maestro before its publication, I cannot remember whether by my mother or by me. He read it at once. He told me it was not bad. The Italian *non c'è male* is both cooler and kinder than our phrase; it denotes a little more approval, but without condescension. "But," he asked me, "why Mozart? Why not Beethoven?" He pronounced the names in his own way, not teutonically; the one was Mo-*zarr*, the other Beeth-*ov*en. He knew that I had been bewitched by Mozart all my life. I had learned long since never to plague him with requests to play that music or, in fact, any specific music. A whole ritual, if not a mystique, and finally, a game, was involved in the risky matter of asking Maestro to play something. A direct request amounted to a certainty that he would not play it. He played Haydn more than he did Mozart, particularly with the Philharmonic; and his reasons were fascinating. In his husky, sometimes squeaky voice, he talked freely about these reasons; I remember him many times after dinner at his house or mine, often at Chotzie's, relaxed and amused by burning a brandy-soaked lump of sugar in his coffee spoon. Intimate friends around him and a novelty or two in the form of a pretty face invited to add a dash of spice, he would lean back in his chair and pick up some question about music which one of us had touched on.

"Mozart," he used to say, "is perfect. Perhaps he is too perfect." Since he spoke Italian to me, my quotations of what he said are translations, and I eschew any attempt to write a phonetic transcription of what his English sounded like. This has been done often before, sometimes very well, but it is not germane to my knowledge of him. His English was fluent, but pronounced like Italian by giving full articulation to every syllable; and accents fell where they might have been had he been speaking Italian. His Italian speech was as beautiful and euphonious and classical as his music and when he lost his temper at rehearsals and let fly with full artillery it was intoxicating.

"Mozart," he said, to return to his talk, "is so perfect that you are in the presence of something superhuman. All other music has faults—beautiful faults. They make it more human."

And so of eighteenth-century composers he leant rather more to Haydn. "Haydn is more human," he said. But when he played a symphony or other work by Mozart he was confronted by his own concept of superhuman perfection and it may be imagined what he demanded of himself and the orchestra. That was how I stumbled on one of the great joys of my life, the acoustical phenomenon of a certain box in Carnegie Hall.

Maestro was playing the G minor Symphony that week. This work is a matter absolutely alone and apart for me in all of music; and as Maestro played it, it was and remains for my lifetime a rite. Always in the Philharmonic days I went to the concert on Thursday night and on Friday afternoon, usually also on Sunday afternoon or Saturday evening. In addition I was often at rehearsals; in later years, with the N B C Symphony, invariably. At the Philharmonic the Cerberus was Bruno Zirato, the assistant manager, who had been Caruso's secretary. Maestro trusted him sufficiently to leave in his hands the minor fiction that nobody except the Toscanini family were ever admitted to rehearsals. The reason for the interdiction was Maestro's chagrin at his outbursts of temper when he could not get the perfection for which he fought. His orchestra understood him and his violence and passion in pursuit of the composer's intent, but it was out of the question to permit outsiders to witness what they would have demeaned with their misunderstanding. When the rehearsals went more or less peacefully—rather less, in those days—we few snoopers, intimates, of course, smuggled into the back of the dark hall, were breathless and grateful. When they were stormy we were terrified.

At that rehearsal of the G minor the orchestra had come to the last bars of the first movement, the resolution in slashed octaves which Maestro brought from the strings like lashes of a whip. The fiddles muffed it. There followed one of the worst Toscanini rages I ever saw. He tore the place apart, he threw the score at the first violins, he screamed imprecations unquotable in any language, and finally, kicking his music stand in an arc right out into the empty hall, Maestro ran moaning from the stage.

Bruno came creeping white-faced through the dark back corners, motioning the handful of us to get out and be gone before Maestro should return to the stage, if he were coming back at all. I was desperate. If it had been any other work, I would have run out to Fifty-seventh Street, hounded by my own guilty conscience. But the G minor Symphony overrode everything. I fled down the side corridor and into the back stairs, which all habitués know, and kept on running to the second tier hall, dark and deserted. I slunk along the hall, trying the doors of the boxes, all locked until I hit one that had been left ajar by oversight. I slipped in, shut the door tight, and lay down flat on my stomach on the floor. After a long time Maestro returned to the rehearsal, look-

ing far more pitiful than the chastised fiddlers. I saw the stage
by resting my chin on a chair, my eyes level with the edge of the
box. The G minor began over again. And I had stumbled onto a
most wonderful discovery. The box was (and is) the centre of an
acoustical sharp spot. Carnegie Hall is glorious, and more so by
contrast with the lamentable Philharmonic Hall in Lincoln Center; but nowhere else in the old house is the sonority so total,
the instruments, together or individually, so brilliant and penetrating. The sound comes out of the walls and surrounds one like a
cloak. At first I thought I was overwrought by the tempest of the
afternoon and by emotion about the tragic, agonizing music
evocative of all the suffering and frustration in Mozart's brief
life. But as time went on, and I made deliberate comparison of
that spot with others in Carnegie Hall, I found I was right. It is
different; and for all the years that Maestro played there, I contrived to sit in that box. When I told him about it he said, "You
are crazy."

CHAPTER EIGHT

N OW in the late winter of 1966, as I come to segments of manuscript and notes of experiences of some thirty-five years ago, I read them with consternation. As a student of history I have been told by historians that it is frivolous, if not superficial or ignorant, to state that history repeats itself and to cite current happenings as examples of that fallacy. I wonder then how we should regard repetitive evidences of resurgent nationalism which take as many forms as there are variations of humanity, and which sooner or later turn violent and destructive of efforts to put areas of the world into some form of viable cooperation or unification. We have been seeing this throughout our lifetimes and this is not the place to catalogue the instances. But nobody of my generation can forget that the treaties of Versailles and St. Germain paved the way for Hitler; that the division of Germany since the Second World War has left dangerous questions unanswered and a perilous ferment at work. By cautious degrees we become apprised again of the emergence of extreme right-wing elements in localities of Germany and of Austria too. It is impossible not to see this in its real frame of reference.

I have no qualifications as a political reporter like my friends John Gunther and William Shirer, Edgar Mowrer, the late Dorothy Thompson and H. R. (Red) Knickerbocker, and others of the brilliant American group who covered Central Europe through the rise of Hitler and thereafter. I was merely there. My purposes were unrelated to the turbulence and the looming menace that pervaded every aspect of life. Savagery and barbarism have a smell; so has fear; and Germany, later Austria too, reeked with those smells. On the side, one remembers with despair the shrugs and the voices of those who said, "It's only a rabble, it will pass." "He's a madman, nobody could take him seriously." The complacent Austrians in their coffee-houses: *"Es kommt nie her."* The Czechs said it over their beer. Any perceptive person moving and working in the midst of that attitude was marked by it. It penetrated my mind and my feelings along with the elements which first drew me to Central Europe and held me to some parts of it more fixedly than I have been gripped by any other force. Central Europe was the breeding-place of music and its supreme creators; of fairy-tale and fantasy; of an architecture which feeds certain hungers of mine as nothing else can. It will be remarked that Italy in respect of music and architecture was the progenitor, and I have lived responsive to that truth. But the all-encompassing growth flowered in the heart of Europe, beneath that sky which to my eyes is uniquely high and wide, across the broad rolling lands which have been called by many political names that do not specially matter. Nationalism is a tragic and terrible delusion. It has diverted the life stream of these lands into the sewers of oppression, persecution, war, revolution, dictatorship, anti-Semitism, anti-Christ, and all the perversions of humanity and inhumanity spawned by the horrors of this century. When there was no entity called Germany, when Austria meant the hodge-podge, ramshackle empire of the Habsburgs, when nobody took fire over which boundaries included Munich or Salzburg or Dresden or Trieste or Prague or Weimar or Vienna, there was more space for the mind to soar and the creature to breathe than after the wars which made the word 'liberation' the cruellest of travesties.

All this is hindsight, the outgrowth of experience and age. And from the same view, when I come to my own recollections of the emergence and proliferation of the Nazi mania I am dismayed by present-day evidences that this is not entirely of the past. I know too that it is not peculiar to one national mentality. I know that it ferments in my own country, an inevitable generation later than in Europe. I know that the domination of any people by a national or supranational despotism can come from any extreme, be its color brown, red, or any other.

In January of 1933 my husband and I went to Central Europe, I in pursuit of an idea which emerged later, diffused between two wholly unrelated books, and not consequent on what I thought I had planned. Russell Davenport decided to accompany me mostly because he was unfamiliar with the parts of Europe to which I was attached. He was a francophile and I was not. To him Europe was effectively France, with peripheral touches of Italy and Switzerland. I thought and saw and felt very differently. Midwinter is no time to go where we went, but the farm was preempting his attention in the pleasanter seasons, so I suppose the winter was some sort of compromise. Our objectives were Prague and Vienna, and since I always travelled on German ships, and took along a car—how clumsy and complicated all this seems by contrast with flying and hiring cars anywhere one goes today—we landed at Bremerhaven and drove to Berlin. It was as good a route eastward as another, and he had never seen the capital of Germany, which was then in a state of extreme tension from the rising pressure of Hitler and his Nazis. Russell felt as a journalist that he should see it, and he saw much more than he bargained for. We arrived at the Bristol, and a superlative hotel it was, on Sunday night the 29th of January. Next day at noon Hindenburg appointed Adolf Hitler Chancellor.

The people I knew in Berlin were the remarkable group of American newspaper correspondents I have mentioned; I had met them previously at Dorothy Thompson's house and the Edgar Mowrers'. They had been living for years on the lip of the volcano and when it finally erupted they went into action which they have recorded in their own books better and more accurately than I could do here. During that Monday they were in and out of the Bristol and the Adlon Bar, where we found ourselves, between

their calls at the Foreign Office, covering the uproar all over
Berlin, and rushing to file their cables. By afternoon they told us
that hundreds of thousands of Brownshirts, arriving from every
accessible part of Germany by truck and bus and innumerable
special trains, were assembling in the Sportplatz, a vast outdoor
arena, to form squads for the torchlight parade that was to take
place that night. Sheer horror and revulsion from this, enclosed in
the evil fact that it was a drama of primary historical impact, is
something I have never forgotten.

We were in the Adlon Bar at the end of that day with Red
Knickerbocker and some others, when John Gunther rushed in,
still in the ski-clothes in which he had left Vienna, interrupting
a holiday. He was a young and massive Adonis with curly blond
hair. It is no longer possible to remember who said what, but
the sense of shock which was at the same time no shock is vivid
to this day. They said we must go with them to the Wilhelmstrasse
that night, where the Press Section of the Foreign Office had windows fronting on the street, directly opposite the Chancellery
and Hindenburg's residence. Of course we had no accreditation
and no time to obtain any.

"Never mind," somebody said. "The guards will be too excited to check anything carefully and most of them can't read
English. Find some piece of printed paper and wave it at them."

So we searched our wallets and Russell unearthed an ancient
reporter's card from his early days on *Time*. The best I could
find was my New York driver's licence. Our friends formed a
flying wedge around us and, waving our phony accreditation at
the guards, we were rushed through the control and into the room
with the windows on the Wilhelmstrasse. It was packed. The
American press corps was only one of many. They came from all
countries. Each huddled more or less by itself, taking turns in
the front of the crowd at the vast open windows. The night was
bitter cold. Somebody gave me a perch seated on the window-sill
with my feet hanging out and people holding me from inside as

they looked out over my head. Directly across from us old Marshal Hindenburg stood at attention in his window, immobile as a statue. He was past eighty, and his bearing so fantastic that people were laying bets as to whether he was propped up from behind. Somebody cracked that he was already dead and embalmed. He stood there all night as if frozen in place. In the next building down the street, also in our direct view, stood Hitler at the Chancellery window, his arm raised in his damnable salute, motionless like the old field marshal. And below in the Wilhelmstrasse the drilled marching mob, platoon after platoon, as far as the eye could see, flowing in solidly from miles away. They wore their brownshirt uniforms and their swastika armbands, they carried rivers of Hakenkreuz banners and flaming torches that made the dark lurid to the limits of one's vision. As they passed Hitler's window they turned eyes left, all clockwork, roaring their horrible *Sieg Heil!* with the straight-arm salute. Bands blared and blatted, the nauseous Horst Wessel song, Prussian military marches; I have never since heard the Kaiser Friedrich march without shuddering. The pavement below us was jammed with spectators solidly lining the street, standing on one another's feet, each waving a swastika flag on a stick and screaming *Sieg Heil!* with the storm troopers. Fat, wild-eyed, red-faced, pig-necked, the people one had told oneself were not the real Germans. A few hours ago their flag and hooked cross had been illegal. Now it exploded everywhere.

It was the thoroughness of all this, the impeccable organization, the precision, the plannedness, on a scale involving hundreds of thousands and taking all night to execute, that filled us with sick terror and revealed the total pervasion of the German people by this filth. They had been preparing this for years, every household had had banners and shirts and armbands hidden against this day, even when only six months before, the feeble electoral process of the Weimar Republic had given them but 37 per cent of the national vote. And we did not know at that time what was really to happen. All we had read or heard of the paperhanger's ravings could not convince us or any people of normal outlook what the future was to hold.

Red Knickerbocker told us a day or two later, when we were recovering from the colds we had caught and impatient anyway to move on, that the sooner we got out of Germany the better. We were incredulous. Did he mean they would molest us? Americans?

He looked doubtfully at me. "You never know." He quoted some of Hitler's monstrosities from *Mein Kampf*. Everyone had been revolted by these but had thought them the ravings of a madman. No one supposed they would be implemented literally. But Knick said, "There may be pogroms and physical violence very soon. To wipe out the Jews and confiscate their property is the basis of the whole thing. And it is revolution, don't underestimate that." He sounded over-alarming to us and some of his colleagues disagreed with him. After the fact, and after what the world saw in the following years, it is impossible to realize that none of us could envision sudden arrest, torture, transport, the concentration-camp, the gas chamber, genocide. It was inconceivable until it began to happen.

I wanted to visit Dr. Wolf at the Staatsbibliothek and was urgently advised not to. "Leave him alone," I was told. "You might call attention to him in some way that would do him harm. Don't communicate with any German Jew you know. Just get out."

Driving through the Erzgebirge to Prague by way of Leipzig and Dresden, the villages along the way were more sickening than Berlin had been. From these and places like them all over Germany the trained mobs in the trucks had streamed into the capital. Every window flew a swastika flag, every main street and town square was crowded with fat shouting fanatics waving things and reading proclamations plastered on the public buildings. Loudspeakers had already appeared. Youthful bullies in brown shirts with armbands and knee boots swaggered about heiling one another. In the shop-windows were printed signs: *Hier grüsst man nur mit Heil Hitler*. And overhead across the road outside most villages and towns was strung a banner with the words *In diesem Ort sind Juden unerwünscht*. It was the first time I had ever been confronted by the bare fangs of rabid anti-Semitism and the first time I had reacted with roused and curdling blood. Russell was pale with rage and disgust. We did not stop anywhere except to buy gasoline. When we reached the Czech frontier after a hair-raising drive on mountain roads lacquered with frozen sleet, and the German barrier pole with its garnish of swastikas went down behind us I burst into irrational tears and the Czechs in the little mountain hut plied us with hot coffee and slivovice before they looked at our passports and motor documents.

Shortly before I was married to Russell Davenport we had talked at length about my ancestry and about religion. I started that by asking him if he was sure he wanted to marry me, born a Jew and raised a believing Christian. He answered, "That is one of the reasons I want to marry you." He was fascinated by the little I knew of my forbears and baffled that the Old Testament was as much as I had ever known about the Jewish world, which is altogether different from knowing Jewish people. He gave me the great works of Jewish history and of Jewish classical and folk literature. I read them with ardour. I suspect I have read more of them, and thought and learned more about the culture from which they spring than some of my friends, particularly women, who have been of the Jewish religion all their lives. When my husband encouraged me to explore the philosophical and historical grounds of my ancestry I found myself wondering why my mother had been shut off from them. I understood when I learned how Jewish ritual postulates the presence of the paterfamilias, the dominance of the man and the quorum of men in the religion. Its lack of hold upon my mother must have been due to the absence of a father in her life from earliest childhood and to the family of women in which she grew up. She herself drifted on the agnostic sea-of-consent where so many barks float or founder or merely keep on circling, but she did not think that right for her children. So I emerged what I am, married to the descendant of generations of Protestant clergymen; and there on the icy road out of Hitler's newly exploded hell, we both had the same shattering confrontation with what would have been an assault upon ourselves but for the accident of nationality.

It was anyway an explosive year. We were in Vienna in March, having a very good time which seems not to fit at all in the retrospective frame of reality. Austria was still reeling from the crash of the Creditanstalt which had detonated ominous political and social dislocations and shaken all Europe in reverberation. And when Franklin Roosevelt was inaugurated President on the fourth of March, chance had put Russell Davenport in a most unlikely place for him to be. The United States was in its worst crisis since the Civil War, the nadir of the depression, with seventeen million unemployed, industry and business paralyzed, banks failing, and financial chaos at hand. Transatlantic radio transmission was primitive but we listened to what we could hear of Roosevelt's inaugural address. He proclaimed the ten-day bank moratorium and spoke the words which have gone into history. Russell was flummoxed at being so far away. Every inclination and instinct in him protested his being in the heart of Central Europe at such a moment in the affairs of the United States.

I was shaken by the dramatic twist that had made us witnesses of Hitler's accession to power rather than Roosevelt's in such close juxtaposition. Russell's mind had leapt to New York and Washington. It was his way to grab at any reason, intrinsic or fortuitous, when he made an impulsive decision. This time the propellent came in a sudden cable from his mother. His brother was seriously ill and Russell said we must leave on the next ship. That was the Conte di Savoia from Genoa. We had twenty-four hours and nearly a thousand kilometers in which to catch the ship. We left Vienna at one o'clock in the morning and drove non-stop except for gasoline to Genoa, spelling each other every hour. The weather was the Austrian mixture-as-before, fog, cloud, rain, snow, sleet, ice, and the dreadful roads which in truth I used to like better than the speedways of today.

There was a final stroke of phobia in the strange interlude that had swept us through history and headlong towards the culmination that lay ahead three, six, twelve years in a dire future which also spanned the best years of our lives. We came out of cloud-bound and streaming Austria over the frontier to the unlikely accident of brilliant 'Italian' weather. Of course it is all one part of the world, and Mussolini, the other jackanapes, had been battering hard at the unreconciled people of the former South Tyrol. But there was bright sun and strong blue sky, and as soon as the houses began to have flat yellow-washed walls and knobby red hip roofs, it did feel like a familiar friendly face. But every yellow-washed wall was defaced by a painted slogan from one of Mussolini's harangues. Though the people went about their business, if they had any, with indifference, the Blackshirts were evident, and Fascism which until then had been a matter of contempt and cracks about trains running on time, suddenly revealed its kinship to the obscenities in Germany.

A trifle caused me to explode. On the dock in Genoa a gaggle of customs functionaries, the eternal supernumerary bureaucracy, put on one of their classic shows: we could not load the car on the ship. I forget the reason, some piece of paper that had not been prepared because of the telephoned arrangements from Vienna. The car, they said, could not leave Italy. I had not often spoken Italian up to then. I had it in my head and my ears, but not the facility of speech which later became automatic. About all I had said in it since childhood had been little remarks in reply to Maestro. In my mind these bullies with their strutting Fascist overseer suddenly became the whole filthy thing wherever it was; here in Genoa, in Bologna two years earlier where they had physically assaulted Maestro; in Berlin or Nürnberg or anywhere.

I opened my mouth and out of it came a fluent stream of Italian abuse. I called them names I did not know I knew. I said they could rot before we would bribe them as they expected. I talked like a fishwife. I told them to get the hell out of the way and I got into the car and drove it over the motor gangway into the hold. Russell stood gaping on the dock with the ship's whistle blasting overhead. He ran aboard just as they started to raise the gang-planks.

And yet there were years to follow which were neither black nor white in the countries where I like to be, but grey as life really is. If you looked below the surface in Austria you found rudimentary civil war, a seething pot stirred from his nearby eyrie by Hitler at Berchtesgaden. The Austrian Nazis were at first cautious and surreptitious; the Socialists in Vienna were struggling to hold the momentum of progress they had made; the *Rotweissrot* patriots headed by Chancellor Dollfuss were standing in the breach. I was not there for political reasons nor were any of the people with whom I spent the loveliest summers of my life. We did not want to peer beneath the lid of the pot, we knew that it cooked and boded nobody any good, and as I look back on it I am surprised that even then people seemed to have come to terms with a basic fact of twentieth-century life: pursuing existence in spite of threats to security or survival or decency or hope, living as we have all grown used to living, in danger and with sangfroid contrived to meet the particular peril closest to each life or each community of lives. Incredulity always pervades this attitude, I suppose one of the fundamentals of the instinct for survival; the bullet is for the other chap, some other plane will crash, my country won't go down the drain, nobody will dare to drop the bomb. Twenty-one kilometers from Salzburg Hitler screeched and egged on Streicher and the liquidation of the Jews. Up in Prague by 1935 the great old founding father of his country was telling his son Jan that terrible times lay ahead for the nation, and predicting too accurately what was going to happen. But for three years in Salzburg there was the best of the good life, the best in my lexicon meaning music and its peripheral wealth of drama and spectacle, a magnet which drew a world public who participated in an excellence that has never since been approached.

I had work to do there and that is my measure of satisfaction in any experience. Some time after the publication of *Mozart* the small magazine distributed to Theatre Guild subscribers had been expanded to become a national monthly called *Stage,* devoted to what has since come to be called the performing arts. I continued as its music critic. This is the most difficult kind of periodical to make and keep successful; it has been attempted many times, but has never permanently succeeded, in part because of technical problems of publication in relation to such a fast-shifting scene as the New York theatre. The musical world is more stable, and I was given carte blanche to cover it as I chose. Writing for a monthly made it unnecessary to hear everything that a daily or a weekly newspaper critic would have had to cover, but I received all the critic's tickets and could make my choices on the basis of what was genuinely important. I always heard many more concerts, recitals, and operas than I had space to write about. When anything of major importance was presented outside New York, I went to San Francisco, Boston, Chicago, Philadelphia, or whereever; and of course to Salzburg in those years when Maestro, beyond the presence of the other leading musicians of the world, made it for one month unique in the annals of music.

My fascination with Lotte Lehmann had been reaffirmed in many visits to the Staatsoper when I was in Vienna, and at the end of 1933 she finally came to New York. Oddly enough, neither she nor I remembers just how we met, but I think it was because *The New Yorker* had commissioned a Profile of her. The profile took off from the basis that I rated her the finest singing actress before the public, and thirty years later I can add that I have never seen or heard her equal. But Lotte as a person, Lotte with her cosiness, her simple tastes, her jokes, her warmth, was what *The*

New Yorker wanted, just as it had wanted the hilarious tale of Efrem Zimbalist's weakness for shills and auctions and gambling. Neither subject was pleased with his portrait and a good deal of pacifying had to intervene. "However," Lotte wrote in a memoir, after protesting that I had written nothing but details of her everyday life which annoyed her terribly, "wherever I went, reporters spoke of it." She got over her annoyance and we became friends for life. When she made her début at the Metropolitan as Sieglinde I took my mother, who reacted exactly as I had done when I first heard Lotte in Vienna. My mother was stubborn in her own way, and having taken the attitude that I had gone overboard with exaggerated enthusiasm, she gave me some agreeable moments as I watched her trying to conceal her own open-mouthed enthrallment so as not to capitulate outrightly to me.

The five years between 1933 and 1938 were propulsive, crammed with activity and hard work, with treasured and productive friendships. Those are the years, between the ages of thirty and thirty-five, which should be the catalytic years in a working life; not necessarily the peak of a writer's creativity, but the upward thrust in energy and growing mastery of his medium which will culminate somewhere in the next decade in the major work he has it in him to do. After that it is a descending curve. Refinement and subtlety may increase, taste and skill replace sheer drive, good work be done along the gradual descent; but almost without exception the middle years are the peak of a writer's achievement and the years before them the height of the stoking process that brings his powers to their apogee. I can pick up those five years now almost as if they had been a crystal sphere in my hands, in which the power of divination or the courage to act as though I had it, shows me how much of the substance of my life was determined inside that sphere. Those were the last five years of my mother's life, and they were also the last years before Hitler and his works put an end to the world I had loved. They were years in which I saw Max Perkins constantly and wrote my first novel.

They were years when I was in and out of Czechoslovakia all the time, running up there for whatever time intervened between Maestro's performances at Salzburg and any others which it was necessary or my own wish not to miss. They were years when the tensions and pressures of a difficult but rewarding marriage drove me outward and apart to make a life of my own, and friendships and acquaintanceships which were mine alone and often the germs of characters who appeared, filtered, transmogrified, fragmented, superposed, combined, and otherwise metamorphosed in novels that I was later to write.

1935 was the first summer that Maestro conducted a whole season of opera at Salzburg; the year before, he had played only two symphony concerts there. The first of the operas was *Fidelio,* with Lotte; then *Falstaff* with a fine cast from La Scala headed by the great baritone Mariano Stabile. In 1936 he added to these *Die Meistersinger,* and in 1937, *Die Zauberflöte,* the only Mozart opera he conducted except for a *Don Giovanni* in Buenos Aires early in this century. He had not conducted opera since he had left La Scala in 1929, and for me, for any of us close enough to him to be allowed to hear all the rehearsals, those weeks were the most thrilling of our lives. I look back on those three summers as perfection. I suppose, philosophically, that nothing can attain such a pinnacle until the last moment or hour or year—whatever its nature and its relation to time and circumstance—before its decline and ultimate disappearance.

The first of those summers I shared a house with Lotte and her husband, Otto Krause, at Aigen, a village outside of Salzburg. My German quickly evolved from incorrect to a mishmash of Viennese slang and howling laughter. The sublime side of it was living with Lotte through the weeks when she was rehearsing and singing with Maestro what I consider the most inspiring and the most exacting dramatic soprano role in music. Her voice was the glorious organ it had been throughout an operatic career already over twenty years long, and she was then forty-seven years old—a matter which was only recently and affectionately authenticated when we celebrated her seventy-fifth birthday. I cite this to give present-day people something to think about. Today there are no artists like Lotte and some of her contemporaries and many of her predecessors. There are some beautiful voices and some fine musicians (particularly, as Maestro used to exclaim after he got over his surprise, those trained in the United States). But not the circumstances that produced artists of classic stature and repute: the long permanent tenures in the great opera houses, and the long intervals of rest free of the hectic pressures of competitive money-making, snarled up in stereophonic tape and whipped about the world in jet airplanes.

Maestro had consented to conduct opera at Salzburg without pay, as he had done at Bayreuth in 1930 and 1931. On that basis he could devote himself to the production and performance of opera as close to perfect as he could make it. The Festival direction gave him exactly what he asked for: his own choice of artists; as many rehearsals as he thought necessary, which could be any number at all; autocratic power over each of his productions. Nothing of this sort had been known in the United States since Maestro's time at the Metropolitan and perhaps not there, at the end, since his rehearsal demands had been one of the rocks on which the Golden Age had foundered. The Vienna Philharmonic, which is the orchestra of the Vienna Opera, is a state-subsidized entity, and whatever were its contractual arrangements with its employer was no concern of Maestro's. He called the rehearsals: cast rehearsals with corrépétiteur (piano accompaniment, and the pianist was a young man of about nineteen named Erich Leinsdorf); cast rehearsals with orchestra, individual and group rehearsals for singers, for the chorus, and for various subdivisions of groupings; orchestra rehearsals, separate rehearsals for different choirs of the orchestra, and so on to the grand finale, the dress rehearsal, by which time—in the case of *Die Meistersinger*—there had been a total of some sixty rehearsals altogether. I heard every one of all the rehearsals of all the four works that Maestro conducted, and every one of the performances in all three seasons.

I learned those four works as I have learned and retained nothing else in my life. Through having seen as well as heard Maestro in the long, intricate labor of rehearsing any work one gains a knowledge of the music and of its composer, in a way which could not otherwise be possible. Maestro was sixty-eight years old in 1935; he looked and could have been half that age, and he thrived on a schedule that would have killed an ordinary mortal. He lived with his family in a villa at Liefering, outside of Salzburg; a spacious house, but crammed to bursting with his daughters and their husbands and children, his wife's sister and her husband and other relatives, and a constant parade of guests for luncheon or for dinner on his free evenings, all in an uproar of noise and busy games played by the feminine company to contrive to sit next to Maestro. He had his own vague way of seeming not to look at the pretty women, but his famously myopic eyes missed nothing and he saw whom and what he wanted to see. In those days some of us were deployed as a sort of buffer. There were troops of beautiful women dressed as we all were in Dirndls from Lanz's, and those he liked were placed next him. But a few of them bored or annoyed him, one English lady in particular who pursued him with brazen determination. She applied herself to knowing his daily whereabouts and being where she would encounter him, and he enlisted three or four of us—Pauline Chotzinoff and her sister Elza, Virginia Wallenstein and me, to make a shifting barricade that would fend her off. When one of us was placed next him it was often because he wanted not to be bothered by somebody else and he could say anything he liked or equally, nothing at all if that was his mood.

He was of course the idol and the autocrat of Salzburg. The townspeople used to line the streets to watch him drive by, sitting in the front seat of his Cadillac limousine beside his chauffeur Emilio. The back of the car was filled with his wife, his family, and various guests, all talking and gesticulating at once. Maestro often wore a beret, his concession to summer informality, and much of the time a broad smile; he would even wave to the cheering people, a most uncharacteristic gesture, but the place seemed to make him good-humored. One evening a lot of us took him to a local wine-house after the opera and though we warned him that Austrian red wine can be ghastly, and tried to see that he got the local white wine to drink, he asked for red—either because he ordinarily preferred it or to put us in our places. The red wine was worse than ghastly and the beaming proprietor stood by while Maestro drank glass after glass of the dreadful red ink and pressed it on the rest of us. I was sick all night. He used to tease me because the American car I drove, about the same size as his own, was too big for the narrow streets, but I lived thirty kilometers out of town and with all the runs up to Prague I really needed the car. Maestro's house at Liefering had a devilish entrance with two stone gate-posts built in the horse-and-carriage era, placed at a sharp turn from the narrow highroad. Emilio had a hard time manoeuvering the Toscanini car through this gate and the feat was no easier for me. Maestro all his life had an endearing way of receiving every guest on the front steps of his house, wherever he was living, and at Salzburg he spiced that sweetness with an invariable barb about my big car, and what fools American women looked driving such things themselves. Naturally I was on my mettle to negotiate the damned gate without visible difficulty, but one day something distracted my attention as I was twisting through it and sure enough, I scratched my fender. Maestro capered off the steps as I arrived, pointing and shouting, "Look! Look! She did it!"

He was a wicked tease, always about trifles, but his formidable memory kept trifles fixed in its clear amber as precisely as the hundreds of scores it retained. Once in New York he came to a supper-party at my house after a concert, and like the guests, the seating, and the wine, the food had been carefully planned to please him. (He never touched shellfish or caviar and was revolted if others were eating them.) He always said that he ate nothing but soup and a piece of bread, but that was subject to his whims and many variations. He was bored by the length of most meals and having finished the minestra, the first course which could be rice or pastasciutta instead of soup, he sat back and watched everybody else eat his way through three or four courses more, muttering to me if I were next him, "The pigs! How can they eat like that!" But if, thinking to please him, I held back from the delicious dishes at his own table he would scold me and say I was rude. The particular supper I remember included a rice dish that had pieces of chicken, mushrooms, and other things he liked cooked in it. He asked me what this was he was about to eat and thoughtlessly I answered, "A risotto." It was not a risotto, it was a kind of pilaff, which is not an Italian way to cook rice. *"Un risotto!"* he jeered. "Carla," he called to his wife at the other end of the table, "look what she calls a risotto!" Signora Carla, who was eating with appetite, made some reproachful answer, but Maestro paid no attention. For years afterwards he taunted me about risotto.

It used to be said that 'everybody' was at Salzburg, and in some sense, everybody was. There were groups, and groups within groups, the innermost ones the keenest and most cognizant devotees of music, the fringes full of glittering names and beautiful faces from all over Europe and the New York scene; they came primarily because it was the place in all the world to be. I was no more interested in that milieu than I have ever been, nor it in me; and while I went occasionally to Max Reinhardt's Schloss Leopoldskron—I remember chiefly its magnificent inlaid floors—which was destined to a beastly fate in the hands of Goebbels and Goering, and is now an American study centre, I was never part of the gilded world which flitted there. I had a much better time with Lotte in her simple *Landhaus*, or with Maestro and the old musical friends from New York. But one did see nearly everybody one had ever met or heard of, at the Festspielhaus, respectfully in their places before curtain-time (there was no admission after and we all enjoyed the slapping-down of a certain royalty who had expected an exception to be made); eating *Würsterl* in their fingers in the intermissions, supping and gambling later at the Mirabell.

Whenever I have walked since through the lounge of the Oesterreichischer Hof, the leading hotel which used to be in a queer way both chic and cosy, and is now enlarged, crowded, and hectic like the rest of the world, I think of the one time I met Somerset Maugham. It was there, and someone in a group of us introduced him and his friend Gerald Haxton. I have lived through the long years when Maugham was tossed off as a clever tale-spinner and a slick commercial writer; and I have always expected to witness the current posthumous 'discovery' that he wrote some masterly fiction and can give most of us tough lessons in the writing of spare and lucid English. I had heard, as anyone did who listened to any mention of him, that he had a horrid disposition and was no fun to know. It was too true. He must have been bored or vexed, or simply hating Salzburg. He sat there silent and scowling, with the corners of his mouth turned down, sniffing suspiciously at a dry martini. I could imagine what an ass I should have made of myself had I said anything admiring of his work, which I did and do admire very much. So I said nothing and went away.

The weeks in Salzburg, the gaiety and constant occupation and above all, the music, were all-absorbing, but never so much as to quiet my worry about my mother. In that year she became very frail, she lost weight and aged all at once. Until she was in her late forties she had kept the vivid features of her beauty, the clear brunette skin, the classic head with its great dark eyes and serene level brows, the beautiful carriage, the splendid throat and shoulders which were so lovely in evening dress. Suddenly, it seemed to me, she was very thin. The skin was loose on her fine arms and heavy hands. She let her hair grow out in the grey which has been

hereditarily premature in all of us and which she had kept tinted
to its original chestnut brown ever since she was before the public.
Plainly she was very ill. But she staved off questions and was
stubborn about doctors; she had as little to do with them as possible. In those years she took to travelling to the far parts of the
world with Efrem Zimbalist on concert tours in Asia, Central
America, and other places where she ought not to have gone,
specifically to countries where there was no milk—and much of
the time she lived on a milk diet. She insisted she could manage
if she had a supply of American dehydrated milk, a product called
Klim, which came in bulky five-pound tins. That year I had
arranged to have these tins of Klim sent ahead of her before she
left on a long journey, so that she would find a supply at each
major stop. By late August she was in Russia and on her way to
Karlsbad where she was going to take a cure. I persuaded her to
come by way of Salzburg and when she was to arrive I went to
meet her train.

I had a piercing shock when I saw her on the platform and
I had to wrench myself in line to hide my terror. She was emaciated. I doubt if she weighed much over a hundred pounds. She
was very weak, but she tossed that off, saying how exhausting the
long train journey had been. But worth it, she said; she was full
of the Soviet Union, where she had been a specially honored guest
and vastly interested in all she had seen there. I found out later
that she had also been a patient in the diagnostic clinic in Moscow
reserved for the Russian top brass. The doctors in New York had
known for a long time that she had a grave disorder of the liver,
but they had not given this a name for reasons I suppose were
valid; evidently they had their own way of timing such discussions.
But the Russians had told her that she had cirrhosis of the liver,
and with frigid calm she told me. She spoke as impersonally as
though talking about a stranger, looking into my eyes and commanding me with her prodigious will-power to face this as she
was facing it. She did not have to tell me it was a mortal illness,

I could see that by looking at her even had I not known what it was. I had no way then of learning enough to give me something to go by, what the course of the disease would be, how long she would live. I had to wait until I was back in New York and my dear Connie Traeger could 'stand me by,' that wonderful phrase from *Fidelio,* with his honesty and his wisdom, so that I could be and do as my mother wished. "Nobody else," she said, "is to know about this, nobody but you. You and I will take it together."

And for a long time we did. She recovered somewhat from the extreme debilitation in which she arrived at Salzburg and for a year or more appeared to be much better. She gained some weight and when occasionally she made the effort to go out, to a concert or the theatre or a party, or to have friends at her house, she could still by a combination of courage and art and will-power look amazingly beautiful and seem to be herself. But the obverse of that was the life of an invalid which she lived most of the time, hiding it from everybody except me, and relying for companion-ship on a few intimate old friends who stayed with her in the country, and in New York came for quiet games of bridge or backgammon. She learned how to keep going by rationing her strength, but when she emerged from Russia that summer she had had an exhausting journey that would have pulled anybody down. After a day or two of rest she went with me to hear Lotte sing the last *Fidelio* of the season, which thrilled and moved her deeply. Afterwards we went back to see Maestro, and to a strange and tragic reversal of a happening of long ago. I had told him beforehand that she was not well and that we could not have supper with him after the opera, but I had not told him she was very ill, one never told him such a thing because he was always frightfully upset by the illness—or worse—of old friends. In the green-room there was the usual crowd and Maestro was surrounded by Signora Carla and Emilio with their ministrations, fanning himself and in a smiling mood since the performance had gone well. He greeted me warmly but in his face there was no recognition of the wasted, grey-haired woman with me as she took his hand. I was heartsick, but my mother said, *"Maestro! Non mi conosce più?"* He started, looked hard at her, and the tears came into his eyes. "Alma, *cara!*" he said, very upset. "How could I not know that voice?"

He embraced her and held her hands tightly and she said something about the performance, but it was heartrending. We left quickly. I was always grateful that that was not his last impression of her. When she was stronger in the following winters he saw her sometimes and they could laugh and reminisce about the old days. He used to like to tell stories of the Metropolitan spring tour in 1910, when the company went to Atlanta, and my mother, only twenty-six years old, was the mischief-maker who kept them in an uproar. *"Dio mio!"* he used to say, "how beautiful she was, those great dark eyes, and full of jokes, full of laughing. Always in such a good humor." He never forgot the day when he had called a morning rehearsal and neither he nor any other man in the company had a pair of trousers to put on when they started to get dressed. My mother had bribed the hotel valet to take away every pair of trousers from every man's room.

And many years afterwards, when he was very old, Maestro used to tell me, "Yes, you are intelligent. You have brains, you are musical, you are interesting. But your mother!" He would pause. "Your mother—*she* was beautiful!"

CHAPTER NINE

IN January, 1935, Marcella Sembrich died at the age of
seventy-seven and her funeral took place in St. Patrick's
Cathedral. My mother had been her intimate friend for
many years. We went together to the funeral. As I sat in the
Cathedral beside my mother, sensing the weight of musical history, thinking of Madame, as we always called Sembrich, and of
Lilli Lehmann and Melba who had died in the past few years, a
thought came into my mind with a curious slow push. Nobody
had ever written a realistic book about a singer such as these or
their counterparts. There was no book about a singer which, in
my own eventual words, told the truth, which had everything in
it, all the trouble and ugliness as well as the glamour and
triumphs. Only this much as I recall it, occurred to me at that
time; but that funeral is the opening scene of my novel, *Of Lena
Geyer.*

The question ever since has been whether the book is really
a novel. It is, but I achieved its fictitiousness crabwise. I wrote
it as the biography of a fictitious singer. I knew I possessed the
knowledge and the material to write such a book, I knew I could
write biography, but I did not know that I could write fiction.
For a few weeks I turned the idea over in my head without seeing
what to do with it. Then there was a conversation with Carol
Brandt, when one or the other of us said how impossible it is for
one person to know everything of a rich and complicated personality; that a fully dimensioned portrait must be compounded
from all the people who knew the subject intimately in all the

different phases of his life. The sudden click in my head alerted me, I saw how to go about my book, and I told Max Perkins. By this time I knew Max well. I had seen a good deal of him in the past three years, though I was diffident with him, mostly because I was a woman. Max was the editor and friend of as many women writers as men, but the men were then, and time has proved them permanently, of such stature that it would have been an egomaniac who thought herself in their class. Besides, Max's family life was over-supplied with women. He and his artistic, high-strung wife had five beautiful daughters and no son; most of my visits with Max were set to the tune of his soft groan, "Women!" wrung from him by the events and crises of his daily life. There was always something to relate about Louise, or about Zippy or Nancy or another of the girls. Max at this time was deeply engrossed with Tom Wolfe. Wolfe's second book, *Of Time and the River,* was about to be published, and during the years of Max's enormous labors with it I saw him often. I realize now that this was both patient and generous on Max's part. I had nothing in preparation and was living through one of the long blank intervals which have always followed the completion of a book and persisted until something finally happens to galvanize me to begin another, the substance of which has long been there.

Tom Wolfe was as unlikely an acquaintance for me as a wild buffalo, which he rather resembled; huge, hulking, shaggy, clumsy, with an obsessed look in his eyes intensified by drink. I used to see him occasionally with Max, but not at lunch or 'tea' as Max called an afternoon drink—those were kept for his sole attention to whomever he was seeing. Max introduced me to Wolfe in his office, the small cluttered corner room on the fifth floor of Scribners, which was so full of books stacked everywhere and the famous hatrack which stood by while Max usually kept his hat on his head, that Wolfe seemed to make the walls bulge. He had no idea who I was or a notion of a reason for my existence. But I was curious about him because of Max's belief in him and the prodigies of work that Max poured into Wolfe. He gave Wolfe more time than any other writer, and involved himself more deeply in the confusions and torments of the man.

Max's habits were rigid except when Wolfe barged in and upset them. For years Max had lived in a spacious book-lined house in New Canaan to which he commuted every day, using the hours in the train as undisturbed time in which to read manuscripts. He also read them throughout weekends. He had no recreations, he took no time off, it was impossible for Charles Scribner or anyone else to induce him to take a vacation. Every day he met one of his authors for lunch at a small restaurant called Cherio's in East Fifty-third Street or, very rarely, in the Grill of the old Ritz. And every afternoon he met by appointment another author, usually one in deep trouble, for 'tea', in winter in the small bar at the Ritz, in summer in the garden of the Chatham. Tea consisted of two dry martinis for Max, stretched over an hour, and for me when I was with him, one weak whisky and soda. The teas somehow were more magical than the lunches. There were times when I was working on a book and would get into a paralyzing slough of confusion or frustration. Sometimes I would sit (and still can) all day long, either writing nothing or writing drivel which ends in the waste-basket. Sometimes this went on for weeks. Then one day Max would telephone and ask, "How are you getting on?"

"I'm stuck," I would answer. "I'm in a terrible mess."

I always had the feeling that he knew this and had called just because of it. He would ask me to meet him for tea next afternoon. We sat and drank our drinks and talked not very much. If I mentioned the problem I had been wrestling with, Max somehow changed the subject and the change often ended up on the head of Franklin Roosevelt, whom Max did not admire. Nor did he like the New Deal. I was a good audience for this since I agreed with Max's views and I enjoyed hearing him talk about them. Or he talked about "Women!" or about one of his other authors; and often he did not talk at all. We just sat there and thought. Suddenly Max would say, "Time for my train," pick up his briefcase from under the table, and bid me a hasty good-bye as he started down Madison Avenue to Grand Central Station. I would go home, feeling both calm and exhilarated at the same time; spend the evening as I had planned it, nearly always at a concert or the opera, and next morning my problem would have disappeared.

This was the essence of what Max did. In his own words, written or spoken and paraphrased many times in the seventeen years I knew him, "You can only help a writer to get out what he has it in him to say." His drifting, sometimes inarticulate talk, his slightly husky voice, his fine eyes, his peculiarities of dress like the thick, loosely-knotted wool neckties he wore; his marked deafness in one ear which I understood well since my husband had exactly the same thing; his confidence in me, which was the root of confidence in myself as a writer—these were the qualities, tangible and intangible, which gave Max his power to help writers to write. Editing in the literal sense, correcting the style or structure or language of a book, fussing with minutiae of punctuation or spelling, concerned him not at all. He stood by a writer with his wordless communication of belief and encouragement for as long as it might take to get through to the end of a manuscript, and it might take years. Max would only say, "Don't worry, just get it all down on paper and then we'll see what needs to be done."

Sometimes I think I would never have come to writing fiction if it had not been for Max. He understood the nature of each writer and made himself part of that writer's capacity to write. Himself an extremely shy and reticent man, he was not confounded by extremes of behavior or taste in anybody he believed in; and it was self-evident that he understood the hesitance of a person like me to write derivatively of myself. When I had been at work on *Lena Geyer* for some months I found myself in trouble, and Max wrote to me:

"It is the good book that gives a writer trouble. You do not like to call this book fiction, and there is no need of doing it, but when I read the Mozart, it did seem to me very plainly to indicate that you could write fiction. And certainly, that you could write such a book as this one. So don't lose courage."

It was at about this time that Louise Perkins persuaded Max to try living in town, which she had wanted for years to do. He was full of protest at the idea, and appalled at changing his habits, but I wonder if he did not finally consent because Tom Wolfe preempted so much of his time, keeping him in town anyway. He gave in to his wife and they bought a house in Turtle Bay, almost directly across Forty-ninth Street from my mother's house, and next door to my old friend Katharine Hepburn. Louise engaged a fashionable interior decorator to do up the town house and invited me to dine there as soon as they had moved in. Max came home to the new house, bringing Tom Wolfe with him. The drawing-room was very elegant and highly stylized, with swagged turquoise blue silk draperies, decorative wall panels—and not a book in sight. Max looked utterly miserable, like a displaced person. Wolfe looked stranger still. His enormous bulk, blundering around that pretty room, cautiously settling into a dainty chair with a whopping drink in his ham of a hand, was a sight to remember.

The absence of books in that room pivoted on the famous story of which there are several versions, but mine is the one I had from Max himself at the time he was upheaved from New Canaan. Partly because he was against the whole idea, partly because he was preoccupied, he paid no attention to Louise's preparations to move. But the first time he came into the newly arranged New York house he ignored the decorations, the changed furniture, and the rest of it. He took one hard look and asked, "Where are my books?"

He meant specifically his collection of first editions of Scribner books by some of the most distinguished authors of the twentieth century, inscribed to him by Galsworthy, Barrie, Fitzgerald, Boyd, Hemingway, and all the others. Louise, finding that there was no room for them in the town house, had sold the lot to a second-hand dealer for twenty-five cents apiece. "Women!" was what Max said to me about it, but he ground out the word through clenched teeth. The books were retrieved one by one, as I remember the story, with Max paying their current price, but this is not the version related by Malcolm Cowley in the profile of Max that he wrote for *The New Yorker*. There he says that David Randall of Scribners' rare-book department got the books back by a genteel bit of blackmail, suggesting to the dealer that the books could have been sold him by a dishonest housekeeper and might get him into trouble if they were found to be stolen goods.

I finished the first draft of *Lena Geyer* at seven o'clock in the morning of February 4th, 1936, having stayed up writing all night. I had done the same thing with my first book, and I did it as a talisman through several more. In each case I took the manuscript to Max Perkins at four o'clock on the same afternoon, which meant that my typist had been keeping up with me day by day and that she typed the final pages—my own originals are undecipherable—while I slept through the morning. There is much about all this that I do not remember, but I do remember taking that manuscript to Max, shaking with trepidation and sure that I had made a hopeless mess. The manuscript was in two thick binders and I laid these on the edge of his desk. I suppose I was so tired that the actual happenings were a blur; and they took place thirty years ago. I cannot remember a word that was spoken, but I can still vividly see Max putting aside the top binder, picking up the bottom one, and turning it over to open it at the last page. He read the final paragraph, curiously enough with a slight moving of his lips as though silently reading aloud. I sat and watched him and I saw him nod. His approval was plain, but I was still half-sick with suspense. It was a Tuesday and I knew he would not have read the whole manuscript until after the following weekend, but when I was out in the street I began to walk round the block, east on Forty-eighth Street, north on Madison Avenue, back on Forty-ninth Street to Fifth Avenue; and I kept walking round and round that block, I have no idea how many times. It was as if I thought he might have scanned through the book in that short time, and followed me out to the street to tell me that it was no good after all and not fit to publish.

As a matter of fact it was the book about which he made the fewest suggestions, he said because of the peculiar technicality of the musical material about which he knew little. As a novel it was and is faulty. But neither Max nor I could have found a way to surmount the basic problem—the interweaving of factual and historical settings and personalities with the fictitious ones who were the protagonists of the story. It seemed to me preposterous to attempt to create an imaginary opera house in any of the cities where the action took place; why contrive names for the Hofoper or the Metropolitan, or for dozens of instantly recognizable musical and historical personalities upon whom the authenticity of the book depended, and with whom I neither wished nor needed to take any liberties? What I did, in effect, was write a history of the Golden Age of opera in Berlin, Paris, Vienna, and New York; and superpose on it the central figure of Lena Geyer and the individuals through and with whom her musical and personal life was lived. At the time I was writing the book I was saturated in the milieu, beyond lifetime knowledge of it through my mother. Lotte Lehmann was my intimate friend; I was up to my eyes in the Metropolitan, the Vienna and Salzburg operas, and all the musical events where every critic had to be; and I was writing from inside the emotions and the body of deeply-experienced knowledge.

Who is Lena Geyer? The question rained on me in hundreds of letters when the book was published in the autumn of 1936; and with persistence but in diminishing quantity, the rain has continued ever since. Some people insist she is one or another of the great singers of her time, and a surprising number insist that a singer named Lena Geyer really existed, and that they or their parents heard her sing. I was very busy in those years. I had my pages to write for *Stage* every month; I wrote many articles on musical subjects for other periodicals; I collaborated with Russell Davenport on several *Fortune* articles where I was useful; in Salzburg in the summer of 1936, I was the commentator when the National Broadcasting Company for the first time broadcast the opera performances to the United States; in the winter of 1936–37 I talked (ad nauseam, in my opinion) in all the intermissions of the Metropolitan Opera broadcasts; and I answered my mail about Lena Geyer with variations of what my mother used to call a bedbug letter—the Pullman Company's form letter in reply to a certain complaint.

Lena Geyer is not my mother, and I have been enraged by statements that she is, or that the book is "the story of my mother's life." With the exception of two isolated instances which I have cited in this book, and a minor parallel concerning choices of music sung in concert, there is no element of my mother in Lena Geyer. Lena Geyer is what I believe a sound fictitious character should be. She is about half a composite of prototypes, and half sheer imagination. The prototypes are nine or ten of the supreme dramatic sopranos of musical history and the imagination is mine own. Elements suggested by the musical accomplishments or the private lives of the prototypes have been taken as I felt they fitted into the character, and blended together. The private life of Lena Geyer is fiction out of whole cloth, but some threads of the cloth are drawn from the prototypes. Anybody who knows the history of opera can name the prototypes. The element that has a true origin in a single person is the voice, the capacity of the artist to sing the repertoire she did, and the model is Lilli Lehmann. I never heard Lilli Lehmann sing, but I do possess the phenomenal gramophone records that she made late in life,

Alma Gluck, 1913

Myself, about two years old

With my mother in Como, 1907

Tam at work, 1942

My mother in 1928, at the age of forty-four

Maxwell E. Perkins in his office

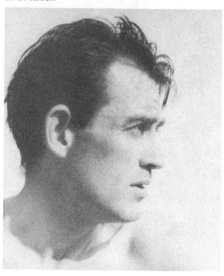

Russell W. Davenport in 1940   Wendell L. Willkie in 1940

Maestro rehearsing the Schubert C major Symphony, No. 9; 1941

Prague: the Charles Bridge and the fortress Hradčany

Old roofs

Jan Masaryk: Prague, 1946

aged between fifty-six and sixty. Technically she was probably
unequalled in the whole history of singing; but I conceived of
Lena Geyer's voice as having had more physical size and splendor,
more warmth, and more dramatic coloration than Lilli Lehmann's.

But I had one insuperable problem. I wrote and rewrote, cut
up the manuscript and the character, used every device I knew of
or dared to invent; I could not solve it. In March, when I was
revising the manuscript and Max Perkins was doing what he could
to help, I wrote to him:

> "As for Vestri, he is a wooden Indian, he leaks sawdust, he drops
> the whole book, he invalidates Lena, his joints creak, most of the
> time he has only one dimension, the rest of the time he does not
> materialize at all. Oh my God."

No wonder. Unless I could recreate the authenticity of the
seven years between 1908 and 1915 when Maestro at the Metropolitan made operatic history that has no parallel, there was no
book. At the same time I would not write a fictitious mock-up of
Maestro himself. I did what other and better writers have done
in analogous situations. I put a conductor in the opera house and
in musical relation to Lena Geyer, giving him such powers as
would evoke the quality of performance that really existed, and
in sketching the man personally I deliberately contradicted each
and every attribute and feature that could have been ascribed to
Arturo Toscanini. A clumsy business, and one that made me
heartsick, because I had to accustom myself to living with the
sophistry that this was not Maestro, and in all truth it was not
Maestro as I knew him and saw him in increasing warmth and
ease of friendship. Worst of all was my knowledge that he trusted
me both as a writer and as a friend. As a writer about music he
expected me to do my work accurately and conscientiously. Whatever I wrote about his performances or about him as a musician
was what I was supposed to do and he knew I would do it scrupu-

lously. He used to say that he never read the reviews of music critics. I assumed this was true, and it made my job easier. He did not even object when I asked him before the 1936 Salzburg season if he preferred I not speak on the opera broadcasts to the United States. He had no objection although he was sceptical, if not hostile, to the whole idea of broadcasting; only in very recent years had he consented to let the Sunday concerts of the Philharmonic be broadcast, and to make records with the orchestra.

But about himself as a man—that was a different matter. Time and again he said he would never forgive any friend of his if that person wrote about him as a man or a personality or in any way used the elements of personal friendship as literary material during his lifetime. Maestro knew perfectly well that he was a historical figure and that much would be written about him biographically and reminiscently; "but not while I am alive," he said, and he meant it as a condition of his friendship and confidence. The exaction lay heaviest on me because I did not need the admonition.

He had said that the winter of 1935–36 would be his last year as conductor of the Philharmonic and we who were most devoted to him really believed he would be leaving New York for good, except perhaps for a guest appearance now and then. We had no way of divining the future. So we had more reason than ever not to miss a concert or a rehearsal, and I never did. Every week there were three concerts, repetitions of the same programme, and some weeks a fourth, on Saturday night. It was this heavy schedule of repetitions that was one of his reasons for leaving the Philharmonic, though he was moved by other factors too. On his sixty-ninth birthday he played his last Pension Fund concert, one of the all-Wagner programmes which marked so many special occasions, and on the 29th of April his farewell concert, one of the most emotional public scenes I remember in my entire life. I dined with George Gershwin beforehand and we joined my mother and her party in her box. An audience which stood in tribute to Maestro when he entered the hall was more or less routine, but that audience stood, refusing to leave the hall after the concert, for what seemed like half an hour, most of the people openly in tears.

In the present day any opera or symphony orchestra performance in New York, including rotten ones, elicits shouts and bravos and an indiscriminate uproar which is nothing but evidence that a part of the audience considers this behavior its right of participation in the show. Contemporary ovations are not spontaneously evoked by inspired performance or superlative artistry or a genuine musical experience. They have taken the meaning out of audience response, they are a perfunctory noise made by a mob which may like music but has no standards. In Maestro's time the public did not give out with the same shouting uproar every time he appeared, just because he was he. If he played music that bored them such as works by Castelnuovo-Tedesco or Martucci the audiences responded with a little polite clapping. But when it was a great occasion, an all-Wagner programme or the Ninth Symphony, and later when he did opera in concert form with the N B C Symphony, the audiences demonstrated in a way which stays sharp in memory and is never drowned out by the meaningless pandemonium of the present day. And when he played the Verdi *Requiem* the response was more moving still in deference to his wishes. There was no applause at all. There was a long pause after the final hushed notes, in which one had the feeling that everybody was holding his breath and then, knowing that Maestro would not return to the stage, the audience would silently get up and leave.

When I arrived in Salzburg in July Maestro was beginning the *Meistersinger* rehearsals. I used to think as I watched him at the most exhaustive and exacting labor I have ever seen how he had said at the age of sixty that he was too old to conduct opera any longer, and at almost seventy that he was too old for the

Philharmonic; but three months after that retirement he was driving himself and the huge complex of elements in *Die Meistersinger* with the energy of a man of thirty, and a demonic one besides. After the preparatory work with the singers, and the first orchestra rehearsals, the stage rehearsals began. There was no detail of the production that did not get his minute attention and show the effects of his insistence on perfection. He was all over the place. He stayed in his pit so long as the work went to his satisfaction. If not, if he wanted a change on the stage in action, lighting, setting, business (the riot in the second act!) he was up on the stage. Sometimes we heard his hoarse voice call "Graf!" from the dark back of the theatre where he had run to see how the scene looked in perspective; and he did see no matter what he insisted about his own poor eyesight or what legend has said of it. Herbert Graf, the stage director, and all the company slaved for him. Lotte was the Eva, a part she had never liked much, but this time she had potent reason to change her mind. The rehearsals culminated in the historic dress rehearsal which has been cited time and again as one of the great moments of operatic history. It was a performance in which every participant was genuinely inspired. It went without a flaw from beginning to end. As I think of the Prelude, which Maestro played so often in concert, I wonder now how the whole opera which followed it could have gone on, building and rising in tension and excitement from that level, but it did. We who heard that rehearsal —and saw it, because the memory of Maestro in his black cassock-like rehearsal coat with the light on his face remains as vivid as on that day—were overwhelmed with emotion. But when the curtain fell on the finale, and then went up again as curtains do at rehearsals for technical reasons, there stood the entire company on stage, every one of them in tears. Maestro himself stood motionless in his place with his right hand covering his eyes. I do not know what may have lain in the hearts of those singers and musicians but I have often sensed that for some of them this was their defiant defence of their German heritage in the face of the obscenities across the frontier.

It is surprising to remember how much time there seemed to be for enjoying ourselves. Maestro was usually in high spirits and some of us gathered in Salzburg were his closest friends from New York. Chotzie and Pauline were nominally his house-guests, but since the Liefering villa was crammed to the roof with Toscaninis and their relations, the Chotzinoffs put up in the *Fremdenzimmer* of a nearby peasant's house whose dairy-farmer proprietor kept the classic and valuable dung-heap in his front yard. He also if I remember rightly made a very smelly cheese. His neighbors in the village were the locals whose shop-signs were *Mölkerei, Metzgerei, Wäscherei,* and so forth. We called the Chotzies' lodgings the Dreckerei, and we used to stumble up the stairs holding our noses and screaming with laughter. They ate their meals at the Toscaninis' or wherever we all met in town. Alfred and Virginia Wallenstein were there—he had been Maestro's first-desk 'cellist at the Philharmonic and then proceeded to eminence as a conductor himself; and there was a passing parade of other old friends. Between rehearsals and other engagements we had a check-point at a certain table in the Café Bazar where we stopped to gossip or make plans.

I must have been the only one who was not wholly on vacation, because I have the cables I sent after each performance to *Stage,* and notes for the material on six broadcasts about which I remember nothing else. But I am astonished at my own temerity at doing the spoken introductions to *Fidelio, Falstaff,* and *Die Meistersinger.* At least I have the satisfaction of knowing that if my superlatives about them at that time might have been thought extreme, thirty years later there is no doubt whatever that those were the definitive performances of the three works and that nothing comparable has ever been heard since. Sometimes a separate element has been finer, such as the N B C Symphony instead of the Vienna Philharmonic, or a certain singer in some part. But only Maestro gave us the experiences which told us: this is the ultimate, this is the most authentic you will ever hear; remember it and hold it as the standard.

With all that going on I was not thinking about my novel which was to be published in September. And a very curious veil has intervened to confuse me. I cannot remember nor does my red book for 1936 tell me where it was I saw Maestro late in that year. It could not have been in New York because he did not come that autumn or winter as he had done for ten years past. It could have been in London. Anyway, it was not long after the novel had been published. It never occurred to me that he had seen it, which was a fatuous idea because of his insatiable curiosity. But I was at a large evening party for Maestro and the moment we met I began to quake. I do not remember whether he kissed me as usual, but I suppose not, for his face was cold and like a stranger's. He was in a towering rage and I knew why. I wondered with despair how he had come by a copy of the book. (Harold Holt, the London concert manager, had sent it to him.)

"Tu!" he said, and though I translate them, the words he actually spoke burn much hotter on the page. *"Che brutto pasticcio hai fatto, tu?"* (You! What kind of ugly hodge-podge have you made?) He had turned aside from the people and separated himself with me in a corner. I was sick with terror. I tried to say, "It isn't you . . . believe me . . ."

"No!" he said. I had never heard him speak so harshly. "It is not me. This fake, this charlatan"—*pagliaccio* was the word he used—"this Vestri. It is not me, not at all. *Vergogna!* Shame on you!"

I was in tears and I wonder that I dared say anything more. If Maestro turned on a person in anger it was almost surely the end, but I suppose I was too desperate to reckon with that. I did say, "Don't you see what the problem was? Maestro, what was I to do? You know the man himself has no resemblance to you."

"You had a problem, yes," he said. "But a novel should be

a work of art, a work of the imagination. If you are not skilful enough to create a whole imaginary world you should not write novels. You are a bad artist. You made a *pasticcio,* you tried to mix a story with reality. You are not an artist," he said. "Not at all."

And raising his heavy hand he struck me lightly across the cheek and turned away. It was not a real blow, it was a gesture, it hurt only in meaning. He did not really intend to strike me and long afterwards he insisted he had never done such a thing and said I had imagined it. Of all people he was the one whose hands most vividly conveyed what he wanted to say. That was the essence of it. And when it was past, it was past. When I next saw him I had been forgiven. He never mentioned the novel again, and I found to my surprise that as I sent him the later books I wrote he read them word for word. I heard nothing more about the bad artist but when Maestro taught a lesson, one had learnt it.

I had a strange experience on the ship returning to New York. I have always been a congenital seasick, and when transatlantic flying began I was released from a private hell. I have never crossed by ship since. In the ship days I used to stay in bed in my cabin for the whole voyage, reading two or three books a day, since I was only comfortable lying flat. Once in a while if the sea was dead calm I might venture on deck for a breath of air and a short walk. That was what I was doing when a huge figure barged up to me with a boisterous greeting. It was Tom Wolfe.

"Come and have a drink before lunch," he said.

I could not tell him I was afraid I would be sick shut up in the ship's bar, and since my only link with Wolfe was Max Perkins I had no idea of ducking. Wolfe wanted to talk. He always wanted to talk, and his talk was a river in flood exactly like his books. The subject was himself, only and always. We sat down at a corner table at right angles to each other, Wolfe ordered drinks and began to talk. Five hours later we were still sitting there. Lunch was ignored, Wolfe had God knows how many drinks, I had the little which is all I ever want, and I have no memory of whether I felt sick or tired, or in fact, of anything except of rage and outrage. We had a quarrel which lasted all day.

Wolfe began with his German love-affair in Munich, which had ended, but he was both truculent and defensive about the Nazi setting in which it had taken place. I told him there was no excuse for falling for anything German after the onset of Hitler and his filth. Yes, said Wolfe, he too now saw that Germany had put itself beyond the pale and he was going to show that in his next book; it was written already. Then came the crux of what was on his mind. Obviously I cannot remember verbatim the long stream of his talk but the core of it was his intention to prove that he was not, as he claimed the literary world believed, the creature of Max Perkins. They all said that Wolfe could not have written his books without Perkins, that Perkins was his Svengali, that Wolfe was nothing but confusion of himself and would never have published a book but for Perkins. Wolfe said, his loose lower lip dithering and his eyes wild, "I'm going to show them I can write my books without Max. I'm going to leave Max and get another editor. I'm going to leave Scribners."

"How about the dedication in your last book?" I said. "Are you that much of a hypocrite?"

Only the year before he had dedicated *Of Time and the River* to Max in words of such emotional extravagance that Max was distressed. He was also touched by Wolfe's tribute but he said many times that he would never have allowed the dedication to be printed had he had the chance to see it. Wolfe took care that he should not.

Wolfe returned to his diatribe, ignoring my scornful remarks. He said that Max had kept some of the best parts out of that last book. He fulminated about other details that I have forgotten. Over and over he said he had to get away from Max. I said, "I think you're a rat. You're ungrateful and treacherous. That dedication was disgusting. It didn't mean devotion to Max, it was just spilling yourself. You have no devotion and no loyalty either. Where would you be without Max, and Scribners too? You can't face the truth."

This is a difficult thing to reconstruct because it is almost impossible to clear my mind of the mass of comment about the matter when Wolfe did leave Scribners and after his death in 1938, leaving Max Perkins his executor with the tragic duty of seeing Wolfe's last two novels through publication under the editorship of Edward Aswell of Harpers. At the time Wolfe was talking to me I knew nothing about his unpublished work or his current relations with Max or in fact, anything except that Max believed passionately in Wolfe's talent and cared for him personally more than for any other writer and friend. I could not bear to have Max hurt. I did not think Wolfe the genius which some, but by no means all, of literary opinion acclaimed him. I had many reservations about his work and more about him; but I tried to separate the man from his books. Tom Wolfe made that separating difficult. His books were himself and nothing but himself.

I knew how much Tom Wolfe and his work meant to Max, but of course I had then never seen Max's letters which have since been published and which attest this poignantly. I only learned after Wolfe's departure the vastness of Max's generosity of mind and heart, and the selflessness which he showed by insisting he cared most of all that Wolfe should fulfill himself as a writer by whatever means he found necessary. If that meant severing his relation with Max in order to prove himself and write his books, then that was what Max wanted. So Max said; and I never knew a man more scrupulously honest.

None of this could I know when Wolfe sat all those hours doggedly reiterating his egotistic obsessions and his intentions to

jettison Max. I replied by castigating him for treachery, ingrati-
tude, insincerity, and disloyalty. How could I know that this was
not the position Max would have had me take? I made no impression on Wolfe. He had seized on me as the nearest sounding-
board; he was really talking to himself. I never saw him again.

CHAPTER TEN

WHEN we lived in Vermont we used to go over to Barnard to see Dorothy Thompson and Red Lewis at Twin Farms. Occasionally they came to us. In the flood of talk around the table there was one word which glares in my memory like an airport beacon. The word is IT. It was Red's word. He sat at the head of his table, wanting if he was in a good mood and relatively sober, to be a genial host. At times he could be a very entertaining man. He had a talent for extemporizing rhymed verse, doggerel, but amazing. He would tell a long burlesque story of some foolery like a village maiden wronged and spin it out in a twanging chant, all rhymed lines, which streamed from him without a pause. He liked to entertain an audience and in his own house he never had a chance. At Dorothy's end of the table there was always a clutch of Central European politicians or intellectuals, and some of her own colleagues. Their talk would rise in a heavy swell, louder and increasingly impassioned, until it broke over Red like a wave, the spume a froth of idiomatic German which he did not understand. He would take several of these breakers, his thin scarred red face twisting with boredom and frustration. Suddenly he would shout, "Goddamit, can't you ever stop talking about IT?" And kicking back his chair he would storm out of the room.

IT was the world situation, particularly in Europe. IT was Dorothy's overriding passion. She talked about IT too much, too vehemently, she monopolized too much conversation. But she was seldom wrong. Her clear, penetrating voice in excited talk came

to be called breast-beating and she herself Cassandra. She was a
primary force in rousing this country to the dangers and horrors
of Nazism; Britain too, some say, but rather too late. She was indeed the High Priestess of IT, as Red called her. But one did not
need to be Dorothy to be aware of what was happening.

I had much too close a view in Austria. It was widely said of
the impoverished nobility whose castles—rented out or full of
paying guests—were scattered through the Salzkammergut that
most of them were Nazis at heart, but how could this be surprising
when they had been pressing for Anschluss with Germany ever
since 1919? The peasants and ordinary townspeople, tradesmen
and working folk, were mad for Hitler. He was one of them, born
in a small Austrian town and formed by the same forces that had
shaped them. Only in Vienna was there opposition from the
Socialist working class and from the whole intellectual and artistic
articulation of the country, largely Jews. I should have sensed that
1937 would be the last year of Salzburg. There was an under-
current of alarming rumors about the activities of the Austrian
Nazis, but people wanted not to believe it, just as many wanted
not to keep their sights on the Spanish Civil War which my
political and journalist friends were already calling a dress rehearsal.

That summer of 1937 I had taken the ground floor of a small
house with a garden on the edge of town, and a maid came with it.
There was something sly about her and I did not trust her. I perceived that my possessions and the papers in my desk were gone
through when I was out, but the woman was not a thief, nothing
was stolen. She was sullen and grudging, unusual in an Austrian,
especially one who is being paid a generous bonus by a foreigner.
I did not sleep well in that house, and after I woke several times
in the small hours, only shortly after going to bed because we all
stayed up late, I realized it was not restlessness that disturbed me,
it was something I heard. I began to listen as I lay awake. The

maid did not sleep in the house, she lived nearby with her husband who worked, she said, in the post office. I had thought I was alone. I believed I heard whispers and something like the clink of crockery. I got up, turned on all the lights, and went and threw open the kitchen door. The maid was there, serving a meal to a man who sat at the kitchen table. He wore a black leather jacket and a motorcyclist's helmet, with goggles pushed up on his forehead. He did not stand up and the maid eyed me defiantly.

"What's going on here?" I asked.

"This is my husband," she said.

"And I am feeding him?—at four o'clock in the morning?"

"The post office works at night."

"On motorcycles? I never see them around here. You must be one of those Nazi messengers that go back and forth to Rosenheim at night," I said to the man. This was the kind of tale we had been hearing and not wanting to believe. He did not answer. His wife slammed something down. I fetched my purse. I had enough cash to pay her for the whole time I had taken the place and I gave it to her and said, "Give me the keys you have and get out."

"I work for Frau X," she said, the owner of the house whose name I have forgotten.

"I'll speak to her tomorrow," I said. "She can take you back if she wants to after I've gone. I won't have Nazis in the house."

"What do you think everybody is in Salzburg?" the woman shouted. "Everybody! You foreigners with your money, you think we want you here? No. Soon we won't have rotten foreigners any more. *'Raus! 'Raus* with you! *'Raus* with you dirty Americans and Jews! *Ein Volk, ein Reich, ein Führer!*" she screamed. "*Wir wollen heim ins Reich!*"

I thought of sending for the police, the polite smiling police who cleared the way for the celebrities' cars and held back the townspeople who crowded the pavements to watch the famous foreigners. And I knew that every policeman in Salzburg must be like this couple, probably the leaders of Nazi cells, which was exactly what the police proved to be.

Except for my friends and the music, Salzburg was horrible after that and I spent as much time as I could in Prague and roving the Bohemian countryside. I never went up to the northwest corner of the country, the Sudetenland where Konrad Henlein was already laying the groundwork for the tragedy of Munich. I was not informed politically, I knew nobody in such circles, and my impressions were all personal ones absorbed through the pores of my attachment to the country. I did not need reportage and documentation to tell me that the Czechs were different from the Austrians. I loved the valley of the river Vltava, the country between Ceské Budějovice, Tyn, and Tábor, the town of Jan Hus, beautiful in architecture and spirit and tradition. The village of Hluboká and the lands all round it, the ancestral lands of the Schwarzenbergs, fascinated me for reasons which never became apparent until I found them at my fingers' ends four years later when they took their place in *The Valley of Decision*. Long ago I stopped wondering why I have felt impelled towards certain places and compelled to burrow through them like an earthworm. I have learned to know that this is a blind instinct which will not reveal its purpose until I am ready to write about it and I may not be ready for a discouraging length of time.

That year Russell Davenport was appointed managing editor of *Fortune*. The long leaves of absence and intermittent spells of work came to an end, and he had only a short vacation when he came to join me for the last week of Salzburg. Then we went to France to a glorious adventure through the Côte d'Or in the company of the late Henry Hollis, once a Senator from New Hampshire, once a teetotaller who had never been in Europe in his life until, already elderly, he went on a holiday to Paris— and never left it. He had a natural palate for wine, discovered and respected by some of the great growers of France. He became one of the foremost judges and experts of wine and was a fascinating person to dine with, to listen to, and to learn from.

With him we visited the vineyards of the Côte de Nuits, that unbelievable slope of stony hillside on the right side of Route 74, the road from Dijon to Beaune. He knew all the proprietors and growers, the *vignerons* and *cavistes,* he was welcomed with open arms and open bottles, and we trailed along, learning, marvelling, and savoring the wonderful experience of seeing legends come to life. Each name was a step in a pilgrimage through the lore and the delights of wine. We visited historic vineyards and cellars at Gevrey-Chambertin, Chambolle-Musigny, and Vougeot, and finally we arrived at the Domaine de la Romanée-Conti. It was a beautiful early September afternoon with hot sunshine and richness in the air, some weeks before the vendange. The grapes were heavy on the vines, small and dark with a dusty bloom. The maître of the Domaine was an old, handsome man in a blue work blouse with a chain round his neck with a tasting-cup hanging from it. He had calm, wise peasant eyes in a brown wrinkled face, a long-winged moustache, and a courtly manner. He showed us the difference between the vines of Richebourg, grafted to American stock after the phylloxera, and the tiny plot of Richebourg Vieux Cépages, still at that time growing on its original native stock. He watched us gazing dumbstruck at the most valuable piece of cultivated land in the world, the four acres of Romanée-Conti itself, which shows no visible difference from all the vineyards round it. He only shook his head when asked the question he must have heard to satiation all his life: why? What explained it? *"C'est le sous-sol, Madame."*

He took us to the cellars where they were bottling La Tache of the vintage of 1935. "It is not ready to drink," he said, although he himself tasted the wine from the cask, and invited Senator Hollis to do so, "but it will be a *grand vin, un vrai grand vin.* It will have a very long life."

How right he was. I opened the last bottle of mine, the last of many cases that Senator Hollis sent us until the war, less than six months ago. I ought not to have kept it so long, but who can bear to open such wine for anyone not truly capable of appreciating it?—and the ranks have thinned. Besides, I had kept it as a curiosity. The wine was extraordinary. The cork was sound. The mighty bouquet, which once used to fill the room when the wine was poured, had faded to a shadow. The color was more mahogany than ruby. But the wine, at thirty years of age, was pure silk velvet. It was all there, filling the senses with magnificence and my mind with some of the best memories of long ago.

Life became very different when Russell was responsible for every issue of *Fortune* instead of for a single story whenever he wanted to work on one. The intervals between stints at *Fortune* had been filled in theory by writing of his own. He had had a long poem in progress for years, and pieces of prose manuscript, all kept together in one battered black binder. But whenever he took a leave of absence from *Fortune* the bulk of his time went into something so egregious, to any opinion but his own, as manual labor in Vermont or six months devoted to an exhaustive project in astrology, in which he firmly believed. Russell was a brilliant man and he possessed the faculty of holding the confidence of people who wanted to believe in him, even when he was doing something that appeared quite mad. If you could hold on long enough, through periods of apparent confusion or irresponsibility or absurdity, you might find that he would emerge ready for some remarkable accomplishment. He was a visionary, but his vision, which concerned this country and its fate and force in the world, was something weightier both in realism, the knowledge of the essential United States, and in idealism, the heritage of his preaching New England ancestors, than the spectacle we are in the world today.

With the permission of my old friend, John K. Jessup of the editorial board of *Life,* I am quoting his description of Russell

Davenport's editorship of *Fortune*. Jack Jessup wrote this as part of the biographical sketch which prefaced *The Dignity of Man*, the posthumous book compiled from Russell's unfinished work after his lamentably early death in 1954. There is no better description of Russell at work than Jessup's, and I feel that this colleague's view of him is both objective and authentic. Jessup describes Russell's decision to accept the managing editorship as the outcome of a weekend, mournfully taken to decide between the old manuscript and the new job. The decision had been made easier by the fact that he had lost the manuscript, binder and all. (He had more than lost it, he had left it in a taxi; and when I began to commiserate with him and suggest we try to trace it, he said, "Hell, it's a relief.")

Jessup writes, "Davenport was in important ways the best managing editor *Fortune* ever had; in unimportant, the worst. As an executive, he was a fountain of anarchy, indecision, and disorder. He inherited a small staff of able and somewhat pampered writers and researchers who were used to a good deal of autonomy in fulfilling their assignments. Davenport took this machine apart and put it together again, and also doubled its size. . . . his editorial antennae, so readily agitated by remote inscrutabilities, often led him to change signals in mid-story; and in view of his noon-to-midnight working habits, there was not always time or occasion for him to make the signals clear to his staff. In the resulting crises he sometimes rewrote whole stories himself overnight, offending the writers and researchers who considered themselves responsible. Before he had been in office a year the researchers drew up an all but unanimous protest against his methods.

"He surmounted this brief uprising by a long, candid memorandum and by the personal charm with which he could solve any problem of human relations, once he was reminded that he had one. He was always ready and able to talk anything out with anybody, when there was time. But a shortage of time, whether real or manufactured, was an indispensable working condition for Davenport. No other managing editor found it necessary to maintain a permanent night shift of typists and proofreaders. None went so often on emergency trips to the printer's in Jersey City on closing nights, or made so many changes of copy at the eleventh hour. Sometimes he went there direct from the opera, in full dress, black cape, and crushed black hat from his Paris days; sometimes, if time really pressed, he dictated direct to the linotypers. When the last proof was read, he and his exhausted help would roar back through the Holland Tunnel and sleeping Manhattan in his big Chrysler, and he would reach his apartment at East End Avenue at dawn."

The personal side of what Jessup calls Russell's "chronic crisis and disorder" was an existence charged with the same explosives. It was stimulating and exciting, too exciting since it precipitated an endless series of domestic crises reverberating from those he detonated at *Fortune.* Those all-night sessions of dictating to the linotypers were followed by late-sleeping mornings and noon-time breakfasts in a dining-room knee-deep in newspapers, manuscripts, proofs, telephone wires, and cigarette-ends. Charlotte, who had been with us long enough to weather everything else, gave out under the stress, and I had two or three years of struggle with a revolving door through which trooped uncountable cooks, maids, and housemen. Nobody would stay because, they said, nobody could keep up with Mr. Davenport's day-long demands for coffee, tea, milk, soup; for three o'clock lunch, ten o'clock dinner, and his room never free for cleaning until the end of the day. Bells rang day and night, the telephone all the time, the doorbell with messengers, his room while he stayed in it in a fug of tobacco-smoke, doing his best work there while his writers and researchers tore their hair at the office.

But the end product of all this uproar was memorably excellent. I took an anonymous part in it, sometimes unofficially, and sometimes paid by the powers that were. I was between books, that wrung-out state of self-perpetuating paralysis, and when Russell had an article in work in which some special knowledge or aptitude of mine could be put to use, he used it. I suppose the *Fortune* staffers were irked by this too, but I found them wonderful colleagues on the occasions when I worked with them. Jessup notes that Russell turned the *Fortune* searchlight on a series of "opaque subjects" which in fact were all part of a prescient study of changing social mores; on the organization of the Vatican; and how unionization came to Big Steel. As a result of the latter I was to find out some years later how greatly I benefited by Russell's friendly relations with Philip Murray, Clinton Golden, and other labor statesmen of Big Steel. As a beginning to the Vatican story Russell was invited to lunch in private with Cardinal Hayes at his residence. Naturally I wanted to hear all about the meeting, but Russell only said, "Gee, I never tasted such sherry in my life."

Early in 1937 the American musical world was electrified by the announcement that Maestro Toscanini would return to New York at the end of the year to conduct a new orchestra to be formed for him by the National Broadcasting Company. His departure from the Philharmonic had left a dreary void. I am aware that there were mutterings in some circles which held that certain orchestra politicians and personalities were relieved to have him go. I know some of the motives which prompted the mutterings. It has been said elsewhere too that Maestro in the long run had a bad effect on orchestras, that after he had left them the men deliberately sagged from the extreme discipline he imposed on them (and on himself even more) and never played so well again. I do not consider steady mediocrity preferable to perfection in the rare instances when that can be attained. But I am not an orchestra player. Without Maestro the joy went out of concert-going for me and I had less appetite for my duties as a music critic. And I missed him, missed the feast of rehearsals and concerts every week, the frequent visits and parties, the cracked voice on the telephone ringing up to chat and gossip. The news about his return was a surprise to everybody except the few of us who had been concerned in its making, but nobody foresaw that this would be the longest continuous tenure of his long career, that it would carry us through the war years and another decade, and leave the priceless legacy of most of his repertoire on records. The creation of the N B C Symphony was an unprecedented departure in American corporate affairs. Any major broadcasting company had a house orchestra, but the N B C had promised Maestro the finest symphony orchestra that could be assembled.

The idea was David Sarnoff's, and the feat of persuading Maestro to return to New York to conduct the new radio orchestra was pulled off by Chotzie. I was the small but functional insect, the connecting link. Chotzie wrote an account of his experience in a book about Maestro in 1956, and there is no reason to quote here what is widely known. The origin of these narrations was a dinner-party, shortly after Maestro had left the Philharmonic, when David Sarnoff asked just why the public had such fanatical admiration for Maestro and why he was considered the greatest conductor in the world. Sarnoff was in no doubt about these phenomena, but he demanded they be documented for his shrewd analytical mind. I undertook to answer his questions and the talk went on to what a calamity it was for the American public no longer to be able to hear Maestro, in person, or on the Sunday afternoon broadcasts of the Philharmonic. Maestro, who had not yet been persuaded of the virtues of reproduced music either in recording or broadcasting, had been indifferent about the Sunday afternoons, but it was the broadcasting aspect of the matter which visibly challenged David Sarnoff. He threw out like a bait the speculation that symphony concerts could be played expressly for the radio. Great symphony concerts, he went on, expanding to the notion. "Why—suppose you had Toscaninny"—so he pronounced it—"to conduct them!"

This was an intoxicating idea, but what in the world could be done about it? Maestro had said he would never again be the

permanent conductor of any orchestra. His mind was closed to reproduced music because his ears, attuned to perfection, could not
accept the imperfections of radio reproduction as it had been
up to then. We who knew him knew what an immovable
object his made-up mind was. But David Sarnoff did not know
him, and eventually he asked me who, if anybody, might be the
person to send to Milan on the risky mission of trying to persuade
Maestro to return and conduct what was then a hypothetical
orchestra. I suggested Chotzie. Sarnoff had never met him either.
Chotzie was then the music critic of *The New York Post,* but he
had been saying for some time that what he would really like would
be somehow to get into broadcasting. He had the vision to foresee
that radio (television was still far in the future) would be a tremendous factor in the musical life of this country. It was like
Chotzie to have such an idea and also no notion of a way to implement it. He was by temperament an artist, impractical, quixotic,
lazy, and subject to the intense enthusiasms—also dislikes—without which real taste and appreciation do not exist. I hoped that
something might come of introducing Chotzie to David Sarnoff, so
I had them and their wives and some other people to dine and the
two men, in heredity and instinct cut from the same piece of cloth,
hit it off immediately.

Chotzie recounts how he was eased part-time into the National Broadcasting Company without knowing what he was going
to do there, and tells the story of his two shivering weeks in Milan
before he could drum up the nerve to explain his errand to
Maestro who by then was suspicious. It ended with Maestro's
astounding "Why not!" which marked his capitulation, and
Chotzie returned to New York to join Artur Rodzinski, Maestro's
choice for assistant conductor, in putting together the finest symphony orchestra that could be assembled. Bitterness and panic
swept through the nation's orchestra managements as first-desk
men were lured away; solo virtuosi and chamber-music players
eagerly came to audition; the jazz world contributed the finest

brass players in the United States; and when Maestro arrived in December he pronounced himself content after his first rehearsal with the new orchestra. As time went on he became strongly attached to the orchestra. He felt proprietary about it and spoke of it in words he never used about others such as La Scala about which he was sentimental; but he never put that or any other European orchestra in the class with the best American ones. He called the N B C *la mia orchestra, la mia bella orchestra.*

The first broadcast concert on Christmas night has been often and widely described, even to the programmes printed on white satin so that no rustle of paper would be picked up by the microphones. The invited audience, very gala indeed, in Studio 8 H of the N B C were a negligible fraction of the real audience listening on their radios, but I was so ecstatic that I remember only Maestro and the music he played. He played the Vivaldi Concerto Grosso in D minor, the Brahms First Symphony, and the Mozart G minor. It was of course the latter which moved me most and marked that particular concert with red letters in my lifelong memories of special performances that Maestro conducted, and their equally special associations. He had played the G minor at his farewell concert with the Philharmonic when we had believed we would not hear him again in New York, he played it to mark his return, and he played it many other times, when I would try to thank him because, in spite of his teasing, he knew what it meant to me. The most he ever said in reply was, *"Sciocca che sei!"* (Silly!)

Where I was silly was in failing to realize that broadcasting would eventually lead to the recording of most of Maestro's music. My husband and I were so determined to possess what we could of it that we undertook a surreptitious plan to have a commercial studio make recordings of every broadcast—at a cost I am ashamed to remember. We could not afford it but that was never a deterrent to something we counted really necessary. We kept the recordings a black secret on the principle that Maestro would have been furious had he known I was doing such a thing; and of all self-deluding follies, that was the most absurd. Countless numbers of other people were doing the same. The contraband acetate records would arrive each week in a bulky container. After a couple of seasons they overran the available storage space; and worst of all, they were faulty and inexpertly reproduced. We were royally swindled. By that time the first of Maestro's approved records with the orchestra were beginning to go on sale and I stopped the blood-letting. Years went by, the wonderful recorded repertoire steadily increased, and not until long after Maestro's death did I confess to my dear friend Walter, his son, that I had many hundreds of dollars' worth of illegal piratings hidden away, all a disgraceful botch.

"I must have them," he said. "There may be some fragment in them that I want to compare with other recordings taken off the air." In the Toscanini Archive at Riverdale he has every sound that was made in all the rehearsals and concerts of Maestro's years with the N B C Symphony—and much else besides. I loaded the mess into the trunk of my car and took it and thankfully dumped it on Walter.

I had a friend who was one of the editors of a magazine with a large circulation. She was a very strange woman—a freak by any measure. I met her through Carol Brandt, who had arranged with her for a number of articles I wrote about various aspects of the musical world. Her name was Mabel Search. To anyone who remembers her—she is long dead—the name recalls a stout, red-faced, loud-voiced woman with cropped dark hair and a violent temper. She dressed always in black and had the affectation of never wearing a coat, even in the coldest winter weather. She had an air of swaggering toughness which concealed a mass of eccentricities and emotional twists much better not fathomed—and I never tried. She was clever and able but so contentious that she quarrelled sooner or later with everybody.

Like other people I have known she had the idea that I might be lured more or less deviously into writing short stories, since I had never felt any direct impulse to try them. I have such respect for the serious short story that I have been too aware of its technical exactions to dare them; and the commercial short story has positively never been for me. One of the reasons why I respected Carl Brandt's judgement so implicitly was because he said to me thirty-five years ago, "Don't try to write magazine fiction, ever."

One day Mabel Search came to see me. She settled with a stiff drink and began to talk about an idea she said she was turning over in her head. It would be a character study of a person who would go through life with a collective ideal about a family, an ideal which would attribute to the family qualities better than they really had, and expect of them acts and attitudes superior to their own capacities. A subordinate person, an outsider, but one who would know all the members of this family better than anybody else could; somebody who would, in sum, become the conscience of the family.

"You would need to carry that through several generations to make it stand up," I said.

"Well—" She had seen this in the scope of something the length of a two-part story or a novella.

While she was talking I had jotted down the salient points of the idea on the back of an envelope which lay on my desk. I doubt if it came to twenty-five words. I said, "Mabel, this isn't a novella or a story. This is a full length novel. A long one."

She swore.

That was the origin of *The Valley of Decision*.

I did not see it all at once or realize for some time what I had got into. The central character presented herself to me immediately. But what I was to do with her, where place her, who this family would be, what the central force that would occupy them and carry them through several generations—the span of one woman's long life—all this came about by degrees. It began to ferment at a time when I was particularly interested in industry because of my closeness to the subject through Russell's work at *Fortune,* and constantly meeting industrialists and men of business big and small, whom he brought to our house. The family in which I would place my woman must be an American family concerned in a basic American industry. Perforce this must be somewhere in the industrial heartland of the U.S., somewhere that was most emphatically America and not New York. I had no experience of any such place. Every taproot of my being that was not in New York was in Europe, except—"Pittsburgh!" I screamed, all alone, pacing up and down a closed room with the gramophone going full blast, playing Maestro's Philharmonic recording of the *Semiramide* overture—a hair-raiser, unconditionally guaranteed.

In a way I was shaken. I am not a person who looks for mystic significances in life. The arcane, the occult, the stars in their courses and consequences had never taken me in tow in my husband's wake. But the sense that there really is a grand design in life, the insight into a reason for the absurd irrelevancy of having lived for eighteen months in Pittsburgh fifteen years before; this made chills run up my spine. I needed an American industrial city and I needed its major force, the steel industry. I had them! —in my own rudimentary experiences, which were only impressions up to then. But the essential sense of place was there. What I did not possess I could learn by application and study and digging in. The moment I had seen that far, I saw the rest of what I cared passionately about, and its natural place in this schema: the coming of the Czechs and Slovaks into the steel mills of Pittsburgh, and the subsequent links between them and the creation of their post-war republic and its story.

I was off to Pittsburgh. It was the first of many long stays, and I had not been there twenty-four hours before I knew I was on the right track. I was not ready to talk to Max Perkins about the idea, nor in fact to anybody. Mabel Search was never a factor in it again. She had thrown out the baby with the bath-water be-

cause I had seized upon my own medium, a book, instead of looking for a way to write short fiction. Pittsburgh and an intent preoccupation with it proved to be a godsend just at the time I was
being cut off from Europe; this was between Hitler's annexation
of Austria and the looming doom of Munich. I would not anyway
have gone abroad that summer because my mother was so ill. But
it was a time when nobody could look ahead to anything but terror, mounting tragedy for Hitler's victims, and the shadow of on-
coming war.

1938 was a watershed, a year marked by shattering events in
the world and in the lives of my friends who were uprooted and
their fates violently changed; and for me privately by the death of
my mother. I was thirty-five years old and from this view I see that
that was where my life divided exactly in half. I have now lived all
but seven years of the second thirty-five. I am a realist and I know
that no significant new force will enter my existence henceforward; so I can weigh and measure in perspective. It is as though
all the forces, influences, and interests that formed me were a
network of small streams which flowed towards a confluence that
centred on 1938. I liken the elements of life and of work and of
character and personality to streams of water because they are
fluid, because while it is possible to dam up water it is also impossible to prevent it from penetrating living substance. Thus in
that fateful year the central confluence came to a halt as if blocked
by a dam, marking the termination of elementary ties and roots
from which I and the work I had done had grown up to then: my
mother, her presence, her company, her physical self which was
the greatest love I have ever known. The first part of my long life
in Europe. The first part of my work as a writer, whose basis was
entirely music. The end of Central Europe as it had been for me,
and of the little country for which I had formed a powerful
atavistic attachment without understanding why. The confluent
stream had certainly met a terminal dam.

And yet, being water, it did not stop flowing. It penetrated, seeped, divided, found outlets around and past the dam, and gathered force, enlarged by new runnels but always deriving from its original source, to make new courses which were the designs of others, the people whose influence and activity gave me prepotent experience. And as I said at the outset of this book, I think of my function in life and work partly as that of a sieve: water flows through it.

The autumn of 1938 was a landslide of disastrous coincidences. I remember saying later to Max Perkins that if I had constructed this as fiction he would have taken exception to it. Once he said that there was too much coincidence at the climax of a novel of mine, and I changed it. I am afraid such coincidences come about in fiction because they really reflect reality, but artistically they seem contrived. I did mischievously ask Max what he thought about several extremes of coincidence in *The Forsyte Saga*. He looked rather nonplussed, but he mumbled, "Oh—well, he was Galsworthy, you see."

That autumn would have been too much for any contriving. Six months before, in March, we were celebrating the end of Maestro's first season with the new N B C Symphony, at the famous surprise party which he ruined with his bad humor simply because he did not like surprises. It seemed to me that Chotzie, who was a ring-master of parties for Maestro, should have thought of that. But Maestro said, "I will stay to the bitter end," and stay he did, twisting his moustache with his eyes turned away while a burlesque vaudeville show of rowdy amateurs—and some mere professionals like Heifetz and Zimbalist, Marc Connelly, and Vladimir Horowitz—made sacrificial fools of themselves. Six of us girls, coached and costumed by the Radio City Music Hall, did a can-can that we had rehearsed for weeks. Each of us stepped out front of the line to do a solo turn, and mine was a split which looked fine but which left me with a tetchy back for life. Maestro did not once look at the performers. He sat beside my mother and spoke not a word all evening except to her. She never told me what he said. But he always remembered that it was the last time he saw her. He sailed for Italy a day later.

That was the week when Hitler swallowed Austria. The coup meant tragedy and terror for my Austrian friends, and the end of the wonderful days of Salzburg. Maestro immediately withdrew from the Festival. But the Nazis were welcomed with hysterical joy by the mass of the Austrian people who like the woman in my house were the most fanatical Nazis of all. The Anschluss had barely taken place before the shadow of the hooked cross swung northward over Czechoslovakia. The next six months were hideous with fear and suspense. I remember the harried arrival here of friends and friends of friends who had escaped penniless from Vienna, and the efforts we were constantly making about visas and guarantees and bonds and jobs; the ones who did not escape and who vanished into concentration camps; the ones who committed suicide.

Among the other terminations of that curiously final year was the journal whose music critic I had been, and thus the end of the articles that I wrote before turning into completely different channels. Since then with negligible exceptions I have written only books. And because it was written in passion at an explosive time when nobody could conceive of the world as it is today; because it stands as the summary of what I felt most deeply then, and proves to have foreseen accurately the effect of the Nazis on a country that has never been the same again, I quote parts of the final article. It was written in April, 1938.

"Before the world events of the past month and their impact on music, the writer of this column is overwhelmed in mourning. . . . To have breathed the atmosphere of Vienna is to know why every creator of German music, with barely three exceptions, chose it for his home . . . The passionate pilgrim feels this. He cannot resist, nor would, the rite of the visit—in this personal case, the annual visit—to the sacred bit of ground which is the

most precious musical shrine on earth. I mean that part of the
Central Cemetery called the Music Corner, where amidst trees
and flowers these names on simple tombstones speak a message
before which barbarians should shrink in shame: Beethoven.
Schubert. Haydn. Gluck. Brahms. Wolf. Strauss. And, in the
centre of this circle, the mourning Muse above the name of
Mozart. These are the Germans who will redeem their heritage
after bloodthirsty maniacs are lost in history.

It was in Vienna, Hitler has written, that he learned to hate
the Jews. It must also have been in Vienna that he learned to
hate the free blooming of the spirit which music is. Vienna has
little to offer a devil-ridden hysteric. But for others it has been
called the home of the soul. To know this Vienna is to drive out
to Lichtenthal to visit the humble tenement in which Schubert
was born; to wander amongst the shabby cafés of the old Inner
City; to know that in the yellow *Deutsches Haus* back of the
Stefferl young Mozart declared his independence and cast his fate
for a brief life in Vienna; to tread the rough floors of the cramped
rooms where Beethoven composed the Pastorale and Mozart *Le
Nozze di Figaro*; to see the suburbs in the summer sunshine and
the wine-houses with their green bush waving for the *Heurige;*
to drink the tart young wine amidst the foolish, shiftless folk no
bit more obscure than Schubert who spent his life as one of them;
to know Vienna in winter, the grey, smoky, odorous time of
dampness and crackling porcelain stoves, and crowded coffee-
houses where, like Brahms at his beloved *Roten Igel,* the bearded
men sit day and night, reading, talking, dunking, sipping, and
smoking their long curved pipes; to visit the shop of Artaria,
whose safes still contain letters that Beethoven wrote to the firm
when they were his publishers; these are experiences to be rever-
ently savored and long remembered. This has been despoiled
and defiled, its gates slammed in our faces. But more terrible is
the onslaught of the Vandals on the living flesh and blood of
Austria and its music . . . The name of Salzburg is appearing
for the last time in these pages, Salzburg which was the last German expression of the international spirit of art. Its artists, gladly
accepting the modicum of compensation, went there for the sake

of making music at its best. Where are they now? Scattered, like birds before a tempest. Many are men and women without a country . . . The Cathedral Square where *Jedermann,* despite the bombast for which I ridiculed it, was an honest pageant of ideals, echoes now to the tramp of ruffians and rabble. The candy-box houses and toy trolley-cars which used to flutter with red and white bunting are plastered with the hooked black symbol of terror. For once, the incorrigibly slouchy shopkeepers and head-waiters of Salzburg will do things on time, will step lively and on the mark; but nobody will be there to care . . .

Our own musical scene will be expanded to take care in some measure of the broken lives and careers of musicians who are Hitler's victims. But the artistic life of Austria has come to a dead halt. Beyond music, the theatre and the cinema lie in wreckage. So too do Austrian literature, education, science, research. The great plays and novels are burnt, the foremost artists are destitute and many under imprisonment and torture . . . The dark ages have closed like a tidal wave upon the Austria and the Vienna of sacred and deliciously profane musical memory."

These paragraphs tell more of my state of mind at that time than anything reminiscent I could write today. Lotte Lehmann had come here to live with her delightful husband Otto Krause, after she had defied Goering and his edict that she confine her singing to German stages. Otto was an Austrian cavalry officer and a member of the troop of incomparable horsemen who rode the white Lippizaners in the Spanish Riding School. He was Viennese to the core and had not Lotte's touch of the artist-gypsy which makes a wandering life appealing. He suffered more than Lotte did over the loss of their homes in Vienna and the country, and he died the following year of a sudden onslaught of pulmonary tuberculosis—but I think really of a broken heart.

There is much that I can no longer remember beyond grief for Austria and terror for Czechoslovakia, because I was so concerned about my mother. As her health failed I believe her will strengthened. I was alone with her a great deal and to me this was the last segment of a design that enclosed my whole life: I had the best of my mother, at the beginning and at the end. I know I idealize her, but I am not so deluded as to claim she had no faults and shortcomings. She had many. But her strengths outweighed them. If she had lived in the realm of precept and morality; if she had been a teacher, or some kind of occupational keeper of her collective brother in humankind, her character might not have seemed so remarkable. But she was a charming, beautiful, provocative, inwardly tragic woman of the world and there, I think, one does not look for the granite of which her graceful backbone was made.

Most of us have known the great courage with which those we have loved have faced long and mortal illness, too usually cancer. It is one of the resources latent in otherwise unremarkable people. Anyone who knew her would take that for granted in my mother, and so did she. It was not her stoicism that was extraordinary but her detached, rational attitude. Little was known at that time about cirrhosis of the liver. It was thought to be a disease of heavy drinking and rich eating; nothing could have been more preposterous in relation to my mother. So she was a study to the doctors not only in the treatment but in the cause of the disease. And she said, "Since I'm stuck with this damned thing, the least I can do is try to be of use with it."

She asked her intimate friend Abe Flexner what was the progress of research in the disease. He told her that the Rockefeller Institute, whose director was then his brother Simon Flexner, was engaged in a study of cirrhosis under Dr. Cornelius Rhoads, the late brilliant research pathologist.

"Very well," she said. "Tell them I want to volunteer as a guinea pig."

The patients in the hospital of the Rockefeller Institute were sent there by their own physicians and hospitals because they were suffering from the diseases that were under study in research projects. This was the way my mother chose to live out her fate.

She could not endure an emotional approach to her condition, nor any attitude but a scientific one. She never permitted anybody to delude her with the false hope that she might be cured. Cirrhosis of the liver still remains incurable and fatal, but the studies to which she contributed in her own way have greatly lessened the suffering and prolonged the lives of its later victims. She was not in the hospital all the time. In the last months of her life she was mostly at home, either in New York or in Connecticut. At intervals she became acutely ill and then she went to the hospital and cooperated cheerfully in every treatment they experimented with. She liked Dr. Rhoads because he had the objective mind and personality of a man of pure science. She asked him to tell her how long she might expect to live and she proceeded with the utmost calm to make her plans accordingly. She told him I was the only person who could be trusted to share this knowledge without panicking and laying on her the burden of tragedy and fear. So he talked to me frankly and, I felt, with relief. Once he said, "I'm afraid I haven't got a bedside manner, but that is not what your mother looks for here. She is a remarkable woman. She has the greatest self-control I have ever seen."

It was not easy for me to learn to simulate courage like hers but she forced me to it by saying, "I can talk to you because you can take it. You're tough—like me. You can stand up to it as much as I can. The others could not."

To me this was invoking the early years when she and I had had each other and nobody else. But we did not reminisce and sentimentalize about them. We held them as a bond of silence; she knew perfectly well how vivid my memories were, how I had worshipped her as an artist, how possessive I felt about her voice and her beauty and the career that she had deliberately subordinated to her husband and her other children. Remarkably, I think, she kept me from feeling embittered about this, which I have never been; but I have recognized the elements which might have been the seeds of bitterness in me if she had not for-stalled that. I do not know how she did it, except by the strength of her convictions and the warmth and tenderness of her personality. Though it may hurt my sister and brother at this late time to learn what I have hidden until now, my mother did say to me towards the end of her life, "I had you first and I made you mine alone. I have been both mother and father to you, and to me you are different from the others."

September came, the beginning of the loveliest season in New England and in Europe too, but that was a September of horrors to distinguish it from all others. In the light of my later involvement with Czechoslovakia, it is hard to realize now what a complete outsider I was in relation to all that was happening in Prague, and in the other cities where cynical and cowardly and wool-headed politicians were preparing the betrayal of their own countries along with the victim whose throat they cut. Since the appearance of the Runciman mission in Prague in August I had hung on the news, seizing every edition of the newspapers (in those days we had many newspapers, with many editions each, in New York) and glued to the radio. News broadcasting from Europe was still a relative innovation. Edward Murrow whom I knew well later, had put together the brilliant CBS foreign news staff, and had engaged Bill Shirer to cover Central Europe. My agonized memories of the day-by-day nightmare in Prague; of Berlin, Godesberg, and the eternal shame of Munich, are personified in the gentle voice of Bill Shirer. Later his *Berlin Diary* revealed much of the human and personal detail behind the horror. It made a powerful impression on me, and sharpened the immediacy and intimacy with which I visualized the city I loved so much. I could actually see and feel it and the faces and voices of its people in the streets. I was then reconstructing the tragedy in *The Valley of Decision*; and also by then I was deeply involved with the exiled Czechoslovaks, their fighting forces in the war, their resistance at home, and their government in London. But when the crime of Munich was being committed I did not know, in spite of my anguish, that the threads of my own fate were interwoven, to resolve five and seven and ten years later.

My mother was my even more acute concern. She had been in the hospital in August and when she was stronger I drove her back to Connecticut, where she was planning to spend the autumn. She was alone there with her maids. My sister had been married the previous spring and was travelling with her husband, my brother was at Yale, and my stepfather away on tour. I went back and forth constantly to my mother but it was the time of year when I had to get my daughters ready for school, the house organized for the winter, and I even tried to take a few whacks at the scaffolding of the novel I was attacking. I spoke to my mother on the telephone every day. However ill she was, her beautiful voice would say, "I'm fine, darling!" and that lovely silvery sound remains as real to me today as it was then. Her speaking voice had all the charm and delicacy of her song. It does not follow that a singer's speaking voice is beautiful; quite often they are not. But my mother's voice in speech had the crystalline soprano sparkle of her singing; it was not high-pitched or low; it was spoken music.

By the third week of September the crisis in Europe was almost unbearable. It seems to me I seldom left the radio, necessarily a big, clumsy piece of furniture in those days when foreign broadcasting was uncertain in reception, and one stayed by the most powerful instrument one had. There were no small portables then anyway. I was trying to catch every word about the imminent meeting of Hitler and Chamberlain at Godesberg, while a tremendous nor'easter howled outside and torrential rain beat the windows—with the usual consequence of flood inside the house, wrung-out curtains, and profane invective for the architect who had thought of casement windows for the most exposed location on Manhattan Island. In the midst of that there came a local news flash that New England was being devastated by a hurricane.

I ran to telephone my mother. The lines were already down.

It was impossible to get through. I wanted to start at once to go to her, but it was late afternoon, the twenty-first of September, and the radio alarms were about equally divided between the crisis in Europe and reports of the terrible storm in New England. The hurricane was at its height and I realized it would be insane to try to drive to my mother then, with dark coming on. Her house was in a remote bit of country west of Hartford to which there had never been access by rail; there was no way to go directly except by motor and that was what we had always done. I supposed she must be safe in her house, but the radio kept reporting unbelievable damage—enormous trees uprooted and thrown around like weeds, roofs blown off of houses and windows shattered, flood, electric and telephone wires ripped from their smashed poles. I was frantic.

Early the next morning I started out to drive there. It was about ninety miles and ordinarily took three hours. I was almost nine hours on the way and never, except in the aftermath of wars, have I seen anything like the devastation. The platitudinous calm following the storm had settled in, and in its baleful metallic light it was impossible to believe one's eyes. The glory of the countryside, its giant elms and maples, had been snapped like matchsticks, the oldest and grandest the worst victims. The trunks and boughs lay all over the roads. The roads themselves in many places were gone, flooded out or burst by the pressure of broken culverts beneath them. Most bridges were down, and where they had not gone, the rivers were like rough seas, throwing violent waves across the bridges which, of course, were closed. I would not have believed that one torrential rain could make every stream in that part of the country overflow or burst its banks, but that is what happened. Every bit of road was thick in torn leaves and branches, mud and silt, the ruin of nearby gardens and barns and sheds, débris of every kind. The hurricane was the worst in the history of the New England coast and the inland countryside. It became

the motive of an extraordinary novel by the late Christopher
LaFarge, called *The Sudden Guest,* to which I pay the highest
compliment—I wish I had written it.

Fortunately I knew that part of the country intimately, and
when I was stopped in my low-gear crawl by a barrier on one
road I would back down to a crossing and turn off to try something else. There were barricades closing the roads every few
hundred yards, while crews of men labored to saw up the big
fallen trees or make emergency repairs to get the roads open. My
mother was safe enough when I finally arrived, and the curious
thing is that I have little memory of details of the damage to her
house and to the garden and the trees. There was severe damage,
in fact, and we camped without electric light or the telephone
for several days. There was some kind of battery radio in the
house and we hung over it, trying to follow the crisis in Europe;
but the radio must have been weak or the transmission bad, because the frustration was even worse than the suspense. We heard
only in snatches.

Predictably the weather turned beautiful and my clearest
memory of those days is sitting on her bed in the mornings with
the sun streaming into the room. No matter how ill she felt her
hands were never idle. She was working on one of the eight
needlepoint seats she had begun to make the year before for my
dining-room chairs. She wanted the design to be something original and of special significance to her and to me, so she chose Tom
Cleland's beautiful classic ornament from the title-page of my
Mozart. This includes a violin and a clarinet, the masque of
drama, and the opening notes of the G minor Symphony. In
Vienna I had had it enlarged and drawn on fine canvas, and she
worked it in natural gradations of shading from the white of the
scroll of music through all shades of grey to the black of the
notes and symbols. The background is Burgundy red, suitable indeed to our dining-room where much wonderful Burgundy was
drunk, with my mother admiringly inhaling the bouquet of the

wine but shaking her head as she watched me drinking it. A total ascetic herself, not by prejudice but by physical taste, she used to say, "You'll end your days in a wheelchair, Marcia, crippled with gout."

Her own days shortened remorselessly as she worked on the chair seats. She did the whole set in a race against time. She kept at the needlework with dogged perseverance and amazing speed. Towards the end of the stint, in her last weeks, she would say while her heavy brown fingers flew with their astonishing delicacy and precision, "I've got to finish these. I've got to finish them before I die. I know I won't die before I finish them."

If this was agony for me, my part was not to let her see it.

When she was working on the last piece and we both knew the awful brevity of the time left to her, she said, "I know I'll last until I finish this. I've got to."

She finished the last piece on the day she went to the hospital to die. For months I could not look at the chair seats. I rolled them up in mothproofing and locked them away. The thought of putting them on chairs for people to sit on seemed sacrilege. Then one morning I was staring at the telephone. I was still in the numbed but raw state when I could not believe I would never speak to her again. The habit of picking up the telephone to call her every morning was painful to break. Suddenly it seemed as if I really did hear her lovely voice; and whatever my imagination was reaching for, I listened. "You fool," said the beloved memory. "Is this why I rushed and slaved and drove myself to finish those chair seats? So you would keep them hidden away like a coward?"

The next day I got out the seats and had them mounted on the chairs.

I think her toughness of mind was more prodigious even than her tenderness, and she had a vast endowment of both. Only very late did I attain that certain niche in the painful ascent towards maturity where she and I, in monosyllables, or with an eyebrow or a shrugged shoulder, could enjoy the knowledge that we shared. Her wisdom was elusive; only in the quizzical depths of her eyes could I see that she knew all about something that had been troubling me. Once I would have dreaded her knowing that. Now those fears were gone. I leaned back against the footboard of her bed and laughed and in a couple of words said what I thought about my own dilemma. The remark included a certain reference to men, which opinion coincided closely with her own. Her rejoinder was pungent.

I reached over and took her hands and looked at her, studying the extraordinary serenity of her straight brows and the ageless beauty of her eyes. The rest of her face was sallow and wasted. She sighed. She said, "What a nuisance I have to die now just when we have such a good time together."

Another day she began to tell me her wishes about a long list of matters that would have to be dealt with after her death. She was calm and precise, telling me how she wished her personal possessions divided, and filling out the formal provisions of her will with her private reasons for the dispositions she had made in it. Then she began to give me directions for her funeral; extremely brief and simple, in her own house, and the Quartet to play two pieces of music. The first was an arrangement that Sascha Jacobsen must make of the aria of the Happy Shade from *Orfeo*. At this my whole life rose before me from my earliest childhood worship of her; everything I loved most dearly was wrapped up in this and I struggled not to break down. I was not as strong as she; suddenly I said, "Oh, must you put us through this?"

She pulled herself upright in her bed. Her huge, sunken eyes widened as they used to do when I had been naughty as a child.

"Look here," she said. "Who's doing this dying, anyway? If I can have the guts to do it well, you can have the guts to listen to me now!"

She died on the twenty-seventh of October, at the age of fifty-four. It was a Thursday. On the previous Monday she had been in her box at the Town Hall for the second of a series of sonata recitals that my stepfather was playing. She looked lovely; heart-rendingly fragile, but beautiful and gallant, with her straight back and her proud carriage. I will never forget her smile as I kissed her good-night. The next day she collapsed and was taken to the Rockefeller Institute Hospital. By the time I got there she was in a coma and never regained consciousness. All that day and that night, all the next day and through the next night I stayed beside her, holding her right hand in mine. Her strong heart and her magnificent lungs could not give up, though the rest of her body had reached the end. I did not understand what was this long slow dying. I looked beseechingly at Dr. Rhoads. He said, "Believe me, she is not suffering. Please believe me." At ten minutes past nine in the morning she died. I laid down her hand and went to do as she had bid me.

LIFE with Russell Davenport had never been easy but even
more surely, it had never been dull. Jack Jessup's phrase
which I have quoted was one that I should have had the
wit to coin: Russell could solve any problem of human relations,
once he was reminded that he had one. The problems did not
always stay solved. And when they reappeared they took a discouraging variety of new forms. I never knew what to expect,
but in the two years following my mother's death I never had a
chance to wonder.

I was only beginning to find out what I had bitten off in my
Pittsburgh project. It was enormous in span, depth, and detail.
I had prompt and generous help in proportion. Through Russell
I was introduced to men in all branches of the steel industry—
management and finance, production, technology, labor. He had
met many of them at sessions of a discussion group called The
Fortune Round Table. Once a month at some agreeable place
outside New York this group met for a weekend for the purpose
of discussing a topic of economic, industrial, or political importance. The participants were chosen for their eminence in their
fields of activity and in the course of time they included leading
industrialists, bankers and financiers, scholars, scientists, labor-
union leaders, lawyers, sociologists, economists and technical
specialists. Each meeting was followed by a report in *Fortune*
of its discussions and conclusions. The one that set off a national
explosion took place early in the summer of 1939. It included
Wendell Willkie.

TOO STRONG FOR FANTASY

We had moved for the summer to a house in Connecticut between Norwalk and Westport. The question of a country place had always been one of the burning disagreements between my husband and me. After the financial and temperamental fiasco of the farm in Vermont, which was now safely rented to Mr. Beal, I was tough and wary. Nothing would ever again entrap me into the horrors of the inland countryside. Russell was equally adamant in his spurning of 'suburbia.' But he was working so hard that he himself was the first to admit that unless he would settle for something accessible to New York he would never get off Manhattan Island. I wanted no burdens like running two houses at once, no summer-resort life with the men there for hectically social weekends, and ghastly week days for me fringed round with women and children first. I intended to close the town apartment (and make some major alterations in it meanwhile, since an attack of Builder's Itch has always been one of my primary reactions to disaster like the concatenations of 1938.) I set out to find my idea of a place for the summer.

After I had first nosed it out alone I took Russell to see it one Sunday in March, and the next day we leased it. It was called Great Marsh. It was a big property directly on Saugatuck Harbor, with beautiful old trees, wide lawns, a vegetable garden, an old-fashioned barn and stable, a dock and a boathouse. The house was large but completely unpretentious; shabby, ramshackle, a nondescript pile of about the 1911 era, with gimcracky porches and no style whatever. It was casually but comfortably furnished, its rooms were big, and it could hold a lot of people. Life was delightful there for us and for the two little girls and for a great many others. It was close to most of our friends. It was everything that Russell had said he did not like. He loved it. He and his brother John took one good look at the harbor with Long Island Sound outside, and went off and chartered a sloop, which was soon replaced by a fast and comfortable forty-four-foot auxiliary cutter which they bought together. I had learned from

Vermont that Russell's reaction to any place would be functional; if a farm he had to farm it, and when there was salt water he had to sail. Cindy III was a joy to all of us. I who am prostrated by one whiff of a steamship, the larger the more fatal, dearly love a sailboat, and proved it for years by being ship's cook as well as one of the five unpaid hands who were the whole crew.

My birthday came along shortly after we moved to Great Marsh and Russell was late that day coming out from town. He had driven in in his horrible old black Chrysler instead of taking the train. When I heard it come snarling in from the highroad I glanced out the window of my room where I was changing my dress. Russell had driven down to the barn instead of stopping at the front door. I wondered what he was doing there. It was out of sight of the house. There was a long delay. Then I saw him walking slowly across the lawn. He was holding what looked like a long rope and on the other end of it—"Damn!" I said aloud. I thought of the arrival of the cows in Vermont. In the dusk I could not see what he was leading but it looked big and tawny in color. I thought he had bought a Great Dane. I was ready to kill him.

Then my cat Tam who was crouched beneath my hand on the window-sill suddenly began to swell like a blowfish. His spine went up, his claws came out, and he let out a noise that was both a hiss and a yowl. His eyes were sharper than mine. Russell had a lion on the end of a long chain. She was a cub three months old —my birthday present. She was enchanting. I named her Kitty. She was a perfect kitten in maximum. She played with strings and balls and bouncy toys; she rolled over and waved her huge paws when she was happy; she cried when she was lonely; she purred with a noise like a large electric motor. Her affection and enthusiasm were a little dangerous since she had no idea of her own strength—she weighed about sixty pounds—and she would fling herself at me, asking to play, or wrap her paws around my ankles. Stockings went at the rate of dozens a week, and lion scratches,

even those from love-pats, can be toxic unlike those of felis
domesticus. I settled for strong denim overalls, a long-sleeved
jacket, and gloves when I went out to play with my pet. Tam
was miserable. When Kitty was not in her loose-box in the barn
she was tethered by her chain to a long wire between two trees,
and Tam remained in my room, yowling with jealousy on the
window sill.

At first sight Kitty petrified most people, including the ice-
man, who asked me, "Is that there what I think that is?" Her
favorite treat and toy on hot days was a lump of ice. She had
sprung onto the first piece of ice when it slid off the back of the
truck, and thereafter she bounded joyfully on her tether to greet
the ice-man whenever he came. I assured him that Kitty was
harmless but soon the local game warden came round. He could
not make up his mind what he was supposed to do about Kitty.
I offered to take out a licence for her. He hadn't thought of that.
In fact, there was no such thing, and no precedent for this situation. Was there a law applicable to Kitty? Well, not exactly. He
stood watching Kitty who was amiably playing with a spray of
rambler roses. He pushed his hat to the back of his head and said,
"Aw, shucks, it can stay."

Russell came home from his Round Table meeting and
walked into the house saying, "I've met the man who ought to be
the next President of the United States."

"Whose idea is this?" I asked. "His or yours?"

Russell said, "It's spontaneous. You see him and you know
it."

I knew of course that he meant Wendell Willkie, at that time
president of the Commonwealth and Southern Corporation. He
had just taken his company through the famous legal battle with
the Tennessee Valley Authority, locking horns with President
Roosevelt's New Deal, and emerging on the public scene a marked
man, variously defined according to people's views. Some called
him a Wall Street malefactor from the utilities industry, which

had had a malodorous connotation ever since the time of Samuel Insull. Some called him the advocate of free enterprise; some, the spokesman of big business against the government. These were mostly mistaken summations of Wendell Willkie. He was an old-fashioned, hell-raising, hard-wrangling liberal, with some of the evangelism of John Brown and the Boston abolitionists. But his concept of American democracy was middle-western. He was the small-town Indiana grandson of German immigrants who had fled Europe in the revolutionary upheavals of 1848. He was a Democrat, a man of the people, well educated, self-made, belligerently independent; the antithesis in birth, temperament, tradition, and education to the Hudson River Valley patroon in the White House. He was also better-read and a brilliant student of American constitutional history. Willkie only left the Democratic Party after Roosevelt's first term in office. Those four years confirmed Willkie's concept of the difference between the classic tenets of the Democratic Party and the power ploys and economic manipulations of the New Deal. "I am still a Democrat but not a socialist," he wrote in one letter at that time; and in another, "Franklin D. still causes me great worries and concern. All my life, as you know, I have been an ardent Democrat and here I find myself after one is elected with almost a phobia on the subject."

In the time of Franklin Roosevelt there were large numbers of thoughtful, responsible American people who were instinctively mistrustful of the man and opposed, not so much to what he did or aimed to do, as to the way he did it. This definition rules out the rich and privileged, the angry oligarchy who called him a traitor to his class, the diehard Republicans to whom he would anyway have been anathema, the reactionaries who viewed all social change or reform as communism or the next thing to it. The people who were inherently opposed to Roosevelt (other than the blind opposition I have defined) were moderate—moderate of means and in social ideas, open-minded, independent in their occupations and in their capacity and desire to think for themselves. They were revolted by the remark of Harry Hopkins which was the distilled essence of the New Deal: We'll spend and spend and elect and elect. They were alarmed at the imminence of a third term for Roosevelt, already too deeply entrenched for the good of the democratic process, even while they approved his foreign policy, his outspoken contempt for Hitler, his implied support of the Allies in the coming war whose outbreak by then was only a matter of weeks. Hitler was screaming and fulminating over Danzig, German troops were manoeuvering on the Polish frontier. Americans who saw their country, its Presidency, and the world in this balance were early promulgators of Willkie for President.

Russell told me he had invited Mr. and Mrs. Willkie to stay the weekend of August 19th. While they were there he wanted them to meet certain people who, he thought, would be as impressed by Wendell Willkie as he was, and for the same reasons. The Willkies accepted our invitation and I began to plan the sort of weekend which in my experience presidents of large corporations usually enjoyed. We had not played golf for years, but I arranged with a neighbor for the courtesies of a golf course nearby. I had our moth-eaten tennis court patched up. I planned that a good bridge game and a good poker game should be present in the making on each evening of the Willkies' visit. I lined up some of the brightest of the many bright people who lived in the vicinity, and they agreed to drop in for cocktails or a meal if I thought such an impromptu party would go well. I planned the menus and did the marketing with the care that had made our food, if I do say so, deservedly well known. Long beforehand I went in to town to carry back some of our best wines from their resting-place. I laid in plenty of Uppmann cigars. Everything was in readiness and on the Friday afternoon, the Willkies arrived.

Wendell was a personality to charm a bird from a tree—if he wanted to. He was a big, shambling, rumpled, overweight, carelessly dressed man, and he radiated a stunning combination of intellect and homely warmth. He spoke a twanging Indiana burr in a rumbling bass voice, grating down hard on the vocal cords as many midwestern American men do. He had a delightful, instantly responsive chuckle. Mrs. Willkie was tiny, pretty, self-effacing, and, I thought, shy. She was visibly content to stay in the shadow of her striking husband.

I took her upstairs to their rooms and left her to get settled while I went down to see what I might offer Mr. Willkie in the way of relaxation and refreshment. He had attended to that himself. He was out on the porch with Russell, sprawled in a wicker armchair with one leg thrown over the arm of the chair. He had taken off his jacket and necktie and opened the collar of his shirt. He was drinking a whisky and soda and chain-smoking cigarettes in such a way that most of the ash fell on his shirt-front and most of the butts missed the ashtray at which he threw them. He was talking hard; emphatic, concentrated talk, with his blue eyes fixed on Russell's absorbed face. He noticed my appearance only to the extent of a smile and a nod, and a gesture of one hand which implied, "Here, sit down and listen and be intelligent, but don't bother us."

And there he sat, except when he was at meals or asleep, for the whole length of his visit. Tennis, golf, bridge, poker, and social chat had no reality to him. Food and wine were tossed down unnoticed. Wendell's leisure, such as it was, went into a rolling boil of ideas thrashed out with other brilliant and challenging minds; into voracious reading; and into writing, eventually speaking too, as he began to evolve the points of view, rooted in passionate beliefs, which transformed him from a tough, smart corporation lawyer into the articulator of constructive opposition to the monopolistic governmental theories of the New Deal. He was equally outspoken in opposition to what was then the classic isolationist position of the Republican Party. Actually, he wound

up in the middle—hated by the Democrats as a renegade and by
the Republicans as an interloper. He polarized the real centre
of American political feeling and implemented that in a popular
vote of 22,304,755, larger than that won by any Republican candidate before Eisenhower in 1952.

Theodore H. White is the current undisputed authority on
the politics of American Presidential elections. In *The Making of
the President 1964* he takes a backward glance at 1940, which he
rightly terms the world of yesterday, and states that the Eastern
Establishment "had compelled the party to name Wendell Willkie
as Republican nominee by a combination of every kind of pressure
the publishers, broadcasters and bankers could collectively exert
around the country. Through the provincial banks, then in
trailing-strings to New York banks, the Wall Street men could
mobilize for their Indiana favorite almost inexorable pressure
on local businessmen who controlled delegates." It may be that
Mr. White's statements are true. But I was at the nerve-centre of
the Willkie pre-nomination and Presidential campaigns, working
with my husband, when Teddy White was a brilliant twenty-
five-year-old journalist in China. I saw something rather more
genuine and spontaneous than the collective pressures that Teddy
White describes.

For that matter, every Presidential nomination and campaign
since 1940 has been increasingly a phenomenon of pressures, in
recent years particularly by advertising experts and the hyper-
tensive techniques of television broadcasting; and bankers have
not been idle bystanders either. It is demonstrably mistaken to
assume that support by newspaper publishers and their editorial
staffs will get a candidate nominated or elected. But the manipula-
tion of popular opinion from obscure ripples to a national ground-
swell or even a tidal wave is more sharply understood and more
cynically practised today than it was twenty-five years ago. It is
true, however, that publishers of newspapers and magazines,

through their editorial observers and writers, were early pro-
ponents of the Willkie-for-President idea. And one of the ripples
started in our house.

The Willkie ground-swell was not, as partisans of both political parties have claimed, a conspiracy, a take-over, a purchase, or
a pressure manoeuvre by the big interests of the Eastern Establishment. In its origins it was more an extraordinary series of coincidences. At the time of this writing I have turned to one of the
surviving activators of the early Willkie boom, Oren Root, who
has confirmed my own belief that the idea of Willkie for President struck simultaneously a number of eloquent people who
promptly proceeded to express themselves and go into action.
Some of them really believed the idea was original with them but
it has never been possible to attribute it to a single person, not
even to Wendell Willkie himself. In Mr. Root's words, Wendell
"happened" to these individuals, and to certain elements of natural
(not pressured) public opinion all at about the same time, or over
a very brief span of time. It seems to be the case that he happened
first in print to Arthur Krock of *The New York Times.* In just
what order he happened to successive elements it is impossible to
state, but happen he did in their newspaper columns to Raymond
Clapper and to Dorothy Thompson (who later deserted him.)
He happened to Russell Davenport in 1939, and thus to Harry
Luce and other members of Time, Inc., who met him in our house,
the first of them during that initial weekend. He happened to
Oren Root, then a young lawyer, who started the prairie-fire of
the Willkie Clubs in April, 1940. He happened to John and Mike
(Gardner) Cowles, the publishers of the Minneapolis *Star* and
Tribune, the Des Moines *Register,* and *Look.* This was at our
apartment on a Sunday evening, April 23, 1940, cook's night out,
and my notebook reminds me that I cooked, that nobody was
present but the Willkies, the Cowleses and ourselves, and that we
were up until nearly three o'clock in the morning. Wendell also
happened to business men in general who liked the idea of a

business man in the White House, and to Big Business which wanted to overthrow Roosevelt. He happened to many leaders of the legal profession and then he began to happen to the financial community, headed by Thomas W. Lamont. Then came a series of influential newspapers whose persuasions were neither those of the New Deal nor the isolationist-reactionary arch-Republican Chicago *Tribune*.

Wendell did not happen to the Republican Party.

The idea of Willkie for President, gathering speed and size as it snowballed in some ten months from a thrilling notion to a national clamor, was promulgated almost wholly from outside the Republican Party; and much of it was pushed in our house by constant meetings between Wendell and the amateurs who brought it off. Several times each week we had people to dinner, sometimes by careful plan, when it best served the purpose to enclose the occasion in the form of an agreeable social evening. Sometimes the gatherings were impromptu and hard-working, interrupted only by thick roast beef sandwiches, plenty of drink, and the incessant ringing of telephones. The telephones multiplied like flies and drove me almost mad. Every time I turned around another telephone had been installed and Charlton MacVeagh, the first political technician from inside the Republican Party, was manning a battery of them, talking to men all over the country on whom he was working to light the Willkie fuse among delegates to the coming convention.

All this was happening against the backdrop of the war which had begun with the invasion of Poland on the first of September 1939. I was standing on the stair-landing at Great Marsh on that day, when Russell came out of the library where he had been listening to the radio and said, "Hitler has attacked Poland. They are expecting Britain and France to declare war."

"Why couldn't it have been a year ago," I said, with bitter retrospect of the Czechoslovak sellout. The Allied declaration came two days later and the annihilation of Poland followed swiftly. Then came the evil interlude of the Phony War. We moved back to town and to the hardest-working, highest-pitched winter I have ever known. Running the house for its purpose in the Willkie drive, with the help of a superlative Czech cook and her able husband Alfons Buzek, for many years since the head steward of the University Club, was a full-time job. But I was also up to my eyes in Pittsburgh and the steel industry. A new and treasured element came into life with the settling of Maestro and his wife in a large house overlooking the Hudson at River-dale. I went there constantly, as I was to do for the remaining years of his life, and he came often to us. One evening when he and his family and some old friends were dining with us we had just finished dinner and Maestro was settled in his chair in the drawing-room when I was called to the telephone. Whoever it was (I have forgotten) told me that Artur Bodanzky, the eminent Wagnerian conductor of the Metropolitan, had just died, and I had better tell Maestro. This was a duty dreaded by anyone who knew Maestro, because he was always very upset by the death of any person he knew, a matter unrelated to his real estimation of the deceased. He had had a low and shockingly frank opinion of Bodanzky as a musician. Nevertheless, when I told him about Bodanzky's death, he clutched his head in his hands and rocked back and forth, moaning, *"Oh, che triste! Che disastro!"*

That evening Katharine Hepburn, among others, came in after dinner, eager to meet Maestro but also much inhibited by her innate shyness and her distaste for gatherings of any but her intimate friends. She was at the height of her career and to me always a fascinating actress and personality. Maestro for his part was curious about any woman of whom he had heard as an artist or because of her looks or any facet of attractiveness. Whether or not he expected a counterpart of Eleanora Duse I do not know, but when he saw Kate, thin and flat as an arrow, freckled, un-adorned, and silent with timidity to boot, he was dashed.

"Is this what you call a beautiful actress?" he asked me later.

A year or so before there had been a similar episode with Helen Hayes. It was when she was playing in *Victoria Regina,* and her deserved celebrity was impressive. On a Saturday evening when a lot of us were dining at the Chotzies' with Maestro, Helen Hayes and her husband Charles MacArthur were to stop in after the play on their way home to Nyack for the weekend. When the doorbell rang we moved on cue to make room on the couch beside Maestro for Helen, and he waited for the "grande artista" with eager curiosity. In came Helen Hayes, pale, without makeup, her mousy hair dragged flat as it had been under her wig, wearing a plaid skirt and a sweater. She looked like a high-school student tired out from a long exam. Maestro was visibly crestfallen and Helen Hayes too dumbstruck with awe to say a word. Nobody knew what to do. The MacArthurs departed shortly, but she had summoned the courage to ask Maestro if he would like to see her play. And he had not known how to avoid the yes, with pleasure, which was all he could say in spite of his doubts.

A number of us accompanied him some days later to the theatre, because it was always necessary to surround Maestro, right, left, and behind, with friends so that no stranger could get at him to ask for an autograph or otherwise intrude. It was always arranged that he sit in the front row because of his extreme nearsightedness. *Victoria Regina* began and Maestro was enthralled, more and more impressed as Helen Hayes carried through the prodigious feat of recreating the royal character from girlhood to extreme old age. Afterwards he insisted on going back to her dressing-room. When he arrived there, she was once again the small, quite plain woman with the colorless skin and the drab hair. He took her hands and said, "My dear, you are a very great artist." Niagara gushed forth over the dressing-table.

Present-day emphasis on youth in politics and in public life might imply the contrary a generation ago. That is not true. The age of whiskers and Prince Albert coats was already long past and the most striking thing about the main movers around Wendell Willkie was their youth—after their inexperience. Wendell himself was forty-eight years old when he was nominated. Russell Davenport was forty in 1939—an old man compared to Oren Root who was twenty-eight when he sent out the first copies of his Willkie Declaration. It was organized on the round-robin letter principle; it had space for fifteen signatures of people ready to work for Willkie's nomination. Each signer was to undertake to produce fifteen more. This was the beginning of the Willkie Clubs; by the time of the convention in June they had multiplied to seven hundred and fifty clubs who fielded fifty thousand volunteer workers and sent out over 750,000 pieces of Willkie literature. The other starters in the Willkie movement were all about forty years old or younger. The three Republican insiders whose work was the first leverage in moving the mountain were Sam Pryor, National Committeeman from Connecticut; Charles Halleck, then a young Congressman from Indiana who briefly saw the light and made the speech putting Willkie's name in nomination; and Harold Stassen, the then "boy wonder" Governor of Minnesota, only thirty-two, who was the Willkie floor manager at the convention.

Russell came to be called Willkie's personal representative because he had to be called something. He was also called Willkie's manager, which is laughable to anybody who knew Wendell Willkie, most unmanageable of men, and most so in the face of the expediencies and compromises demanded of political candidates. Russell was also called Willkie's speech-writer, which was a closer approximation to the truth. But Wendell all his life had been speaking his own mind with force, originality, and independence. He spoke best extempore, having prepared his arguments as he had been trained to do in the law. He also wrote well, not in the literary sense, but with the clarity and skill that had gone into his legal briefs. During the winter of 1939–40 he published articles in a variety of periodicals ranging from highbrow to popular. These were climaxed by "We, the People" which was published in *Fortune* in April, and which does bear the polish and style of Russell's editing. It created a national sensation. Wendell received over two thousand requests for public addresses in its wake, and it was reprinted in enormous numbers and distributed by the Willkie Clubs.

This article in pamphlet form, accompanied by a second pamphlet, the reprint of Russell's *Fortune* editorial about Wendell Willkie, were the culmination of some eight months' intense association between the two men. Such intellectual and temperamental affinities are like the anvil and the hammer, between which the forged iron takes form—in this case the form of a weapon of ideas hurled by a man of dramatic political magnetism. Wendell had to have a confidant upon whom he could rely in every way; who could be his alter ego in words when the pressure of time and events and the terrible contentions of politicians made it impossible for him to deliver his speeches off the top of his head or to prepare them personally as he would have preferred to do—and sometimes, in spite of everything, actually did do. Like other novice candidates for major office Wendell found it hard to realize that Presidential campaign speeches are beyond the capacities of an individual. They depend on a mass of research and of experts to sort it out and make telling use of it. The color and eloquence that carry the speeches across, the impact of his personality, are the candidate's part, beyond the prior requisite that unless he knows what he wants his speeches to say and lays that down as the foundation of each of them, he has no business running for office.

Early in April the Phony War came to an end with Hitler's onslaught on Norway and Denmark. Only a month later the Blitzkrieg was unleashed on the Low Countries and swept on to overrun half of France. By the tenth of June the Nazis were at the gates of Paris and Mussolini stabbed France in the back. To Russell and me, to our friends, to everyone who felt and believed as we did, this was primary anguish which would have swept every other consideration out of mind, except for the fact, grotesque in its way, that we were passionately committed to nominating Wendell Willkie in opposition to President Roosevelt—who was at his best as the war engulfed and the Nazis enslaved the free countries of Europe. But it had never been Roosevelt's foreign policies which Wendell had opposed. He was outspoken in his support of President Roosevelt's assurances of aid to tottering France and to Britain about to be left fighting alone. From that view I marvel today at the audacity of a handful of amateurs who drove in the nomination of Willkie over the heads of the whole Republican Old Guard. And so to Philadelphia.

It was hot. It was hot as only Philadelphia can be—thick, filthy, sweating June heat many years before there was air-conditioning. It was angry. It was crowded. It was tense. It was noisy. It was a conflagration of confusion, excitement, rumors, and counter-rumors. It was swarming with partisans of the Taft and the Dewey forces, with runners from the camps of Senator Vandenberg and countless favorite sons; with delegates mostly committed to Taft or to Dewey, but a precious few not, who swarmed by the hundreds to the cramped suite in the Benjamin Franklin Hotel where they wanted to meet Wendell Willkie and get a look at this man who was—the word was then the newest in the news—"blitzing" the delegations.

I do not attempt to reconstruct all that went on. I am competent to record only what I witnessed. The Convention Hall was a hell of sealed-in heat; the night sessions were torture because of the blazing illumination. Before leaving for Philadelphia on Friday, the twenty-first of June, when the whole Eastern seaboard was sweltering, I had realized I would have no time to think about clothes or the processes of keeping them in order. Russell had preceded me to the old Ritz in Philadelphia and told me on the telephone not to rely on laundry or dry-cleaning services there, that the hotel was packed like a cattle-car. I went to

Macy's basement and bought half a dozen of the plainest, cheapest white summer dresses they had, which cost about four dollars apiece. Every night I threw one away and started with a fresh one the next morning.

What I did in Philadelphia during the days up to the nominating speeches and the balloting was stay with the telephone and keep on top of the urgent and secret messages to Russell, who was most of the time with Wendell, or conferring with the handful of wonder-workers who made the miracle amongst the delegates beforehand and on the convention floor. These included Sam Pryor; Sinclair Weeks of Massachusetts; Congressman Kenneth Simpson of New York; Governor Baldwin of Connecticut; Bruce Barton of New York; Rolland Marvin, the Mayor of Syracuse, who cracked the Dewey-committed New York delegation; Governor Ralph Carr of Colorado; Harold Stassen; and Charlie Halleck for whom Russell was writing the Willkie nominating speech.

Every time I have heard such a speech since, I have realized anew the brains and the freshness of what Russell and Halleck did. They abjured the hackneyed prolixity of the "man who" speech, which bores its audience through the intoning of leathery chestnuts like "this great nation" and "our high purpose" until the punch-line when the candidate's name is finally pronounced and the signal fired for the delegation demonstrations on the floor. Halleck spoke a few opening words and said, "I am here to nominate Wendell Willkie." The galleries exploded. "We Want Willkie!" had been a scattered shout up to then. Instantaneously it seized the initiative from the platform and the floor. "We Want Willkie!" turned into a mounting tornado of genuine popular will. It was not rowdy and it was not ugly like the hoodlums who made a disgrace of the Republican Convention of 1964. It was irresistible and it spread like grass-fire. Behind it were the Willkie Clubs which had sprung from the real convictions of individuals all over the country, and behind them was Oren Root. I have heard and read what has been claimed by politicians, reporters, and historians, to the effect that the galleries were packed with stooges or hirelings usually attributed to Sam Pryor; that the tickets distributed to them were crooked; that "We Want Willkie!" was planned, rehearsed, conspired, bought, and paid for. None of that is true.

Sitting in the front row of the balcony, with the terrible arc-lights generating a temperature of well over ninety degrees, Russell and I sweated out the balloting in the most literal sense. We were too tense and too exhausted to react with voice and stamping feet like the excited people around us. The storm of chanting took us by surprise. "We Want Willkie!" was the voice of ordinary people demanding the nomination of the man they wanted. They were far ahead of the delegates on the floor. Oren Root tells me that he made it his business in the galleries to find out how most of the people there had obtained their tickets. They had got them from their own state delegations, which in turn had gone to the convention overwhelmingly committed either to Taft or to Dewey. Members of the Willkie Clubs were scattered throughout, and there were some of the invariable bright young people who always wangle their way in or otherwise crash the party. Oren Root believes that the original shouts of "We Want Willkie!" came from the Clubs and from these stragglers; but as the proceedings went on, he saw more and more others joining in each outburst, until at the end "We Want Willkie!" was a nearly unanimous roar from galleries packed with people wearing Taft and Dewey buttons. Among the pages on the floor of that convention were a pair of eighteen-year-old twin brothers from New York —David and John V. Lindsay. More than twenty years later, when he was my Congressman, John Lindsay told me how he had been impressed and influenced by Wendell Willkie. The influence lives on in the Mayor of today and the man of tomorrow.

Wendell was nominated on the sixth ballot, at quarter past one in the morning of June twenty-eighth. For more than eight hours the savage tussle had gone on. The first ballot was a juggle

between Dewey in the lead, next Taft, next Vandenberg, various
favorite sons, and 105 votes for Willkie, scattered among twenty-
four states and the Philippines, all in straggling small numbers
except the solid sixteen votes of Connecticut—our cornerstone.
Ballot by ballot thereafter, Dewey's votes diminished, Taft's
almost negligibly increased, the favorite sons began to fall away,
and the changing votes went bit by bit to Willkie. The suspense
was so acute that I can feel it to this day; also the bitterness of the
Old Guard, the adamant resistance to the interloper, the hatred
against him and against all of us who had worked for this aim
which was, after all, visionary and fantastic. I looked at Russell,
pale and sweating, with his green eyes glittering in the hot glare.
He was watching the floor where the splitting delegations were
roaring and cursing at one another, the New York one where they
were almost at blows, with Rolland Marvin fighting to grab the
New York standard and lead the rush to the aisles.

When the big breaks came on the sixth ballot, when Vandenberg released Michigan, when the last six votes from New Jersey
made that state unanimous, when the roll-call came to O, and
Oklahoma gave the thirteen deciding former Taft votes to Wendell, each time to greater thunders of "We Want Willkie!",
Russell wrote the tallies with a trembling hand and I leaned
forward to see Governor Bricker of Ohio, the mainstay and general
of the Taft forces, making his way to the platform.

"He's going to move to make it unanimous," Russell said, but
I was too wrought up to believe him. From then on it was pandemonium. Joe Martin continued to poll the delegations, but he
was wildly interrupted by chairmen jumping up to shout for
recognition to change their votes. The bandwagon was rolling
and when it roared to a halt there were 998 votes for Willkie.
I have little memory of the ensuing half hour, during which
Senator McNary was nominated for Vice-President; only of the
intolerable heat and of the superb comportment of Senator Taft
when Wendell and Edith appeared on the platform. Not for many

years could any person of my views find common ground with those of Robert Taft, but he was a great gentleman, a patriot, and his gallantry when he lost to Wendell who in his eyes was no Republican at all, was of a quality rarely seen in politics or elsewhere.

Wendell made a brief and moving address to the convention, his spontaneous best. I wept: who would not? If I could have seen the real future, instead of the lofty dream we held for Wendell and our country and the world, I would have wept more.

The campaign began. It was one thing for a small group of inspired men to incite the American people to demand the nomination of Wendell Willkie and ram him down the throats of the Republican Party. It was quite another to mount a Presidential campaign on the shoulders and through the resources of that party, with the candidate standing off its lifetime professionals and relying on a gaggle of what they called wild-eyed amateurs (and worse). And this through the fall of France, the ominous summer of 1940, the Battle of Britain, the overriding issues of aid to Britain and of a military draft in the United States, in both of which Wendell unconditionally supported his opponent. By these stands he did his country and the Republican Party a historic service, recognized now, but sometimes obscured in smoke and brimstone then.

The Willkie campaign train has roared off into political legend under the name of Organized Chaos. It may well have been Russell who dubbed it that, but I am doubtful only because Russell was the organizer of the chaos. The jet airplane and television have erased from any but old memories the classic Presidential campaign as it was for most of a century, based on the mighty train which for three to four months crossed and recrossed the country. Every night it stopped at a town or city for a mass-meeting in the biggest hall or arena the place afforded, so the people could see the candidate and hear him speak in person. All day the train chuffed on, up and down, back and forth across the land, making frequent whistle-stops with the candidate waving and shaking hands and making short speeches from the end of the last car. I suppose the last such full-scale campaign was that of 1948, with Harry Truman giving 'em hell off the end of his train.

I had thought my job finished after Philadelphia, and I retired to Great Marsh to catch up on my responsibilities and go back to my sidelined book (a piece of self-delusion which has impinged on my probity all my life; I have never written a line in the country or anyway, one that stayed written). Russell, against Wendell's advice, had resigned from *Fortune* at the beginning of May to put all his time into the nomination. Wendell rightly wanted no such responsibility but he did not reckon with his man. Russell told the press that he was working on his own without any authorization from Mr. Willkie; that he did not contemplate forming any organization, raising any funds, or making any of the routine moves of a campaign. He never made them. Routine was a foreign language to him.

In August we went to Wendell's birthplace, Elwood, Indiana, for his formal notification and his acceptance speech at a colossal outdoor mass-meeting. The record has it that the temperature was 102 in the shade; I personally saw a thermometer on somebody's porch which read 112. The whole thing was hell—the journey, the crowds, the blasting heat, the noise, the confusion, the gnats that bit, the plans that went awry, the speech which was not good, the early wrangles with the Republican National Committee. Thankfully I went home to move back to town and really get to work, at the same time organizing the benefit concert which Maestro and the N B C Symphony were to play at the end of November to raise the initial funds for the Memorial to my mother, a part of the Roosevelt Hospital. Maestro when I saw him during the summer was incredulous and scathing about my excitement over Wendell.

"Why politics?" he asked. "Politicians are pigs! Dogs! Criminals! *Tutti*—all of them! They are all the same as Mussolini. This man of yours will be a criminal too, you will see!"

My remonstrance that America was different was slapped down with the noise that sounded like a mastiff muffling a growl —*Mmmppppffff!*

In mid-September Russell left on the Willkie train, heading West. With him went a team of experts to do the hard content of the speeches. They were brilliant and skilful, masters of their specialties, and I doubt if more than one of them had ever been heard of by the Republican old-liners. The idea-thrashing with Wendell and the finished speech-writing were Russell's part; and there were also claims, some abusive and furious, that it was impossible to get to the candidate except through him. This was untrue. The man who stood guard over Wendell and ably filtered the clamoring demands to see him was his brother Edward. But the train had not been gone a week before the reports came back, first in trickles, then in a shower of sparks, that the train (like *Fortune,* like any undertaking of Russell's) was a fountain of anarchy and confusion. The press began to crackle with these stories; Lippmann, Clapper, Moley, and other columnists rushed into print with them. The real basis of the anarchy was not so much Russell's disorganized methods as the bitter warfare between the Republican professionals and Willkie's wild-eyed amateurs. Russell caught the brunt of the blame, though, and it occurred simultaneously to him and to several others that I had better be there; in his view to help out, in that of others, to keep him in some kind of order. He telephoned me from California when he had been gone a week, telling me to fly to Portland, Oregon, to join the train next day; and at the same time Carol Brandt, relaying the urging of several insiders, told me I must go. It had been a delusion anyway that I would sit in New York writing my book. I was much too wrapped up in the campaign to do anything else. And Max Perkins, who ardently wanted Wendell to remove That Man from the Presidency, also told me to go.

The train consisted of about eighteen cars. Behind the engine, or engines, were a dozen compartment or bedroom cars, full of the press. The newspaper men kept the platforms of their cars stacked with cases of beer. Next came the press diner, one or two, hitched and unhitched with murderous shuntings at dawn and late at night. Then came the research car, jammed to the roof and the platforms with filing-cases and working material, crowded with typists and detail experts and office machines; I believe also the mimeograph machines that ground out the copies of speeches for release—but those may have been in a baggage car. Then came our car, where about ten of us lived and worked in a travelling approximation of Andersonville. Then another diner, for politicians and guests and for us (except for rare moments of escape to the cynical company of the newspaper reporters, who sat killing time with beer and poker). Then came the reception car. Last of all, the private car carrying Wendell and Edith and their entourage, headed by Lem Jones—a loyal stalwart donated by Tom Dewey. Lem Jones remained Wendell's right hand to the end of his life.

Russell and I had two adjoining compartments. One was his office. Any office or room of Russell's was a prodigy of disorder —but this one had dirt and cramped space to distinguish it. In the other compartment we slept (when we slept—an average of three hours a night). When the room was made up in the daytime I worked in it and so did a lot of other people. The facilities connected to our bedroom included a shower-bath which never had any water in it. Everything related to physical order and cleanliness, including laundry, was a nightmare. Some of the wildest tales of the Willkie train are stories of lost laundry which never caught up with the men who had left their shirts in a town which seemed to have slunk off the map when anybody tried to connect with it again. This was years before nylon, drip-dry, and the habits they brought with them. We lived like that for six weeks.

In the car with us were Raymond Leslie Buell, the well-known economist and presider over The Fortune Round Table, who had invited Wendell to that fateful meeting; Elliott V. Bell, financial expert and later Banking Commissioner of New York State; Pierce Butler, Jr., of Minneapolis, one of the leading Democrats for Willkie; Bartley Crum, a shrewd young San Francisco lawyer who years later went far out to political left field; Paul Smith of the San Francisco *Chronicle;* John B. Hollister of Cincinnati, a law partner of Senator Taft's and a member of his Ohio organization. He was the only Republican politician of the lot—some said, the only real Republican. Oren Root joined us at intervals. So did various others. Looking back on it I wonder that I had anything to contribute.

Apparently Wendell and my husband thought I had. Russell called me in on the language of the speeches and on what we called ear impact as distinct from eye impact. I was invoked in another area where Russell with his poetic gifts would have done better had he had time, but he had no time. Wendell conveyed a passionate personal emotion about the United States, a powerful drive sprung from his small-town Indiana roots. Sometimes there came a place to bring this through the text of a speech. It has to be done well or it comes out corn. When I was confronted with such lines to write, I would sit alone in the grimy compartment with the door locked, looking out the window as the train rushed across the endless spaces of this country. Sometimes I wondered how I dared to do this, I who knew only New York which they say is not America. I did not see it so. I did not attempt synthetic paraphrases of Wendell's sentiments, for I had a wellspring of my own to draw on—the memory of my mother talking about the home towns and the plain people of this country. She had travelled the length and breadth of every one of the forty-eight states, had sung in all of them, and was very proud of that. She was known and loved by everyday people, was met in county seats by fire-department bands and banners strung across Main Street saying "Welcome, Alma Gluck." Her annual concert was the big event of the year; and while she had no phony sentimentality about prairie ovens and tank towns, she knew what moved men and women who were like Grant Wood subjects, and she knew that it had to be genuine. I held this memory as the measure of the words I wrote, and it did not fail me.

Somebody found that I spoke a number of languages and I was drafted for occasional duty in the reception car, the province of our sworn enemies, the Republican National Committee. But actually most of them were friendly people, bewildered at the invaders who had put over this maverick candidate on them. When the train stopped at towns along the route the local committeemen and women came aboard, to be entertained in the reception car and passed through to the end car to shake hands with Willkie. All these politicians obviously spoke perfect English, but some of them came from what were later, I think, called nationality groups. It was supposed to be good politics to slap around a few phrases in the old mother tongue. It was Italian in San Francisco, German in Milwaukee, and so forth.

In the evenings I discharged the most responsible of my duties. The train would stop in the scheduled city, to be met by a motorcade to take Wendell to the arena, followed by a stream of cars carrying the reporters from the train, who had already received and transmitted the mimeographs of what they were about to hear. Every town put on the same hullabaloo and neither Russell nor I ever got to a meeting or heard Wendell deliver a prepared speech in person, except the final one at Madison Square Garden. Russell stayed shut up on the train sweating out the next day's speech, and I went ashore to do the private telephoning. In each town a hotel room was reserved for me, to which I went when the candidate and the mob had departed for the meeting. I had a list of the telephone calls that Wendell wanted made. The calls went all over the country. I would first give the hotel operator the whole list of numbers and ask her to put through the

calls as fast as she could complete them. Then I would draw a hot
bath and take off my clothes, dying for that bath. The telephone
would ring. I would take the call stark naked, make my notes,
start towards the bathroom, and the telephone would ring. So it
would go until I had finished the last call without ever getting as
far as the bathtub. Usually then, just when I was stepping into the
water which had cooled, there would be a battering at the door
and some voice outside would shout, "Hey, for crissake, the train's
leaving." Into the clothes again and back to the train, without the
bath. I have thought of this in recent years when I have seen
candidates' wives and lady politicians on television, groomed and
coiffed impeccably, and heard of their personal hairdressers going
along in the campaign plane.

It should not be thought because of my lighter memories
that we were unrealistic or frivolous in estimating what we were
up against in Franklin Roosevelt and his hold on the nation. We
were not. The domestic and the foreign forces of history combined
against us were in essence insurmountable, and the President
played on these elements with the virtuosity of the political cathedral organist he was. Resting on the worship of millions who
held him their redeemer—though some ten million of them were
still unemployed; backed by organized labor and by the Democratic machines of the big cities, to whose venality he held himself
superior except at convention and election time; a mighty spokesman for the free world embattled against Hitler—Wendell did
not underestimate any of this, nor the disdain with which the
President pursued his initial policy of dedicated preoccupation
with the problems of the nation and the world. He would not
stoop to notice his opponent or condescend to the campaign arena.
Some of our amateur blunders in the early weeks were glaring.
Wendell made mistakes in judgement and he was reckless in his
relentless grind on his voice, which gave out several times. Throat
specialists and advisers in voice production came onto the train
and were of some help, but nothing could keep Wendell from the

platform of his car when the train slowed down and even a handful of bystanders were gathered to hear him speak off the top of
his head. He was at his best then. Nobody who was there will ever
forget that burly, tousled figure, the impassioned face with the
long, stubborn upper lip, bearing down hard on those raw vocal
cords, haranguing the cheering people in rural areas and the sullen people in industrial ones, the hoarse voice crying "Production!
Production! Production!"

By the middle of October the tide began to turn. Wendell
was getting through to the people, the polls showed steady gains,
the mistakes were less catastrophic and the successes more positive.
We had our sources in Washington and around the country who
informed us before it became public that Roosevelt and his advisers were beginning to be alarmed. They convinced him that he
would have to come down from his disdainful height and make
some campaign speeches.

He consented to descend to a little campaigning with the help
of Boss Flynn and the voice from Chicago's sewers. Nobody
claimed the Republican Party contained no such elements but
nobody was being pious about them. Two Roosevelt speeches
were announced, which were shortly increased to five. They are
well remembered, and by me with bitterness, for they initiated a
disgraceful slugging-match in which neither candidate wholly kept
his integrity. By this time the election was approaching and the
air was greasy with lies, hysterical accusations and the mephitic
effluvium of whispered scandal. Roosevelt in a speech in Brooklyn referred to the candidacy of Willkie as the "unholy alliance
between the extreme reactionary and the extreme radical elements
in this country." He charged that Wendell Willkie was stirring
class hatred. Wendell blew off in a tearing rage, and rightly, for
nothing could have been a falser accusation. His final speech was
in preparation, the one to be delivered in Madison Square Garden on the Saturday night before Tuesday's election. He wanted
the speech to build up to an apostrophe to the American people,

pledging them his total allegiance to civil liberties, equality for all, and what today we comprise in the term civil rights.

At one point Russell gave me the drafted sentences to work over, and I, having heard Wendell passionately express these ideals in his own words, worked them into the text in terms which I was too naïve to understand were then absolutely taboo in politics. Russell when he read them whistled with surprise, himself strengthened and improved them, and incorporated them in the finished speech. The speech went to the Republicans around the candidate and the fight was on. That was one of the instances in which the story is true that men almost came to blows. The disputed lines were taken out by them, put back by Wendell, taken out, put back. When the final draft went to the mimeograph and the final copies went to the press, the lines were out. They therefore do not appear in the newspaper versions of Wendell's last campaign speech.

But when Wendell in Madison Square Garden before twenty-three thousand people, with many thousands more listening to loud-speakers outside in the streets, came to the place where the disputed lines had been deleted from the big-type copy in the notebook before him, he paused. Then he made his pledge, interpolated and freely spoken, in the words that had been fought over: his allegiance to equality of life and liberty and opportunity for all, without discrimination of race, creed, or color; to all the American people of every strain and origin; to Christian and Jew, to Catholic and Protestant, to Negro and to white. Loud and clear he spoke all the tabooed words.

The crowd exploded. They stood up in a mass, they leaped onto their chairs, they shouted and clapped, they cheered and whistled, they stamped, they blew horns; they made a noise like no noise I ever heard before, and they made it louder and longer. I was perched on a railing at the back of the platform crammed with party big-shots, and beside me on the railing was one of the biggest Republican shots of all; able and tough and heavily armored in elephant's hide. I stole a glance at him. He was wiping his eyes with his handkerchief.

Three days later Wendell was defeated. But he polled the biggest popular vote a Republican had ever won, possibly the most constructive defeat a candidate ever met. It was the opposite of the classic Pyrrhic victory. It changed the direction of Republican policy during the war and in the harried years of non-peace afterwards. Old Guard Republicans feared and hated Willkie more after the 1940 election than they had before, and did their utmost to insure that no such maverick and his wild-eyed crew ever again repeat the incredible feat of Philadelphia. But no Republican since has taken a leading place in American and world affairs who did not follow the path that Willkie blazed. And when the Old Guard, after twenty-four years of battling his ghost and his echo, nominated one of their own for the Presidency, Goldwater went down to the most crushing defeat in Presidential campaign history.

The night after the 1940 election Russell and I were alone at home, in a state of exhaustion and near-shock which was like too sudden emergence from a decompression chamber. The doorbell rang, about eleven o'clock. I went to open the door—to Harry Hopkins. I had never met him, though Russell had, more times than he admitted. Hopkins was like a walking corpse, bone-pale, emaciated, bent and stooped with weakness. He shuffled into the drawing-room with me, saying to Russell, "Tell me all about it. Tell me how you did it."

Hopkins asked me for a glass of milk and something very light to eat. I gathered that the fatal gastric ailment above which he rose so many times to do heroic service to his chief and to our cause in the war, required him to eat frequently in minimal quantities. This was a man on whom we had concentrated as much mental and verbal opprobrium as on any personification of the New Deal. But his appearance at that moment was corroboration of the great crisis beyond domestic politics, which was the real concern of both Wendell Willkie and Franklin Roosevelt; of every man who put first things first and understood what our country was about to face. I brought the milk and a chicken sandwich and sat with the two men for a little while. Then I retired, leaving them to talk until past two o'clock in the morning.

THE *New York Times* has spoiled my plan for the opening sentence of this chapter. The sentence stood in my manuscript for perhaps eight months and was to have been: "Where were you when you heard about Pearl Harbor?" Then in November, 1966, the *Times* began a series of advertisements for a documentary record album called "Dec. 7, 1941" and headed its dramatic full page: "Where were you when Pearl Harbor was attacked?" I decline to be accused of plagiarizing the *Times,* but the *Times* has underlined my reason for stating that universal question, which people have been asking one another ever since. The question is dramatic because the moment had a uniformity unusual in the motility and restlessness of American life. So it remained in memory: the quiet of a winter Sunday afternoon when nearly everybody had finished the traditional midday dinner and had settled down to the rest or the Sunday newspapers or whatever he most enjoyed. There was no television; it was not a time of year for sports or outings; the skiing weekend was far in the future; people were mostly at home. Thousands of them were listening to the radio broadcast of the Philharmonic concert, among them my husband. I have no idea why, because we had been at Maestro's concert with the N B C Symphony the evening before, and the Philharmonic had as little attraction for Russell as for me. They must have been playing some work he specially wanted to hear. I was at the other end of the house when I heard Russell shouting for me in a high, tense voice. I ran to the room where the music had been interrupted by the radio news flash about the

Japanese attack on the American fleet. We were too stunned to grasp the full import of this, or even really believe what we heard.

"Japan?" we asked each other. *"Japan?"*

Our vicarious participation in the war had been so bound up with Europe that for all our intensity, and all our conviction that our country had to join the fight to crush the Axis, Japan had not had immediacy to us. The recent meetings between Secretary Hull and the Japanese envoys had not hinted at the dénouement that followed. Nobody knew at those first moments or for long afterwards what really had happened, but by the time we understood that the report was true and not the wild hoax which some people first thought, we knew we were at war—or would be when the President had addressed Congress next day at half past twelve. The progression which evoked the German and Italian declarations of war on us four days later was not yet clear, but its ultimate certainty was.

At that time Peggy and Lewis Douglas lived in our apartment building, and on the same floor. We had asked them to come across the hall for a pick-up Sunday supper and I do not remember who else was there, but we were six or seven people. We were all stupefied by the news and wholly in the dark as to what to do. Our first idea was that Hitler might have planned a sneak attack on the East Coast in some way synchronized with Pearl Harbor. We actually expected it. I do not remember how we thought the Nazis could have effected this; presumably they had no bombers of transatlantic range and no carriers to bring smaller bombers near us. But what did we really know about that? We sat talking in low voices, each of us particularly calm because we expected that of one another. Presently an air-raid siren began to wail. In recent months there had been some rudimentary precautions installed in the event of 'emergency.'

We stopped talking and sat looking round the table with raised eyebrows. What was the right thing to do? Was there really an air attack approaching New York? I went and turned on the radio and turned off all the lights. It was a long time before some station informed us that the sirens were only being tested because of the day's events. Incidentally they were totally inadequate had they been needed to alert the whole city; there happened to be one in our vicinity, I suppose because of the proximity to the East River with all its bridges. For years no military man entered our drawing-room with its five long windows overlooking the river who did not say, "What a target!" I wonder if today I am supposed to take comfort in the thought that the science of destruction has advanced so far that precision bombing is no longer the instrumentality which would eradicate New York.

In a certain way we were crestfallen here when we realized that the United States would be immune to air attack, not because this deprived us of the chance to be heroic like the British; but we felt ashamed. It did not feel like holding up our end for our own country to go unscathed, or to compare ourselves with the peoples of occupied Europe who were suffering the horrors of Nazi rule. All of us, my friends and associates, everybody I knew, wanted to plunge into war jobs, but the only effective thing that most men and women of my age and range of profession could do was stay in our own fields and find ways to make them contribute to the war effort. I doubt that any of us really accomplished much individually, and the combination of confusion, delays, bureaucracy and know-nothingness was maddening. The men were naturally overtaken by restlessness and the frustration of seeing the younger men join the fighting forces. There was a rush on Washington. Alphabetical agencies and administrations sprouted like mustard-seed; jockeying for titles and rank was hectic; lawyers swarmed to the proliferating war agencies; coordination and coordinator became dirty words; and the United States again, as in the First World War, required nearly a year to put troops into action and start to fight. The landing in North Africa in November, 1942, was hailed in our circles with literal tears of excitement and thanksgiving. It is a notable fact about the Second World War that each person who was passionately committed to it had his own orientation to it. It is commonplace that the European war was the East Coast's war, and the Pacific war that of the West Coast and the middle west.

But some of us had been ahead of events for a long time. While I was immersed in the Willkie campaign I had left *The Valley of Decision* simmering like a pot-au-feu on the back of the stove; and when I shut myself up for the major work on it at the end of 1940, I found that writing such a book has further analogies to the soup-kettle. Ingredients are not only added from time to time according to what is on hand or what you must go out and fetch; but nourishing food comes out of the pot during the long, slow cooking, like the boiled chicken or the marrow from beef bones that is so delicious with plenty of *gros sel* on the heel of a loaf of rye bread. What I brought out beyond all else was intensifying concern and involvement with the Czechoslovak people. My first attachment to their land and their architecture and their music and the strange spell of Prague had been strengthened and made much more realistic through knowledge of their history both ancient and recent, the traditions weaving back to the Bohemian Kings of the middle ages, to Jan Hus and the Reformation, to the sources of and reasons for their emergence as an admirable modern democracy in the Masaryk Republic. It was intolerable that that country and that people should have been Hitler's first victims, abandoned to him by the shameful and futile appeasement of Munich. By 1940 I saw it all in the round, and I cared, and acted, to the utmost of my ability. But the Czechoslovaks by then were not alone in their terrible plight; the situation of all Europe was desperate.

Hitler had overrun the whole continent except for the classic neutrals and Stalin's Russia, still poised in the bad dream of the Nazi-Soviet Pact of 1939. The Nazi extermination machine was grinding ahead unchecked. Purges, transports, concentration camps, gas chambers, crematories, torture, slave labor, and the whole hideous apparatus for "the final solution of the Jewish problem" and for bringing free nations to heel were proliferating everywhere. There was collaboration in some conquered countries, but in most, heroic and fanatical resistance—in divided France, in Holland, Denmark, Poland, Bohemia. There in November, 1939, the Nazis had perpetrated the bloody, obscene massacre of university students in retaliation for an attack on one of their satraps. Like the later destruction of Lidice and the slaughter of its inhabitants this horror roused the whole world. But it was anyway a time of horrors. Britain was standing alone in the breach, braving the first winter of the Blitz, with Winston Churchill voicing his immortal words of defiance and inspiration.

It was impossible to remain unimpassioned. To me and to the people I knew and trusted it was our cause and our war. The late political campaign was racked up in history while President Roosevelt effected Lend-Lease for Britain and sent fifty destroyers to initiate it. Wendell Willkie went off to England in January, carrying the President's letter of introduction to Winston Churchill with its much-quoted quotation from Longfellow. The journey was a magnificent manifestation of statesmanship rising above politics, the message of American solidarity with Britain dramatically personified. Here, we pitched in with everything we could muster as individuals and in groups, to support Britain, and to help Hitler's victims in the limited ways that were possible. The moral question was paramount. I remember now and then encountering people whose isolationist views were those of an organization called America First, bred in the medium of the Chicago *Tribune*. The fights were furious. Our own activities consisted of outright propaganda and every form of exhortation to fight Hitler. We were very active members of The Committee to Defend America by Aiding the Allies, but we called ourselves the Let's Get in the War Now Society. One of the tasks we could do here was raise funds to send supplies and foodstuffs to Britain. I spoke at many rallies for the first of these agencies, then called the British Relief

Society. Later it became British War Relief. But quite as soon I found myself working with Americans of Czech and Slovak descent, who since the nineteenth century have formed large communities all over the United States. They were supporting the Czechoslovak soldiers and fliers fighting with the British. These men had escaped from their own country, many of the fliers in Czech Air Force planes, between Hitler's final annihilation of the Republic in March, 1939, and the assault on Poland which precipitated the war six months later. Thousands of Czech civilians had escaped too and were scattered all over the world, living in hardship. At this stage of the war it was not possible to get help to the people inside Czechoslovakia. Everybody knows what happened to the Jews amongst them; but time has rushed on, dimming the memory of the savage Nazi reprisals against the families of the men who had escaped to fight outside, and against the underground resistance at home. Their heroism was usually suicidal and their exploits were communicated mysteriously and promptly to their exiled government in London.

All the time I was writing *The Valley of Decision* the war in Europe was like a continual high-voltage charge which not only spurred me along but gave me extra work to do on the side. Twenty-five years ago it did not seem particularly effortful to keep four or five activities going and do justice to them all—but I was thirty-eight years old. If at that age one were not at the top of one's powers both of intake and output, one would never be. I worked with the Czechoslovaks in this country at fund-raising and at war propaganda. The long-range sense of my feeling for these people and their country would emerge in the book I was writing, but more immediately there was work to do with them day by day. I needed all the material I could get. Much of it came from the Czechoslovaks here, from their Washington Embassy and their New York Consulate; but presently it began to arrive from their government-in-exile in London. I had not asked for it, and do not know who ordered that it be sent me. Some of it was unknown to the world in general, like the details of the student massacre at Ruzýň, which went into my book. Every week I received dossiers of private information, remarkably specific, about what was happening inside the occupied country, which I could use in any way I thought would serve the cause.

After Hitler invaded the Soviet Union in June of 1941, the issues of the war became, so we thought, absolute. Hindsight today clouds the mind with all that we have learned since 1943, when Soviet political objectives in the war became apparent, and the inability or unwillingness of our leaders to recognize or to counter those objectives led to the eventual communization of half of Europe. In 1941 we saw Russian participation in the war as a mighty club with which to smash Hitler. The Russian war effort and the terrible devastation of the Soviet Union evoked massive response in this country and in Britain, who had agonies enough of her own. The then Mrs. Churchill headed the British fund-raising drives for Russian relief, and Mrs. Roosevelt did the same here, enlisting me as one of the chief speakers for Russian War Relief rallies.

There was a short-wave radio station in Boston which used to broadcast to the occupied countries. They asked me to speak on their broadcasts to Czechoslovakia. Nobody knew how well such broadcasts got through, or whether there was any use to them, since the great morale arm of the Czechoslovak cause was the weekly talk on the B B C by Jan Masaryk, the Foreign Minister of the exiled government in London. The Czechs and Slovaks listened to him clandestinely on pain of death, on secret and often home-made receivers called bed-spring radios. His talks were unique in the whole realm of war propaganda, for Jan Masaryk, beyond his identity and personality which his people adored, had a highly personal gift for colorful speech. His thoughts and his way of expressing them were devoid of hortatory bombast. He was eloquent but not oratorical. He knew how to put himself close to anybody he wanted to reach, and he spoke to the people in his beleaguered country as if he were huddled over their secret radios with them. The Czechoslovaks are largely a peasant people and he told them plain truth, even when it dealt with the unendurable. They were surrounded by lies and threats and terror. He encouraged them with truth and with messages of reassurance and affection, couched in his own intimate language which was tender and also pungent; witty, and full of the earthy humor that was primarily humanness.

I could not see that broadcasts in English from the Boston radio could be of supplementary use, but if their value was non-neutrality from a then non-belligerent country, I was willing to help. Once or twice it was decided that I read phonetically some short phrase in Czech translated from my English text. This was not the first time I had been stumped by mere confrontation with the language and I decided that that would not do. I was constantly surrounded by purposes and by material which made me feel stupid and hampered by not being able to read and speak Czech. The language is too difficult to pick up by ear and by instinct, as I have done with others, as a decent linguist often can do. I remembered that my mother had first learnt Russian by pronouncing it phonetically without knowing what it meant, but I found that this was no way to break in my jaws on Czech. And behind and beyond all the current efforts and the war itself, lay my intention to go to Czechoslovakia again as soon as it was free— and I never doubted that it would be. The time had come to learn Czech. Never again would I stumble around Czechoslovakia asking people if they would mind speaking German with me. One of the refugees from Prague who was working at the Czechoslovak Consulate in New York came three times a week to give me lessons. It was fascinating but confounding to be confronted for the first time by a Slavic language, whose roots are unrelated to a syllable in any other language I knew, and whose grammar so intricate and heavily inflected that it is really impossible for anybody to master perfectly who was not born in it.

Nobody I knew was more impassioned about the war and more combative in his own way than Maestro. His way was music; and also a private arm of immense generosity to victims of Mussolini and Hitler; to their families and their desperate necessities for refuge and work. Maestro had always been virulent in his detestation of Mussolini and the Fascisti. He was reckless in his denunciations of the dictator. Most of the time he was safe from reprisal because of his prestige in Italy and throughout the world. He was universally called the greatest living Italian and nobody would have risked the obloquy of molesting him. He belonged by birth to a hard core of tough and resistant men, the artisan and working class of North Italian towns. He was called by his compatriots "Parmesan of the rock" which well describes this breed, and means a native of the city of Parma. But the whole province of which it is the capital produces the same strain, one of whose endowments is musicality and another, rebelliousness. Giuseppe Verdi was of almost identical nativity; the only difference was Verdi's birth in a rural town. In the last year of Maestro's life I was asked to write the text for the record album of Verdi music played by Maestro, titled *Verdi and Toscanini*. In it I traced the remarkable similarity of origin, intellect, temperament, and character in the two titans, creative and interpretive, of Italian music. I read the essay to Maestro who was then in frail health, his eyesight failing badly. He was moved to tears and with much less control, so was I.

At the height of the war he was in his middle seventies. He had commanding vigor and the drive of furious hatred of Mussolini and Hitler. He was a very proud man of incorruptible personal and intellectual integrity. To him the debasement of Italy by Mussolini and his cohorts was an intolerable humiliation; the situation of Italy allied with Hitler and excoriated by the free world was grotesque. Maestro's father, Claudio Toscanini, had fought with Garibaldi. Like his native affinity with Verdi, that was of the texture of his passionate *italianità*. Only twice did the

Fascisti dare to challenge him; in 1931 in Bologna when he flatly refused to play *Giovanezza,* the Blackshirt anthem, before a concert and was physically mauled by some hoodlums; and in 1938, just before he was to leave Milan for his New York season with the N B C Symphony. Mussolini confiscated his passport—it was said, at the insistence of Hitler in retaliation for Toscanini's cancellation of Salzburg. The passport was returned through pressure that was quietly understood to have come from President Roosevelt. Maestro and his wife arrived in New York to remain throughout the war, honored guests in this country, of special status which disregarded the wartime classification of Italian nationals as enemy aliens.

The Toscanini house at Riverdale became headquarters of the musical world's resistance to Fascism and Nazism, and a refuge in transit for many of Hitler's victims. Maestro had been playing all his life with Jewish musicians. His precise, rather rigid mind, which categorized people and their collective and individual personalities as accurately as all the other elements of his knowledge, beginning with music, had its own orientation to Jews. He was immensely respectful of them and of their natural gifts and achievements; musicality first, of course, but intellect and enterprise and all the rest. He could also be mischievous and outspoken about their faults, as he was about anybody's defects and lapses.

When Hitler's pogroms broke up the orchestras of Germany and then of the occupied countries, sending their musicians into flight if they escaped the camps and death factories, Maestro and Signora Carla were a first recourse for those who arrived here. To this day only the recipients know the full measure of the quiet and often anonymous generosity of the Toscaninis. Maestro helped innumerable exiled musicians to find work. And his house was, naturally, the gathering-place of the anti-Fascist Italians who had made their way here, mostly to teach in American universities, like Gaetano Salvemini, G. A. Borgese, and Giorgio La Piana. Maestro had always played great benefit concerts to raise funds for causes he wanted to support. His original contract with the National Broadcasting Company stipulated that he be given the services of the orchestra and Carnegie Hall in that season for two benefits of his choice; and this continued every year. At such concerts the orchestra and the rental of the hall were paid, but Maestro gave his services. The beneficiaries were various American and Italian institutions; hospitals, welfare agencies, and the Casa di Riposo in Milan, the home for aged musicians founded by Verdi.

After the war began the American public met a Toscanini they had not known before; the one who had left the Metropolitan in 1915 to conduct a military band on the Italian Front in the First World War. Every summer during the war he conducted a series of popular concerts under the sponsorship of the Treasury Department; admission (except for members of the Armed Forces) could only be had by buying a War Bond. Wearing a white coat, and starting off with a Star-Spangled Banner orchestrated by himself which raised shivers of excitement, he played Sousa marches, popular overtures, and light music that brought people out of their seats with howls of enthusiasm. The waltzes and other dance music made it impossible to believe his grumpy statement, "I never danced in my life." He made everybody else dance sitting down. It was in the midst of one of those War Bond concerts on 25th July, 1943, during the intermission, that the programme was interrupted by the news flash that Mussolini had fallen and was in flight. Maestro's face and bearing when he returned to the stage was a sight I shall never forget. He was playing an all-Verdi programme which took on the quality of a sacrament in the circumstances. Some of it was repeated, together with *The Hymn of the Nations,* the following spring, at a concert in Madison Square Garden for the benefit of the Red Cross. The N B C Symphony and the Philharmonic were combined in an orchestra of over two hundred men, with a body of massed choruses, to make a monster concert that raised an enormous sum of money.

It is hard to realize a quarter of a century later that such uncomplicated sincerity in individuals, evoking chain-reactions of popular response, could have been the least factor in a war. But war as we knew it then was an unclouded purpose. We of the anti-Nazi, anti-Fascist world knew who our enemy was, and the knowledge was sharper for being personified in Hitler and his jackal partner. Today we are trapped in the equivocation of undeclared war against a faceless enemy. We are embroiled in the impersonality of what may be an irresistible historic force crunching ahead over the mounting disunity of a fragmented world. In the First and Second World Wars we were perhaps brash and overly idealistic or juvenile in personifying the enemy as Hun or Nazi, Kaiser or Hitler; but those enemies carried the seeds of their own dissolution within themselves, and to crush them, we believed, was to sweep clean. Both times the tragic, irreparable American error was losing the peace by failing to fight a political war when others were doing so. In the winter of 1940–41 nobody foresaw such a conclusion. The ultimate and preponderant belligerents were not yet even in the war.

You cannot copyright a title. This fact of life came up one day when I was lunching with Max Perkins and he asked me if I had decided on a title for the novel I was writing. I had, and I told him. There is a point of view which holds that a good title is the title of a good book, and nothing more. But I do not concede this, because any voracious reader is constantly encountering good potential titles, and the analects I had chosen from the Book of Joel seemed exactly right to me. I thought Max would agree. To my surprise, he looked doubtful.

"What's the matter with the title?" I asked him.

He said slowly, "I have an idea it's been used before."

"So have lots of others. What did you do when Galsworthy used *Escape* as a title?"

Max was not fond of being needled about Galsworthy, however gently, but he laughed and said he would look up the title I wanted to use and let me know what he found. Next morning he telephoned. *The Valley of Decision* he told me, was the title of Edith Wharton's first novel. I am a very particular admirer of Edith Wharton's work and I thought I had read all her books. But I had never heard of this one.

"Yes," Max conceded. "It is very obscure, out of print for many years. I think it was published about 1902."

" 'You cannot copyright a title' " I parrotted, from whomever I had last heard it. "But if you have any misgivings, Max, do please clear it with her estate or her publisher. I really want to use the title."

There was a long silence. Suddenly my mind switched from Appletons, where it had lighted, to another perch. I said, "Max. Who published Edith Wharton's book?"

Another long pause.

"We did," came the reluctant reply.

Max sent me Scribners' library copy of Edith Wharton's book to read. Only because of the notable and much deserved re-surgence of interest in Edith Wharton in recent years do people other than literary insiders know that her first novel was *The Valley of Decision*—a static and rather artificial historical romance set in eighteenth-century Italy. She found her stride with her next and probably her finest novel, *The House of Mirth*. Max abandoned his opposition to my using the title and stood by me in his inimitable way while I plugged on through all of 1941 and half of the next year until the revised manuscript—a six months' job of revision—was finished. Max used to write me short notes every now and then, whose point was always the same:

> "I know it is a terrible task, and especially with the world the way it is. Why don't you not go through it too carefully, but just do as you have been doing and then let me study it all."

Or he would say, over what he called afternoon tea, "Just get it all down on paper and then we'll see what to do with it."

One hot summer afternoon when we were having a drink in the garden of the Chatham, and I was very discouraged, a big man came striding over from the entrance. I recognized Ernest Hemingway, whom I had never met. He leaned over the table and began to talk to Max who was attempting to introduce Hemingway to me. Hemingway ignored me completely and continued trying to speak to Max. I saw Max's sensitive face flinching from Hemingway's rudeness, and I was sorry because I knew how much pride he took in the man's work and what close friends they were. Hemingway acted as though I were a gnat. Max said, "You can tell me that tomorrow in my office, Hem. I'm not free now." He turned to me and Hemingway left. I felt more chagrin for Max than resentment at Hemingway. I never knew Ernest Hemingway at all and had no reason to admire him personally—except for his loyalty to Scribners until the end of his life. One up, I thought, on Tom Wolfe.

But Max was stronger-minded about writers and their necessities, and less moved by sentiment than I was. Some months after *The Valley of Decision* had been published I was dining with Charles and Vera Scribner and Max. I was still in a state resembling post-anaesthesia, feeling as though Max had been the surgeon who had got me through a critical major operation. Tom Wolfe and his problems came into the conversation, and Max said he felt that Wolfe could only have gone ahead with his work by leaving Scribners as he had done.

"Oh, no!" I said. "He needed you as much as I do. I couldn't write a book without you."

"If that were true," said Max, "you would not be worth the work that has gone into you."

A few days later he wrote me a long letter, and here is the best part of it:

"You know there is not any help I could possibly give you that I would not give most willingly. Besides, you could never possibly become dependent in the way Tom did . . . The danger that I meant was that if a writer feels that the public believes he could not function as a writer without some individual's help, he really has to prove that this is not so . . . For instance, Goethe would have turned against anyone if he thought that it was thought he could not create his work without that person's literary help . . . But in a literary sense, one really cannot do anything like as much as the run of the public believe. I was only afraid that in your generosity you might give people the impression that you owed immensely more to me than you did, or could. You simply got tangled up in all the underbrush of a huge book, and I, not being the writer, was not tangled in it and could see your way out. That is, the ways in which you could do what you meant to do. But it was you who did it. That always must be true with a real writer. I only thought that if you did get to think, as Tom did, that you were dependent upon me as an artist, you would get to resent it, and should resent it . . . I know I hung back for a long time in working with your manuscript, but that was only because editing to such a degree is a terribly dangerous thing. Good writers have often been damaged by editors who undertake too much. Apart from these things, I could find nothing more interesting than working with you and will always do it to any degree you wish . . ."

Max had a way of sending his authors books written by other writers of his; rather particularly, I think, when a book was remote from one's own range of subject and style. In this way I came to appreciate the work of Marjorie Kinnan Rawlings; and presently when she was in New York from her beloved Cross Creek in the wilds of central Florida, Max introduced us. I suppose there was not one thing we really had in common except books and the reading and writing and living of them, but we became devoted friends. Marjorie had a heart as big as the Big Scrub she wrote about. She was intensely American in the rooted, regional, earthy sense that I am not. She had a rowdy, bellowing love of laughter, a passionate tenderness for animals, illimitable hospitality, she was a superb cook, and she loved to eat and drink.

I used to go and stay with her at Cross Creek. I would be tempted
to describe the lovely, languorous, sweet-smelling place if Marjorie herself had not done that so memorably in her own books
which are not and I hope never will be out of print. No easier
life for a lazy guest has ever been devised. There were no hours,
no rules, no routine; one day differed from another only because
of whim or of how late we had been up the night before. Some
years after Wendell ran for President we spent a vacation in Florida with him and on the way north stopped at Cross Creek to see
Marjorie. Wendell was fascinated by writers and had greatly admired *The Yearling*, but he never got any of the book-talk with
Marjorie that he had hoped for. She gave us a luncheon so prodigious and delicious that we dispersed in a daze, each to the nearest thing to lie down on, and slept like logs the rest of the afternoon and evening.

I wonder now how it happened that we took such a vacation
in the middle of the war, but the details are gone beyond recap-
turing. Long-distance travel was difficult, short trips were ruled
out by gasoline rationing. Cars were disposed of or put in dead
storage. We never returned to Great Marsh after 1941; the war
made such summers impossible. I had all I could do with the revision of *The Valley of Decision*. The framework of the revision
was a long memorandum from Max, broken down by chapters,
which gave me perspective finally to be able to see the forest for
the trees. It was a very long book and as in any book that is properly constructed, solutions to problems and corrections of faults
throughout the early parts were only to become clear from the
vantage-point of the end.

I had a strange and moving experience recently when I went
to Scribners to look at copies of Max's letters to me whose originals
I thought might be incomplete in my own files. (They are not.)
There in a locked and dusty portion of the file-rooms had been
laid out for me all the folders of correspondence since the begin-

ning of my treasured relationship with Scribners thirty-six years before. And I had totally forgotten that in these files would be all the letters I had ever written to Max. There they were—handwritten or dashed off on my typewriter; never a copy of them made, for I have a phobia about carbon copies. I have never made a carbon of a letter unless it was about business requiring a consecutive record of the matter under discussion. As a result I do not possess a copy of any letter I ever wrote to a person who was a close and vital part of my life. When I saw all at once these forgotten letters spanning the seventeen years of my devotion to and friendship with Max, I was overcome. They were so young in their mingling of brashness, timidity, and enthusiasm; so trustful of Max, so doubtful of myself. I put my head in my arms on that grimy table and wept.

But I laughed too. Back came that awful summer of 1942, with that enormous manuscript ripped apart and its pieces all over the house, and Max encouraging me with little notes or telephone calls, or taking me out to tea after I had staggered into his office with another load ready to go to press, or another wad of corrected galleys. I wrote him:

> "If you want me to come tomorrow to go over this, I can in the early afternoon, but I have to catch a five o'clock train to Philadelphia to dine with my mother-in-law. If you want it to be Friday instead, I could make it earlier in the afternoon but will have to be at home by five on account of the children. If you want my children, my mother-in-law, and all my other encumbrances except my cat, it would help a lot to unburden me of them."

I found too the letter I wrote him after delivering in person, as usual, the manuscript of the next novel I wrote, which was brutally difficult. I described the time years before when I had walked round and round the block, sure that Max would say the manuscript I had just left with him was unpublishable.

"This time" (I wrote) "I am too despairing even to walk around the block. I am just sitting with my head in my hands wondering where I can get a job as a cook."

Even before I was through with *The Valley of Decision* the war jobs crowded in at the rate of two or three a day. In retrospect I cannot feel as though those meetings, rallies, speeches, broadcasts, and articles written for periodicals and propaganda organs could really have been of much use; but what else had a person like me to contribute? My husband too was engulfed. He had returned briefly to *Fortune* after the end of the Willkie campaign; then he moved to *Life* to inaugurate and write its editorial page which has continued ever since. He was restless, and unless he was writing wholly from his own convictions as in some of his best apostrophes to the American people, and all his expressions about the war, he was disoriented. He started and dropped a number of projects. It was a tense and difficult time, when the disparities between the best we had and were, and the worst, were sharper than they had ever been. There had always been a resource of immense mutual purpose in work between us, and for what reason I do not know, this never again reached the pitch that it had in the Willkie campaign. The tensions and pressures that were to culminate in a radically changed existence were already thick around us; but in such a passage one does not see, and even less remember, each step of the way. Much of it is groped through as though blindfolded. That is my recollection of the early war years; that, and constant work for war causes.

In a way that was flippant, I fear, but irresistible in its context, I used to say not very nicely that it was I who killed Alexander Woollcott. Nobody would better have understood what I meant than Woollcott himself. In all the years between my youth and the height of the war nothing had ever happened to soften my bitter memory of his beastliness to me as a defenceless girl. During the war, the Writers' War Board—for late-comers to whom this is ancient history I append that this was a propaganda arm to support the war effort and rouse public opinion—had enlisted most American writers and literary figures and assigned them jobs to do. One of these was speaking on radio broadcasts. Somebody had put together a discussion idea which brought four writers together around a dinner table and tuned in on their after-dinner conversation on some topic concerned with the war. Usually we were assigned well ahead of time. One Sunday afternoon about five o'clock the Writers' War Board telephoned and asked if I could go on that evening's broadcast as an emergency replacement for the woman scheduled, who had been taken ill. The panel always consisted of several men and one woman, no doubt for variations of voice and personality. I asked the subject and who the participants were to be. They included Woollcott.

I knew that Woollcott had had several heart attacks and was a very sick man. I also knew that he had a memory like an elephant and would detest me now as surely as twenty years ago. This might be harmful to a man in his condition. I told them they had better ask Woollcott what he thought about my being on the programme. In a few minutes they called back and said that Woollcott had no objection, so I felt I had to go on. We met around the dinner table in the studio, and unlike the rest of us, Woollcott ate heavily. Our talk was supposed to lead into the subject to be discussed on the air—"Is Germany Incurable?"—but Woollcott continually needled me with sarcastic remarks about books I had written, to which he had referred scathingly in *The New Yorker*. I was no longer my mother's frightened little girl. I told him to forget old scores and stop being beastly and aim his venom at Hitler instead of me. At that point the control booth signalled, the microphones went live, and we were on the air. The question was asked, and two or three of us, including myself, replied in turn. The next turn was Woollcott's. He was just opening his mouth when he tried to stagger to his feet, clutching his necktie and trying to tear open his collar. He collapsed. The control booth signalled us to keep talking. The moderator speeded up the questions, we talked and kept the show going while they carried Woollcott out of the studio. By the time the programme was finished he was being moved to the hospital where he died that night.

I have never prized youth for its own sake. I do not look back on it with nostalgia. I do not envy the young, who form so startling a preponderance of the population today. I have never felt the urge to prolong youth, if only by illusion. My mind finds no meeting with those who act or hope to appear younger than they are. I did not like my youth very much, except for the presence of my mother, and I was content to see it go. When I was in my twenties I wanted to be thirty and when I was in my thirties I wanted to be forty. When I was forty I knew that this was the best part of life. I lived it and savored it consciously, aware that this must be the height of experience, of personality, of living for what I wanted most to contribute to in effort, in resources, in emotion, in totality. After that, life would be a decline and I knew it. Perhaps I knew it with the mentality of women in Europe: black-clad peasant women of southern and eastern Europe, prosaic matrons of the bourgeoisie, wise and cynical upper-class dowagers; old women, resigned to reality, accepting the order of things with patience or with acid humor.

But one must have something to live for. For me it must be something propulsive. Once ambition was the propellent, but I have long outlived that. Conviction and positive belief expressed in action are the surest satisfactions. Yet at my age the purposive requisite of something to live for verges on the unrealistic. I have outlived nearly all the people who were my primary necessities; and the other components of my need have depended on vigor and ability in myself. Naturally those diminish. My dear Louise, who has made my personal world go round for nearly twenty–five years, observes that most people have nothing to live for in this kinetic sense, and she is right. She also proposes that most people are more content than I am. Most people do not want to live propulsively (or can it be, selfishly?) They want to put one foot before the other, never expecting to fling themselves on a surfboard and ride the crests of the waves. They are prudent enough to see that they would also be flung alternately into the troughs. Such prudence did not concern me when I was young and in the necessities of my work it does not concern me now. I have always been reckless and I will always be reckless.

A part of my life and mind has always been solitary. I do not mean the mandatory physical solitude of writing. All writers are conditioned to the unremitting aloneness of the closed room and the fixed solitary hours of their work. The rest of life, the accumulation of all we experience and know and the substance of what we write, is usually not pursued in solitude. My experience has been different. I am limited by that lacuna in my character or personality which in other people is filled by family ties and by gregariousness. There is a line in an old nursery rhyme which says, "When nobody's with her she's always alone." I was teased with this as a child. I was not resentful, I was puzzled. Why was one taunted for being alone? I found out of course that it is because the loner is a freak, and this puts people off. When I was older and could benefit from my mother's example I tried to learn from it and overcome my defect. But whatever its origin, it was there to stay. I suppose it resulted from the intense separateness of my initial and exclusive possession of my mother and my revulsion from family life as I encountered it in those childhood years in Philadelphia. A person who has such a defect and some intelligence will try to correct it, to compensate for what he cannot do or be by working very hard at what he can do or be. A sense of humor helps more than anything else, by which of course I mean the ability to see oneself as others see one.

What I asked of life I got—and had to pay for; tremendous moments on the crests of the life I chose for myself and terrible passages of tragedy in the troughs. My mother was right when she warned me that this would happen to me. She was right when she insisted that a woman could not be an artist preemptively devoted to her work and also a good wife and mother. Yet for all her wisdom she tried to give me the dual indoctrination which she herself knew could not stay in tandem balance: on the one hand her idealization of family life, on the other hand, the absolute compulsion to work. She never defined what such work should be, but one must work; there was no justifiable existence that was not based on work. The question of talent was never touched on. A voice for instance is not a talent nor is it an attribute of creative accomplishment. It is an instrument for the interpretive expression of art and of the singer's capacities and personality. If she is also a fine musician that is where the element of talent lies. It was never discussed whether or not I had talent of any kind. I wanted to be a writer and my initial approaches to writing were concrete, not imaginative. By the time I was ready to write my first book I was not thinking of expressing myself, or concerned with any question of talent. I got such fulfillment out of that book, not only from the writing but from the years of study and travel that went into it, that I emerged a different woman from the one who had gone in. I did not know then what my next book would be but I did know that I would be writing books the rest of my life. I wanted to write books more than I wanted anything else. My husband and I probably met halfway in achieving such family life as we had. But marriage and family life were not the core of our relationship. He was not primarily a husband in his own id, and I was not primarily a wife in mine.

Sometimes I was swayed between the two impulses and then I remembered that my mother had been silenced, her artistic life truncated by the demands of family, passionately abetted by her own beliefs. I made a fierce resolution that nothing like that should happen to me. I knew I had no native gift to compare with hers but I was determined to work out my destiny by the use of whatever writing ability I had. This required lengthy immuring

in solitude; going away alone for long periods to wherever I felt
I had to be; and staying locked in a room at my desk six or seven
hours a day for as many years as it took to write a book. A
grotesque life, in a sense, but if it is the one you can support,
then it is the right one for you.

Whatever my mother felt of ambition she was ready to subordinate to her husband and children. I was not willing to do
that, but it was not asked of me. I had drive and I was selfish. I
had intellect and my mother had heart. She had a God-given
voice and I had aptitude. She was delicate and I was strong. She
was gregarious and I was solitary. She was, after all, ambivalent
—like all of us. She brought me up to have fanatical respect for
accomplishment; not for mundane success, not for celebrity or
money as aims, but for genuine personal accomplishment achieved
by hard work. When I began to show that I had absorbed this
indoctrination and was embarked upon living my life by it, she
stood—the hen on the bank of the pond—calling "Come back!"
to the duckling she had hatched as it swam away.

Early in 1944 I began to live alone. This as a possibility had
always loomed over me. It was not sudden or quixotic. It was
inherent in a relation that was subject from its inception to the
stress of extremes which ranged from splendid to terrible. The
personal side of it had always been either extraordinarily good
or unendurably bad. There was no median jog-trot in it. The
balancing of possible against impossible had gone on for eighteen
years, fifteen of them married. I think too that the circumstances
of the war had their effect; I was prevented from going abroad
to work for long intervals as I had always done, and those had
given us necessary breaks from each other. Nobody could have
lived twelve months of the year in the house with Russell Davenport and I assume that nobody could stand that much of me.
When "chaos" and "anarchy" have been words used to describe a
man's working methods it would be unrealistic to suppose that
they did not enter into other elements of his life. I am not chaotic

or anarchic but I have got qualities that are their irreconcilable opposites.

When people separate without the intention of either to remarry, they part because they can no longer stay married. It is specious to say that one is at fault more than the other. As long as people really want to stay married there is no fault in one that the other will not condone; in fact, that is marriage: the continual workings of tolerance, acceptance, adjustment, and balancing— the balance of positive against negative, good against bad. The balancing may continue for the lifetimes of two people, or it may go off in one direction or the other. With enormous care and effort it may be possible to redress the balance and get the relation even again. But if that must be repeated too many times a kind of exhaustion sets in. The effort becomes too much. It is like stretching a band of elastic so much and so often that there is finally no stretch left and it cannot spring back. The marriage is at an end. This is always grievous and in the case of my husband and myself it gave us a desolate sense of waste because we had married for the sake of our work and not primarily for personal reasons. What made the personal side of our relation viable was our value to each other as writers, and the powerful community of our interests—strong enough for so many years to outweigh our differences. I have never known another man with whom I had such compatibility and he told me repeatedly that the same was true for him in respect of me.

Eventually Russell Davenport's life moved on, like my own, to other ties; and it is the essence of the reticence I mentioned at the beginning of this book that I will not cede my own privacy, nor breach that of others, to write about him in details that are graceless. As the years have lengthened since we parted I find that I remember the bad in him only if I try; when I bring no conscious effort to bear I remember the good. I wish he could know this. He was at his best with me after we were divorced, when I was about to publish in 1947 a novel called *East Side,*

West Side. The book was a work that Max Perkins had believed I must undertake, that sole novel drawn from elements of my own experience. I had talked about it with Russell, for we saw each other often; and he had read the galley proofs. It was a painful book to write and for some people to read; but he was excited about it. He thought it an important progression for me. He was also keenly aware of my agonizing loss in the recent death of Max.

Review copies had gone out and the book was considerably discussed before the publication date. During that interval Robert van Gelder of *The New York Times Book Review* asked me for an interview. I knew him, he had interviewed me before. He opened the talk by saying he assumed that the husband in the novel would be thought a portrait of Russell Davenport, and a savage attack on him. I was appalled. I told van Gelder that this was not true, but he said nobody would believe it; that I was standing on the brink of a literary scandal. Sick at heart I telephoned Russell and told him what van Gelder had said. I was in tears; this was surely not what Max or I had had in mind when he thought I must write such a book. Russell listened to me at length. Then he said slowly, "Is that so? So that's what they're going to say? Well, let's show them a thing or two."

The night before the book was published he took me to dine at Twenty-one. We sat at our old *Stammtisch*, drank a bottle of Romanée-Conti, reminisced and laughed, chatted with all the quidnuncs who were going to see us or themselves or everybody they knew in the book; and whatever else was said of it, nobody said I was attacking Russell Davenport. The book was presumed to be autobiographical but that was gratuitous. It contained portraits, among many others, of a man who was cruel and a woman who was selfish. But those were no more their singular qualities than they are of any creature who must share the frailty of all human character.

I have known my share of tragedy in life but now at this

perspective I believe the ultimate human tragedy to be the failure of the mind or body, the spirit or the will in a man or woman to realize the best of his aims and abilities and powers. Sometimes the failure is inherent, sometimes extrinsic; sometimes wrought by the confusions and harassments of life, sometimes by the truncation of death. But if we have anything to mourn when we mourn, above the grovelling of self-pity, this is what we lament. This is what we seldom dare to face, alone in our reckonings with ourselves. This is what I feel when I read the poetry of Russell Davenport, and what I feel when I weigh the failure of a relationship so very nearly right. When we parted he gave me his copy of the poetical works of Donne, the heart and core of the poetry that we had read together long ago. On its flyleaf he had pasted these lines of his own:

> Life is the sum of perishable things,
> The windy grass, the curved and dappled wings,
> The day of promise, which was clear and bright,
> And the clandestine raptures of the night;
> Of books much briefer than the need, and song,
> However exquisite, which lasts not long,
> And of ourselves, who love, but cannot keep
> One kiss inviolate from eternal sleep.
> All such are petals of the secret Flower,
> Shed year by year and falling hour by hour
> Within the haunted garden of the earth
> Where joy and sorrow have no separate birth;
> And without these the Flower is not seen,
> Nor yet will be, nor ever yet has been,
> But in their forms perpetually grows,
> Shaped as a verse, a symphony, a rose,
> A kiss, a thought, a heart that undertakes
> To love this beauty that the garden makes:
> And only on these surfaces we see
> The breathless chasm of eternity.
> Thus to this book some years ago you came

And found the Flower growing in my name,
The surface of some depth within the mind
Of him who wrote and left his shape behind:
And this I give you now before we part
As in some way the image of my heart,
Where truth endures as that which is not true—
As you endure in me, and I in you—
And marriage binds us not as man and wife,
And love lives on which has no longer life.

So I began the life alone for which I must have been destined from birth. I began it without thought for the long span ahead, twenty-three years already and who knows how many more; years for which I had no plan to make a joint life with anybody. At the time I was compelled by inner forces to be alone. King Lear speaks for me: "The art of our necessities is strange." And barren too. The fruitful art is living for the necessities of others. In the long perspective I denied myself this, or was denied it by my own nature and the force of circumstance. I was forty years old. I could not see ahead in that turbulent time, except to a far plateau beyond the war, when a part of my life would come into being which had the insubstantiality of a dream and yet was built on the stones and the arches, the yellow walls, the needled towers and spires, of the place where I meant to go. There was no personification of this and my imagination fell short of conceiving that the dream would be fleshed out in human reality.

▓[C H A P T E R T H I R T E E N]▓

IT is nearly twenty years that Jan Masaryk is dead. His name
has passed from the world's lips. His memory is suppressed
in his own country and is dim elsewhere except among his
surviving friends. Sometimes there appears a reference to him as
a latter-day Hamlet doomed by his dilemma. Occasionally someone claims to reveal a fragment of knowledge bearing on the
mystery of his death. To me the years have been an immeasurable
emptiness in which some impressions fade, but others have grown
minutely and permanently sharper. In certain ways Jan is as much
alive to me as when I last saw him three days before his death; but
time has also made baffling erasures.

I have never written a word about the Czechoslovak tragedy.
I have not wished to write about it because I believe that that
passage of history should be seen in the frame of the terrible great
design of this century. I have not wished to write anything which
could be considered topical. I have known that I required perspective from which to comprehend and record my experience.
Twenty years is too short a time for a true historical view, but
that has to be the interval from which I contemplate my own
small place in relation to a convulsion of history.

I also feel, as science and geopolitics accelerate to suggest
for us unimaginable dispensations of destiny, that I had better
write what I know whilst the choice is still mine. Life in the
present day is not conducive to reflection, to creative imagining, to
literary lucidity. Each day's haul of alarms and crises assaults the
mind, first fragmentizing it, then passing on to leave it stunned,

indifferent, cumulatively less capable of reacting to the next day's shock. This is destructive to imaginative writing. Novelists and playwrights are flung into despair because the stupendous events of the day make the literary imagination seem futile and piddling by juxtaposition. Novels become for the most part contrived escapes from, or posturing reflections of, the menacing present; and I have no wish to write a novel of either definition. Certainly I would not use the substance of my experience with Jan Masaryk as the material of fiction; the title of this book states why that is so.

The relation grew out of the profound attachment that I had formed in my youth for Prague and for the countryside of Bohemia and Moravia, and for the plain people who are of their essence. I have described the uncanny beginnings of this. It was the second of the two high-voltage power lines on which my life's whole motivation was strung; the first was music, instilled by my mother and formed in permanence by Maestro. Until the time of Munich I had had no personal ties with Czechoslovakia at all, only the insistent pull which drew me there. But after Munich, when the fate of the small country became common cause with every man and woman who stood up to be counted against Hitler, I began to work for the Czechoslovaks as I have noted, and they had been from its first stirrings one of the major themes of *The Valley of Decision*. All this was a spontaneous expression of something I felt intensely. None of it was fortuitous. There was no explaining or rationalizing it. It was the manifestation of an instinct that had permeated my whole working life. I never imagined or foresaw that it would culminate in a personal tie so absolute as to transcend the limitations of two very faulty human beings and become, in the midst of Hell, a corner of Elysium.

I first met Jan Masaryk in my own house in New York. It was in November, 1941, a few weeks before Pearl Harbor. I was brought a message from the Czechoslovak Consulate that the Foreign Minister was in town from London and would like to pay his respects. I thought it very gracious of Jan Masaryk. I sent word that some friends were dining with us on the following Monday, if he should care to join us, and he replied that he would.

Nearly everybody I knew had known Jan Masaryk for years. Time and again, chance or circumstance had effected that we not meet. When it used to be said that 'everybody' was in Salzburg in the great and festive years, he was often there with his old friends George Daubek and his wife Jarmila Novotná, the lovely Czech soprano who sang Pamina with Maestro. Jan was then the Czechoslovak Minister in London, one of the most popular diplomats in England and in Europe. In those days I heard a lot about him, mostly about the charm, the wit, the escapades, the gaiety, some dissipation, and all the other superficialities that had earned him the sobriquet, "Playboy of the Western World." I have never had any attributes interesting to playboys and I may have had a reluctance to risk seeming dull. When I thought about it years later I realized that I had, unconsciously withal, been contriving for a long time not to meet him.

It was characteristic of him that he already knew all the people who were dining with us and was a stranger only to my husband and to me. The other guests had come before he arrived. He entered the room with his slow, light step, and though I was standing near the door, he nevertheless went the round of the drawing-room first. He greeted Wendell Willkie, whom he had met in London, Mr. and Mrs. Thomas Lamont, and the others; he came last of all to me and without any salutation began to speak, in the middle of a sentence, as though continuing an interrupted conversation. I cannot remember exactly what he said, but it was badinage about my enthusiasm and my efforts for his country. In later years he often shook his head and said, "You're crazy, you know," and those first words were in that vein.

It was to be nearly five years before I knew him differently. All during the war he used to fly in from London in R A F or other military planes, on missions for his own country or the Allies. He would appear out of the blue, ring up on the telephone, ask me to go with him to meetings and gatherings of the Czecho-slovaks in New York and in Washington. He dropped in frequently to dine at our house, sometimes with musical or literary or political friends, sometimes just so. He had innumerable American friends and a few relations, too—his American mother had been born Charlotte Garrigue in Brooklyn. One evening he said something about his maternal grandmother whose maiden name had been Whiting. Russell and I looked at each other, startled. He got up and fetched the Davenport book. Russell's paternal grandmother had also been a Miss Whiting from Brooklyn and she turned out to be a first cousin of Jan Masaryk's grandmother. Since this went back to the early 1800's when Brooklyn was a tightly-knit community of a few interrelated families, it was probably not so strange. But it seemed uncanny to us that Jan Masaryk and Russell Davenport were related.

To many Americans Jan seemed like one of themselves, not a foreigner at all. Many of his British friends have told me that they too thought of him as more American than otherwise. He had real roots and ties here, and a backlog of kicking around the United States long before the First World War. And he had lived long in London, with the intuitive perceptiveness of English character and life which endeared him to friends far beyond the circles of diplomacy. Above all there was his fantastic command of any and all shades of the English language; of nuance and argot and profanity and slang in either British or American idiom. He spoke as many kinds of English as there were variations of origin and accent among his friends. So gifted a linguist and raconteur will always echo what he is hearing when he is talking. But I knew Jan as a Czechoslovak; and that was a different man.

He was very tall and bulky; corpulent, in fact, when I met him at the age of fifty-five. He used to say that he had begun to get heavy and to change in many other ways, from the time of

Munich. Until then he was (he said) slender and careful to keep himself so, riding in the Park every morning for exercise. Though he was over six feet tall he was small-boned. He had small, fine feet and hands and used them precisely. He walked lightly, often on the balls of his feet; and he used his hands graphically to illustrate his entrancing talk. His head was striking. He was bald and jowly, with long-lobed ears and a domed forehead above witty, mobile eyebrows and extraordinary eyes. They were the deep, dark brown of his Slovak ancestry, the mirrors of a character which ranged from profound moodiness and an intimation of tragedy to outrageous clowning and electric wit. His left eyelid had a distinct droop. His nose too was asymmetrical, a prominent beaked nose with a sharply-carved point, and a slant to the right. I never thought to ask him if his nose had been battered in some boyhood fight but I should not be surprised had that been so. His face, in summary, was an astonishing dual revelation of the man. If I cover the left half of Jan's face in a photograph, down the middle, the right side is the face of sadness and bears that intimation of tragedy. The man is withdrawn, remote. Reverse the motion and the left half of the face is the other person—the wit, the warm and intuitive companion, the man of the boisterous laugh and appetites and rich expletives. This man is intimate.

Almost anybody who knew Jan Masaryk thought he knew him well, for his ease of approach and his quick perception of people's characters and quirks—and frailties—were startling and disarming. I think his whole life had been a pattern of sizing people up and hitting the right notes with them, another way of saying that he was an artist as a diplomat. The same art went into the complex tapestry of his friendships, long-standing and varied, many of them compartmented to suit a nature which beneath a surface of booming expansiveness was reserved, even secretive. He was a man of diverse and multiple tastes in people and associations. He kept many of these apart from one another. Most people did not know him as well as they thought or as he let them think. He had enormous charm and many faults. After frivolous people had been dazzled by the charm and solemn owls put off by the faults, there remained only a few who really knew him. Fewer still had any knowledge of the blood or the earth or the strangely mingled forces which had formed him.

Jan Masaryk was twenty-eight years old in 1914. He had been on his own for ten years and he had accomplished nothing. As a youth he must have been a disappointment to his father— scholar, philosopher, professor, politician, at that time unknown outside Austria-Hungary—a parent much troubled about a son who abhorred study and had never attended a university. Jan's school years in Prague where he was born in 1886 had been one escapade after another, his restlessness uncontrollable, his resistance to personal or scholastic discipline unbreakable. He told me that his father beat him again and again, but chastisement neither weakened the deep and tender love between them nor effected any reforms in Jan. He was a wild boy and at the end of his ordinary schooling his father gave up the struggle and consented to let Jan go his own way.

This was a few years past the turn of the century. Tomáš Masaryk and his American wife, whom he had met in Leipzig when he was studying philosophy at the University and she the piano at the Conservatory, were intellectuals within the austere circumambience of plain living and high thinking. In both there was a measure of the puritan; but where this was deep-dyed in Charlotte Garrigue Masaryk, their son told me that his father was never far in mind and tastes and humor from the earth of his peasant parentage. He was, of course, the son of a Slovak coachman on an Imperial estate in Hodonín, in Moravia, and of his wife, a Moravian girl who had been in domestic service in Vienna. Only the year before the birth of Tomáš Masaryk in 1850 had the serfs on the feudal landed estates of Austria-Hungary been freed by decree of the young Emperor Franz Josef, a direct consequence of the revolutions of 1848. Tomáš Masaryk made the long step from his father's illiterate serfdom to the professorship of philosophy and the seat in the Austrian Parliament which was the beginning of his historic destiny. He was profound and idealistic in character, abstemious and spartan in his mode of life; but he had a streak of barnyard humor and a native fund of lowdown stories which he told with relish and which were a strong bond with his beloved but rather wayward son. Jan used to tell this one, which was a favorite of his father's and which might have come straight from the character of Švejk (Schweik):

A conscript in the Imperial army was troubled by an infestation of the body-lice called, in plain language, crabs. The poor devil tried every remedy suggested by his barracks-mates but nothing gave relief and the man was frantic. One winter night a fellow-soldier advised an old remedy; to poultice the site of the infestation, its tormented members and their habitat, with snow. This was done, more snow was packed on during the night, and in the morning when reveille sounded, the barracks gathered to inspect the results of the treatment. The patient was shivering violently; in the habitat of the crabs every hair was standing straight up on end; and on the tip of each hair stood a crab vigorously thrashing itself with its front legs in the manner of coachmen thrashing their arms on frosty mornings. Jan of course illustrated this with realistic gestures and so, he said, had his father.

At the time of his marriage Tomáš Masaryk adopted his wife's surname as his middle name and thereafter was called T. G. Masaryk. The Masaryk family with two sons and two daughters lived in Prague on the meagre scale of a professor's stipend. Jan described their home, a flat in a dark nineteenth-century dwelling-house far from the beautiful and aristocratic quarters of the city; so cramped that his bed was a shakedown on a couch in the parlor-dining-room where the family's communal life went on. He said he used to grow so bored with the high-minded intellectual conversation of the evening that he yawned his head off waiting for the group to disperse and let him go to bed; but very soon he took the alternative of slipping out after supper to enjoy the company of his own friends and the mischief they found to get into.

He had two skills which possibly were attributable to heredity. Like his mother he was musical, he played the piano easily and charmingly, mostly by ear and largely by improvisation. He knew an enormous repertoire of folk music—Czech, Slovak, Russian, Polish, Hungarian, Rumanian—the natural music of the peoples who were the flesh and blood of the Habsburg empire and the Slav world. And he was a good horseman, like his father, like his grandfather the coachman. But neither of these, nor any other native aptitude, pointed to a serious occupation for a young man almost twenty years old. He was restless, he wanted to rove, and he was half American. His mother had taught him perfect English.

He told his father that he wanted to go to America. T. G. Masaryk gave him such money as he could—something under a hundred dollars—and Jan went off on his own. He entered the United States as an immigrant. He did not get into touch with his mother's relations, and he did not seek out his father's only American friend, Charles Crane. Mr. Crane was the head of the Crane plumbing manufacturing company, a rich man who had endowed a School of Slavonic Studies at the University of Chicago. He was a Slavophile and presently a Czechophile at a time when this was so unusual as to be eccentric. He had travelled to Prague in 1902 to invite Professor Masaryk to give a course of lectures at Chicago; thereafter the connection ramified to bring T. G. Masaryk to the United States and into touch with the large communities of Slavic peoples in the middle west; to bring the Crane family into close relations with the eventual Czechoslovak Republic and its founder.

Jan Masaryk spent nearly ten years in the United States. When I knew him he seldom talked about that part of his life, but sometimes a word or a chance reference would bring out a brief burst of reminiscence. Once when he had asked me to play some of my mother's records for him I said, "What a pity you never heard her in person."

"What?" he roared. "I used to come down from Bridgeport to go to the opera in a seat in the peanut gallery and sit up the rest of the night in the train going back. Of course I heard your mother! I heard them all!" He had known the whole panorama which at that time was forming me, a child seven or eight years old. He used to love to hear me talk about Maestro, "the most important friendship a person could have," he said.

He went to work in Bridgeport after a chance meeting in the street with Charles Crane. He had arrived broke in New York and taken the first job he could find, filling inkwells and running errands. Mr. Crane substituted for that a job in the Bridgeport foundry of the Crane valve works, at a wage which Jan supplemented by playing the piano in movie houses. He kept his distance from the Crane family, not wishing to presume on his father's friendship and also, he told me, preferring to keep on the farther side of his own independence. He said very little about those years, during which he worked also in Chicago. In a dual sense inherent in Jan himself they were lost years but they were a lasting strain in his personality. He told me that he liked gambling and girls, and that the only serious thing he did was teach English to illiterate immigrants from all over Europe who worked in the brass foundry. But his most characteristic act was finally to get fed up and go home. He was a European, he always said so; repeatedly I heard him invoke the spirit of this when he spoke of "Mother Europe." That was his term for a state of mind, a point of view, a set of instincts. They were strong enough to draw him back to Prague and the Old World when almost any young man in similar situation would long since have become naturalized and made a permanent life in America.

He arrived in Prague in time to be drafted into the Imperial army shortly before the war broke out. His father was by then a

Parliamentary leader in the politics of the dissident peoples of the Habsburg house of cards. There was a Czech question, a Hungarian question, a Croat and a Slovene question, a Slovak question in its own frame of reference to its subject status as a province of Hungary; and the war was only a few weeks old when the activities of T. G. Masaryk came under suspicion and he under surveillance. His son Jan in the army was probably considered a sort of surety for the father's reliability. But that did not deter T. G. Masaryk in December, 1914, from escaping through Italy to the long wanderings and labors which were to end in his return at the end of 1918 as the first President of the Czechoslovak Republic. Because of his father's subversive activities, and because Czech and Slovak soldiers by hundreds of thousands were deserting the Austrian armies to cross over and fight for the other side, Jan was assigned to non-combatant jobs in a Hungarian regiment on the Polish front. He told me he never fired a shot. Except for a series of Schweik-like stories and some colorful additions to his linguistic repertoire he had as little to say about the war years as about the ones that preceded them. In 1919 the Masaryk family were reunited in Hradčany, the castle of Prague, the fortress-palace of the Bohemian Kings. It was one of the great unlikelihoods of European history.

In front of my fire there is a small couch upholstered in light blue velvet. The velvet is a fragile color and has been renewed several times; impractical, but I am fond of it. Jan used to sit on that couch, cross-legged in the manner of a Buddha. It was a habitual position of his. Once in a while he would look over at me with a grin and say, "See? Never touch it." He pointed to his feet, curved up in such a way that his shoes could not touch the velvet. I would not have cared if they had. It was when he was relaxed in this way, smoking his Players cigarettes, with a drink beside him, that he talked of the years I have described. There was never a consecutive account of those days such as I have written; it was snatches and fragments of reminiscence, touched off by some name or face or episode that had come to his mind. I have laid the pieces end to end, so to speak, to form at least an outline sketch of the man who found his métier because, in his own words, he chose his father wisely and was thirty–two years old when the Republic was created.

But he did not escape the grumbling of Czechs and Slovaks who ascribed his assignments in diplomacy to nepotism, and who were jealous of his ease and popularity in the world to which most of them were strangers. The arts of government and the niceties of protocol were unknown to them. Most did not at first perceive the advantages to their country of a man like Jan in Washington and London, but his father did; and also Edvard Beneš, the Foreign Minister and right hand of the President. The Czechoslovaks when I first knew them took an attitude of reverence towards T. G. Masaryk much like the American schoolchild's worshipful concept of Washington and Lincoln. Realistically we know that neither Washington nor Lincoln could have achieved what he did without a due measure of toughness, shrewdness, and the knack of making the most of opportunities. T. G. Masaryk had his share of these. He was also assisted, in the curious workings of fate, by the personal friendship of Charles Crane with Woodrow Wilson and his Secretary of State, Robert Lansing. Masaryk had access to Woodrow Wilson not shared by any other leader of an eventual Succession State. It is true that in drafting the Constitution of the Czechoslovak Republic in Philadelphia in June, 1918, he drew in part upon the American Constitution as a model. But it is also true that he was influenced by Woodrow Wilson's stubborn insistence on self-determination for all peoples, away from Masaryk's own original broader concept of a post-war reorganization of the Habsburg empire into a democratic confederation of the hitherto subject provinces. The failure to achieve this after the First World War laid Central and Eastern Europe open to Hitler; and Russian obstruction of any similar plan (which was

Jan's own best hope) after the Second World War brought about the Communist satellite countries of today.

The Masaryk-Crane friendship branched on to further connections which might appear surprising except to those who know the peculiar pull of the Czechs and their country—by no means everybody's dish. The taste is special; it has never touched vast numbers of travellers and foreigners like those who have made Italy, for instance, a land of heart's desire. The Czech virus is small and singular and it chooses its subjects cannily. It certainly chose Charles Crane. His son Richard was sent to Prague as the first American Minister to the new Czechoslovak Republic, and his daughter Frances Crane Leatherbee was married in 1924 to Jan Masaryk. The childless marriage lasted less than five years. When it took place Jan was Counsellor to the Czechoslovak Legation in London. He had spent two years before that in the Foreign Ministry in Prague, and the year from 1919 to 1920 as Chargé d'Affaires in Washington. In 1925 he was appointed Czechoslovak Minister to the Court of St. James's. The next thirteen years were the grand and brilliant ones when the Legation in Grosvenor Place was a centre of the last great epoch of diplomatic and social life, and its bachelor host the fascinating charmer I used to hear about in the 1930's. It was the time when I did not know him and everybody else did. My interests abroad were on the Continent. I was seldom and briefly in London, and never a part of the great scene recorded in hundreds of memoirs, which we have all read. It came to an end in the tragedy of Munich.

The design of this book rules out as much as possible narration of historical events to which I was not a witness. Otherwise I would be embarked at this point on an account of the Munich crisis, to which many books have already been devoted. They relate it from every view, including my own in the version I rendered through the fictitious characters of *The Valley of Decision*. Munich now, as it did in the years when I shared the last of Jan Masaryk's fate, concerns me as it affected him. Anything I know of his acts and words at that time is what he told me himself. But he did not mention his own nobility and objectiveness of mind when he rose above the searing humiliation not only of betrayal and abandonment by Britain and France of their ally to Hitler; but of the way it was done. The reader should remember that after the initial meetings of Chamberlain and Hitler, the Munich Conference of those two with Mussolini and Daladier excluded the Czechoslovaks themselves and their ally and France's, the Soviet Union. At the time, no protest was heard from the Russians. The Czechs were treated like lackeys and their country like a pawn. From the Diplomatic Gallery of the House of Commons Jan Masaryk witnessed the scene of hysterical joy with which Neville Chamberlain's announcement of his imminent Munich settlement was received. Afterwards Jan Masaryk confronted Chamberlain and Lord Halifax alone. He said to them, "If you have sacrificed my nation to preserve the peace of the world, I will be the first to applaud you. But if not, gentlemen, God help your souls."

Seven years later Jan gave me in running retrospect a sense of that time which I had felt only vicariously. It will be remembered that 1938 was the autumn when my mother died and when the anguish of Munich penetrated to me through a wall of personal grief. I was too crushed by the loss of my mother to take notice when Jan Masaryk came to this country at the end of that year for a series of lectures, and when Edvard Beneš, who had left Prague in October, went as an exile to lecture at the University of Chicago. Only after the war began a year later was I forging my working links with the Czechoslovaks. Long before then Jan was back in London, settled in a small flat in Westminister. Beneš also took up residence in London. With other exiled members of the Republic's Government and Parliament they formed the Czechoslovak National Committee which from then until July, 1941, had a bitter wait in the wilderness of post-Munich policy until the then Anthony Eden replaced Lord Halifax as Foreign Secretary and brought about recognition of the Czechoslovak Provisional Government in exile. Dr. Beneš was again President, and Jan Masaryk Foreign Minister. It was another full year until the British Government completely repudiated the Munich Agreement and declared its provisions void.

But there was, in effect, a second Czechoslovak government in exile, a shadow cabinet which functioned all through the war in Moscow, and in Kuybyshev when the Soviet Government moved East as the Germans were threatening Moscow. Today it does not seem possible that during my constant association with the Czechoslovaks in the West I hardly heard them mention by name the leaders of the Czech Communist Party who had fled to Moscow at the time of Munich and thereafter—some also before. None of those Communists denounced the Nazi-Soviet Pact of 1939, or supported the Allies in the war until after Hitler invaded the Soviet Union. My friends made much mention, however, of the many thousands of Czechoslovaks who fought with the Red Army. In our illusions until the first uneasy whispers about Teheran we thought of them as a sort of parallel to the Czechs in the First World War. We were wildly mistaken, which must have suited Soviet purposes very well.

I cannot any longer recapture the sense of urgency and conviction of the war years. I am thankful that this book is not fiction and that I need not strive to recreate those feelings in imaginary people who would have to act with the passion that we felt at that time. I realize now that I have not been able to feel it for many years. The reasons, in two words, are Teheran and Yalta—but I did not know that in 1943 and 1945. The compendium of what we did not know, were not told—necessarily at that time, disgracefully in later years—dared not guess, and could not have believed, is now an old, familiar tale of horror. The commitments of Teheran and Yalta made fools of those who had believed the words of the Atlantic Charter; who thought they were fighting for, or upholding the armies who fought for, beyond the destruction of Hitler and all his works, the security of free democracies throughout Europe. Since I pretend to no omniscience, and am holding closely to my intention to write only about what I saw and heard and was part of, the small country of Czechoslovakia is my measure of the long-range political war aims which made the Soviet Union the master of the heart of Europe and of all the lands to the East. Compared to this, the American war aim of clear-cut military victory, smashing the Germans to pulp with the least loss of American lives, an aim unrelated to post-war *Realpolitik,* was simple-minded, as Roosevelt's attitudes at Teheran and Yalta were irresponsible.

What I know of Teheran and Yalta, beyond the mass of published material, memoirs, and such White Papers (surely with parts suppressed?) as have been released, was told me by Harry Hopkins and by a man still living who was a high-ranking member of the British Foreign Office. He was present at both conferences. I gave him my word that I would not quote him by name. He told me, for instance, that Czechoslovakia was never mentioned at Yalta. He said that that had been made unnecessary by the actions of the Czechs themselves after Teheran. At Teheran, Stalin made the specific demands which resulted in the ultimate partition of mutilated Poland, ceding the part east of the Curzon Line to the Soviet Union, and throwing Poland the prospective sop of a chunk of East Prussia. At the same time Stalin insured that the Lublin Poles should be the future government of Poland; Communist and 'friendly' to the Soviet Union. The London Poles were to be resolved by a hazy equivocation turning on the word 'democratic' which, of course, means one thing in Communist dialectic parlance and another to the rest of us. The shape of eventual post-war Central and Eastern Europe under Soviet hegemony was discernible to many participants and observers at Teheran. Nobody summed it up more succinctly than Edvard Beneš in his memoirs: "This conference also showed the first signs of the intention to fix military—and therewith also political—spheres of influence for the Eastern front as well as for the Western front. . . . Where these spheres should or would meet was not definitely fixed. But it can be supposed that the Soviet Union was already hinting that it was counting on its sphere including in any case North-Eastern Germany, the whole of Poland, Czechoslovakia, Rumania, and Hungary. . . . *we were not told anything of these plans at the time either by the Soviets or by the Western Powers.*" (The italics are Beneš's.)

This piece of chilling prescience lies most curiously on the same page with Beneš's smug and characteristic summary of Teheran: "I am convinced that at this Conference these three leading men . . . did great service to their countries, to all Allied Nations and to their war effort, and above all, to promote the final victory. The Conference at Teheran therefore has a really important place in the history of the Second World War though some of its decisions caused differences to arise later but not till 1945 and the years which followed."

Like many other instances in the tragic story of Czechoslovakia this straddle means that Beneš had decided long before Teheran to go to Moscow to sign a new treaty of alliance with the Soviet Union. He had been in the United States in May, 1943, to be received by President Roosevelt and to address a joint session of Congress as heads of state ceremonially do. He had been honored at a series of Czechoslovak gatherings in New York, where I met him for the first time. Thereafter he pursued the policy which seemed so reasonable and ended so hideously, the balancing of Czechoslovakia between East and West. Beneš arrived in Moscow twelve days after the end of the Teheran Conference. The same British statesman who spoke to me of Teheran and Yalta told me that his government had attempted to dissuade Beneš from Moscow and the 1943 treaty, but that the Americans had urged him to go. Jan Masaryk never told me any details; but he did say during the last phases of the war that if Beneš had not gone to Moscow in 1943, had not signed the treaty, and had not conferred with the

Czechoslovak Communists in Russia, the Czechoslovaks in 1945 would have found themselves in the same situation as the Poles: the Lublin Communists foisted on the nation as its government, and the London Poles shut out altogether.

My knowledge of Jan Masaryk moved both backwards over all these matters, and forwards from the time in 1945 when I began to know him well. He was then already ensnared in the toils of the decisions—or were they deals and compromises?—of Teheran and Yalta. He used to call it *force majeure;* perhaps really historical inevitability. From within those coils he used to take some solace in talking at random about the past, about the old days, about his father, and about promises that he had made his father. One of the first bonds between Jan and me, which he pointed out, was that each of us was the child of a very great person (his own phrase) whose character and accomplishment we could not equal, while we literally worshipped the parent in each case. Obviously, I pointed out the difference in stature between a world-revered statesman and a widely-loved artist, but Jan stopped me, shaking his head. He said, "No, the principle is the same, and my father would be the first to say so. He had tremendous regard for artists, any artists—musicians, poets, painters. He said its artists were more important to a nation than its politicians."

In the autumn of 1944 I looked around me with disbelief that life in all its elements had changed so much in four years. Another Presidential campaign was on, an exhausted Roosevelt running for a fourth term against the candidate the Republicans had nominated after the savage Wisconsin Primary where Wendell Willkie went down fighting for his liberal and world-minded beliefs. They were on their guard against him and he was past the time for wild-eyed amateurs and heaven-sent brainstorms. They eliminated him as a Republican figure but not as the spokesman for millions of enlightened Americans. Early on the morning of October 8th, Russell telephoned to give me the heartbreaking news that Wendell had died in Lenox Hill Hospital at the age of fifty–two. It was not known that he had had several heart-attacks and had been a patient in the hospital for some time. His death was a very great loss to this country. His most influential services had been rendered as a private citizen after the 1940 campaign and before and after Pearl Harbor. Nobody knew that better than Franklin Roosevelt.

Life was much changed for me personally, too. I had spent years at the war jobs which were exciting and urgent and seemed of real importance then; but I had no book under way. I have always lapsed into long intervals of nothingness after finishing a book and have listened shamefaced while my counsellors have reproached me, particularly by holding up examples of the Great Ones who have disciplined themselves to those invariable four hours or fifteen hundred words every day of their lives. When I have a book to write, I say meekly, nobody is more disciplined than I am, and for more than four hours a day. But until the thing happens which means there is a book . . . "you are poison," says Carol Brandt dryly, and she should know.

My existence was duller in some ways than in the days of "chaos and anarchy" but the peace was welcome to me and my friends. Much of this was due then and has been ever since to Louise. Louise's surname is Weil; but that is not part of her inimitable personality. She is Louise. She is my loyal, brave, unselfish friend. She came to work for me in 1944 in a prosaic capacity whose details as I described them in our first interview seem ridiculous now. She thought she was taking a conventional job in New York. In a way, so did I. Since then Louise has lived and made life function for me and for others in Prague, in England, in Italy, and in other places, not to mention a prodigious amount of travelling, which she takes with a shrug. Her particular faculty is instant communication with people; neither strange tongues nor other barriers obstruct this, and everybody feels it. Her energetic walk, her cheerful whistle, her beaming smile (unless she has her own good reason for withholding it) set the mood that people feel when they come to my house.

So with Louise and her old friend and mine, Marie Nusser, who was my cook and housekeeper and—any friend of mine will confirm—one of the very great cooks any of us has known; and with Tam who was growing old and waiting for me to begin a new book, I had the requisites for perfect contentment and for good work. And what did I want?—to get to Prague. I could think of little else. Max Perkins had brought me to the verge of the idea which was to emerge as my next novel, but it was so difficult to move in on, and Max so understanding and patient, that I had to follow my nose and come to it in my own way. Meanwhile I was giving most of my time to the United War Fund into which the many different war relief agencies, one for each belligerent country, had merged. All of us who were officers of its member agencies worked hard to raise the funds which were distributed proportionately among the member agencies. I was an executive of the Board of American Relief for Czechoslovakia and long before the end of the war we were already assembling personnel and materials for the rehabilitation work to be started inside the country as soon as possible.

Throughout the war we had been receiving detailed information about the effects of Nazi depredations on the civilian population, particularly on children who were gravely undernourished. We were planning to send trained social workers from Czech and Slovak-speaking communities in New York and Chicago. I was intending to go because I am a fairly resourceful wrangler and wangler, and trained by profession to be articulate on paper and in speech, which had a bearing on whether things would or would not get done. Also I would go at my own expense. My other and even more urgent motive in wanting to go to Prague was my own work. I knew that I would first have to keep my promise to Max and write the New York novel, which meant that I could not yet stay in Prague indefinitely; there could only

be trips back and forth until I had finished the New York book.
But beyond that lay the book I cared much more about; for years
I had been living with the roots of the major novel I meant to
write, most of them planted deep in Czechoslovakia. I wanted to
be there to witness the return of the nation to its own people,
paraphrasing Comenius, after the tempest of God's wrath should
have passed. I was there, and I have not written the novel.

During the war years I had met most of the Czechs and
Slovaks in the Foreign Service of their country who were stationed
here, and through them, many other Czechoslovaks and Americans of Czechoslovak descent. I have put so many of these people
partially and collectively into novels, along with glimpses of their
ways and their views and their speech and their folk-songs and
their hospitality and their heavenly cooking, that to go into such
details here would be repetitious. My closest friends amongst
them were Ján and Betka Papánek and Vladimír and Olga Hurban. Vladimír Hurban was the Czechoslovak Ambassador in Washington and Ján Papánek was Minister Plenipotentiary stationed
in New York. Both the Papáneks and the Hurbans came of old
Slovak Protestant families with traditions of intellectual and social
enlightenment very different from the mass of Catholic Slovak
peasants. Both men had fought with the rebellious Czechoslovaks
in the First World War and both had been in the diplomatic service since the beginning of the Masaryk Republic. They were old
and trusted friends of Jan Masaryk. I was often with him at their
houses, together with others of the Czechoslovak community and
many of those who had escaped here from the Nazis. The composer Bohuslav Martinů was among these; dead now for years; a
gentle, timid man whose music was always respected but is now
played as widely as that of any twentieth-century composer. The
great team of theatre comedians, Voskovec and Werich, were here;
so was young Rudolf Firkušný, the pianist; so were writers,
journalists, illustrators, and other members of Prague's literary
circles. Several of the latter were working for the Office of War

Information in Washington and New York—some, like the car-
toonist Hoffmeister, later to prove undeserving of the refuge they
received here.

By March of 1945 the end of the war was in sight. The American and British Armies were rolling up the Germans from the
West and the Russians were closing in from the East. The Yalta
Conference in February had insured that the Red Army should be
the conquerors or the 'liberators' of the capitals East of the Elbe;
capitals of all the countries (now excluding Austria) which are
the Communist bloc of today. East and Southeast of Vienna the
Russians were already on the scene as conquerors (and depredators.) This fact is repeatedly cited by American apologists as a
basis for the realities of Yalta. The British have not by any means
concurred, nor others who know much that we do not. In passing,
since I was shortly afterwards in several of those capitals, I saw no
distinction drawn by the Red Army between conquering and
liberating. Nazi victim or Nazi ally, they were treated alike. It
was rape and rapine, pillage, plunder, drunken savagery and terror, wholesale looting and wanton destruction of anything left to
destroy. And everywhere, the NKVD. This had been going on in
Slovakia since the Red Army had entered it in the autumn of
1944. The Germans were still holding Bohemia and Moravia.

In the middle of March Edvard Beneš carried out his long-
laid plan to lead the members of his London Government to Moscow, to meet there with the Czechoslovak Communists and put
together a permanent government. The Westerners were a nu-
merically balanced representation of the old multi-party political
structure of the Republic, and the Easterners were all Communists except for a fellow-traveller named Zdeněk Fierlinger who
had once been Beneš's trusted associate. Beneš had sent him as
Czechoslovak Ambassador to Moscow at the beginning of the war.
It proved to be one of the gravest mistakes that Beneš made. The
only non-partisan, who had never belonged to a political party in
his life, was Jan Masaryk, the Foreign Minister. He had to go

with Beneš and the others to Moscow, where—he told me—he had his first confrontation with Klement Gottwald, the head of the Czech Communist Party, a drunken brute who wielded power with crushing insolence and took every opportunity to scorn if not insult the name and tradition of Masaryk. The new Government of some twenty-five Ministers and many subordinates went early in April to Košice in eastern Slovakia, which was to be their temporary seat. They were treated like convicts by the Russian occupying troops and secret police. From Košice they would proceed westwards behind the Red Army which, having gloriously 'liberated' Prague, the Government would come home in the wake of the nation's deliverers.

Long before Košice the Soviet Union with the ready concurrence of the Czech Communists in Moscow had lopped off and swallowed Subcarpathian Ruthenia, the extreme eastern province of the Czechoslovak Republic. This, combined with the revisions to ravished Poland, juggled the map in such a way as to create a contiguous frontier (and direct access for the Red Army) between Czechoslovakia and the Soviet Ukraine—a juncture that had never existed before. Always concerned not to rock the boat, the non-Communist Czechoslovaks acceded helplessly to this piece of cynical larceny, though Jan Masaryk protested violently to Gottwald. The forcible change of nationality and handing over of the Ruthenians to the Red police state was hedged round by the Czechs with face-saving pronouncements about Slavic Brotherhood and Solidarity that did not hide the brutal truth from anybody who could read a map. This was the first alarm bell to ring loud in my mind long before I got to Prague. I was even stupid enough to protest bitterly about it in private to Jan. When I heard his booming verbal reassurances and at the same time saw the haunted look in his eyes, I shut up.

He would have had to go with his Government to Košice except he was to head the Czechoslovak Delegation to the initial Assembly of the projected United Nations at San Francisco, like

the Foreign Ministers or heads of government of all the partici-
pating countries. For that reason, Jan instead of going to Košice
and thus to Prague in the wake of the Red Army, went from Moscow to London to San Francisco. That Assembly was the first of
the series of unrelenting public humiliations at the hands of
Molotov and the Red bloc, including the Communist robots
among the Czechs, which were visibly to tear him apart. But his
presence there was reassuring to the West, and at that stage of matters a useful façade over the ugly structure designed by Gottwald
& Company ultimately to replace the original Czechoslovak Republic.

April opened in high excitement as victory in Europe came
closer day by day. On Thursday afternoon in the second week of
the month I was sitting with Carol Brandt in the projection-room
of the motion picture company that had made the film of *The
Valley of Decision*, which was about to open at the Radio City
Music Hall. We had seen most of the film, and I was just beginning
to relax in relief and reassurance over the fine cast and the faithful
and gripping representation of the third of the book which had
been used, when Howard Dietz made his way to us across the dark
room, leaned over our shoulders, and told us that President Roosevelt had just died. Like everyone in the nation and the world we
were stunned. Our first reaction was tears. How difficult it is now
to suspend that moment in the recollected emotions it evoked
and separate it from all that we were to learn and understand
later. How could we know that Harry Truman was to prove a
President of immense courage and decisiveness; and how could we
know until we saw it in distant, agonized perspective that Franklin
Roosevelt was almost a dying man when he ran—we did think,
irresponsibly—for a fourth term; and in the brief months of that
fourth term cast away fully half of the victory over tyranny against
which he had stood so splendidly in the early years of the war, and
before?

I was in the country with Carl and Carol Brandt for the

weekend of April the twentieth. On the Sunday morning, Ján Papánek telephoned me from New York to say that he had received a code message from Jan Masaryk who had left London by air on his way to San Francisco. The message asked that I be at home that afternoon, as Jan wanted to speak to me. I left for town immediately and had hardly reached my apartment before Jan was there, hurried, preoccupied, and dishevelled. He had come straight in from the airport and was returning there immediately to catch his plane for San Francisco.

He took an envelope from his pocket and said, "Here you are. I always forget everything, you know, but—"

He had brought me letters signed by President Beneš and himself, an official invitation to go to Czechoslovakia at the request of the Government immediately the military situation permitted. He smiled in a secretive way he did when he was pleased with himself about something and said, "There, that's one promise I've kept anyway."

He said he had just time for a drink. He put down his glass after taking a swallow and sat for what seemed a long time, silent, looking round the room. He was distrait. He had always disliked the long transatlantic flight in military planes and he looked tired out. Only later did I learn piecemeal and by deduction what he had been through in the past weeks in Moscow. Several times his eyes roved round the room. Then he turned to me and made a gesture, circling the air with his right hand. "When all this is over—" He paused. I have never known just what he meant by "this." I thought then that he meant the constant travelling and hair-trigger pressure which were all I had ever seen of his existence. The awful realities, the confusion, contention, frustration, mortification, I would only realize as time went on—and never from admission by him. "When all this is over," he said, and characteristically, nothing more. His face was serious, his eyebrows raised —for question, for emphasis? There was another long silence. Presently he nodded his head slowly.

"I must go," he said, getting to his feet. "I'll be in touch from San Francisco. I'll see you in Prague—or here, before."

He paused at the door of the room and once more he looked slowly all round it and then again at me. Nothing could have been plainer than his weighing my changed situation and my life alone here now.

"That's that?" he said.

"That's that."

"God bless." He left at once to go to his plane.

THERE was the day at the end of April when the Army
Information Service telephoned and told me to be at a
certain loft building between Ninth and Tenth Avenues
at three o'clock sharp that afternoon, bringing specific identification with me. They did not say what for. I found there a number
of writers and editors waiting until the whole group should assemble. We were carefully screened and sent into a long bare
room with rows of wooden seats in it. A cinema screen hung before us. An Army Colonel told us that we were about to be shown
the motion pictures taken by Army photographers of the Third
Army's breaking open of Buchenwald. This had happened three
days before. The films had been flown to New York. As members
of the Writers' War Board and other war agencies, we were to
see them in secret.

The world knows what we saw. Fragments from these reels
have found their way in subsequent years into documentaries and
narrative films, but I do not know that they have ever been seen
publicly in their entirety. Nothing that the ablest, best informed,
most impassioned amongst us had ever written or said about Nazi
depravity had conveyed the reality that unrolled before our eyes.
The cameramen had gone step by step with the first American
units as they entered the concentration camp, neatly gardened at
its gates; and then into the alleys of horror between and inside
the barracks. We saw young American soldiers with their boys'
faces rigid under their helmets, their mouths locked against
nausea as they opened the doors of the charnel houses where

barely living skeletons were piled on top of one another in the bunks. Now and then a fleshless limb would stir or an eye open in what was no longer a human face. The shaven skulls were filthy and thick with scabs. Almost none were able to move, unless they could manage to crawl, towards the open doors. Outside, the walls along the barracks were piled with corpses that had been dumped out as the Nazis made their last frantic rounds before the Third Army fell on them. On the railway siding, always part of the apparatus of death camps, there stood long trains of open box cars, piled to overflowing with naked corpses. Our imaginations supplied something of the frightful stench under the bright spring sun. Alongside the tracks more emaciated cadavers had been piled like cordwood; those piles, those masses, with a skeleton hand or foot jutting out stiffly; those skulls with open dead eyes; to keep telling oneself that these had been human beings no more deserving of this fate than any of us who sat there trying not to groan or curse or rush outside to be sick; this was only the first of several such proofs I had of what Hitler's genocide and his death factories had been. I was to see some of the actual places very soon.

This was never out of my mind as I returned to the continent which has bred and nurtured the utmost extremes of man's nature and his works, from sublimest beauty to foulest degradation. The war in Europe whirled to its end, Hitler followed Mussolini to Hell, and not many weeks later I was meeting men and women who had survived years in those concentration camps. Not Jews, manifestly; they had been exterminated. But others whose identities had condemned them because they were a nation's thinkers and articulators and creators and patriots. They were ravaged mostly beyond recuperation, and they were repatriated from that same Buchenwald or from Dachau or the unspeakable women's camp at Ravensbrück. There were even scattered survivors of the still more terrible camps to the East— Oswiecim (Auschwitz) and Treblinka in Poland, Mauthausen in

Austria, and Terezín not far from Prague. This screen stood between my mind and any other immediate grasp of the realities
of war's end. The screen was weighted with the crimes of Hitler;
ponderous and difficult to move. When finally I had to heave it
aside to see around me there stood forth the spectre of revolution, itself veiled in what seemed inevitable confusion. The confusion was maddening, sometimes disgusting, but still a natural
consequence of occupation, persecution, war, and liberation (a
word to be read with reservations.) Long after the fact, years after
thirty-three months of struggle, agonized hope, and looming despair, I see that the confusion was largely deliberate, a master
key to the awful truth that the Communists, carrying out plans
made in Moscow, had been preparing the final fate of Czechoslovakia behind the screen I have sought to describe; and behind
other screens too; of Munich, Nazi occupation, Slovak separatism,
the war itself, partisan infiltration into the Resistance, and the
finale of Red Army penetration into the country.

By the seventh of May the Germans had surrendered everywhere—except in Prague. As it had been the first city they fell
upon, so it was there they made their last stand. Here we hung
in suspense, knowing that General Patton's Third Army was in
Plzeň, stopped there; knowing that the people of Prague had
risen and were fighting the Nazis in the streets—with the Russians to the East taking their time about the triumph they would
stage, entering Prague with their hordes and their tanks (many
Czechs spat at those) to 'liberate' the capital. I was not there then,
I am not party to the facts recorded in the memoirs of the Gen-
erals whose decision (or obedience) it was not to order the Third
Army on to Prague. The real Czech people were kneeling in the
streets praying for them to come. I would not confess to such
naïveté as the belief that this move, had it been made, might
have changed the course of history. I only know that the decision
against it cast away a most vital part of the victory.

The actual matter of getting to Prague, with the war in

Europe but five weeks ended and the Japanese war still at its height, would have been impossible without the help of the Air Force and the State Department whose Central European desk took an approving view of my mission while its Passport Division, a matter now for retrospective smiles, did not. How Mrs. Shipley fought to keep the sheep in the sheepfold! At last the arrangements were made and I was told to report to Washington ready to be transported. I would be flown to the Allied air base at Caserta, and from there some way of getting to Prague would be devised.

I went to say good-bye to Maestro. He had been commenting on my increasing involvement with the Czechoslovaks as almost any other European would comment: Why? Why the Czechs? I have no answer to that question more concise than this whole book. Maestro was cross. He said, not for the first time, "All Slavs are primitives." Sometimes he was even less polite. In my wish to get him off the subject, I told him I would be landing first in Italy, whereupon he sprang up and said, "Why didn't you say so? That *is* important! I want you to go at once to Milano. Go to La Scala. See everything. Have pictures taken of it. Send me the pictures and write me all about it, everything you find out." Up to then nobody had told him, or anybody in the United States, just what had happened when La Scala was bombed.

One did not counter such an order from Maestro with the reservation that it might not be feasible. But when I told the Air Force, whose guest I was, what Maestro had said, the officers in charge chose to consider it an assignment. They sent along an Air Force photographer in the plane that flew me from Caserta, and ordered us to make a stop at Milan. By that time I had seen so much devastation in Italy that I no longer reacted with sharp personal explosions of distress. I had been at Monte Cassino, whose destruction, however barbarous, was necessitated by the last stand of the Germans there. But nobody had ever understood why the British, in the great bombings of 1943, had hit La Scala when their objectives were the marshalling yards and the main railway station which is a long way from the heart of the city. The station, a Mussolinian vulgarity which could have stood a good bombing or two, was relatively intact while La Scala got firebombs through its dome. As we made our way on foot through the frightful mess in the Piazza, with the Palazzo Marino (the City Hall) in ruins and the heart of Milan in rubble around us, I looked up at the dear old face of La Scala, its pediment intact, and said, "But it wasn't destroyed. There it is."

"Wait," said the Air Force Major who was with me.

In their way, incendiary bombs in the Second World War were the most obscene form of destruction. They left the façades of buildings seemingly intact—the Cathedral in Vienna got the same treatment—when they crashed through the roofs and started holocausts in the interiors. The façade became a tragic deception, only comprehended when one had seen what it hid.

Inside the theatre I stood with the superintendent and some other officials of La Scala, in the centre of the auditorium. Beneath our feet was damp thick grit, the residue of the water that had been knee-high until the work of reconstruction had begun shortly before. High overhead ragged black tarpaulins flapped and let in daylight through the shattered dome, as they had done through all the weather of two years. All around us was a maze of scaffolding, and everywhere piles of construction material. The fireproof curtain had been down when the firebombs hit, so that the stage and the working areas were not burnt out. But the theatre itself was gutted. It was beyond reality to imagine a fire which had consumed this vast interior; and it was unreal to see workmen moving like flies on the face of the boxes as they scraped the mess from the surface to find what could be salvaged. I was very upset, more shocked by the destruction than reassured by the work under way.

"But, Signora!" said the superintendent. "Don't be so distressed, I implore you."

"All that beauty," I lamented. "All that lovely gold gesso! All that wonderful red damask!"

"It is all made again," he said.

"Impossible!"

"I assure you. Every silk mill in Italy has been making that damask for months. It is all ready."

"And the chairs," I said. "The beautiful red velvet!"

"That is ready too."

"And the carpets!"

"Also ready."

It began to dawn on me what he meant. Instead of exclaiming any more I listened to what he told me. They had gone to one of the historical archives in Milan (their own was destroyed in the fire) and there found the original plans of Piermarini for La Scala in 1776. They had turned them over to a group of the best architects and engineers in Italy, who drew plans for a perfect replica of the original theatre, using modern methods and materials where they would be improvements, but keeping—thanks to the genius of Italian artisans—the hand work in wood and stucco which makes the theatre a jewel visually and acoustically. "The work is well ahead of schedule," the superintendent told me. "La Scala will be restored before anything else in Milano. It must be so."

And it was. Ten months later, one year from the end of the war in Europe, Maestro returned to open the rebuilt Scala with a triumphant concert of the music of Verdi and Boito. He had not been at all upset by my letter about what I had seen, or by the Air Force photographs I sent him, including one of the enormous sign that the people of Milan had hung on the ruined theatre the day the war ended: We Want Toscanini. The city of Milan is phenomenal anyway in its energy and enterprise. During that summer of 1945 I was in Paris and London and Munich and Vienna, as well as all over Italy and of course in Prague which, like Paris and Rome, was never bombed. But Milan was a shambles, not so bad as the German cities or many parts of London; but bad. And Milan was the only Continental city which had trams and other transportation already functioning; taxis without gasoline but with charcoal-burning fuel bombs on their roofs; shops open, selling goods that the stubborn Milanese had been manufacturing in their bombed factories; and food which the equally stubborn Lombard farmers produced in spite of the lack of seed and fertilizer and livestock. When I was in Paris at the end of that summer I do not remember seeing a shop that was open.

That was a fantastic day. I had got up before dawn in the VIP guest quarters at Caserta where the Air Force lodged me. We took off from there for Milan in a B 25, dismantled of its armament. After the visit to La Scala and lunch with the top brass who were using my dear Hotel Principe e Savoia as headquarters, we flew on towards Plzeň. Our way took us northeast across Germany and the Major suggested I might like to get a good look at things while the photographer was taking pictures. In fact, he said, since I knew Germany and its cities well, I might be able to spot points of interest to the others in the plane. So they put a pile of parachutes in the nose of the bomber where there was the place to look through that had formerly housed the bombsight. I lay on my stomach on the parachutes while the pilot flew very low, almost buzzing Nürnberg, with my face in the bombsight housing, talking to the crew on the intercom. The destruction was almost total. I felt no regret at the sight, no compunction whatever. I said, "They asked for it," and I feel the same to this day.

By mid-afternoon I was riding in an American Army jeep from Plzeň to Prague, a distance of about fifty-four miles. It was a beautiful midsummer day when in normal times the broad rolling land would have been golden with ripe barley and rye, the harvest in progress, the funny slat-sided farm wagons trundling behind sturdy teams and followed by booted men and kerchiefed women singing as they loaded up the sheaves. The hop-vines would have waved tall on their tepee poles, and the dusty pink of poppies raised for their seed called *mák* would have patterned the land with artless loveliness. Geese would have marched by the brooks under the alders, and squawking hens scattered before our wheels as we rolled through the villages. But there was none of this. There were no beasts or fowl, the fields were rough with the weeds of neglect, the crops were scattered in sparse patches which a few women and children had had to tend while the men were off at forced labor in the armament works at Plzeň, now bombed to rubble, and the coal mines of the region. But once again as we slammed along in the hard-riding jeep, with the peasants cheering and shouting greetings when they saw its American insignia, I felt the commanding pull of love for the sight and sound and sense of that strange little country. I was particularly silent, there was nothing to say to the party in the jeep to explain why I was taut with emotion when they were merely curious at sight of another strange place. In the back of the jeep with me were the Air Force Major who had commanded the B 25, and a Russian-born U.S. Army Colonel, long a naturalized American, whose mission I assumed to be more secret than otherwise. In front were the sergeant driver and another non-commissioned man. We were going to Prague by road because Ruzýň, the airport of Prague, was occupied by the Russians and they had refused permission for an American Air Force plane to land there. I still react with the flare of rage that I felt when I heard that.

Suddenly the driver stopped the jeep. Before us in the road stood a mouzhik, armed to the teeth, covered with guns in and out of holsters, cartridge belts, and a bayonet. He had a tommy-gun trained on us. Russian road-block. We produced our papers, every form of paper that it was necessary to have, all written or printed in Russian as well as English. We submitted them to the Russian soldier for inspection. He looked at them upside down. Clutching them in his non-trigger hand he told the Russian-speaking Colonel in our jeep that we would have to stay there and

wait in the road because his superior officer was off duty and nobody could pass in his absence. So for the best part of an hour we
sat there in the jeep, covered by a Russian tommy-gun: Allies.
At last the Red Army officer appeared. He had been off somewhere drinking; he reeked, and his exaggerated scrutiny of our
papers was in slow motion like a burlesque. Finally he prepared
to let us pass. Our Russian-speaking Colonel asked him something,
which the Colonel told me later was a request to mark our road
permits so as to get us through any further road-blocks on the way
to Prague without other such delays. The Soviet officer shrugged
and said he had no pen or pencil. We produced handfuls. Then
he shook his head and said he had to get an official stamp from
his command post, a barnyard hut some distance off the road. He
returned empty-handed. I offered him a mechanical pencil which
wrote in four colors of crayon by twisting the barrel. He stood in
the road playing with it like a child. We in the jeep exchanged
looks of despairing fed-up-ness. Suddenly I blurted in Czech,
"Keep it! It's a present!" Our Russian snickered, the Soviet
Russian nodded and grinned; laboriously he marked our papers
with his new toy, and we were on our way.

No detail of this is important enough to remember, and
every detail is a facet of the thing as it was in its grotesqueness. I
learned all too soon that what we had met west of Prague, and
what I was to see in the capital itself, was the Red Army on its
best behavior. The worst was yet to come. As we approached the
city, the Major asked me if I remembered Prague well enough
to direct the driver. I thought so but I was not really sure. I had
not been there in more than seven years and I did not want to
make a fool of myself. But instinct stood by me, and it is anyway
not a complicated matter to come down the Plzeňská to the west
embankment of the river. But I wanted to go a certain way. My
excitement and emotion were choking me, all I could say was
"Right", "Left", "Turn". I managed to direct the driver so that
we came down through Malá Strana with a right turn to the

river, where the towers of the Charles Bridge soared before us in the golden summer afternoon. I had done my best to restrain my feelings, which could be of no concern to my companions. But at the sight of the Bridge I was overcome. The Bridge is an emotion, not only the emotion of response to unique beauty; but it is visibly and tangibly the spirit of Prague. I think every memorable place has its comparable talisman, but I do not know of any other that casts the personal spell of this Gothic miracle. Some call the spell baleful. And I cannot call it other than tragic; but tragedy as a groundwork of the human condition comprises all the other elements of our fate and some of these, like our own characters, are the obverse of the dark and the dire that is in us. I looked up at Hradčany on its hill, from the sweep of green and leafy trees to the ancient grey stones crowned by gold-whiskered spires sparkling in the sun, and down at the old red roofs huddled below; and I vowed that nothing ever again should cut me off from this place that I loved so much.

I had been told beforehand that I would not be able to stop at the Esplanade where I had always stayed in Prague. All the hotels, like all living space, had been taken over by an *uřad,* the Czech word for office, a bureaucratic parasite that had already attached itself to every facet of existence. The Esplanade as the best hotel was reserved exclusively for members of diplomatic missions who were just arriving to reopen their embassies and legations. Presently they would all be scrambling for villas and desirable apartments. I was to go to the Alcron Hotel where rooms had been booked for me by the Foreign Ministry. The Alcron is the archetype of ugliest Central European Bauhaus architecture, built about 1930; a dungeon of dark grey concrete, gloomy and hideous inside and out, with massive chunks of dusty plush furniture. It fronts on a street called Stěpanská, just off the Václavské, and just far enough from the corner to get no sunlight at all. It bespeaks something of my feeling for Prague that in all my stays at the hideous Alcron before I moved into my own dream-house, the ugliness and gloominess never got me altogether down.

I had just been shown into my rooms when there was a loud knock on the door and Jan came in, taking off his mashed black hat. He stood staring at me with his mouth open. I was wearing the WAC Captain's uniform I had been assigned in order to travel in Air Force planes and Army vehicles, and I was windblown and dishevelled. My face was dirty—all those miles in the open jeep.

"You look," he said delicately, "like The Old Oaken Bucket in The Well of Loneliness."

I began to take from the pockets of my uniform blouse and trench-coat the lipsticks and stockings with which I had filled them. He transferred quantities to his own pockets. Every woman in Prague was starved for such things and I had brought as many as I could carry. Every ounce of my forty-pound luggage that was not needed for a few summer clothes consisted of things to give to people.

Jan looked round the stuffy rooms with fastidious distaste. I had had all the windows opened, but the place was oppressive. "It stinks of them," he said. It did. It had surely been well house-cleaned since the last of its Nazi high-brass occupants had been booted out, but there was something about it even more repellent than the banal hotel smell of coarseness and stale cigar smoke. Within a day or two this began to lessen as people sent me flowers and flowering plants in surprising profusion; surprising because every kind of agriculture was disrupted, but horticulture evidently not. The production and distribution of food was at a standstill. Even then at the height of summer there were no fruits or vegetables at all. But when no other shops were yet open a few florists' were, and the flower vendors' stalls along the streets were as charming as they had always been. I have never understood this.

Leaving to keep some appointments, Jan said he would come by later to pick me up for dinner. And so, having had the hot bath which was the luxury I least expected—abundant hot water

was a rarity everywhere in Europe except Prague—and resumed
my own identity, I went down to the hotel entrance to find Jan
sitting in an ancient black car and his small smiling chauffeur
Dohnálek waiting to escort me to it. The car was a rattling old
thing and Jan said, "This will have to do until they find me something else. They expected me to use the Mercedes that was
Neurath's and I refused to get into it. Bad enough to live in the
rooms he occupied."

Jan himself had arrived in Prague only a few days before,
coming from San Francisco to Washington, where I had last seen
him, and stopping briefly in London. He had taken up residence
in the private apartment of the Foreign Minister on the second
floor of the Czernin Palace, the Ministry of Foreign Affairs. The
vast eighteenth-century pile crowns the height overlooking the
church and square of the Loreta. The name of the Ministry
in Czech is Černinský Palác and we referred to it always as
Černinský, which comes to me more naturally than the anglicized
name. It was past sunset of a perfect summer evening as we drove
westwards again over the Bridge and up the hill through the steep
ancient streets of Malá Strana, round the serpentine whose name
means Towards the Royal Castle, out onto the magnificent square
on which the Hrad faces, with the most superb baroque palaces in
Europe to right and left; on through my beloved Loretanská to
the Černinský. If I was thinking—and I do not remember, curiously—of my first sight of all this on that long blissful day afoot
fifteen years before, I said nothing to Jan about it. We were silent.
The silence was a mingling of emotion about returning to Prague
and the first probings of the ominous and the unknown. The car
stopped at the north door of the Černinský. We went inside to a
hall so immense in height that even Jan was dwarfed by it, and
into a small private lift which took us to the Minister's apartment.

There the door was opened by an elderly manservant whom
Jan introduced affectionately as Příhoda, who had been his
father's valet and had been with the old President until he died.

We walked through a series of magnificent rooms, none of which Jan ever used unless he gave a very rare party for personal guests, to the last room at the northeast corner of the building. Here Jan lived altogether. It was a very long room, somewhat narrow in proportion to its length and great height, with a lozenged, richly decorated ceiling and three enormous windows overlooking the Loreta. At the far end of the room was a plain brass bed, so lost in the proportions of the place that the other furnishings took precedence. The room was a sitting-room and library in which Jan also slept and ate his meals. He received his friends there and any person with whom he wished to talk alone. There was a couch at the end of the room farthest from the bed, with several arm-chairs surrounding a low table. There was a writing-table under the centre window. The wall opposite the windows had many doors, some to cupboards, and some to passages leading to other rooms; but Jan took no personal tenancy of any of them. He made a face as we entered his room, saying "Hanči"—President Beneš's wife—"had this room painted and made decent for me before I got here. Nothing is the same as when Neurath was in it except the ceiling." He looked up with a pout of disgust at the splendid frescoed ceiling.

We had a drink; he had brought some gin and whisky from London and even remembered a bottle or two of sherry for me. Then Přihoda and another man carried in the supper-table all set with a silver tureen of soup and the usual cold *smaženi řizek* (fried veal cutlet) with potato salad. Jan dismissed the men, saying he would ring when he wanted the table removed. He served the food himself. It was very quiet in the high, rather dark room, and we appreciated the isolation from the bustle and confusion and constant tramp of booted feet that were the sounds of downtown Prague. It was either nine o'clock or ten o'clock, I cannot remember; but through the open windows we heard the lovely carillon of the Loreta Church begin to play St. Mary's Hymn. We were very close to it. We left the table and went to the window to lean on the wide sill and look at the ornate belfry in the starlight, and listen to the mournful melody, an ancient Slavic folk tune. In my ear it echoes in the key of A; but I might be mistaken. As it ends, the great bell a fifth lower tolls the strokes of the hour. For the ear this is the same haunting spell that binds the eye to the Gothic beauty of Prague. We leant there with our chins in our hands and looked out over the darkening loveliness, the onion domes and fairy-tale castles floating in the summer sky.

"Did you cry?" Jan asked me.

"Of course. Did you?"

"Like a fool."

We turned from the window after a time and I realized I was exhausted. It was twenty hours since I had wakened that morning in the palace of Caserta, outside of Naples. Now I was here, telescoped through space and time and history and the horrors our world had been through, and an intimation that struggle and grief were not altogether in the past. I knew also that it would be my part not to admit or appear to believe this. I am not sure that I really knew it on that first day of my return to Prague, but it made itself evident and imperative so soon that I cannot place its inception in my mind. It was one thing I could do for Jan that his other Western friends, British and American, could not or would not do. Perhaps they were reluctant to appear less acute than they really were. I did not care. I wanted to help; to help him and help the people, the ones I call the real Czecho-slovaks, who clung to him and believed to the end that he could save the Republic that his father had created. He had to believe it himself or he could not have endured what he did.

When I went out alone next morning to walk about the city and get the feel of things, I saw Prague swarming with the Red Army. Considering that it was the Red Army they were on their good behavior—armed to the teeth, which was offensive in a 'liberated' country—but relatively untroublesome. These were members of Konev's divisions which had spearheaded the westward thrust against the Germans, and most of them, I was told, were European Russians. But in their wake moved far larger numbers of the armies of Malinovsky, and those were what we saw east of Prague; primitives, largely from the Urals and from Central Asian Soviets, who made no feint of being correct. I was wracked with shame and disgust at the sight of them and what they did. Yet no such reactions could be unilateral and untouched by a double-kick deriving from equal or even greater detestation of the Nazis. I went that morning to look at Staroměstké Náměstí (The Old Town Square), the heart of mediaeval Prague. The Germans had blown up the Gothic Town Hall there in a last burst of vandalistic fury, just before they surrendered; vindictive barbarism exactly like their destruction of the approaches to the Ponte Vecchio in Florence. But where the Florentines have chosen to replace their lost treasures with ugly and commonplace contemporary structures, the Czechs decided to leave the Town Hall permanently in ruins, as a memorial of those times and to those who died at the hands of Hitler. Any way you look at it you know you have touched the crux of this tormented century.

As in all conditions of emergency and upheaval you find yourself close to people quickly and without the preliminaries of acquaintance that pertain in ordinary circumstances. I met a great many people all at once, it seems now; most vividly I remember those who were just returning home after years of indescribable suffering in Nazi concentration camps. Most of those survivors were so shattered by starvation, torture, and brutality that they had not enough residual health or mentality to regain their original strengths and powers. I met women who had been years in Ravensbrück and worse places to the East. One memory about them all streaks through masses of impressions: their preoccupation to wear long sleeves at a time when there was little clothing to be had. They wanted to cover up the blue number tattooed on their forearms by the Nazis. Some had had their legs hideously scarred by the 'experiments' of the bestial 'medical doctors' at

Ravensbrück. "Thick stockings for X—" reads an item in the memo book I carried; "long skirt for Y—"

And food for everybody. There was no food. There was nothing to eat but potatoes and the makings of a black bread that was heavy and sour compared to the normal *chleb* that is the people's staff of life. *Chleb,* the national black bread, is good when it is good; but this had admixtures of God knows what, to make enough to go round. In the mornings when I rang for breakfast I took what I got, a small piece of this bread and a cup of undrinkable brown liquid without any sugar or milk. (Before the war Czechoslovakia had been the biggest exporter of refined sugar in Europe.) Of course there was no meat. There was no fat. There was no milk. There were no eggs, no fish; there was no protein food of any kind. Out of the potatoes and breadstuff the Czechs contrived food that had some taste. They are wonderful cooks, and somehow they made thick soups, dumplings, and stews that were edible. This was the food situation in reality and in the Alcron whenever I ate there, but more often I was with Jan, whose kitchen, like those of all officials, was supplied with food that ordinary people could not get. I also found as I went with Jan to the houses of old friends of his that there was some sort of black market in operation. I went to several houses where we had very good dinners because the Foreign Minister was coming. There was meat and there were other foods which you never saw elsewhere. I was miserable at such tables because it choked me to eat the precious bits of meat which the people needed so badly, yet the hostess would have been mortally offended if I had not eaten it, or had left a scrap on my plate.

Much of what I saw was in Jan's company. He took me about with him for some reasons that were not personal at all. From the first the ubiquitous Communists and their stooges inevitably labelled me The American Woman. This suited his purposes. As he said and restated many times, publicly in Prague, privately to swarms of interviewers and Western journalists, "I will stand on my hind legs and yell my head off to prove that we have freedom of speech in this country." He was the personification of Czechoslovakia's tie to the West, and if this was emphasized by the presence of an American woman friend who was in the talk business, written or spoken, and would also do some subsidiary yelling, he thought it useful. Typically, he never put this in words, he would never have been so obvious. He would suggest almost as if by accident that I drop in on so-and-so; that I go to some meeting like a gathering of writers already coralled into the beginnings of a Syndicate, which was an element of the Communist Ministry of Information. What I said when I got there was up to me. I said what I believed and what was also consonant with his efforts. Occasionally I asked him beforehand if he really wanted me to sound off. He would throw his hands in the air with a grimace that meant, "What the hell do *you* think?"

One place I went without him—he could not have stood it —was the cellar of the Petschek banking-house where the Gestapo had had its torture installations. At that time the Czechs had done nothing whatever to change it. It remained as the Nazis had fled from it. There was a series of dungeons obscenely white-tiled in a demonstration of German hygiene and order, each room arranged with strapped benches and tables, and instruments and implements whose details I will spare you. The Petschek was the place reserved for the highest grade of Czech prisoners, leaders of the Resistance, wives and relatives of Czechoslovaks fighting abroad, informants who worked with the Czech parachutists sent in by Allied Intelligence. The centre of the installation was the guillotine in the middle of a bare room. There was a drain in the floor in front of the machine, and a long hose to facilitate quick flushing-away of the blood. All round the walls, near the ceiling, ran a heavy metal rod and from it hung meat-hooks, exactly like a butcher's cooling-room. The guillotine itself had not been cleaned when I was there; its blade was dark and caked with dried blood. Across it lay a tattered Czechoslovak flag and a small, dried-up wreath.

One day soon after I arrived we went out to Lány, the village west of Prague where the President's country residence is situated in a fine park, and nearby the village graveyard where Jan's father is buried. President Masaryk had spent his last years at Lány after retiring from the Presidency in 1935 and turning over the reins of government to Edvard Beneš. He died in 1937. Jan took me up to the room in which his father had lived and died, a study-bedroom very plainly furnished, with a pigeon-hole sort of bookcase, all in small compartments, along one wall. Jan said that this had been his father's invention for keeping papers and notes in order. The room was arranged in typical European spirit, quite as the Founder-President had left it. In glass cases were the death-mask of his face and a cast of his right hand. The sun shone gently through the high windows.

There was a particular simplicity in Jan that afternoon. I felt his love and reverence for his father in his bearing and in his few understated words about the last months of the old President's life, when Jan came frequently from London to be with him. "He died on the fourteenth of September," said Jan. "My fifty-first birthday." We stood in the quiet room, saying nothing more, and I knew that no other emotion or attachment in his lifetime had had the strength or the permanence of his feeling for his father. It was as he had said, like my love for my mother.

We walked slowly through the halls and out to the garden. The castle of Lány was now President Beneš's official country residence, but he was in Prague at the Hrad. The old servants and attendants spoke to Jan with touching affection. We strolled through the garden and Jan plucked a small red rose and gave it to me. It is on this table as I write, dried, but still red and fragrant. We went to the stables, where there were beautiful white and dapple-grey horses, each horse in a roomy loose-box with its name and pedigree on a card in a scrolled frame over the door. They were of the same strain as the Lippizaners of the Spanish Riding School in Vienna. It was a curious echo of the early century, and I stood there silent, thinking of the years before fury was unloosed to spawn and re-spawn horror and violence and agony. I doubt if I could ask myself then, in that ambience and atmosphere, whether anything now was a better disposition for humanity than the blundering old hodge-podge Habsburg world; but I have pondered the question since.

We walked through the park and across the highroad and down a short way to the village cemetery. There at the far right corner, under the wall, was the unmarked grave of T. G. Masaryk. It was covered with fresh flowers in small bouquets, field-flowers and the humble blooms that grow in cottage gardens.

"The people bring them fresh every day," said Jan. "They have done it always, they did it all through the Nazis and the war. They were forbidden and threatened, there were guards to keep them away. Every day the Nazis took the flowers away and every night the people brought fresh flowers and got them over the wall in the dark onto the grave."

Twenty years later I would make another pilgrimage to that place where Jan lies beside his father in an unbelievable today when Czechoslovaks themselves impose on their people an effort to obliterate the name of Masaryk.

We were driving some days afterwards east of Prague on the way to Pardubice. This is beautiful country, laced with rivers and smaller streams, the heart of agricultural Bohemia. The peasants lived in villages strung a few kilometers apart, typically with a single street on which the low houses face, pretty stucco houses tinted yellow or pink or white—or even pale blue. There was a big barnyard beside each house, with high wooden gates. Inside were the farm wagons and machinery, the animals, and the valuable dung-heap. The people went out from the villages every day to work the land which, from the beginning of the Masaryk Republic, they had owned in consequence of the land distribution programme. This limited the acreage that any one owner or absentee owner could possess, and required the hereditary Austro-Bohemian nobility who had owned most of the land to make proportions of it available for purchase by the peasants who worked it, with the government helping them to finance their purchase. The nobility grumbled to some extent but it was a fair and democratic measure.

These peasants had a high standard of living and were intelligent, substantial elements of the body politic. Illiteracy was unknown amongst them and they sent their sons and daughters to excellent high schools in the larger nearby towns and very often, on to universities or technical schools. They were fiercely resistant to the Nazis after 1938, and were the heart and guts of the underground all through the war.

And now when the war was over and the Germans gone, they had Russian occupation. This was terrible to behold. Wherever you saw the Red Army you saw the crudity and poverty for which the men themselves could not be blamed; but to saddle this to the backs of a people who had had seven years of Nazi hell was too much. The Red Army lived off the land, and consequent upon the devastation of the Soviet Union and their own scorched-earth resistance to the Germans, they took it as their right to eat up the substance of whatever place they found themselves in, whether as conquerors or allies. There was a story going round that their government would leave them wherever they were because it was the easiest way to feed them until their own country could absorb them again. It was probably a canard. And I have heard the claim, meant to be a balanced point of view, that all armies are equally brutalized by war and equally vandals whenever they pass through or occupy foreign territory. It simply is not true. I saw the American and British forces in Italy and Germany, also the French, and while the Americans brought a detestable black market into being, the Western forces did not plunder, steal from the people, or eat up their substance.

That summer afternoon we had not gone far outside Prague in an easterly direction when Jan said quietly, "From about here on, they are all Malinovsky's divisions. And, we understand, moving towards home—thank God."

Their only resemblance to the Russians in Prague was that they carried as many guns and other weapons as could be loaded or strapped onto them, and wore as many stolen wrist-watches. They were filthy. They were shaggy and unshaven, their uniforms shapeless and thick with dirt, their bearing brutish. They had set up the usual chain of road-blocks that we had seen west of Prague, but we were not stopped because Jan's car bore official identification and a Government flag. Dohnálek and the body-guard beside him in the front seat had a whole portfolio of documents, which nobody asked to see—I assume because nobody could have read them. We had been moving along for perhaps three-quarters of an hour on roads which had, of course, no normal traffic whatever, when our car slowed down. Ahead of us was a long, crawling queue, moving at snail's pace and stretching as far as we could see. It consisted of farm wagons and carts, two-wheeled and four-wheeled, the craziest assortment of non-powered vehicles imaginable. The Russians were pulling out, it is true; in utter disorganization, taking with them everything that could be moved. Each stolen wagon or cart was piled to overflowing with furniture, pots and pans, crockery, carpets, farm implements, window curtains, sewing-machines, an occasional plumbing-fixture, sometimes a piano or other musical instrument, mattresses— it was said there was not a mattress left when the Russians had finally gone—quilts and other bedding, toys, sometimes a telephone ripped out of a wall, anything and everything they could have found in the houses and barns of the local population. Many of the articles could have been of no use to them, and many others they would not have had an idea how to use. The wagon or cart or whatever the vehicle was, was pulled sometimes by a wretched farm animal, or two—an ancient, trembling cow would be harnessed together with an emaciated goat. But there were very few animals left in the country at all, and sometimes a couple of men had harnessed themselves to the cart and were dragging it along. On top of the looted stuff overflowing from every wagon there were several mouzhiks, dead drunk or sound asleep, their booted or wrapped feet dangling over the sides; and somebody trudging ahead leading the starving, stolen animals.

These people were thousands of kilometers from their own country. We could not know or care how they would get there, but if this was their method of movement it would take months, and their plunder would be abandoned along the way. I sat in the car with tears of rage—not grief, but blazing rage—running down my face. I could not look at Jan, but he said later that he looked at me, and saw me digging my finger-nails into the palms of my hands, and heard me trying to stifle a flood of furious profanity in my clenched teeth.

When I was in New York again that October I saw Harry Hopkins at dinner. It was within weeks of his death, and he was so plainly a mortally ill man that I would not have challenged him with questions. But he catechized me. He asked me searching questions about Czechoslovakia. He listened attentively to my answers. No detail appeared to be too small for significance. I told him all I had seen of the Communists and of the Red Army. When there was a pause I said, "Harry, couldn't your Boss have foreseen this at Yalta? Couldn't he know this would happen if the Russians got into Europe?"

Hopkins said, "They were already there. But the Boss thought that when Stalin got tough, he'd be able to wheedle or bargain him out of each thing as it came up."

Jan took me to the Hrad to see the President and meet Madame Beneš. There were only the four of us at afternoon coffee. I had met President Beneš in New York two years before.

At that time I did not know Jan well enough for him to talk to me about Beneš with the frankness he did later. Jan treated Beneš with the greatest respect, always called him "Mr. President" or "Sir" and in New York or elsewhere abroad stood watchfully at Beneš's side with a protective attitude as if to assist Beneš's halting command of English. He spoke it uneasily; his natural second language was French, in which he had been educated. But I never heard him speak French; only his limited English or, after he realized with surprise that I understood it, Czech.

I saw him many times, but I never knew him any better than at first. I think few people did. I thought him a didactic little man. I am not among those who are prejudiced in impressions of men by the accident of their physical stature. Maestro, for instance, was short by Anglo-Saxon though not by Mediterranean standards; but he was a giant. Beneš was a pygmy in my mind, and would have been had he stood six foot three. I know that he was a very skilful statesman, that he had been instrumental in the creation of the Republic, that he was the architect of its foreign policy (whose failure was primarily the fault of France); that he was a staunch democrat, personally and symbolically important to and deeply respected by the Czechoslovaks as the political heir of T. G. Masaryk. The betrayal of Munich shook him and embittered him, and influenced him towards compliance with the Russians even before the full pressure of the Czech Communists was turned on him. I know much about him that is admirable. But the man when he was alive, and my memories of him since, are cold.

Beneš was accustomed to be oracular. He discoursed, declaimed; he never conversed—not that I should have expected him to converse with me. His mind and manner were devoid of wit, grace, or flexibility; particularly of course, in contrast to Jan. In Beneš's presence Jan seemed to suppress his natural play and sparkle of speech. Beneš talked that afternoon with rigidity and positivism as if to rule out the political imponderables, domestic and foreign, which hung over his country. He said arbitrarily that the Soviet armies would have quit the country by the end of the year, and he proved to be right. I was grateful for that when I was assailed in New York and Washington with taunts that Czechoslovakia was already down the Communist drain. The remarkable truth is that at that time, and for nearly three years afterwards, it was not, in terms of the lives and liberties of its ordinary people. But Beneš was not right when he stated with equal positiveness that the Soviet Union would absolutely respect the political and economic independence of Czechoslovakia because Stalin had promised him that. He was not right when he leaned on the multi-party pre-war political structure of the Republic, which proved to be a pile of jackstraws when the Czechoslovak Communists were ready to kick it over.

I never understood why there should have been Communists, with strong ties to Moscow and the Communist International, in Czechoslovakia from the beginning of the Republic in 1919. As an American I suppose I oversimplify the motivations which explain Communists. I look for the reasons which made them that way. And in the Czechoslovak Republic there were few logical reasons. The working class had no cause to be radical or rebellious. In social legislation which protected workers from exploitation and assured them of wide state benefits—pensions, medical care, education, and such—the country was one of the most advanced in Europe. There were no conditions of social injustice. There was no dispossession of peasants and the working class. There was no feudal primitivism such as existed in Poland and Hungary. Unemployment, starvation wages, and a vast disparity between the very rich few and the very poor many, which for instance explains the Italian Communist Party, did not pertain in Bohemia and Moravia, the industrial heart of the old Habsburg Empire, which later made the Czechoslovak Republic one of the foremost industrial nations of Europe. Communism was also incompatible with the nationalism of the Czechoslovak people. There did exist, in the so-called Sudetenland of northwestern Bohemia, a mal-content German minority of nearly three million people who suf-fered extensive unemployment and ascribed their situation to the policies of the Government in Prague. But their discontent led them not into the Communist camp, but into the arms of Henlein, Hitler, and the Nazis.

Why the Communists? Jan explained it to me as a matter partly of theoretical orientation, dating back to the nineteenth century and the influence of Marx and Engels on the working class of Germany and Austria-Hungary; and partly to the powerful mystique of Slav solidarity. The Russians have pulled the stops on this all the way back to the dim times of Rurik. It was inherent in their machinations throughout the Balkans and Eastern Europe in the time of the Tsars. It spread from the Communist heartland of Lenin and Stalin to draw to Moscow the leading Communists of Central and Balkan Europe for training and for the promulgation of revolution. The leaders of the Czechoslovak Communist Party headed by Gottwald, who was Stalin's own choice for the Execu-tive Committee of the Communist International, had been attend-ing Congresses and training schools in Moscow since the early 1920's. The membership of the Czechoslovak Communist Party before Munich was not large, but it was vociferous—because the Masaryk Republic was a true democracy in which no political party was outlawed or suppressed, as the Communists were in Poland, Hungary, and Yugoslavia.

Tough and ruthless, free to push their party and sit in the national Parliament, where Gottwald, in his first speech in 1929 looked around him and said, "We are here to wring your necks"; cynical and, we would say, wholly unprincipled in changing and switching the party line for their own ends through all the up-heavals from 1938 to 1945, the Communists used every situation to promote their aims. Wherever they were—in Hitler's concen-tration camps, in Moscow, in the armed forces, a few in the West, or in the underground at home—they used every device to undermine what they called bourgeois Czechoslovakia. They collaborated with the Nazis, they formed cells in the camps whose purpose was to betray Czechoslovak democrats, they laid the groundwork during the war for the entities called National Committees (Národný Výbor) which mushroomed in every community as the tanks and guns of the Red Army crunched westward. The National Committees were to take over for "protective" reasons the local administration of their communities. In reality they were central implements for the seizure of power and for other purposes such as the confiscation (stealing) of the property of vanished Jews and of anybody whose house or business or goods or land they wanted; such people were denounced as collaborators.

The strange thing is that the time-table for the communization of the country was so leisurely, and so veiled by semblances of conciliation with the national sentiments and democratic traditions of the people. Any Communist with whom you talked (and those Ministries which were not headed by them were full of their appointees) would say, "We are Czechoslovaks first and Communists second." Of course it was the correct line. It was supposed to be disarming—and I am afraid in the beginning it really was. They bided their time, preferring to make their revolution within the framework of normal Parliamentary elections and of the coalition Government which included all (and too many) political parties. The Government as put together in Moscow and shipped to Košice had Communists at the head of the four most strategic ministries: Interior (police), Defence, Information, and Education. In addition there were Communist deputy and vice-ministers in the Premier's office, the Foreign Ministry, and the departments of Industry, Agriculture, and Social Welfare. Effectively, a stranglehold; but one with curious sliding loopholes that were left slack, through which the people had a degree of freedom: free speech, free communication of every kind with the West, religious freedom, a free general election in 1946. They had to fight for this freedom (particularly within the Government) but they did fight.

The Communists knew that too flagrant a stranglehold would have alarmed and alerted the nation and the West—particularly the United States from which Czechoslovakia sought loans and other assistance. Not until another general election was imminent in 1948 did they pull hard on the slip-knot and move in for the kill. In the beginning they even preferred the screen of a stooge as Prime Minister. This was the contemptible Zdeněk Fierlinger, their own designee in 1945; not a Communist but worse, since he betrayed what had been an honest democratic party and his own former friend, Edvard Beneš, by serving the Communists as collaborator.

I saw him one day in his office. He had a terrible face, narrow and pointed, with slitted eyes that never looked straight at you. Rat, I thought; I have never seen a human being whose face was so rodentlike. I went to see him because Jan had said, "He is worse than Gottwald; I'd rather deal with the devil face to face than with something crawling in the woodwork."

It is difficult to say long after such a lost struggle when and in what degree one's illusions ceased to be illusions, and when they were succeeded by reality—which at times was as good as I had always thought it. I had no plan to write articles or reportage or any kind of topical comment about Czechoslovakia. The place was swarming with journalists who were doing that. Their summaries were necessarily superficial no matter how expert they were at news-gathering. My concern was the novel I had long planned. It would span perhaps eighty years of time down to the present, which would no longer be the present when I should come to it. But I never thought until the end that the majority of the people could be overcome by a Communist minority. I did not believe the country could become a police state. I did not like the extreme socialization, and the nationalization of industry in the post-war régime, but I saw why it had to be in the wake of Nazism and the disruption of the capital structure of industry and finance, much of which had belonged to Jews who had been exterminated. (Some had fled in time, taking their moveable assets or exporting them beforehand.)

Laurence Steinhardt had just arrived to be the American Ambassador. During the war, as Ambassador to Turkey—and a good deal else—he had proven tough and effective not only against our enemies but in dealing with our recalcitrant allies. He was not a prepossessing man, not ambassadorial of manner, not suave or smooth-spoken. But beneath the appearance of a materialist and a shrewd New York lawyer, he had heart and courage. He was ideal for the post and the circumstances, a rough diamond. He was a strong and loyal friend to Jan, unfailing in any support it was possible to give him. And a most valued friend to me. I saw a great deal of Laurence in three years; and from the first he conveyed his silent understanding of a tortuously difficult situation. But I refused to concede it a hopeless one and Laurence was stalwart in support of my belief (naïve in essence, but I did not care) that Jan could succeed in his efforts to hold Czechoslovakia in a viable balance between East and West.

A few days before I was to leave, Jan rushed in one afternoon, very upset. He had been at a meeting of musicians, former members of the Czech Philharmonic Orchestra, who had been for years in Nazi concentration camps. A special effort was being made to get these survivors repatriated and rehabilitated as fast as possible, replacements for the murdered Jews recruited, and the orchestra ready to play again. Jan told me they had found that through vandalism or looting or sheer confusion, all the instruments of the woodwind and brass choirs had disappeared. There were none in Prague and none to be had in Europe. He had told the men that somehow he would get them an entire complement of woodwinds and brasses; then he came to me and said, "Can you?"

How should I know?—but of course I said yes. I knew that there had been a time when the best woodwinds were made in France and the best brasses in Germany and, indeed, Czechoslovakia; but it was plain that nobody would be making musical instruments for a long time to come. I said I would send the instruments from New York. And this was done, with the help of Phil Spitalny, the contract man of the N B C Symphony. He asked the first-desk players to go with me to the dealers who sold the instruments and select the best ones available. They were all assembled in my front hall. Maestro's daughter Wally Toscanini was here on her first post-war visit from Milan, and when she saw the hall stacked with a truckload of orchestra instruments in cases, she screamed, "Have you lost your mind?" Then my friends of the Air Force flew the load in a cargo plane to Prague; fine idea, they said, just the kind of thing the U.S. should do. Jan met them at Ruzyň (the Russians had suddenly quit it) and gave them a party.

The evening of the day we had been at Lány Jan talked for a long time about his father. As I remember it, he had never before spoken so personally of President Masaryk, or perhaps it seemed so because I had just seen the old President's room where he spent the last of his days, and could imagine Jan there with him. Always in contemplating the father and son, one weighed the contrast between the great man, the scholar and ascetic, and the son who was so entirely the opposite, but perhaps for that very reason bound to his father by bonds even deeper than filial love.

"My father was on his deathbed," said Jan. "It was late in the summer. Hitler had been more than four years in power. My father had been watching him and seeing all too clearly what he was up to. He said to me, 'Very bad times are coming for the nation . . . and for Europe.' I was alone with him. I never forget how he spoke and what he said."

There we were, sitting at opposite ends of the couch in Jan's room, he cross-legged, moody, subdued, his lower lip protruding in a face he made when he was concentrating. By the tone of his voice, or an occasional gesture, he recalled the quiet, plainly-furnished room in the castle at Lány, and gave me a mental picture which I still keep, of the frail, partly paralyzed old man with the pointed white beard and hanging moustaches, giving his last words of guidance to his son. Jan of course repeated them to me in English, and I quote what he said as he said it.

"Beneš will have to bear the brunt of it. He is not equal to it alone. He is not big enough." So spoke the old man.

Jan said he thought, neither am I; and his father touched on that. Then he said, "You must help Beneš. You know much of the world better than he does. Stand by Beneš always. Promise me that you will never leave him alone."

Jan promised. He committed himself in a promise to stand by Beneš to the end—though to what end, or when, he could not know. And he was not personally attached to Beneš. I never heard him utter a word of personal criticism of Edvard Beneš, but also never one of affection. He was fond of Hana Benešová, a woman who was so reserved and so studied of presence that I could not imagine anyone really at ease with her. But Jan knew her well and said, with a waggle of his eyebrows, "She has had her troubles with him, believe me."

He went on, talking about Beneš, and said, "He was, or he was willing to be if necessary, a martyr for my father's sake. All public men, no matter how noble their characters or high their position, come under attack. All politicians and statesmen have enemies. All have dirty political linen to be washed, unpleasant errands to be run. My father as President was no different from others in these ways, though Czech legend would have you believe he was. And every time that any political difficulty confronted him, Beneš stood in the breach. For any mistake, Beneš took the blame. Beneš was the whipping-boy. Beneš got down in the ditch and did the political spade-work that left my father clear of it all, to remain the saint the people thought him and the saint he really was. For this I will be loyal to Beneš until I die."

CHAPTER FIFTEEN

T HOSE were the years of commuting across the Atlantic in propeller planes by way of what I called Shander: any place (Gander, Shannon, Iceland, Greenland) where the plane made a fuel stop and sometimes remained, fogged in or grounded by engine trouble, for hours or even days. Oh, the dreary air-fields, the Nissen huts and barn-like hangars, where you stood around with nothing, nothing, nothing to help kill the time! At military fields you were not even allowed outside to walk up and down in the Arctic cold and at least get some fresh air. No news-stand, no snack-bar, sometimes not even places for all the grounded passengers to sit down. They would never let you simply stay in the plane and sleep. All those experiences have gone into a retrospective blur through which weird or hilarious moments poke their clowning fingers. I exempt Shannon from the generality of places where we used to be grounded; if you were lucky enough to land there at dawn after that interminable overnight hop from Newfoundland you got the best breakfast in the world when you desperately needed it: Irish bacon or sausages with fresh eggs, grilled kidneys with a mushroom and a popping little hothouse tomato, thick-crusted hot soda-bread with sweet country butter and delicious jam, all the good Irish tea you could drink—scalding, mahogany-colored, strong as liquor. Or if you didn't think that, they laughed when you put a shot of Irish whiskey in it.

Each journey was a messy twenty-four hours or more, and at each journey's end an essential and absorbing part of my life was taking the form I had long intended—moving between New York and Europe with total contrasts of occupation and surroundings, different languages, different rhythms of existence, different air to breathe. I had known for years before the war that I would one day live in Prague but I never intended to leave New York altogether and certainly never be an expatriate. My aim was to have a home in each place and go back and forth between them. I could not put the plan into effect until I had finished the book I had to write, but I started moving towards it in the winter of 1946 during a flying trip to Prague. I made inquiries about the possibility of leasing a flat in one of the houses in the street called Loretanská, which runs from the great square on which the Hrad faces to the Loreta Square I have described. To my eyes this was the most beautiful street in Europe. Its yellow baroque houses had taken their grip on my imagination the first day I ever saw Prague. I wanted to live in one of them. The houses were old family properties divided, like most Continental town houses, into flats, with all the desirable ones occupied by members of the owners' families or by tenants who had been there for lifetimes or generations. There were no vacancies. There was anyway an acute housing shortage which has remained ever since. I made my wants known and also that I was in no hurry; but I asked certain people to keep an eye out in case a flat such as I wanted should become available.

In "The Treasure," a short story written with a surgeon's scalpel, W. Somerset Maugham makes this aside:

"Now it is a funny thing about life, if you refuse to accept anything but the best you very often get it; if you utterly decline to make do with what you can get, then somehow or other you are very likely to get what you want."

I knew what I wanted. I had not dreamt for more than fifteen years of living in one of those houses only to settle for something less. I also wanted to write the novel I was committed to write, which meant staying in New York for eighteen months or however

long it took, with a few flying breaks. At that time it was not a
trial of endurance or a punishment to stay in New York, as it can
too readily be now. Maestro was here—concerts and rehearsals,
and the companionship I treasured. Max was here—the guiding
hand that gave me confidence. I see now at this distance that each
of the people, long dead, who stood in primary relation to me had
the faculty to do so without impinging on the others. As I said at
the beginning of this book they were the forces that shaped me or
my work or my fate (all intertwined.) At that time those relations
were distributed in almost equal balance; death had not intervened and I had not been pushed or even gone voluntarily to a
point where any one of them took precedence over the others.

It was important to me to write the novel about New York
that Max Perkins believed I was peculiarly fitted to write. I consider it the best novel I have written. Nobody else thinks so to my
knowledge, but nobody else has written my books. Max asked it
of me because as my editor he had been dealing for years with
the obstructive factor that in writing fiction I had refused to draw
directly on myself and my life for my material. All fiction reflects
the personality and experiences of its author but I had used these
sources only indirectly. I have a certain faculty for the limning
of characters. I construct them painstakingly from elements of
reality and of imagination. If they then come alive to me and take
over the working out of their own destinies, I have a novel. I have
been told that this is craftsmanship and not artistry; but I must
work with the capacities that I have. I once said to Charlie Scribner
(Senior) that my dearest wish was to write a book that would be
called a work of art and sell twelve hundred copies. Charlie shud-
dered.

East Side, West Side is not literally autobiographical but it is
more nearly so than anything else I have written. This made it
difficult to handle in places where I forcibly re-shaped the material.
In some ways I defeated myself in the result and a good deal of
the best work I had ever done in the drawing of realistic people

[369]

went unremarked. The book itself was not; it had a long life as novels go. A film was made from it which I was told was a horror. I have never seen it. It wholly distorted the purpose and scope of the story and concerned itself chiefly with the murder of a degraded woman. In the novel this murder was a minor thread woven in to show that it was and always had been possible in New York for a murder mystery to remain publicly unsolved when the truth was known to the police and the newspapers, the victim was a disreputable person, and exposure of the truth would have ruined the lives of innocent people. The Elwell, the Dot King, and the Starr Faithfull murders were of this kind. I studied all three cases in working out the murder I devised, and I was generously helped by the late Meyer Berger, for many years the star crime reporter of *The New York Times;* and by the Police Department.

Since that year I have realized that I must have been less perceptive about Max than people I knew who said later that they thought he seemed much older; suddenly frail or tired. Max was a foundation of my world and you do not think of a foundation as other than indestructible. I find to my amazement that he was born in the same year as my mother. It never crossed my mind that he was eighteen years older than me. Max was ageless and Max was timeless. He was the instinctive contemporary of every writer with whom he worked—and they ranged from old parties to this century's giants to brash or timid youngsters writing their autobiographical first novels through which Max discerned the talent that they had. Max was the extension of each writer's self. Yet there never was a man who was more entirely himself. He had strong views, robust prejudices, his own scrupulous code of life. But he never invoked those in judgement of his writers who were a weird lot like any assortment of writers, moved to write about worlds and more importantly, their inhabitants, amongst whom Max would have been appalled to find himself in reality. As usual, he made no suggestions and avoided any current discussion of what I was writing. But he was intently present with his kind of help, visits at luncheon or tea, his telephone calls which came as if by telepathy when I was stuck or about to get stuck, his assurances that it would all come right when I had got it down on paper and "we" would see what would then have to be done about it.

And I still had Tam. I see that up to here I have never described Tam at work. I expect to be stigmatized as feeble-minded for ascribing the ability to write a book to the presence of a cat. The conviction may well be a superstition or a fetish; but if I start to name the writers since the beginnings of literature who have been dependent on cats, this will turn into a catalogue. My present cat, in passing, is satisfactory. He spends the entire day on a couch beside me where my working material is laid out in a succession of folders and boxes. He chooses a spot in the middle of this and goes into the admirable trance which to an ordinary person is a cat asleep, but to an ailurophile means the essence of concentration and also of relaxation. The sight of such a cat soothes and stretches the mind and the nerves. I think it is also the difference between dry desolation in one's solitude and the sense that there can be a living creature who wants nothing more than to share it in total silence and grace.

But Tam involved himself even more in what I was doing. He was with me every moment of the day and the night. When I went from one place to another, in the house or out of doors when I was in the country, Tam walked ahead of me. In the mornings when I went to my study to work, Tam—like my present cat— was already at the door. Tam then leapt onto my desk, always with the trill by which he announced himself. He took his place on top of the pile of manuscript at my right. There he stayed all day, most of the time asleep, sometimes watching me from an eye closed to the merest slit. Tam always knew when I was coming to the end of a page, just before I was ready to remove the sheet of paper from the typewriter. He would then stand up, stretch, arch his back, say something to me, and move aside so that I could put the page on the pile of manuscript; then he would settle on the manuscript again and wait for the next page, asleep unless you knew the nature of his awareness.

At dinner, when I was alone or with intimates, Tam always sat on the corner of the table at my right hand. He would poise himself as close to the edge of the table as he could without falling off, his front paws hidden beneath his frill. He never begged. He purred from the beginning to the end of the meal, which seemed to me a generous tribute to other people's good appetite. I always kept a tidbit for him on my plate but he pretended with grave courtesy not to notice it until I took the morsel in my fingers and offered it to him. Even then he did not move or disturb the symmetry of the table to which he had contributed. He ate his treat daintily and looked for nothing more. He paid no attention to anybody else; to him that would have been a breach of manners. He did not like strangers but he was polite. If I had a party he absented himself and would appear only at the end when I was saying good-night to the last of the guests. He was an imposing personality. Whenever Maestro came to my house he would ask eagerly, "Where is the cat? I want to see the cat." And if some-body was there who was not impressed by cats, or had never met Tam, Maestro would say, "What? You have not seen this cat? But he is extraordinary!"

Tam died in the summer of 1946, a bad and suffering time in every way. I was in the hardest part of my book and it was out of the question to go away. I was lonely (not at all the same thing as solitary); tense, worried. Jan was in Paris at the so-called Peace Conference—the savage wrangle in the Palais de Chaillot where Molotov and Vyshinsky and their satellite lackeys closed in on him publicly, with the Czech Communists running hardest at the heels of the pack. Jan disliked Paris at any time and in those conditions loathed it. His infrequent little scribbled notes were discreet but troubling; his voice on the telephone was depressed.

The summer dragged to its end. Jan arrived on the twenty-first of October for the General Assembly of the United Nations at that grimly misnamed place, Lake Success. He came to my house that afternoon, looking ill and stricken. The session in Paris had been harrowing for him—he never said so—and here it would all be repeated in a more glaring spotlight. I had not seen him for six months, when I had last left Prague after spending a month there. It was never necessary to catch up. Between communicative silence and his resounding talk when he wanted to talk, the threads of understanding spun on, strengthening and increasingly resistant to the savage stresses around him. He was the centre of a tug-of-war which would have torn apart a younger, stronger, and less sensitive man. He believed in the U.N. with a degree of passion —perhaps it was despair—that could not be understood by those whose countries were in command of their own destinies. There was nothing else on the world scene in which he could believe.

I do not suppose that his well-meaning American friends had an idea of the suffering they caused him. He had a great many friends in New York, and more invitations than he could have accepted. He was so approachable, his manner so disarming, his wit so quick, his company so easy, that people said anything to him without stopping to weigh whether their remarks were tactless or whether they knew enough to have the right to remark at all. Many of them took a challenging attitude, remonstrating because he did not do this or that. Most of them had no notion what his motives really were. In a sense they forgot that he was a Czechoslovak and he did little to remind them of it. They did not know that his position was vastly more influential inside his country than abroad, that its internal situation was by no means so definitive as its external one, that the struggle to keep the country free was real and that to all non-Communist Czechoslovaks he was the personification of that will to freedom. The only place he was of great importance was inside his own small land, to whose smallness he referred abroad in terms of slang and banter. "Jerks" was his word for small countries and their spokesmen, and sometimes I winced at seeing him taken too literally at that valuation.

"I don't know which are harder to take," he said more than once. "My friends or my enemies."

His Czechoslovak friends, the non-Communists, were also trying to him at times. Understandably, they clung to him. Some of them were insular and provincial, which inevitably bored a man like Jan; at other times he was consoled by their devotion. They were possessive about him, which was natural, but he did not like anybody to be possessive and I often saw him make great efforts to be patient with them. He lived in New York at the Carlyle Hotel, but he spent much of his time at my house—time that he took by ducking the social gatherings of U.N. delegates whenever he could. He liked to be alone with me or with a few intimate friends who would not interrogate or harangue him. Sometimes he was summoned at an outlandish hour to a conference with Molotov and others of the Communist bloc; he would be tense and distraught and it made me boil to see him humiliated, required to report when he was ordered to. The important thing for me was to keep still, to seem not to know what he was going through.

He used to swing between extremes of dejection and plunges into naturalness—outspoken, boisterous, funny, profane; or quiet and contemplative. He often accompanied me to Maestro's broadcasts which that year took place on Sundays late in the afternoon; but there were times when music was too affecting to his nerves. He was straining to stay in a position that assaulted and offended everything he inherently was. One Sunday after a week of rough going with Molotov and his henchmen, when Jan's delegation had voted and he perforce with them, contrary to the West, he said he was too tired to go to the concert. So we stayed at home and listened on the radio. Maestro played the Scherzo and Adagio from the Beethoven Quartet in F, Opus 135—the next but last work that Beethoven composed, perhaps the most tragic expression of his struggles and sufferings. Jan burst into tears. I went to turn off the radio. He put up his hand to stop me, shaking his head. "The ruin," he said. "I can't bear the ruin."

He got through the month of November and at the end of it he decided to stay on in the United States for the Christmas holidays. He had not had a vacation in years; he said with a snicker, "not since Munich. Before that I had a thirteen years' vacation."

Marjorie Rawlings lent us Cross Creek for a fortnight, preparing the house with the most loving thoughtfulness, herself moving out to stay at a beach house she owned near St. Augustine. It was a time lifted out of the stream of reality, remote from every other association and every harassment. Nowhere else could there have been the gentleness and the simple beauty of that place. Marjorie had created it out of a ramshackle Florida backwoods farmhouse and a rundown orange grove on a country road, lost in a wilderness of palmettos and pine trees. Her lovely book, *Cross Creek,* is a vivid pen-portrait of the place, the life she led, the animals who belonged there, her few neighbors with their violent feuds and stubborn loyalties, the Negroes who lived on and mostly off her place, like old Martha Mickens who must be dead now, "with her deceptive humility and her face like poured chocolate" in Marjorie's words; her maid Idella who welcomed us, along with Martha and Will Mickens when we arrived, with courtly hospitality. I thought they could not have pronounced or remembered Jan's surname, and anyway not known who he was, so I introduced him as Mister John. He got on the cosiest terms with them at once. Idella loved to see him come tiptoeing into the kitchen to look inside the pots on the stove, watch while she made her tiny crisp biscuits or some other unique specialty. Marjorie had taught her to cook beautifully the game and fish and shellfish that abounded there.

Marjorie told me that in 1948 on the eleventh of March Idella went to the mail box to bring in the letters and newspapers.

Marjorie said Idella came running across the yard, sobbing and crying, "It's Mister John! Oh, Lawd, it's Mister John!" Jan's picture and the terrible news were on the front page of every news-paper in the world.

The days were a succession of minor blessings; the gentle winter sun, the graceful, fragrant orange and grapefruit trees, the enormous tangerine tree that overhung the gallery around the house—you reached up and plucked a tangerine warm from the sun and ate it; the clucks and cackles and quacks of barnyard fowl, particularly the flock of tamed (wild) Mallard ducks who were Marjorie's pride and joy. They actually made a frightful racket, as loud as the uproar of guinea-hens, but it was a funny noise, not a disturbing one. Every day at the same time they sounded off and Jan would tip his chin in their direction and say, "Dooks!" Long afterwards in Prague when he had to listen to prolix talk he would tip his chin at me in the same way and silently say, "Dooks!"

He was then sixty years old, I forty-three. We knew a great deal about each other and we knew it by intuition, by deduction, by hearsay, by inevitability, by the logic of relating ourselves to life and the world. He was the most articulate man I ever knew but the substance of our accord was not words. I almost never asked him direct questions nor he me. Unless a matter were specific, like making a plan or fixing the time or place for it, it was unnecessary to pin anything down in talk. Words were in-trusive; a glance, an eyebrow, the flick of a hand could be enough. He was a complex man full of variables and contradictions; of deep loyalties and rooted attachments and also of abrupt with-drawals behind the closed doors of his moods. His sense of the ridiculous was so riotous that nobody was spared; he made fun of me, of his sisters, of Beneš, of his closest friends, of the Russians and other Communists, of diplomats everywhere (his burlesque of a South American making a speech in broken English was devastating), of the whole world. A quarter of an hour later he could be sunken in gloom.

I believe the strongest bond between us was that each of us was solitary at heart. This was at variance with the personality the great world had known in his brilliant London years. Nobody then had been more gregarious; he had had immense popularity on the most polished of all diplomatic scenes. But even then he would retreat suddenly into his privacy. He was at ease among people as I had never learned to be, he had presence and those amazing gifts of language and wit and charm. But of himself he was actually withdrawn and very shy. The better I knew him the more reticent I found him, the more subtle and delicate his instincts, quite often in the same breath with a roaring expletive about some external trifle.

He was a man who preferred people who had lives of their own, into which he could dip when it suited him; people who would not be dependent on him emotionally or socially, who would not intrude on his privacy any more than he would have intruded on theirs. Intimacy with him in some elements of friendship did not imply or invite intimacy in all or other elements. I liked this; I do best in such relationships. Independence and self-reliance are essential to me and I am most useful to others functioning from this orientation. It suited Jan. He could not have found me witty and amusing, which had long been one of his criteria in choosing feminine company; nor an energetic hostess in whose house he would find important and entertaining people. I had ceased to make efforts of that sort, having nobody for whom to make them. I was not young, but he had never sought youth as such in his women friends, and surely I was not beautiful. He said he found me intelligent, though with him my intelligence was directed to veiling rather than revealing my comprehension of his problems, his dilemmas, and at the last, his agony of mind and spirit.

About some things we talked a lot, and after he died I used to recall talks that we had had and transcribe them from memory to catch them before they faded, in pencil on sheets of my yellow manuscript paper. I am using them now. It was talk about all sorts of things, seldom personal; talk that reflected Jan's greater knowledge of history and philosophy than his public utterances suggested. Old memories, old flavors, glimpses of vanished worlds; talk about his father, about Europe—he loved Europe in a physical, filial sense as I do though I was not born there. Long evenings passed before Marjorie's fire, outside the total quiet of backwoods country in the mild southern winter, inside the spurt and sizzle of piney logs, the simple room with its comfortable furniture and book-lined walls, the cat Benny asleep on the couch beside me, Jan relaxed in a big shabby chair.

Sometimes a gesture, expression, or tone of voice would make me look at Jan wondering that he had no Jewish blood, for some of his minor and fleeting mannerisms were very Semitic. He understood my unspoken thoughts so well that I had no occasion to say anything; he would laugh and shrug and say, "Of course!"

What puzzled him in turn I could see without questioning him. He would watch me or listen to me, or having asked me something about the past, shake his head and mutter, "I can't find it. Queer. Very queer."

"Find what?" I asked once.

"Your ancestry. It doesn't add up. I watch you," he said, also watching me laugh at his words, for he watched everything that interested him, with positively mischievous curiosity. "I wait and wait for it to come out," he said. "It would, if it were there. And it never does."

"What?"

"*It.*" He made a shrugging gesture of shoulders and hands, a certain expression of face. "It, that's all. I can't find a trace of it and I watch like that cat at a mouse-hole."

"But that's all there is in my heredity—what I know of it."

"Rot. You're no more full-blooded what you think you are than I am. I must be Jewish somewhere, though the presentable story doesn't say so. And you! How the hell do you know who you are?"

"I don't."

"And neither does anybody else who comes as far back as he can tell, from the parts of Europe that were the battlegrounds of the Napoleonic wars. You think you have no Czech ancestry. You're wrong. Some forefather of yours came through there as a conscript in the Russian armies, and if he didn't leave a souvenir on some local *slečna* (unmarried girl), then it was the other way round and some Czech in the Austrian army had a bit of fun with some pretty girl in Galicia whom they married off to your great-grandfather. You're like everybody else whose people fled to America in the eighties and nineties—all the villages and the synagogues with the family records in them were burnt up in the pogroms. Nobody knows anything."

Jan went on to elaborate this theory of his, which cannot but make one think whether one agrees with it or not. He described Central and Eastern Europe in the first quarter of the nineteenth century, repeatedly invaded by the armies of Napoleon, which were a hodge-podge of all the nationalities of Western Europe; and which met with two still greater hodge-podges, the armies of the Austrian and the Russian empires, full of conscripts of more different nationalities than could be named without recourse to reference-books.

"Furthermore," said Jan, "after taking into account the usual occupation of soldiers in the field, which wouldn't leave a virgin in a hundred square miles, or a pretty married woman without something to think about, you must reckon with the population upheavals which began with those wars and have been going on ever since. Especially among Jews, who have been on the move not only for two thousand years, but particularly in the last hundred and fifty. Look at the Jews of Europe now—six million murdered and the rest scattered to God knows where. Will any descendant of those exterminated people be able to produce records to prove who he is?"

He paused to let silence answer his question. Then he added, "And neither can a lot of other people in those parts of Europe, even though there are church and village records to say who they think they are. My father was the son of a Slovak coachman and a Moravian housemaid, who were serfs. I can't prove what the blood of their parents was and neither can anybody else. You can't prove anything about yours. And if you ask me, nobody else in our half of Europe can prove it either, between history and human nature. As for the nobility, with their Gotha and their thousand-year-old genealogies, there," said Jan with relish, licking his thumb, "you get into the fun and games department."

I was fascinated, for I have always felt my attachment to Prague to be an atavistic thing stronger than conscious experience can explain. "Of course it is," said Jan. "Some Czech around 1810 planted this thing you've got, there's nothing else to explain it."

Some time before she died in 1953, Majorie Rawlings sent me back some of my letters to her, I believe to console me in my desolation. Several times I had written her what has proved to be permanent truth, that in her house that winter I knew the only perfect happiness I have ever had. Inevitably this means a measure of unreality. There is no such thing as happiness if we seek it as an objective. Happiness is a mirage, a gleam like magic in the imagination of a child; it becomes dust if touched by a clutching hand. It is only true in illusion and in memory. It is not meant to last except as a lingering fragrance that we never expect to breathe again. I had many other unforgettable experiences with Jan, some before and most after that beautiful stay at Cross Creek; but they were real and tied to actualities of time and place, to the struggle in which he was engaged and the torments by which he was wracked. I was grateful to be able to share those cruel realities. We knew them for what they were, and against them it gave us surcease to remember cooking our own dinner when

Idella was out—he used to cook too in his flat in London; to smile at a little five-note whistle of his, which meant he was strolling along the gallery peeling a tangerine; to remember him sitting on a rail fence talking all morning with Martha Mickens. At midnight on New Year's Eve he blessed me and made a cross on my forehead with his thumb, some Slavic rite that was both atavism and a shy expression of something in him which very few people knew, that in his secretive way he was religious; an instinct, not a dogma. While we were there he wrote a speech which he made a few days later in Cleveland, a cry in the wilderness, in its way, for the world to make sense before it was too late —for him, but fifteen months away. He concluded, "Oh, let us have peace!"—and repeated the word in the eight languages he spoke so well.

In the middle of January he left for Prague and I settled in for the last three months of work on my book. One of my bird-dogs in Prague wrote me that I might be able to get the choice flat in the largest house in Loretanská. I begged him to proceed and succeed, which he eventually did, and this was the cap to the incentive that spurred me to the end. I finished the manuscript at quarter past four in the morning of April the eleventh and took it to Max that afternoon. Now when I look back on those few days in April which proved to be the last times I saw Max I realize that he did look tired and frail, that I was alarmed by a marked tremor of his hands. But it could not occur to me what was going to happen. Max said he wanted plenty of time to read the manuscript and make his notes about it. I was desperately anxious to get off to Prague and Max encouraged me to go. We arranged that I should do the revisions there, sending him sections of revised manuscript by air mail, which was already functioning reliably; he would cable me to confirm the arrival of each parcel. He worked over the manuscript for two weeks, and on Monday the twenty-eighth of April, I went to his office to get the typescript and his suggestions for the revision. This was the remarkable ten-page letter which is such a model of Max's editorial genius that it was published in its entirety in the volume of his letters that appeared in 1950. The fact that I possess the original, that it is the basis of the last book that he edited, makes it one of the indestructible treasures of my life and mind. I think he could not have done this for any writer who would care about it more deeply than I do.

Next day I left. No hindsight can dim the remembered joy of setting out to make a lifelong dream come true; I was going to live in Prague. All sorts of practical considerations entered in; I enjoy those and believe I am good at dealing with them. The first was that I had to have a car and had ordered a small one in England to be delivered in Rotterdam for me to pick up; I would drive it to Prague. I flew to Amsterdam, where Jan telephoned on my arrival, uncharacteristically concerned about my safety on the way across Germany.

"Don't be silly," I said. "I've been driving back and forth alone across Germany since—"

"You will do as I say," he interrupted. "Go to my Embassy at The Hague and pick up the man the Erbans will send with you."

The Erbans (the Czech Ambassador and his wife) were gracious hosts and informed me that a man from the staff was to accompany me to Prague. There had been some disturbances in the British zone of occupied Germany across which I would have to drive; I have forgotten why, but cars had been stoned and personnel attacked. The concern was because I would be driving an English car. But the U.S. Military Mission at The Hague had already provided me with American permits and an emblem to be attached to the car, and also with their own maps which directed me precisely how to go. There was, in fact, no other way to go. But I could not flout Jan's orders and the Erbans' help, so I had to accept the company of the man they sent along. His name was Vojtěch, which comes out Albert in English, and he informed me in fractured something-or-other (neither English nor Czech nor good red herring) that he was an expert chauffeur and knew everything. I had no intention of letting him drive my car, which I had collected the day before from a bomb-site with a tin roof over it in the tragic ruins of Rotterdam. Vojtěch, who wanted to be called Albert, insisted on speaking what he considered English. I much preferred to practise my imperfect Czech on him; at least it was all one thing and really I wanted no conversation at all. That could not be. Vojtěch-Albert rumbled on continuously and prefaced every single phrase with "Jeezcri,' Moddom." Evidently he thought this the height of form. He got so on my nerves that in order to give him something to do I let him hold the Army maps and act as *cartiste*. This was two years after the end of the war and there was still not a permanent bridge reconstructed across the Rhine. The German cities were still flat, the streets still alleys bulldozed through mountains of rubble. There was no way to go except the way the military signs pointed. But Vojtěch would constantly say, "Jeezcri', Moddom, dot better," pointing to nowhere. I decided to let him hang himself with his own rope. I had to cross the Rhine at Nijmegen, because the temporary bridge there was the only one in existence and I also had to be cleared there at the military control. Vojtěch knew much better turnings and crossings than the ones clearly marked on the Army maps and signs. I let him tell me where to turn, right, left, or whatever. From the nature of the terrain and the total devastation it was clear that we were approaching the river, and approaching it by a cowpath. I saw what was coming, a slight rise ahead of us, the top of the river-bank, and no more road. I bumped the car to a stop. Absolutely triumphant, Vojtěch shouted, "Jeezcri', Moddom, dot Rhine!"

Since it is now twenty years past a time of argument about the subject, I expect to be believed when I say that Prague early in 1947 was exhilarating. Problems there were: confusion, anxiety, frustration, chicanery, the savage struggle between the Communists and the democratic parties and politicians. But the struggle was real, and the non-Communists were free to press it. The Red Army had been gone for well over a year and there were no Russian activators or conspirators master-minding the Czech Communists, as I was insistently told by foreigners, especially Americans, who knew nothing about it. The sad truth was that none were needed. The Communists were openly pursuing their aim of overthrowing the Republic and of doing so within a parliamentary framework; and the others were openly resisting them. Czechoslovakia was the only country in the Russian orbit which had not yet had a Communist régime imposed on it from without or engendered from within. The Czechoslovak intention was to stay firmly allied with the Soviet Union in foreign policy and on the international scene, but to remain a free parliamentary democracy internally. Beneš was committed to this impossibility, so was Jan as its foremost spokesman, so were the non-Communists in the Government, the Parliament, and the nation. It was the only accommodation that could be attempted in the wake of the Nazis and the war and the bad and broken agreements of the Great Powers. It was inevitable, I suppose, that foreign observers dismissed this hope as preposterous and wrote off Czechoslovakia along with the other Soviet satellites long before the Communists really moved in for the kill. But the Czechs themselves did not submit to this. They had had a free and unrigged general election in 1946, in which the Communists won 38 per cent of the seats in the Parliament. There were six other parties—the fatal flaw as in most Continental political structures—no one of which had won a total equal to that of the Communists. Klement Gottwald therefore became Prime Minister of a coalition government in place of the Judas, Fierlinger, who was to align his Social Democratic Party with the Communists in the coup of 1948; and most Czechs, in and out of the Government, were of the opinion that it was better to have Gottwald, the devil they thought they knew, than Fierlinger who was distrusted and detested by all.

Gottwald at this time was still functioning from the position of "We are Czechs first and Communists second." Hard to believe and hard to rationalize; but for a time it was believed, especially when non-Communists were free to promulgate their views, fight for their political parties, and work for gains in the next general election, scheduled for May, 1948. The Communists for their part were consolidating the gains they had already made and doggedly infiltrating every element, organization, and instrument of industrial, agricultural, social, and other aspects of national life. They were loudly proclaiming their aim of winning 51 per cent of the vote in the next election, with the democratic elements determined to cut down the 38 per cent they then had. The universal opinion was that the Communists would lose seats in the next election and the democratic parties make strong gains— a trigger factor in the timing of the coup when it came.

And there were abundant, visible reasons for optimism. Prague when I returned there was like its old self. Bookshops crowded one another on the main streets and avenues and they were filled with translations of all the Western books, current and classic, that the people had not had access to since Hitler. They had always been a book-buying public. The Czech translation of my *Valley of Decision* had been published in two thick volumes and was selling like popcorn. Kiosks on every street-corner were loaded with newspapers and magazines from everywhere, but those from Britain, the United States, and France were gobbled up first. Russian books and reading-matter were pushed at the people by the Communist Ministry of Information and the people turned away. Efforts were made to get students to study Russian in high schools and universities (this was not compulsory until after 1948) and the vast majority of them elected to learn English. The theatres were all open and crammed, many giving translations of English and American plays. The cinemas were showing American films, to the aggravation of the Communists who had made a trade pact with Moscow involving the export of

Soviet films to Czechoslovakia; people did not go to see them. All these matters were indicative of the people's state of mind. Probably more important was their state of being; Czechoslovakia needed first of all to restore its industries and regain its position as one of Europe's major producers and exporters of consumer goods. This of course is integral with a 'bourgeois' economy and the Communists were savagely opposed to it. But when I was furnishing my flat and needed pots and pans, kitchen utensils, mattresses, wallboard, and a hundred other utilitarian and functional things, I was amazed to be able to buy them. When I said so to Jan he only opened his eyes wide and said, "What the hell do you think we fight about in the Cabinet? The people—" usually he called them 'the little people'—"were stripped bare by the Nazis and the Reds. There wasn't a piece of metal or a rag of bedding left in most of this country. There wouldn't be now if They had their way. I'm damned if we make heavy goods for the Russians before our own people get the pots and kettles they need." It was one of the things he could do of the many he tried and was blocked in.

The street called Loretanská runs east and west along a high open ridge which must have been the spine of a primeval hill before Prague became a city. Parallel to it on the south runs another street cut into the side of the hill and climbing sharply westward, called Úvoz. South of that lie the magnificent hillside sweeps of open park and greensward that are the gardens of the Strahov Monastery and the Lobkowicz Gardens. The houses of Loretanská occupy the space between the street on which they face, and Úvoz above which their rear elevations rise steeply. The Úvoz sides have high walls and within these are gardens, reached from the lower levels of the houses. Such a garden went with my flat. Úvoz is an extension of another narrow, steep mediaeval street called Nerudová, which climbs the great hill up from the main square of the Little Side—Malostranské Náměstí. Nerudová is lined with ancient houses and palaces mostly of the fifteenth and sixteenth centuries, their ground floors occupied by small shops which were the glory of the epoch of artisan guilds. From above each shop there hung over the street a work of art in wrought iron, the sign of the master artisan—the goldsmith, the bootmaker, the apothecary, the weaver, the glass-blower. The signs were kept beautifully painted and touched with golden highlights. The street was so narrow that this little forest of hand-wrought signs almost met overhead; you drove uphill beneath them, transported into a fairy-tale world, before making the sharp serpentine turn up to the noble vista of the Palace with the Gothic spires of St. Vitus soaring above.

The house in Loretanská had, like its neighbors, a vast front door with a smaller everyday door cut into it, which opened into a low vaulted hall. This hall adjoined a courtyard overlooking Úvoz, where a lot of domestic activity, beginning with the ancient rite of carpet-beating, went on every day. The original house had been built in the fifteenth century and must have been austere (and freezing). But at the time about two hundred years later when the nobility brought Italian architects to Vienna and Prague and their country castles, or invoked Fischer von Erlach or Hildebrandt, to turn their old properties into baroque beauty, this house had had the best of many alterations. Its exterior was the tender butter-yellow stucco of all houses of the period and of that street, some embellished with frescoes and some with beautiful white plaster-work. From the vaulted hall a very wide staircase of scrubbed pale wood with extremely shallow steps worn down at the centre by centuries of climbing feet led in a graceful curve to the first floor—the *piano nobile*. The western half of this was my flat, with windows looking north and south. It had a beautiful drawing-room, a small library, and my bedroom overlooking Úvoz, the great open side. The bedroom was a finely-proportioned room whose southern side was set into a square tower, clearly a relic of the Gothic origin of the house. This made a graceful alcove with windows on three sides, furnished as a sitting-room; beautiful—painfully beautiful—inside and out. The west windows overlooked the baroque splendor of the Strahov Monastery with its gleaming onion towers. The south windows overlooked the Lobkowicz Gardens and the high hill called Petřín. The east windows commanded the vista of Prague, with the river Vltava winding beneath its bridges. I could see the river and the Charles Bridge from those windows, the nearer domes and spires of Malá Strana, the farther beauty of the Old Town and the Gothic needles of the Tyn spires, and in the dim distance, the misty countryside.

The Loretanská side of the flat held the remaining rooms— the kitchen and an enormous dining-room on which I made some structural alterations (joy for me! shades of my mother!) in order to carve out comfortable space for Louise. The flat was beautiful architecturally beyond my dreams, but it was also in appalling disrepair. The widowed sister of the lady whose children were the owners of the house under an entail had not had the means for twenty years to keep the place up and that was why she had de-cided to lease it to me. There were no built-in closets, the plumb-ing was archaic, and there were hundreds of square feet of wasted space which would lend themselves to my purposes. I was able to afford to restore the flat and modernize it completely. I had made a good deal of money from *The Valley of Decision* and I wanted to do nothing with it so much as to realize my dream of living in that house. I had no trouble finding artisans to do the work. Masterly carpenters, plasterers, glaziers, house-painters, plumbers, electricians, and other craftsmen appeared as if by magic. They did more for my graphic but broken Czech than anybody I ever saw; they taught me mouthfuls. Jan used to stop in at odd mo-ments from the Černinský up the hill, to find me sitting on top of a stepladder gabbling with the workmen. They were always delighted to see him—"Here's Pan Ministr—*Nazdar!*" they said, and kept right on working.

The ceilings of the rooms were fourteen feet high. They did

justice to wonderful chandeliers, laden with drops and prisms of old Bohemian glass; there was a rare one in my bedroom, like a great cluster of morning-glories, their bells blown in paper-thin glass in delicate blossom colors. The doors and the panelled walls and cornices had beautiful carved mouldings. The handles and hinges of the doors and windows were fine pale bronze with exuberant baroque curves. The doors were so high that the handles were four feet from the floor. It used to amuse me to see Louise open those doors, looking like a dwarf—which she is not. The windows were perhaps the most beautiful feature of the house. The walls were at least two feet thick and there were two sets of casements. The outer ones opened out; then there was the deep sill (often full of potted plants in such houses) then the inner casement opening in. I was told that these double windows had been installed in the eighteenth century. All the panes were hand-made Bohemian glass. The famous hand-made glass in Beacon Hill houses in Boston, is not to be compared with that glass in Prague. It had faint ripples and irregularities which seemed to catch the sunlight as if in a web. To look through those windows at the beauty outside was one of the great experiences of my life. Any person to whom architecture, like music, is a highly personal art, and therefore an emotion, responds to certain forms, shapes, functions, as he responds to the melody of Mozart or Schubert, the majesty of Beethoven. To me, windows in my kind of architecture almost have the power of speech; and so do roofs. They move me profoundly. As necessary to me in life as hearing music is the sight of ancient roofs, particularly of ancient red tile roofs, huddled together for fellowship and humanity. Prague has incomparable vistas of such roofs and the most eloquent ones were to be seen from my windows.

Only later have I wondered why I never took pictures of that beautiful house, of the street or the views or the interior. Could it have been because I could never have endured to look at them since? Was it foreboding?

I had my hands full before the flat was ready to move into. Every day in the dreary Alcron I worked from early morning until early afternoon on the revision of my novel. That famous letter from Max, which is beside me now, was my rod and my staff—an amazing exposition of the art of fiction, personified in the characters and situations of the book with which it dealt. There are three pages of these observations, which were more valuable to me at that time (having four years before published a novel of 790 pages) than if I had been the greenest beginner. Then the letter moves on to specific suggestions, after citing once again what Max used to say so often: Dialogue is *action*. There are seven pages of separate brief paragraphs, each a specific suggestion for changing or re-shaping an action or an episode or some character's behavior. Max used to say when he was talking about a good but unrevised manuscript, "It is all in there, you just have to intensify it . . . emphasize it . . . It is as you say, you can't know a book until you come to the end of it." And with Max's guidance it was more a matter of rearranging what was there than of rewriting. As I finished each of the changes I checked off the relevant paragraph in his letter with a red pencil.

When I had finished work for the day I went up the hill to see how the work was going in the flat. I was also buying furniture for it, which was both a joy and a heartache, for beautiful antique furniture was all too easy to come by. Old families were selling their heirlooms in the upheaval and flux of the time—not as they do for subsistence after they are totally dispossessed by revolution —but because the financial and capital structure of the country had been disrupted by the Nazis and was now almost entirely frozen in the processes of reorganizing the currency and nationalizing heavy industry under Communist pressure. American friends remonstrated with me for pouring money down such a drain but I did not see it that way. I was reckless, of course; that is in character; but I was committed to believing in Jan's desperate efforts to save his father's republic. If I could believe that he might save it even partially, I was prepared more readily to lose money than any of the human and moral values involved. I had asked him if he had any reservations about my taking that flat and I had meant more than I said—always the tenor of our communication. He looked at me with a certain probing stare and said, "None. None at all." He would have been other than himself had he gone on to say that it was up to me to decide on a calculated risk; that either he won or all would be lost, and what did money matter in such a balance?

His life in Prague, like much else there, was anyway a precarious balance between extremes: what he loved and what he loathed, what he trusted and what he feared. He in turn was greatly loved by the people and brutally used by their depredators. He had no personal home in Prague, he had never had one. His existence in the Černinský could not be called a life at all. It was more like luxurious imprisonment in a display case. In retreat from its relentless aspects he kept to that one room amidst the empty magnificence; for the same reason he held on to his flat in London which he seldom had a chance to go to; and in the last eighteen months of his life he turned to my house in New York or in Prague for such peace and privacy as he had at all. In his younger years he would have been bored and restless in the provincial life of Prague but the war and its aftermath left him little energy or taste for the life he had enjoyed before—and it had disappeared anyway. His personal world had narrowed to the old friends who are never numerous in anybody's life; his were in England mostly, a very few in Prague, and those were the people we used to see when he was not preempted by Government affairs, public engagements, state dinners and receptions, the obligatory ceremonies of meeting or seeing off heads of state and foreign ministers and ambassadors at the airport—a chore he loathed so much that he used to roar streams of profanity before setting out to do it.

On the seventeenth of June I dined alone with him in his

room. We were going afterwards to see the Hurbans, who had retired from Washington and were settled in Prague. Jan had sent Dohnálek to fetch me before dinner, and just as I was leaving the Alcron the concierge told me that New York was trying to reach me on the telephone. I had a feeling that bad news was involved but I could not imagine what. I left the telephone numbers where I would be so that the call could be passed on.

At dinner Jan saw that I was uneasy. Instead of reassuring me he too became apprehensive. That was peculiar because there was, after all, nothing startling about a transatlantic telephone call, we were used to them. We stayed at the Hurbans' until about midnight and the call had not come through, so Jan took me back to the hotel. He usually avoided getting out of his car there because it meant the immediate gathering of a cheering crowd; so Dohnálek escorted me to the door. As I was leaving the car Jan said, "Telephone me what it is. Whatever it is. No matter how late."

I stopped at the desk for my key and was handed a cable. I was reading it as I entered my rooms and the telephone was ringing. The cable was from Charles Scribner. It said, "Max died of pneumonia early this morning after two days' illness." Carol Brandt was on the telephone to tell me also. Of course I had not known he was ill, so recently had I heard from him. Utter panic, the sense of falling off the surface of the earth, rushed over me for the first time in my life. I can hear my own voice in memory, telling Jan. I had said to him at some time previously, "Max would be the one loss in life that I could not bear." "Oh, God," he cried. "If I could help you! If I could be any comfort to you now!"

When the faint grey of early dawn began to filter around the edges of the curtains I rose without having slept at all, and went to the adjoining room to my desk. Spread across it were the pieces of my manuscript that had not already gone to Max, and beside them his letter. I sat down, just as I was, in my nightdress, and began to work, praying for courage to finish the revision as Max had expected.

Everybody else who loved and needed Max was in the same despair. I wrote to Marjorie, "The first reaction is, I will never write another book. Which would be a denial of all that Max has done for us. So we know we will indeed write more books and that they will never be the books they could have been."

CHAPTER SIXTEEN

IMMEDIATELY there began the interplay of public and private episodes and incidents which have always seemed too huge and jostling for the ten months into which they were crowded. For me there was the juxtaposition of shattering grief at Max's death with the joy of moving into my flat a few days later. For Jan there was the situation of the country, unstable but at that time full of vociferous hope and activity. He was enormously popular with the people and he knew it and did his utmost to justify their belief in him—"and in my name," he said. He did not tell me anything that went on in the councils of the Government or the meetings of the Cabinet; nothing would have been more incorrect and in spite of his resounding informality he was very correct. He was absolutely fearless when he addressed the people. He talked like Masaryk in the knowledge of what that meant to them. I went with him to mass-meetings in commemoration of war victims, the massacred people of Lidice, the dead of the camps and the fighting forces, whose widows and orphans were assembled. Surrounded by every travesty the Communists could make of these occasions, sharing the rostrum with Gottwald or Slánský, the head of the Communist Party, Jan would wait until they and their howling minions had had their say. Then he stood up and spoke to the people about faith and decency and the brotherhood of man and the reasons why Czechoslovaks had died in the cause of these.

The practical results of his efforts and those of the other non-Communists were visible in the improved life and functioning of the country, but nothing was sure. The atmosphere, the mood, the circumstances of people's lives were all in flux. There was confusion, deceit, constantly shifting pressures of opposites and extremes: of hope with despair, of courage with fear, of laughter at small things while one was harrowed by great ones. Idealism and cynicism went together. A person of whom you knew nothing good could show a streak of generosity or loyalty; somebody you thought rock-solid could reveal a rotten spot. A curious case of this was Vladimír Clementis, the Deputy Foreign Minister. He was a Slovak lawyer from Bratislava, of well-to-do family, who had been a theoretical, intellectual Communist all his life. He had little in common with Moscow-trained roughnecks and bullies like Gottwald and Zápotocký, the head of the Communist labor organization. Clementis had spent the war in London with the exiled government there. He was never quite trusted by either side. But he was clever and able and the obvious choice of the Communists to be the watchdog in the Foreign Ministry; to undercut Jan, to run the Ministry as a Communist bureaucracy particularly during Jan's frequent absences abroad at the U.N. and other international conferences, to stuff the offices with Party hacks and spying supernumeraries. Yet he had a kind of loyalty to Jan, which came from an almost tribal feeling amongst Slovaks. This was evoked by the Slovak ancestry of the Masaryks and it was shown by a thoughtful and courteous personal attitude. Jan never banked unrealistically upon it, but he said that Clementis made his lot easier than some other Communist would have done. Through the spring and early summer of that year hope appeared to run high; and when I dared to think it real Jan said, "Careful. It is when they are likely to lose ground that they will be most dangerous."

Living at last in the flat was a joy for me a joy that could only be measured by the seventeen years that I had dreamed of living there. It was so beautiful that I would stop on my way across a room and stand there basking in it, forgetting what I was on my way to do. Louise arrived from New York and at once made it home. She could manage anything, do anything, fix anything, communicate with anybody. She had been there only a day or two when I gave her a map, money, and a shopping list. She took the car and went off. When she returned, all the errands done, I asked her how she managed with the Czechs.

"Oh, I talk," she said. "When I can't talk with my mouth I use my hands or my feet."

She had brought with her a prime steak from my butcher in New York—meat was still strictly rationed but the food supply in general was much improved—and Jan was to come for the first dinner. He sent flowers, wine, butter, beer, his man Přihoda to offer to help; it was a tremendous occasion. Louise set the small table for two beside the centre window in the drawing-room. It was so beautiful there that we never ate in the dining-room. I wanted the steak to be perfect so I lighted the broiler in the brand new gas-range well ahead of time. When Jan arrived I was flat on my stomach on the kitchen floor in a new Bendel tea-gown, pouring water on the burning linoleum that had caught fire because I was unfamiliar with the stove.

My house was only a few minutes' walk from the Černinský. Jan's elder sister Alice Masaryk, who has recently died in exile in Chicago, had had a flat in the same house for many years, and the neighbors were used to seeing him about. Nobody bothered him, the people up there on the hill adored him and respected his privacy. His friendship with me was not much of a matter for remark and he was indifferent to any susurrus about it; but in a sense he slapped it down before the Communists as though in a declaration of his Westernness. In private he was not a man who spoke or acted with romantic embellishments. Alone with me he was serious and understated—unless he happened into a boisterous clowning mood. He called me Miss, for a funny reason; the most demonstrative variant of this was Miss, dear. But in public in Prague, that is to say, in the presence of the Communists or the stooges or the pile-drivers, he called me extravagant endearments. He meant them truly enough, but they were not his private language with me. It was as though he flung me—American, Western, outspoken—in their teeth and alongside threw himself as committed to that. Sometimes I was embarrassed by his vociferousness in that way; then I realized, because he would never have done it in New York or elsewhere abroad, that he had his reasons and was doing it deliberately, not on impulse. Later I thought he spoke as he did so that their espionage could discover nothing about him that was not already known to everybody.

During that summer he asked me to go to a literary conference in Bratislava and speak my mind. I did so and returned the next evening to Prague. Jan came in for dinner and I reported on the meeting.

"And how are you?" he asked. "You look a little queer."

"I feel rather queer, come to think of it. I think I have a bit of fever."

I had not caught cold and could think of nothing else wrong with me except that I had slept very badly in Bratislava. "Perhaps I have some kind of trifling infection," I said. "I itch."

"Which?"

"Itch," I repeated, embarrassed. "I've got—I don't know—welts on me, or something."

"Show me."

I showed him. A very strange expression came over his face, a mixture of mirth and anger.

"Miss," he said gravely, "you can't be expected to know. You have not been in a concentration camp. Or a Carpathian shooting-lodge. Or a barracks."

"Know what?"

"You have been bitten." He stared at me over the tops of the spectacles he had put on to examine my ailment. "Bitten. By bedbugs."

We howled, we roared with laughter. Slowly Jan let down

his big bulk into a chair beside the telephone and dialled the long-distance operator. He told her to put the manager of the Bratislava hotel on the line. Speaking Slovak sonorously Jan said, "This is the Foreign Minister. Yes, Minister Masaryk. I am calling to inform you that you have bedbugs in your hotel. I wish you please to close your hotel until you have permanently exterminated the bedbugs. Yes, that is all. Thank you. Good night."

Such nonsense was respite in a gathering sense of doom. By the end of June the weather became intensely hot and remained so all summer long. I had never known summer heat in Central Europe fully as bad as a hot American summer, if less humid. There was no humidity that year, there was drought—the worst drought in a generation. The catastrophic harvest that resulted, its effect on the food supply and on the farmers, were used by the Communists to intensify disorder the following winter. The previous year had had a good harvest with the help of abundant replenishment from the United States of seed and breeding-stock; but the country needed enormous assistance in loans and credits and raw materials to speed the rehabilitation of industry. Any such help, had it been forthcoming, would have cut ground from under the Communists. It was then that General Marshall, the American Secretary of State, outlined the plan for international reconstruction with the help of American loans that was called by his name. Invitations were sent to all the war-torn countries of Europe to become participants in the Marshall Plan at a conference to be held in Paris.

A savage fight ensued in the Czechoslovak Cabinet. As usual I was not told, and should not have been told, the details. But the outcome was smashing in its impact. In an all night session the non-Communists headed by Jan forced the Communists—and I do not know how—to a unanimous vote accepting the invitation to join the Marshall Plan. The news intoxicated the people of Prague. I was downtown that evening and I saw what has otherwise been only a figure of speech to me—people literally dancing in the streets, embracing total strangers, exploding in waves of public rejoicing.

Of course it was too good to be true. Probably that was why the Communists had given in to it, while Gottwald was on the telephone to Moscow and the Poles and Yugoslavs were also planning to accept—until Stalin crashed down with the axe. This was in the first days of July. The Fourth of July fell on a Friday and the Steinhardts gave the party that is routine in every American Embassy the world over, an enormous crush to which everybody on every imaginable list is invited. I had to go. It was unbearably hot. The party was in the garden of the monstrously vulgar millionaire's villa, the Petschek house whose owners had fled at the time of Munich. Laurence had leased it for his residence and it has since been bought by the American Government—to me an incomprehensible preference over the noble beauty of the Schönborn palace which is the American Embassy's Chancery. It was the original Ambassador's residence.

I found myself in the crowd face to face with Fierlinger, whom I had not seen since 1945. His rat's face creased into a sly smile and he said, "You have quite settled in our country now, have you not?" I saw his slitted, reptile eyes sliding through the crowd looking for Jan who had not arrived. (Jan was with Beneš, who had been noticeably uncommunicative lately, with the public wondering why.) Fierlinger said, "We will soon be welcoming you as a citizen here?"

"It would not be your doing if that came about," I said. "But thank you just the same. I love my own country too much to change."

The next day, Saturday, was hotter still, a hard brassy blaze of heat. Like all Saturdays for weeks past, it was the day fixed for a parade. Every week there had been a *průvod,* mounted by one of the political parties, or the Sokols, the Communist Youth, the War Veterans, every imaginable organization. Except that all had their turn equally, tying up the town and blowing off steam, they had become a fearful nuisance. This one was the most important of all to the non-Communists, the parade of the Legionaries from the First World War, the legendary heroes of the Anabasis who had fought their way all around the world under the leadership of T. G. Masaryk to found the Czechoslovak Republic. Beneš and Jan were to be in the reviewing stand and each make a speech as the parade paused.

Jan had been tense and distraught for several days. I had seen little of him, enough only to know about the Marshall Plan and hear with a sinking heart that he was to go with Gottwald and a delegation of other Cabinet ministers to Moscow the following week, "to discuss a trade treaty and other matters." He had planned that we were to spend that Saturday evening and the Sunday in the country with friends. I left Prague at midday; he was to come in the afternoon as soon as the Legionaries' Parade was over.

I was very nervous and full of a sense of foreboding. Olga Hurban who was there wanted me to go with her to a nearby town where there was something she wanted to do, but I would not go. I had a feeling I had better not be out of reach of the telephone. I spent that breathless afternoon sitting under a tree on the lawn doing needlepoint embroidery. For the next half year a large part of my time went into that repetitive suspense; waiting; not daring to hope; still less daring not to hope; often not knowing; often knowing too much. And always I stitched at the needlepoint; idiot's delight, I said, while I shaded colors, changed threads, and stitched and snipped and stitched again; a way to keep from thinking. But it was only the forefront of my brain that was short-circuited by the device. It was as if a plate of some inert substance across the front of my head was impervious to the assaults of thought. But behind the plate there was turmoil, dread, anxiety, a multiple load of worry whose burden was first Jan, then the country, then Jan again. The worst of the feeling was its roots in confusion, in what I was not told but could not avoid suspecting. At moments it used to come all together like an immense knot hardening in the top of my head, then starting to plummet, a horrible sickening sensation, down through my chest where it set my heart pounding with fear, and then to the pit of my stomach where it turned in some evil way into an enormous gnawing question-mark. Time and again this happened. I used to stand at the windows of my room in Prague, looking out at the sights I loved so much, wrestling with that brutal question-mark. "I don't know the answer," I used to say. More probably I did know it with fore-knowledge that I had not the courage to face. "I don't know the answer . . ." The words were wrung from me aloud, quite alone and without intention to say anything. But I hear the echo of it still.

That Saturday afternoon in July was the first of those full-scale assaults on my nerves, which inevitably touched off a battle between my heart and my head. One can try to anaesthetize one's intelligence but one is not likely to succeed unless the in-telligence is a particularly feeble one. The Hurbans came back from their excursion and brought with them, or perhaps we all heard it together there on the radio, the news that at the Legion-aries' Parade an hour or two before, President Beneš had been slightly upset by too long standing in the blazing sun. We were uneasy. But he had made his speech, and Jan had spoken, and the report was that the President was now quite all right. I began to think Jan would not come, almost surely having stayed with the Benešes, but at about seven o'clock he arrived. He stepped slowly out of his car, his face smitten with worry. He was pale, and suffering from the heat which he always loathed. He wore one of his short-sleeved summer shirts hanging like a blouse outside his trousers. He brushed aside the anxious questions about Presi-dent Beneš; "nothing but a touch of sun," said Jan, "and he's perfectly well now." From the round, booming tone of his voice I knew better than to believe him. He had kept his dark sun-glasses on, too, though it was evening.

He was silent while we sat about at cocktails before dinner

and then he ate very little. He did not refer to the President again unless it was to insist once more that nothing serious had happened. Late that night he sat alone with me, sunken in a chair and gloomy as I had never seen him. He sat with his eyes lowered; I said nothing. After a long time Jan muttered, "Very worried about Beneš. Very."

He raised his head then and I looked at him and whispered, "He had a stroke?"

A gesture was his answer, a quick affirmative jerk of the head and a twitch of his lips. He dropped his face into his hands and sat silent.

This was enormity. The questions it posed were sheerly appalling. I did not know then nor did Jan tell me until later that Beneš for some time had had symptoms of arteriosclerosis. Some were physical—like the stroke and the speech impairment it caused—and some were mental, the effect of the condition on the brain. Beneš's physician described these to me later. They accounted for changes in his personality; for indecision, for marked fluctuations between extreme stubbornness and sudden weakness; for what the doctor told me was a typical attitude of the arteriosclerotic: refusal by the man to admit that he had the condition and to reconsider his responsibilities in that light. The same was true of Franklin Roosevelt. I did not know on that July night how much of this was clear to Jan, but Beneš had made no indication that he would not fight to the last ditch a Communist attempt to overthrow the Government. In the early stages of the Munich crisis he had been equally firm—only to cave in at the end. So Jan, I believe at least in part *faute de mieux,* for he knew Beneš's weaknesses better than anybody else could, was relying on Beneš to save the Masaryk Republic if a crisis should come. I remembered then every word of Jan's last promises to his father. I knew that they were not only never out of his mind but that they were the governing motive of his life. If Beneš failed in health or in capacity there was nobody but Jan himself to take over. Jan's habit and temperament for thirty years had conditioned him to the auxiliary role—the articulator, the intermediary, the interpreter, the place beside Beneš that his father had assigned him. Beneš was also a politician, a party man, the head of the political (disunited, alas!) opposition to the Communists. Jan was not. If there should be no Beneš, we both thought, sitting there in silence and communicating as if in explicit words, would Jan be able to bear the brunt of the showdown when it came; and if no Beneš, would Jan be able to carry the load of the Presidency? For it was precisely clear that unless the Communists, with or without a total *coup,* put one of their own men into the office, Jan was the inevitable choice.

We spent a heavy-hearted Sunday and Jan hardly spoke all day. He was haunted by worry about Beneš, but the imminent journey to Moscow was even more ominous. Late in the afternoon we drove back to Prague. We always loved the late afternoon light glowing over the towers and spires of Malá Strana and Hradčany. In the sunset the rosy light was reflected like illumination from the twin white spires of Svatý Jiří—St. George's Church—rising behind the mass of the Hrad. It was one of the sights for which we used to wait as one does for a particularly moving passage in music; I think of the 'cellos in the second movement of the Ninth Symphony. But that day as Dohnálek drove up the steep lovely hill of Nerudová and round the serpentine past the main gateway of the Hrad, I must have turned away with a shiver, or winced, or somehow let Jan see the thought I had meant to hide. If he should have to go and live there it would be prison for him, and for the rest of it—I could think no further. He gave a hoarse sigh, almost a groan, and his head dropped like a weight over his chest.

On Tuesday he left for Moscow. I can no longer recall any sense of the brief exultation we had felt about the Marshall Plan because that had been crushed by Saturday's alarm about Beneš. Jan remained in a mood of black pessimism. For me there followed one of many intervals that is now hard to distinguish from others like it, of agonizing blind suspense. If it were my purpose here, I could reconstruct from a dozen different accounts what was transpiring in Moscow; but that was not my perspective then and there is no reason why it should be now. On Wednesday the ninth of July I dined at Laurence Steinhardt's. When I arrived he met me in the hall and took me into a small library. His face was very grave and curiously I cannot remember exactly what he said. He could be a hard man when occasion demanded, and brusque of manner; but he took my hands in his and all I can say is that he was tender and his voice almost heartbroken. He told me that Stalin had forced the Czechs to withdraw from the Marshall Plan. Francis Williamson came in then; he was the head of the Central European desk at the State Department, a very fine man whom I knew because he asked me to see him in Washington whenever I returned to the United States from Prague. The blow was so devastating and its implications so fatal that I remember only the shock, not what was said about it. We were only a few at dinner. I was struggling to keep my frightful worry about Jan to myself; I remember listening to Laurence and Francis and whoever else was there, talking with anxiety about what was going on in Moscow.

Jan returned on the twelfth of July. It does not matter now what were the details of the Soviet crackdown. Jan told me about them but he did not say to me what Bruce Lockhart and others have quoted him as saying at the time—that he went to Moscow as the Foreign Minister of a sovereign state and returned as a lackey of the Soviet Government. He looked stunned; ill and bloated. He was very nervous. He alternated between spates of talk and long dark silences. I was used to the extremes of his moods, the bursts of emotion, the abrupt withdrawals into aloofness, the sudden wild jokes at the expense of anybody or anything, the silence in which his extraordinary, tragic eyes conveyed what he did not put in words. These were all parts of a whole that I accepted exactly as it was. Like everybody close to him I knew the history of mental instability in his family, said to have been inherited from his mother. She died in 1923 after several years of invalidism in a nursing home, her mind failing. Her sons and daughters were all described as neurotic, or in other terms of the psychological jargon that is the paramount feature of modern life. All my life by stubborn preference I have stayed out of the stream of preoccupation with psychiatry and psychoanalysis. I am an anachronism and a holdout but I cannot be otherwise, I must be me. I can recognize a disturbed person when I see one, but I will not glibly use a term like neurotic or psychotic. I am not sufficiently informed to do so. I would never have done that about Jan—and I never allowed anybody to tell me about him what I was perfectly able to see for myself: that he was extremely unstable. In the last year of his life the pressures on him were savage. I felt, at a range so close that it might be said to be with his own feelings, the intolerable despair and humiliation which wracked him. I felt his judgement weaken and sway and wheel from desperate hope to more desperate hopelessness. I could only help him by accepting him completely, whatever he said or did, his faults and his mistakes alike with his virtues—the greatest of which was loyalty.

After he had returned from Moscow I asked him one evening, "How does Stalin treat you?"

Jan picked a shred of tobacco from his lip. "Oh, he's very gracious," he said. His voice was light, actually casual. "Of course he'd kill me if he could. But very gracious."

So often we use death in figures of speech. "I'm tired to death. . ." "This will kill me . . ." "I'd rather die . . ." We are not thinking. But Jan was thinking when he said many times in that same careless tone, "One day they'll kill me."

One day they tried, clumsily. It was the affair of the so-called perfume bombs. Besides Jan the two leading non-Communists in the Council of Ministers were Peter Zenkl, the first Deputy Prime Minister, the leader of Beneš's party; and Prokop Drtina, the Min-

ister of Justice. Zenkl was and is now in his old age in exile a true
Czech patriot. He survived six years of hell in Buchenwald,
scourged there by the Czech Communists as much as by the Nazis,
and returned to his country with his morale unbroken. Drtina
was a distinguished jurist, of the same party as Beneš and Zenkl.
Both men defied the Communists; both, together with Jan, were
the personification of the Masaryk Republic. On the eleventh of
September all three men received by post packages containing
small wooden boxes labelled 'perfume'. Some alert clerk opened
the first of the parcels and effected that all three were turned over
to the police. They contained explosives.

The ensuing uproar was less because of the crude bombs
than because they were traced to their Communist source. The
Ministry of Justice ordered thorough investigation and exposure
of the plot by the police. And the Ministry of the Interior, which
was the police, headed by a Communist named Nosek, scuttled the
orders and began the procedure of purging the police of its
hitherto non-Communist elements and packing it with Party ruffians. This was the fuse that detonated the *coup d'état* the following winter. But I have wondered why the Communists bothered
even until then to move behind the façade of a coming constitutional election. The people's bitter disappointment about the
Marshall Plan aroused them against the Communists and alerted
the waverers who had been confused in 1946. The Communists
lashed back by putting the heat on the labor unions, who were
slipping from Zápotocký's control; and they muscled in on Slovakia, where opposition to them was strongest.

At that point Jan had to go to New York for the General Assembly of the United Nations, convening in mid-September. He
dreaded it. All the mortification of the previous year was staring
him in the face, intensified by the Marshall Plan disaster and the
reverberations of his confrontation with Stalin. The world in
general had written off Czechoslovakia and consigned it to the
Communist bloc, disbelieving with cynicism that there remained

any internal freedom in the country. In the United States neither the press nor Jan's friends understood the realities of his situation: that he could not and would not leave his country so long as Beneš was President and any form of democratic government remained. He shrank from pressure—the pressure of Molotov and Vyshinsky and the satellites in the U.N.; the pressure of his friends. Also he was in pain. At the end of August he had hurt his left shoulder, throwing his weight on his arm to avoid falling when he stumbled getting out of his car. He tore a ligament in the shoulder. It was a painful but not a serious injury. To rest his arm he used a sling.

I had gone to New York with Louise a few days before the perfume bomb incident. Jan was to arrive on the fourteenth of September, his birthday. A typical sidelight of his personality was his feeling about special days in his own life and of those close to him, particularly birthdays and the anniversaries of deaths. He had said in Prague that he would 'sneak' in to New York and we would celebrate his birthday quietly, before he had to face the grinders next day. I said teasingly, "That would be sentimental, wouldn't it."

"But I *am* sentimental!" he said. "And so are you!"

He spoke in a tone of voice that was not actually loud, but seemed so, with a resonance that has no precise definition in a verb. If I say that he shouted I am inaccurate. He made a certain sound when he spoke thus, accompanied by a widening of his eyes to a stare of emphasis; sometimes also with a grimace of his mouth, drawing the corners downwards and thrusting out his lower lip in a comical or a derisive pout.

As it turned out, his plane was delayed and he did not arrive until the fifteenth. There followed ten weeks of hell. He did have the support of some trusted aids, all permanently posted in the United States—Ján Papánek, then Czechoslovak Ambassador to the U.N.; Juraj Slavík, who had replaced Vlado Hurban in Washington; Jan's New York secretary Nicholas Mára, whom I wished

he could have had with him in Prague. They were his only defence (though themselves defenceless) against the Communist-
loaded delegation from Prague, with Clementis calling the turns.
Jan made the conventional address to the Assembly made by all
the Foreign Ministers, and thereafter put himself permanently on
the sick list because of his injured shoulder. In that way he reduced his activities to such committee meetings as he could take
part in with the least abrasion from the Russians and the Communists in his own delegation, who were barbarians. He declined
nearly all engagements revolving around the U.N. He saw fewer
American friends than ever before—because they either harangued
him about his country or joined in what became a barrage of pressure to persuade him not to return there. They meant well and
they put him through torment. He began unconsciously to use a
word with me that he had not used before: safe. He felt safe in my
house—a sad illusion but he leaned on it.

The low point of that autumn was a day when Jan went to
Washington. I knew only that he expected to see President Truman or Secretary of State Marshall or both. He told me no other
details and that remains the pattern of my relation to the events
of those months. I felt and saw their impact at primary range
without knowing facts which, if I possessed them, would make
these pages documentation instead of the personal testimony that
they are. It was obvious that Jan hoped to obtain assurance that
the United States would uphold the democratic forces in his country in the coming showdown. He admired President Truman's
courage and decisiveness and he observed the workings of the
Truman Doctrine in Greece and Turkey with despairing hope.
But that could have no parallel in Czechoslovakia, consigned to its
doom by agreement of the Great Powers. We are always reminded
that this would have been otherwise if the Russians had abided by
their promises—and abided in terms of Western legality rather
than of Communist dialectics. How far could blind credulousness
go? It is a fruitless but inevitable speculation to weigh what might

have been, had the West retaliated in kind when the Russians made their first post-war moves. Suppose after observing what they did in Poland we had put our foot down in Czechoslovakia? But, in the words of Dana Adams Schmidt of *The New York Times,* "the whole withdrawal of American forces from Europe at the time made it obvious that the United States was not equipped to take part in the politics of power."

This was made plain to Jan with crudity that is hard to believe of the admired and respected men concerned. He was not received by either the President or the Secretary of State. In the latter case the act was an affront to a ranking colleague, the Foreign Minister of a sovereign state, no matter to what degree opinion—if not policy—had already written it off. I was not expecting to see Jan until the day after he went to Washington, but the doorbell rang late that evening, and I opened the door. He was deathly pale. His eyes were sunken and seemed unnaturally darker than their usual deep brown. He said nothing. He laid his flat-crowned black hat on the hall table and I helped him off with his overcoat; he winced with the pain in his shoulder. He went into the drawing-room and sat down slowly in an armchair. He was like a person suffering from shock; indeed that was his condition. I did not speak either. We sat in dead silence for I cannot imagine how long. Finally he looked at me as if I had asked him a question and with a small, quick motion, almost imperceptible, he shook his head.

Thereafter I believe he was never the same again. Whatever had happened in Washington had broken the heart of his belief and his hope. He knew that there would be no help from the only place help could have come. From then on he was a frightened man. It is a fool who does not know enough to be afraid, and Jan was no fool. The pressure on him not to go back to Prague became intense. He was offered important and well-paid posts if he should decide to remain in the United States. He appeared to be swayed by the offers; he spoke of them in the curious mutter that reflected uncertainty, or secretiveness wrestling with the urge to confide. But I also heard, "Beneš . . . he is so alone . . ."

I knew Jan would go back to Prague. I knew it because his emotion about his country was inseparable from his emotion about his father. He never said that because he was averse to wordy, introspective talk, the kind of talk that is humorless as well as prolix. He saw life and the world through a sense of humor as much a part of his sensory nerves as his capacity to smell or to hear. This sixth sense, as I think of it, is not limited to the realm of wit; rather its real nature emerges in conditions of tension, sorrow, and tragedy, when the quality becomes transmuted into intuitiveness or tenderness; or in some circumstances into cynicism or a brusqueness which is part of the protective instinct. To have expected Jan, when he saw the full scope of the mess into which the Great Powers had dragged Czechoslovakia, to pull out and quit would have been to demand that he cease to feel what he had always felt for his father. Nor could he have abandoned Beneš or deserted "my little people." When he told me he was going back to Prague, sailing on the Queen Elizabeth because he wanted a few days' rest at sea, I said, "Yes. That will be good for you." I watched him prepare to leave and gave him such smiling encouragement as I could feign. Inwardly I was terror-stricken. I do not pretend that I could foresee the débacle. I only sensed that he was acting with towering courage and I told him I was proud of him.

We lunched alone at my house on the day he left. I remember that we ate frogs' legs, of which he was particularly fond. The year before at Cross Creek we had cooked them together, in a patter of argument about whose way with them was better, his butter or my olive oil. In the end we combined the two and produced a glorious dish which we ate licking our fingers under a palm tree and giggling about the garlic each had sneaked in when he thought the other was not looking. This time we had nothing to giggle about and the lunch was decorous.

Soon afterwards it was time for him to leave. I was driving

him to the place where he was to meet his entourage and go to the ship. I had to stay in New York briefly and would be in Prague in a month or so, but the point had come, or perhaps more exactly we had been propelled to it by what he called *force majeure,* where it was painful to be apart. I went to put on my coat and presently I realized that, with his quiet, catlike step, he had followed me to the room where I was. I turned and asked him if he wanted anything. He stood, already in his overcoat, looking at me with heavy eyes.

"No," he said. "I was just—" he paused. "Just looking around."

The last look, I thought. I fought to hide the panic that swept me. For a moment I stood weighing a wild thought. Suppose I stepped out of character, turned sheerly female, even hysterical; suppose I rushed to him, threw my arms around him, wailed, made a scene, implored him not to go. I was afraid for him—not that he might be going to his death, but that he would never be safe in my house again. Suppose I did it. Would it stop him? It would not. It would only torture him more.

Now I come to the curious imbalance of experienced time: how a few weeks may take on in perspective the span and weight of a long major segment of one's life. It is difficult to reconstruct how one felt *in terms of time* while one was living through such an interval. Fifteen days of my life in 1948 were more definitive in depth and in detail, more permanent in impact, than fifteen years that followed them; than any time since or any time there may yet be for me.

It was five below zero when Louise and I took off for Prague in January and almost as cold when we landed there next day. I was ecstatic. This is literal; it may not be rational but it is the truth. Prague in the snow is so beautiful that it is almost a cliché. Good King Wenceslas of course was Václav of Bohemia, and the snow round about him on the Feast of Stephen was the snow that lies deep and crisp and even in the courts of Hradčany. Of all my arrivals in that haunting and haunted city that one was the loveliest. I had my own home to come to and my joy at being there quelled the dark fears of the autumn in New York. The flat was heavenly warm. Excellent central heating had been installed in the house some time in this century and thanks to Bohemia's resources there was abundant coal. (One of the most interesting days I ever spent there was below ground going through one of the great coal mines.) But better still was the stove in my bedroom, an eighteenth-century beauty of fine white porcelain, scrolled and gilded and crowned with the crest of the family who had then owned the house. The stove was not needed for warmth but I used it as one uses an open fire, for delight, for cosiness and grace. The fuel was little square chunks of wood which were fed into it through a decorative brass grilled door at the bottom. Because of the stove we usually sat in the tower alcove of my room and sometimes had supper there.

Whenever I had been in Prague since the end of the war I had taken it for granted that I was under surveillance, a detestable sensation, dirty and demeaning. I had nothing to hide, taking my cue from Jan, but as he said, Communists are inherently conspiratorial so they expect everybody else to be. While I was still living in a hotel they must have been busy as beavers. When I moved to my flat I supposed that my telephone was tapped but I did not assume that the place had been bugged and there too I was guided by Jan. He could not have believed that it was or he would not have talked there, as he did, more freely than elsewhere. I weigh this now in remembering where he said what in relation to the political crisis and his own situation. He did not imply that his room in the Černinský was wired, but it seems probable he thought it was. He took devilish satisfaction in blurting outrageous remarks there and it seems to me now almost as if he intended them to be heard. He left snoopers in the Černinský nothing to discover about him that he had not already made plain. Yet in the presence of the second manservant who worked with Příhoda and was the major-domo he sometimes warned me with a certain glance or a twitched eyebrow.

To the left of my house the street was covered by a long, vaulted fifteenth-century arcade and in the ground floor of one of the arcaded houses was the district police station. The chief duties of the personnel there were said to be to guard the Hrad and the Černinský. But, unlike the old days before Munich, these policemen were not the comfortable, green-uniformed city police. They were the SNB—the quasi-military arm of the Communist Ministry of the Interior. A certain amount of effort was made to establish the fiction that these toughs in khaki with red flashes were nice Czech boys like the traffic cops downtown. One smiled and said *"Nazdar!"* to them and cooperated cheerfully with a mess of tiresome forms and permits that had to be registered at their station. When Jan encountered these SNB's he was jolly, with a ready joke. But when he walked the short distance to or from the Černinský, he crossed to the other side of the street, the open side, rather than go under the arcade and past the SNB station. He said he preferred them to do their watching from across the street.

Little daily matters—the walk up to Adam the baker on Pohořelec to buy fresh black bread, or down the street to the dairy with the milk jug; greeting the neighbors out on their errands; the trips across the Bridge to buy from my fat old market women in Uhelný Trh; the friends I went to see and those who came to see me; the occasional play or concert or opera; the fact that we could laugh—I cannot remember at what but I remember the laughter; these are incredible now against the ferment of terror that was heaving beneath our feet. Yet I remember the little things in the texture of early February. I knew that a ferocious struggle was going on in the Government because Nosek, the Minister of the Interior, had replaced the last eight non-Communist regional police commanders with Communists—a consequence of the bomb plot—and the Cabinet had instructed him by majority vote to reinstate the dismissed men. When Jan came in in the late afternoon or evening I saw that he was under great strain, but I knew more about the Cabinet crisis from others than he told me in those days. What he did say was that the Communists would push for a show-down long before the election in May. "They can't wait for the legal elections," he said. "They'd lose—unless." Unless meant direct Russian intervention. That must have been at supper on Sunday the fifteenth of February. He told me he would be tied up the next day and Tuesday by a meeting of the Foreign Ministers of all the Communist satellites, who were coming to Prague—"Who the hell is sending them here?" On Tuesday afternoon he telephoned and asked me to come up to see him at about five o'clock. I found him in bed exhausted.

"They've gone," he said. "And I've been lying in the bath for an hour. I need a lot more baths."

Next day he sent for me again. He was still in bed, with a woollen scarf folded round his neck inside the collar of his pyjama jacket. He spoke in a muffled voice. "Got a sore throat," he said. I drew a chair up close to the bed and he whispered, "Sick list. As long as necessary."

I was there every day. On Thursday I found him looking really ill. He seemed feverish. No wonder. He had been unable that day to go to Ruzýň to meet Laurence Steinhardt who had returned from a brief trip to Washington. Jan had been working with him to negotiate a credit for twenty-five million dollars' worth of American cotton. But he said, "It's too late now. Zorin arrived today too. Almost the same time."

"*Zorin!* Did you expect him?"

One of those bitter, negative jerks of the head. Valerian Zorin was then Deputy Foreign Minister to Molotov.

"Do they say what for?" I asked.

"To superintend delivery of the grain Stalin promised me last summer." His tone was thin with sarcasm.

"Oh, no." Intervention, I thought. This must be it. Enormity can be much too crushing for words and between us there was anyway the habit of few words in this realm. Jan was breathing heavily. That was stress, I knew; he had no cold. Zorin called on him that afternoon. Jan rang me up in the evening only to say good-night; naturally no mention of anything on the telephone.

Next day he sent for me in the early afternoon. I had already heard: the twelve Cabinet ministers of the three main democratic parties had resigned in protest against Nosek's failure to reinstate the non-Communist police chiefs. The twelve ministers intended their move as a tactic to give Beneš grounds for calling immediate elections in the event that Nosek failed to comply with the majority vote of the Cabinet. Beneš had been told of their plan and had assured them that he would not accept their resignations without consulting them first. Jan did not tell me whether or not he knew about the plan beforehand. But the reason for his diplomatic sore throat was to make it impossible for Gottwald to hold a Cabinet meeting in the absence of the twelve non-Communists; Jan's presence would have provided a quorum. There was never a question of Jan's resigning. As the only non-party man in the Cabinet he could not take a partisan position.

He was in terrible anxiety about Beneš. The matter of a Cabinet meeting quickly became immaterial, for on Saturday Gottwald launched the first of four days of savage duress on Beneš to accept the twelve resignations. There would follow no elections, but a Government and Cabinet of Communists and collaborators chosen by Gottwald. Beneš stood firm at first, while the long-prepared Communist apparatus of mob action and police terror engulfed the country. In a sense the fatal mistake of the twelve ministers, handing Gottwald the device by which he bludgeoned Beneš to submission, made almost no difference. Some other device or some Communist fabrication as a pretext would have produced the same result. Zorin was telling Jan and other democratic men that Moscow would put up with no more of their nonsense. The Army—unlike 1938, when it had been rock-solid

—was riddled with Communists. The visible police were directed by invisible hatchet-men headed by an operative called Rejcin whose name few of us had heard before those days. At Laurence Steinhardt's on Sunday evening someone told me that this man was said to have a cadre of experts from Moscow stashed in a barracks near Strahov—not five minutes' walk from my house. (That was the last time I dined out in Prague.)

The revolutionary uproar went into high gear. Long and thorough underground preparation erupted in the form of Action Committees which had muscled in on every entity and organization—labor unions, factory works councils, farmers' cooperatives, the newspapers. The Action Committees were gangs of trained ruffians. They plunged into outright violence days before the coup was completed. I never understood how the Communists had subverted great basic masses of people who had once been the solid humanity of a model democracy. It is not rational to say only because their morale had been destroyed by the Nazis. Millions of them had fiercely resisted the Nazis. Over that weekend of February twenty-first the Reds brought in to Prague from all over the country hundreds of thousands of factory workers. These mobs gathered in the Václavské and the Old Town Square to be harangued by Gottwald and Zápotocký and the rest. They were cued to howl and whipped to frenzy and all of it was broadcast on the radio. Mobs are mobs. I had seen them before, in Berlin in 1933. I cannot say that one had no relation to the other.

Up on the hill it was deceptively calm. There is about that quarter the atmosphere of a village, and so it seemed on those winter days and nights. Jan remained in his room. I saw him briefly every day and I knew he was in contact with Beneš but I do not know just how. I had not seen Beneš for a long time. Jan said that he showed no effects of the July incident except some impairment of his speech; that his mind was unaffected, and he worked full time. I wonder. I remember the despairing appeals of the people that Beneš assert himself, appear publicly, give them leadership; above all, speak to them on the radio. Three days dragged by while they hung in suspense waiting for Beneš to do that. Nothing happened. Finally I said to Jan, "Does it mean he can't?"

He nodded.

"You mean—he can't, physically—or they won't let him?"

"Both," he said. His face was ghastly.

On Monday afternoon a friend whom I will call Helena was at tea with me. We had heard a rumor that a mass of University students were going to march to the Hrad to demonstrate their loyalty to Beneš and the Republic, to exhort him to appear and address them. From the Loretanská side of the house we heard the tramp of feet and the chanting of voices. I ran to the dining-room windows; the students were marching past. I have no idea how many they were, but the record says thousands, and it seemed so. Eight abreast, they were carrying the national tricolor and they were singing the national anthem, whose tragic refrain is "Where is my home?" They were fine and beautiful young people and they were the last honest open faces I saw in that country. I seized a coat and ran out of the house to go along near them on the pavement; Helena called after me to come back but I paid no attention. Then I heard another noise, a heavy roar, and another kind of tramping; it seemed to come from many directions. The students were nearing the gates of the Hrad. I stood still for a moment as I saw their ranks break and flailing violence falling on them. Then I heard shots. I knew I should not be in the street so I went back to the house. I stood at the window again and saw platoon after platoon of marching men, in ordinary clothes with red rags tied round their left arms, carrying rifles. Workers' Militia is what their Red bosses called them, but I did not know that or care. I clutched the sill and screamed, "Armed civilians! Shame! Shame!" Helena dragged me away from the window.

I cannot remember just how I heard about the outrages that went on all day long on Tuesday: Action Committees arresting non-Communists in and out of the Government, barring officials and personnel from their offices and judges from their benches, closing newspapers. That afternoon I turned on the small portable radio when Gottwald was making a drunken, lying, rabble-rousing speech to a mob downtown. All I remember is throwing the radio across the room and smashing it. Tuesday evening is a blank.

On Wednesday afternoon Jan telephoned. His voice was very strange, breathless and high-pitched as though he were trying to sound nonchalant. He said, "I'm at the Hrad. I'll be along presently. I have something to tell you."

I thought, why has he telephoned? What am I supposed to say? This can only be because he wants them to hear. I tried to answer in the same vein. Like an idiot I said, "I hope it's something good . . ."

In a few minutes he came. He burst into the room, almost falling across the threshold, wearing his overcoat. His face was like a mask, as if it had looked into the pit and was frozen, still staring at the horrors there. I went to him and he said, "Lost. Utterly lost."

Beneš had given in. Jan was unable to say more, to go into details, to talk about his own situation. There was nothing I could say. We sat together for a long time. He kept his hand on my shoulder and once or twice murmured something that I do not think he knew he was saying. He must have stayed an hour. I cannot remember the rest of that evening and night. When he left me he stopped to see his sister Alice across the hall, and then went up to the Černinský. He was accompanied by his bodyguard, a quiet civilian who had been with him since 1945, a man like our Secret Service men. He always rode in the front seat of Jan's car or walked beside him the short distance to and from the Ministry when Jan went on foot.

Early next morning Příhoda brought me a small sealed envelope. Inside was a note that Jan had written in pencil on a very small piece of paper. He wrote:

"Am staying in this 'govt' for time being. It breaks my heart for you to receive these shocks which you deserve less than anybody in the world. Do not be too sad. Be bitter and be proud—of yourself. I am very proud of you. You believed in a decent hope—so did I. It could not be. But this is not the end."

Thus I learned that Jan was to stay in Gottwald's 'government.' I did not need to ask him why. He stayed—he told me later—because Beneš, bludgeoned and without his full faculties, had stayed. Gottwald had insisted on Beneš staying to give his putsch the ghastly simulacrum of legitimacy. Gottwald had met every demur of Beneš's with threats of civil war: by implication, any war would bring in the Red Army. Munich all over again, said Beneš; "you are talking to me like Hitler." Beneš said afterwards to Jan, "In 1938 I had to bear the brunt of Munich alone when you were abroad. Now you must stay and help me and the country." Beneš was beyond giving help—or receiving it. Jan knew that. He told me that in his mind consenting to Beneš's plea was his final fulfillment of his promises to his father. Beyond that, he had to use the device of 'office' in the 'government' to keep his mobility; "if I hadn't, they'd have arrested me."

They were already arresting colleagues of his, and friends of his and mine. Jan interceded for them, I thought at too much risk to himself. While doing that he also made statements to the press whose irony I feared the Communists would see through: "With this government I shall enjoy governing." We were told that the Western press was criticizing him and questioning his motives. He made a certain vulgar noise expressing his contempt. It was not true, as the Communists later claimed, that he was receiving reproachful and abusive letters from Western friends. He stood in the middle of my room and said, "Is it possible that anybody in any Western country who really knows me is so stupid as not to understand what I have to do? How the hell else can I get out? It's my only chance."

Panic was sweeping Government people because of the arrests. Abroad some members of Embassies and Consulates were resigning, as the good ones had done after Munich, led by Jan himself in London. I asked him about Janko Papánek in New York and Slavík in Washington. He told me that the day before he left New York he had talked to them both and told them what to do in the event of a Communist putsch. (So he had weighed the full possibility before he went back.) Neither of them was to make a move "until they had received a sign from me," he said. "I can rely on them."

On Thursday Jan came in the late afternoon and stayed all evening. We had supper in my room and he told me his plans for us. He had an obsession that I was not safe in Prague; that they would cook up accusations that I was a contact with 'Western reactionaries' or even take action against me without pretext. I begged him not to think about that and Laurence Steinhardt reassured him too. Laurence was magnificent all through the crisis; he gave me means to reach him instantly at any time and told me to rely on him and his wonderful staff for anything. The new British Ambassador, Bob Dixon (the late Sir Pierson Dixon), was splendid too. He had only been in Prague a few weeks. I had met him when Jan and I went alone to see him and his wife in the Thunovská. The situation was already so grave that we met as real people; rank and protocol were laid aside. We became friends in a moment under the weight that hung over us all.

Jan told me that evening that he wanted me to go to London and wait there for him to join me. At that time he did not envisage having to escape secretly. International conferences were constantly taking place abroad, and attendance at the next one was the means by which he intended to get out. When he joined me we would be married. At some other time his mention of this, which was anyway implicit, would have affected me more. I was used to keeping the question out of consideration because that was where political realities required it be kept. And at that moment his agony of mind and the sense of terror all around us prevented me from reacting as I might have done in other circumstances. I was desperate with worry about his safety and his freedom; the rest would come when it might. I did not know until after his death that he had thought more definitely about the matter than he had ever said to me. I learned afterwards that before he returned for the last time to Prague he had told intimate friends in New York and in London, when he stopped there briefly, of his wish about me. When he spoke of it to me he meant it to give us both courage.

But I knew at once that there was something very wrong about his plan for my departure from Prague. I did not consider objecting then and there, I had to think about it carefully and be sure of my own sense, and I had to give him peace. It would have been inhuman to argue or to question him. He decided I should go in ten days' time; not so quickly as to seem to be fleeing; soon enough to get the plan under way. I booked seats to London for Louise and myself on the flight of March the seventh—"my father's birthday," said Jan, with that gesture of his hands—lifting them and dropping them heavily on his knees.

Still I was hounded by worry about that plan. It was all wrong. It made me sick with terror for him. For two days and two nights I wrestled with myself; should I tell him what I thought before it was too late? Meanwhile the horrors and the tragedies piled up. On Friday Dr. Prokop Drtina, the Minister of Justice, was found gravely injured on the pavement outside his house; he had attempted suicide, they said, by jumping from a third floor window. On Saturday the twenty-eighth, Jan came from the Hrad in dreadful depression. Beneš had left the Hrad, he said for the last time, and gone with his wife to his own house in the country at Sezimovo Ústí. He was a totally broken man, his tenure of the Presidency a phantasm. Jan was alone, face to face with the dead Republic and its murderers.

He dropped into the long chair where he rested in my room and I sat on the floor close to him. Much of the time in those days he was too shaken to talk. He lay back in the chair and put out his hand towards me and I sat where he could keep his hand on my cheek or the top of my head. Churning with anxiety lest I trouble him more, I forced myself to ask him if he could bear it if I told him my own thoughts about his plan. Yes, he said; go ahead and tell him.

He listened. His expression changed from immobility to attentiveness. He opened his eyes and I saw him closely weighing everything I said. I told him why I thought it would be a mistake if I left first. I thought it would be better if I stayed there, isolated and out of communication, deliberately letting them watch me doing nothing, as a kind of hostage for his 'good intentions.' He could then take the first chance to get out, and the next day I would join him. Laurence would get me out safely. Or, if they did not want me in the country before that time, let *them* ask me to leave. The bead would be on them, I said; we would not be in the position of having let them think: Watch, she's gone, keep your eye on him. When I stopped talking he thought for a time, then he sat up and said firmly, "You are right. Cancel the flight for the seventh."

So my plan stood until Tuesday, the second of March. Early that morning I was brought another of Jan's little notes. He had written:

"Slavík has resigned and denounced this govt. Extremely bad."

When he came in about eleven o'clock that morning he was in a state of panic. Slavík's action had touched off a frenzied hue and cry. I quote here from a letter that I wrote from London to the Papáneks on the twelfth of March:

"You [Papánek at the U.N.] were noble and magnificent in holding your fire for Jan's sake and doing nothing until you had a sign from him. That was what Slavík should have done. The sign Jan gave was not the one he planned, the one with which he sent me out of Prague . . .

"Of course I understand the morality and motives of Slavík's action but the timing was fatally stupid. That morning began the period when Jan looked and acted like a hunted man; I think they must have threatened him in the full fury of their anti-American frenzy . . . he had the obsession that Slavík's action had torn the American thing completely and that they would suspect me of being his pipeline to outside. He was so wrong—if I was in Prague incommunicado they could not suspect that, and if I left, they would—but I could not add to his tortures and when he said [as originally] that I must go, I said, very well. I had to give him peace or what he imagined as the lesser of a choice of evils. . . .

"Certainly the last week I was there his situation was changed in respect to the gangsters. Jan came to my house every day but in such tension that I felt he was not supposed to be there . . . he never used the telephone again after the Slavík thing. I begged him not to come to see me since it was obviously dangerous for him, and he burst into tears and said if he could not see me he would break."

I had said then that if I were in London he would not be able to see me either. He tried to smile.

"I know," he said. "But if I have to choose between knowing you are locked up here or knowing you are safe at Claridge's it had better be London. If I know you are there waiting for me it gives me something to live for."

The resignation of Slavík and the other events of the weekend produced the shame of two leather-jacketed, seemingly civilian thugs who were assigned to cover Jan; his own man and other security staff were withdrawn. He protested so vehemently to Nosek that some change was made in the orders. His personal guard was restored and Jan thereafter never moved a step without him. He went nowhere on foot except to see his sister Alice and me. But the leather-jacketed thugs were in evidence too. They reminded me of Nazis, dressed the same and looking the same. I found one hanging about in our downstairs hall.

"What do you want?" I asked him in a loud voice. "Are you here on an errand?" He mumbled something and went away.

During the last week Jan asked me to burn every piece of paper in my possession. He did not want me to carry out of the country a word or symbol of anything written in any form. He was afraid that somebody at Ruzýň would make trouble. He was very firm. I had a good many things. There were notebooks and pre- liminary material for the long novel I had expected to shape up; they were rather bulky. Might I leave them with Laurence to be sent out in the pouch? Jan thought for a time and, reluctantly, said "Yes. But nothing else." He raised his forefinger in a way he had. *"Nothing else.* You promise?"

"I promise."

Some of the time he was with me while I burnt everything in that lovely porcelain stove. The basis of this chapter of this book is my red desk diary for 1948, one of a series that I have kept for over thirty-five years. I had been noting in it, in the briefest possible items, the events of each day as they happened. Jan had often seen the book on my desk—being Jan, I suppose he had looked in it—but it was not a private diary, only an ordinary engagement book with one six-by-four-inch page to a day.

"You must burn it," he said. "And everything else. Every receipted bill. Everything, personal or not. Your letters to me."

Those were the letters I had written him whenever we were apart, letters that were too personal to send through the post or by pouch. The ones I sent anybody could have seen; the others I kept and brought to Prague with me. He read them when he was at leisure in my house. He tore them up and I put them in the stove.

I had promised; but I promised for his peace of mind. I dis- obeyed him in one element. I cannot say I was taking a long view or even that I knew very well what I was doing. I was alone when I was about to burn the red book. Before I cut it up and put the scraps in the stove I scribbled its entries on a small piece of thin paper, making an illegible jumble that might have been household reminders . . . names became sugar, vinegar, floor-polish . . . After the disaster I bought another red book for 1948 and transcribed the scrambled entries back into it, carefully noting everything I was reminded of by the keys I had made for myself. I had no thought then that those notes would be used in any book I would ever write, but I knew that if I did not put down the facts while they were fresh—more, raw—in my mind, they would become confused, my memory would lose or garble them, and I did not intend that to happen. The odd thing is that afterwards I destroyed the piece of paper.

I had no trouble at Ruzýň. The paper was folded inside something in my handbag and nobody demanded to examine the bag. They did go through all the luggage, very courteously, and questioned nothing. What almost broke my heart was to have to burn the little notes that Jan had written and sent me by Přihoda all those days, sometimes several in a day. But they were short— often only a single line. And I had read them over and over. There were days of which I remember nothing but pacing back and forth across my room, listening to the Loreta carillon play St. Mary's Hymn hour after hour, staring out the windows at the tragic beauty—I will never forget the full moon on the twenty-fourth of February—and reading Jan's notes. I had memorized them word for word. The first day I was in London I wrote them all down. I do not quote them. They are a language within a language: the outer language is small plain words; the inner language I cannot share.

When Jan had first said I should go 'to London he had given me verbal messages that I was to repeat to his old friend Bruce Lockhart whom I had known since he had stayed with Jan in Prague the year before; and to Sir Orme Sargent, the head of the Foreign Office. The messages were about Jan's intentions to escape but made no mention of a time element. On Saturday evening, the night before I was to leave, he came at half past eight. He looked absolutely ghastly. All those days he had had an exhausted, claylike pallor, but that evening he was even more grey of face. He had come from Sezimovo Ústí where he had lunched with Beneš and spent the afternoon. He told me nothing of what had happened there; I learned that later. I saw only that he was distraught. He muttered, "Beneš . . ."

He rested for a time. We were silent. I was afraid to speak and upset him the more because I was so wretched about leaving next day. Besides, there was nothing to say. I have no idea how much time elapsed. Finally he leaned forward in his chair and spoke to me, looking into my eyes. He spoke slowly, with emphasis, in a very low voice. He said, "When you get to Claridge's tomorrow, don't go out. Do not go out of the hotel. Do not leave your rooms at all. Stay there all the time until you hear from me."

I said yes. I did not ask him a question. He said, "Very soon . . . few days . . ."

I went with him to the door and helped him put on his overcoat, an old loose one that he had been wearing in those last days. I had not seen it before then. It was an odd brown color. He said, "God bless." If I said anything it has been erased from my memory. I think we were nearly insensible with misery. I closed the hall door behind him and stood listening to his slow, light step as he descended the shallow stairs. When I could hear him no longer I ran to the dark dining-room with the windows over Loretanská. I moved the drawn blind a fraction of an inch, to peer through the crack. Jan was just crossing the street from my house. I saw the guard beside him, and another dark figure fall into place behind; the thug, I suppose. Jan walked slowly, with the light from the street-lamp on him. I could see the color of that ugly old cinnamon-brown overcoat. His head was bent as he crossed the street but when he started very slowly up the pavement towards the Černinský, he looked up at my blacked-out windows and walked on with his head turned my way.

He knew I was watching. I stood and clung to his figure with my eyes until I could see no longer.

We reached London on Sunday without incident. I have only the most confused memories of how we had got ready to go. Louise did everything. She was calm, organized, unshaken; outraged and angry too. She packed trunks which later, without my knowledge, were taken over with some of my furniture at Laurence's orders and eventually sent me. But I do not know what I left there, what I gave away, what I dragged across the hall in laundry baskets to Alice Masaryk and asked her to give away. The tension was so frightful that it had to break in small ways that come to people who prefer a bang to a whimper. I did some totally irrational things. I took the telephone, which was on a jack, out of the outlet in my room and locked it up in the wall safe. On Sunday morning Laurence sent an Embassy car to take us to Ruzýň—my memories of that airport and its grisly history! In the plane a startling sense of release shot through me. Jan would get out safely, and very soon. No other possibility entered my mind. I would do as he said and it could not be long. "Soon . . . few days . . ." The words carried me through Sunday and Monday and Tuesday. I must have been so fixed on those words that I got through the time on their echo. Do not go out of the hotel. Do not leave your rooms at all. I telephoned on Monday to Bruce Lockhart who was in Scotland and when he said he would not be in London before Wednesday, I thought it as well since I supposed that Jan's last directions to me had superseded his first ones. Perhaps he will be here before I need give any messages, I thought.

On Wednesday morning before nine o'clock the telephone rang. *Jan is here.* That was my only thought as I seized the telephone.

It was my old friend John Foster, who had been immensely helpful in arranging for my arrival in London, and very kind

[427]

after I got there. His voice was high and choked. There was noise in the background. He said he was at the railway station taking a train to his constituency. He said, "There are newspaper extras just out. I think I had better tell you before you hear some other way."

Jan had been found dead in the courtyard early that morning.

᠁[C H A P T E R   S E V E N T E E N]᠁

THEY said, suicide.

He had said, "One day they'll kill me."

The first idea was imaginable before I knew anything except what they had announced after the hours they took to decide on their story. The story was preposterous. The news of Jan's death had already been telephoned out by the foreign press.

The second idea came forth in blundering lunges, like the steps of the blinded Cyclops, over weeks and months, even years, in which people came to me or I went to them. This one had a fact, that one a contradiction; this one had seen and I could believe him; that one had heard and I doubted. The facts that were believable did not perfectly fit together. Missing pieces had been removed as though lifted from a box of jig-saw puzzle parts and destroyed. They have never come to light. I am certain that they never will.

I am startled to read now what I have not gone back to since the beginning: what I told Tania Long of *The New York Times* when she telephoned me at Claridge's that day. I do not know how she and her husband Raymond Daniell of the *Times* knew I was in London. Tania Long withheld my name as I asked her to do. A week later I would not have been coherent enough to speak to her. That day I told her that Jan Masaryk, although in poor health, was not so ill as to be driven to suicide by his physical condition or by worry over reproachful messages from Western friends, as Nosek and the Communist régime had announced. I said, "No, no, there is more to this than meets the eye.

But whatever traces and clues remain will have been cleaned up by now. The police move fast in Czechoslovakia these days."

That was in the *Times* on the eleventh of March. It was valid then and it is valid now.

Laurence Steinhardt when I saw him after a long interval, spoke thoughtfully and with dry preciseness. He said he had studied the question as a lawyer. He said the conclusion he drew was unique in his experience, and that others in the law agreed. "You can put down all the facts relevant either to suicide or to murder and make a watertight case for one or for the other," he said.

Nobody advised me to wait nearly twenty years before I wrote about this. That came from within myself. For many years I was not sure that I would ever write about it, or in my lifetime publish what I might write. Nobody could have influenced me towards a decision. When I took the decision it was because I felt ready from within. I believe that no facts in addition to those that I know are likely ever to emerge. If I felt that in the future I might be able still more accurately and objectively to recapitulate this record, I might wait some years more. But I am not sure I would be more able years hence. I am now in command of the faculties and the ability to write this. I know that henceforward those faculties and that ability may diminish or I may die. I have therefore chosen this age and this time as carefully, as responsibly, as I could.

Those who believe it was suicide, British public opinion in particular, and the majority of Jan's British friends and some Americans, none of whom were with him in the last months of his life, do not consider his death a mystery. Rather more of a mystery to them were his acts and motives when he appeared to be appeasing, or even collaborating with, the Communists. Some thought him weak, some confused, some irresolute. They dismissed the repellent Communist story that he had been driven to suicide by the reproaches of his Western friends. They stressed the intolerable assault it must have been upon his feelings and his mind to have to attend the travesty of a public commemoration of his father's birthday on the seventh of March, and listen to Communist liars stating that T. G. Masaryk would have approved what they had done. The believers in suicide mentioned Jan Masaryk's long solitary vigil that evening at his father's grave at Lány. They concluded that he took his decision there, a clear protest, the sacrifice of his life to vindicate the name of Masaryk and tell the truth to the world. It is a brave and noble theory and in nineteen years I have been through every process of reasoning and of instinct which could induce me to believe it.

I am not afraid to face the fact of suicide as such. I have not got the Roman Catholic indoctrination which causes Catholics, even lapsed Catholics, to deny that a death is a suicide, especially in the first shock of confrontation. If I had had proof from Jan himself that his death was intentional suicide I could have accepted that. I might have wished he could have been deterred by a desire to stay alive and be with me, but by my own principles that would be rank sentimentality. I am now past the age Jan was when he died and I know that personal emotion at such an age may not be powerful enough to decide a question of life and death, when moral motives can decide it. I can clearly and logically construct a case for Jan's death as suicide and complete this by affirming that I would have done the same in his place.

But the fallacy lies in the *manner* of the death. Jan's death was absolutely untypical of Jan—if it was suicide.

I was groping towards some of these conclusions when Czecho-slovaks all over the world began to state that Jan Masaryk had been murdered. Americans said it too—President Truman among the first. That had been my own first instinct, inevitable because it was the echo of Jan's own words. I do not know how many times I had heard him say they would kill him. I had heard it and seen him, changing from the sangfroid of July to the terror of March. I did not think they had plotted to kill him in cold blood; nothing would more have damaged them before the world. But if they had discovered his plan to leave the country it was wholly realistic to think that his death had resulted from whatever they had done to prevent his going. His escape of itself would have discredited them. They would have expected him to become the rallying-point for resistance to them. (He could not have done that. His revulsion from the thought of fighting his own countrymen and his shattered nerves would have prevented him from taking a stand like the one he had led against Hitler after Munich. He was fleeing for his life when I last saw him and not thinking beyond that.)

People began to arrive from Prague. They talked to me, they talked to others. Eventually some of them talked to journalists who wrote newspaper and magazine articles which presented contrasting views of the subject. I could judge the people who talked to me only by my previous knowledge of them and their relations to Jan and to others concerned. No doubt they believed what they said. No doubt they expected me to believe it. Faced with data from primary witnesses who flatly contradicted one another, what was I to do? What was truth in such instances? I concluded it must be that which most closely coincided with what I knew to be true from my own experience, my own knowledge of Jan and of his plans. One abjuration I imposed on myself to the utmost limits of my will-power: to rule out wishful thinking. I discovered that Jan himself had made confusion—I believe deliberately—by telling directly contradictory things to different people. I believe this was to keep anyone from knowing his precise intentions—if he knew them himself. I learned that during the days when he was telling me his plans for both of us, he was also telling a colleague in the Foreign Ministry [so the man said] that he intended to commit suicide. He even specified the window, in the ancient Bohemian tradition of defenestration which went back to the Thirty Years' War. In my house Jan did not believe

he was overheard by listening devices. In his room in the Černinský he suspected he was heard.

I do not name any of the people who talked to me, nor state
where or when or in what circumstances I saw them. Some are
alive and some are dead. Some have or had ties in Czechoslovakia
about which I know nothing today, people who never had anything to do with any of this. All the persons who talked to me
were men. All had stood in functional, working, or appointive
relations to Jan for years. Each person was a *witness,* by which I
mean that he told me what he had seen with his own eyes, or heard
with his own ears, or participated in with his own presence.

Two men in particular told me what Jan had said to them in
his last days. He told them both, for different reasons, of his
plan to escape by air on the tenth of March. To one of them on
the ninth of March he retracted the plan and said he had decided
to commit suicide. The statements of those two men not only
contradicted each other; they also contradicted what I knew of the
characters of the two men.

The one whose credibility should have been the most reliable
gave the account most tinctured with sentimentality and with
idealization of Jan and of the motives imputed to him: the
hardest to believe. This person also later gave a journalist a
description of Jan's actions in his last hours and of his voluntarily
going out the window, which must be discredited because the man
was not a witness of what he described.

The other person, whose account might have been thought
to be colored by a wish to appear important and to have had a
part in something sensational, made statements that were literal,
factual, and primary: the most believable.

The two accounts met squarely on one point only: both
mentioned an airplane arranged for early on the morning of
March the tenth. From nobody else did I receive corroboration
of this. Either there was no plane waiting (but I think there was

because it is the only point on which the two accounts agree); or the plane was seized by secret agents—whoever they were, and whoever their bosses, Czech or otherwise—and the fate of the pilot need not be guessed.

The sequence of Jan's last days began with the afternoon he had spent with Edvard Beneš on Saturday, the sixth of March, after which he came to my house for the last time, in a state of apparent shock. I do not put the substance of his talk with Beneš in the form of quoted dialogue because that would be inaccurate. I was not there. The talk was in Czech. If I were to transcribe it, translated, with literary interpolation, it would be imaginary and invalid. One person was present at luncheon besides the President, his wife, and Jan. That person told me what he had heard. He was in Beneš's confidence and Jan's; both were accustomed to speak freely in his presence.

Jan asked Beneš what his intentions were, for himself and for Jan. Beneš said that he wanted to resign but that Gottwald would not permit it. Beneš did not answer concerning Jan; he was in no condition to answer. Jan told Beneš that he could no longer stay on in the false position he had assumed. Beneš was indifferent. Jan said he felt he had discharged his final obligation and that further compliance with the situation was impossible. It was now necessary to extricate himself. Beneš became rather excited but said nothing that was to the point. Jan was endeavoring to learn whether Beneš had any wishes or intentions which in Jan's mind would still bind him to Beneš. It was impossible to get an answer. Finally Jan asked Beneš what he proposed they should both do now that Beneš had got them out on the end of a limb. Beneš lost his temper and said he did not care what Jan did. Jan should solve his own problems, get himself out of his own difficulties. Jan replied that he meant to do that if he could. He intended to leave.

It is speculation that Beneš's house was wired, but hard to believe that it was not. I judge this by knowing how sharp the surveillance was around Jan after the first of March. If they did not discover Jan's plans through hearing what he said to Beneš, they could have discovered them in many other ways.

Among the persons who gave me accounts of what Jan said to them or did in their presence, on the seventh, eighth, and ninth of March was a man he sent to Ruzýň on the Sunday when I left, telling the man to be inconspicuous. I did not see him there. Jan asked him if I had got off without difficulty. The man said I had.

"She is really gone?" Jan asked him.

"She is really gone," the man replied.

Jan wept.

That was his father's birthday, when they perpetrated their worst lie. That was the evening when Jan went alone to Lány.

On Monday all the persons agree that Jan spent time going through the desk in his room and destroying the papers that were in it. It has been asserted that this was putting his affairs in order in anticipation of committing suicide; but to me it was simply a continuation of what he had begun to do days before, and had told me to do, in anticipation of leaving the country.

On Tuesday he saw Beneš for the last time, when according to protocol Jan and Clementis accompanied a newly arrived Polish Ambassador to Sezimovo Ústí to present his credentials. Jan returned to the Černinský, having told one man to be ready to leave with him next morning and arranging the signal for departure; and telling the other man that he was going to commit suicide as a warning to the world.

Whichever was true, he chose the tenth of March because on that day the Parliament was to convene in full session for the first time since the *coup d'état,* and be presented with all the members of Gottwald's new government. Jan would have had to be present, and that he had decided he would not do.

The man who said it was suicide told me that on Tuesday Jan had said he was going to write two letters, a political testament (whatever that means) and a personal letter—to me. Neither letter was seen before or after Jan's death. Both were said to have been taken from the writing-table by Clementis and Nosek when they went through Jan's room in the morning. One account describes a quarrel between the two men: does this imply that Clementis found a letter to me and might have had it delivered, which I think he would have done, except that Nosek interfered? Why should Nosek interfere? It was Nosek and the Communists who announced the death as suicide and it was to their interest that the world believe them. If Jan committed premeditated suicide and I think inevitably in that case, wrote and left a letter to me, all they had to do to prove the suicide was see that I received the letter. Clementis did send me certain keepsakes, gold pocket-pieces that I had given Jan; but no letter. I do not believe such a letter ever existed.

On Tuesday night Jan had his supper alone and at nine o'clock dismissed Přihoda, saying he would require nothing more. Every account thereafter notes that in the morning near Jan's bed, T. G. Masaryk's Bible was found open at the page where he—some said Jan—had underlined the words of the 22nd and 23rd verses of the fifth chapter of the Epistle to the Galatians:

> But the fruit of the Spirit is love, joy, peace,
> longsuffering, gentleness, goodness, faith,
>
> Meekness, temperance: against such there is no law.

I have thought ever since that if Jan was moved to read that chapter he must have been shaken much more by the first verse:

> Stand fast therefore in the liberty wherewith
> Christ hath made us free, and be not entangled
> again with the yoke of bondage.

The Masaryks were religious but not doctrinary. T. G. Masaryk summed up his political philosophy in the words, "Jesus, not Caesar."

Between the time that his servant last saw Jan Masaryk alive and the time when the first witness reported finding him dead in the courtyard next morning, some eight hours elapsed. During those hours anything can have happened. There is no proof for the statements of those who said he was alone during that time. It is probably true that nobody went to his room by any of the usual means of access. But I know that there are innumerable entrances to the Černinský Palác other than the main ones. And more cogently, that there are many ways (or there were when I was constantly there) of entering the rooms that were Jan's without using the principal passages and doors. Anybody familiar with the architecture of such palaces knows that all the rooms, approached either by imposing corridors or entered successively from one to the next, are backed behind their inner walls by narrow passages for the use of servants. Great public stairways are also supplemented by narrow inside stairs, again for the use of servants. Jan and I had not failed to explore these features, and we used to shudder after we had counted a total of eleven different means of access to his private rooms. It was possible to enter Jan's bathroom from a service passage without crossing his bedroom; and it was possible to enter the bedroom without using the main hallways and doors which gave access to it.

No person can claim that nobody went to Jan Masaryk's room after he had dismissed his servant for the night.

Here, precisely rendered, is the account of a man who saw Jan in the courtyard on the morning of March the tenth. Jan lay on the stone paving, flat on his back, dressed in blue silk pyjamas. His legs were extended straight out and his arms also, with the palms of his hands flat on the ground. The bones of the heels had been shattered. The head and face appeared intact. There is no reason to believe that Jan was actually found in that position; he might have been placed in it by one of several persons who saw the body before the man did who spoke to me. When he told me, and repeated as I questioned him with some doubt, that the legs and feet were as he said, there came to my mind the memory of the police station in New York where I had been called to identify the body of Parker Lloyd-Smith. I had seen Parker's head and face, completely unmarked, and his upper torso, as the police had rolled the covering down. But there was nothing below the torso. The blanket was perfectly flat. There were no legs and feet. I remembered the dry, considerate, but matter-of-fact voice of the New York policeman who said, "We see this all the time. A typical suicide jump. They go out feet first. The legs and feet are telescoped up into the body on impact."

When I asked my physician and my surgeon in New York what it meant that Jan's legs and feet were in the condition described to me, they both said it meant that Jan was unconscious before his body struck the pavement of the courtyard; that it had landed flat. It could not have done that if he had been conscious at the time he fell.

I was told further that the front of the jacket of the pyjamas had been ripped. The abdomen beneath was scratched, the skin broken. There were traces of plaster under the finger-nails and abrasions on some of the finger-tips. These marks indicated that Jan had gone backwards out of the window, struggling to keep his hold, and that the front of his body was torn by grazing the exterior of the building. Then I was told by the same witness what he saw when he went upstairs to Jan's bedroom and bathroom, with which he was very familiar. Both rooms were in wild disorder. The furniture was disarranged. Chairs were overturned. A mineral-water bottle, a glass, and other articles from the bedside table had been flung about. The bed itself was very mussed and the pillows were missing. They were seen on the floor of the bathroom. All over the bathroom were scattered a large number of safety-razor blades. From a hook on the door hung a cord made of the drawstrings from several pairs of pyjama-trousers, knotted together. These suggest frantic, half-demented indecision between two forms of suicide. Scattering the razor-blades and hanging up the knotted pyjama-cords were impossible to believe of Jan. If he had intended suicide he would have been incapable of opening an artery or of hanging himself. I believe that the blades and the cords were placed where they were after Jan had gone out the window to give an impression of suicidal hysteria and indecision about the means to be used.

I was told about the lying-in-state and about the small bouquet of snowdrops that lay behind Jan's right ear. Various reasons for this were given as time went on. The only point where all accounts agreed was that the flowers were put there to conceal something. What? One said a gunshot wound. Another said the marks of a blow with a heavy object. Another said (suicide theory) to conceal the traces of the autopsy.

The autopsy was conducted in such haste that President Beneš's physician who had been asked by Beneš to attend, was not notified until it was too late for him to get there. The report of the autopsy was suppressed. In 1951, so serious and responsible a journalist as C. L. Sulzberger of *The New York Times* wrote a long article based on the evidence of people who had got out of Prague bringing with them the statements of the police surgeon, Dr. Teply, who was called to the Černinský at five o'clock on the morning of March the tenth. Dr. Teply was forced to sign a report that falsified his own findings as the first medical expert to examine the body. Within a few months Teply was dead himself in police headquarters in Prague. He was given (or administered to himself?) an injection of gasoline.

From the foregoing, every word of it except the contents of Sulzberger's article told me by eye-witnesses, I cannot state as certainty what happened: I was not there. But from all that I know, from the description of the bedroom and the bathroom and the bathroom window-sill, below which there was a window-seat, I weigh the probability that there was a struggle at the bathroom window. This could have followed a surprise intrusion into Jan's room by whoever (probably plural) came to tell him that his plan to escape was known and that he would never get out alive. The disorder in the bedroom suggests protest and violence there; the condition of the bathroom suggests a struggle across the room towards the window, to which he was pushed backwards. When he struggled at being forced over the sill, he was struck on the right side of his head (one version said, shot behind the right ear) and, unconscious, dropped out of the window.

But suppose all this were fallacious. Suppose nothing of the sort happened. Suppose Jan did commit suicide. I still believe he could not intentionally have gone out the window. He had a very great fear of pain, which in my mind precludes a leap from a window: Drtina had not died, and that shook Jan profoundly. There was another reason why the window seems impossible. Jan was a man of peculiar physical modesty and fastidiousness. It would violate every instinct of his nature to choose a death of public gruesomeness, dressed only in pyjamas. In his possession he had quantities of sedatives and sleeping-drugs sufficient to commit suicide by taking a lethal overdose. I believe he would have done that rather than anything which involved violence.

But this is not to take refuge in paralogism—if such that be. Precisely because the idea of premeditated suicide is the cruellest for me I have tried to discipline myself to accept it if it is the truth, or if I ever receive proof that it is. I have faced the possibility that Jan might have intended all along to commit suicide and was determined to get me out of the country before he did it. In that case he would have deceived me—in his mind, for my own protection. And I know better than anyone who has already implied or said it, that his stature is greater as a voluntary sacrifice—greater as his father's son, and as a martyr for his beliefs. I was able to see this when I wrote to his loyal friends and mine, the Papáneks, on the twelfth of March, before I was overtaken by a great darkness. I wrote:

". . . he was left to think in terms of his people and his country and his father and look for the only way once for all to be

Masaryk, to speak as Masaryk to the people and the world . . .
I believe he did it with supreme dedication, true to his faith and
to himself and to honor. Compared with that it must have looked
to him quite a small matter whether he got to London and
married me . . ."

That was an effort of my will, and it may have dealt with the
truth. I knew too how he had relied upon me to accept everything
he did even if I did not always understand it; and to forgive him
in silence if an act of his hurt me—and sometimes he did hurt
me. I followed his reasoning, if he so reasoned, that I would
understand his final act even if it hurt me irreparably. So I told
myself that his death was suicide, decided by the highest motives;
and I have told myself from time to time ever since. I think I
have reached rational acceptance of the unacceptable. For a time
I remain upon this plane. Long vague intervals go by. Then one
day something inside me cries, "You know you do not believe one
word of what you have convinced yourself!" And I cannot tell
whether it is my brain or my heart that is crying out.

I HAD a certain plan for part of this final chapter and I find I cannot carry it out. For more than ten years after Jan died I wrote a journal, something I had never done before and have never done since. It was principally private and personal. I wrote whatever I felt and thought. I recorded my memories of Jan and my continuing sense of his presence. He was more alive to me than most persons I ever saw and my memories of life with him were more real than any actualities. I wrote about my dreams, nearly all recurrences of terror, the unanswered, the lost, the unknown. I recorded the sensations and protestations of irreconcilable grief. I wrote of the day-by-day concerns of a remote rural place of great beauty, occupied by the small matters of country life. I wrote those pages as well and as lucidly as I have ever written at all.

I had not gone back to the journal, securely locked away, nor read it through until I was approaching the end of this book. I had considered putting into this chapter excerpts from those notebooks; not personal or introspective writings, but some that were a running commentary of those years, in which I saw a great deal of beauty, acquired considerable wisdom, and learned to be old. But I am not going to do that. The journal has served its purpose.

I suppose that if circumstances had required me to earn my living day by day instead of in fits and starts as writers do, I might not have reacted as I did to the catastrophe which destroyed every motivation of my life and work at one blow. I might have driven myself back into the everyday world where mourning is an abnormality and the commendable attitude is to rise above it and keep the show on the road. I had no show to keep on a road that led to nowhere. Survival when one does not want it is incomprehensible but one moves through it towards some sort of compromise with existence. I wanted isolation and the illusion of peace; water, beauty, old roofs, and something to do with my hands. In the autumn when Carol Brandt and I were staying for a time at Bellagio on the Lake of Como I saw from a boat a small stone house in a beautiful setting close to the water. I thought I might like to live there.

I could not stay in the United States. This may have been irrational but it does not matter now. I believed that my country could have done more than it had done to save the Czechoslovak Republic—not when it was too late, as in 1945; but when there might have been time, in 1943. It was years before I comprehended in global perspective that Communism is the paramount historical force of the twentieth century; that both the World Wars and the interim of Hitler, the Nazi era, Munich, were components of that force. Confusion was and is a tool of those who manipulate the force; to confuse and divide a major tactic. Franklin Roosevelt was a victim of the tactic. That did not mitigate my bitterness towards him and towards Edvard Beneš too, both men of the good intentions which tritely pave the way to hell. I was bitter and bewildered about my own country, crushed with disillusionment about Jan's. Only from the historical view of earlier centuries and from my experience in this one did I finally learn that the twenty years of the Masaryk Republic were a sublime interlude in a long history of subjection, subjugation, and proof of the adage that the master of Bohemia is the master of Europe. Because those years spanned the most impressionable and responsive years of my own life I thought them a norm. They proved to be a historical impossibility.

When I was briefly in New York in the winter, Maestro said, *"Vieni in Italia."* It was one of the thoughts that he offered as consolation, like his music. He did not talk about the tragedy. He never reminded me that he, with his scorn of *"politici"* and, indeed, of Slavs, had warned me not to go back to Prague the year before and had said that something terrible would happen there. Thereafter, at whatever concert came closest to the tenth of March every year, he played *Vltava,* the Smetana tone-poem. And I never thanked him, we never mentioned it. That was what he wanted. He was not as robust then, at eighty-one, as he had been; he did not spring to his podium with the vigor that was visibly diminishing, but once he began to conduct, at rehearsals or concerts, he was demonic. I believe that the last five years of his music were the pinnacle. I saw him more often then and in the remaining years of his life than I ever had before.

In the spring I went to stay in Milan and look for a house on one of the lakes. At the same time Wally Toscanini was looking for a possible house for her father, because of a question that he might not return to the house he had leased for many years at the Isolino San Giovanni in Lago Maggiore. In the end he did remain at the Isolino for as long as he wanted.

Maestro preferred Lago Maggiore to the Lago di Como. He called the latter "that gloomy pair of trousers" or "that ugly pair of scissors." In a way its geography resembles both. I like the intimacy of Como and the sharp juxtaposition of high mountains to water. At any rate, since houses were being looked at, Wally and I did some of our looking together. One morning she rang me up high-voiced with excitement. She had just heard about a furnished villa near Bellagio, with a beautiful garden, to let for four hundred thousand lire (about $600) the year. It was the house I had seen the previous autumn. Three months before, in January, a woman had committed suicide there. No wonder somebody was giving it away. I knew about it but I said nothing to Wally and we arranged to go out that morning to see the house.

I had been skirting around the place for two weeks. I knew that sooner or later I would go to see it, but like anyone else, and particularly in my state of mind, I was leery of its immediate story. Wally chattered all the way out from Milan; we had something or other to laugh about, and I was feeling well. It was a beautiful windy April day. As I was driving the last couple of kilometers Wally fell silent. I said nothing. Suddenly she said, "Let's not look at that house. I've changed my mind."

"Your mind, *va bene*," I said. "But I mean to look at the house. What's your objection to it?"

"Nothing," she said. "I just don't like the idea any more."

"You mean you are bothered about the woman committing suicide there?"

"How did you know that?" she screamed.

"Try and hide it in a place the size of this. It was the first thing I heard about the house. I've decided I don't care, I want to see it."

"But you can't live in a house where a woman just killed herself!"

I did not labor the point. We arrived at the house, were met by the gardener-caretaker, my dear Giovanni, and shown over the place. The house was deplorable, the furniture monstrous, the condition appalling, the interior ugliness terrifying. But it was exactly the right size, small but well planned. The garden was a dream of beauty. It had been designed and planted by a landscape architect of genius and it was filled with phenomenal roses that were just coming into bloom. The situation was ideal, close to but high above the water, the whole place sheltered by thick plantings of trees. Also I saw it at high noon of a perfect day.

I took the house. It was one of the best decisions I ever made. I had reached for the strongest resource that remained to me— the use of my hands. I must use my hands to do functional things. I have always had this need and I have always been what I once called hand-conscious in the mind of some fictitious character.

Hands are of great significance to me and good hands are hands that are used. At Limonta I had enough occupation for my hands to keep me busy all day long: as much gardening as I wanted to do, though Giovanni was there for the skilled, the heavy, and the boring work; needlepoint; and the cooking. I did all the cooking, because I like to cook, because I had the products of my increasingly splendid vegetable garden and fruit trees and plants, because it is almost impossible to make anything but heavenly food out of the best and freshest Italian raw materials, because my pride and my inventiveness were invoked. I found to my surprise that even then, in 1949, it was difficult in Italy to find a first-class cook and had I hired one, I would have been excluded from my own kitchen and from doing my own marketing, which gives me pleasure in Europe. I like the casual closeness to working-people and peasants, the dialects and colloquialisms, the ridiculous things you see or are part of. Whenever I find myself in a strange town in Europe I head straight for the central market square—again, my need for the functional. After living at Limonta for six months I bought the place.

I had unlimited time free of the pressures and demands which perhaps do not really exist in a city, but which one tells oneself are there to escape the desolation of being alone in the midst of the crowd. It is better to be alone in the midst of growing things and birds and animals and the small immediacies of country life, precipitated by weather or unexpected guests or saving the strawberries from the field-mice or the roses from the *maggiolini* (rosebugs; Italian ones can knock out all others in size alone, but in numbers too.) The daylight hours were filled with small reasons for laughter. I remember how I used to imagine that Jan would have been thankful they were there. The other hours were submerged in books and in music. I read three or four books at a time all during those years; a work of history, one of biography or memoirs, a classic novel and a current one, poetry or essays. Avery Fisher built me the most wonderful gramophone I ever heard and

Louise brought it over by ship, crated and marked, "Property of Arturo Toscanini." I played it at full volume, which was like being in Carnegie Hall. That was how Maestro himself listened to records—to his own with scowling self-criticism; occasionally to one by somebody else, God help him.

The first time Maestro came to Limonta he hopped out of his car carrying a large rolled parcel under his arm. He gave it to me, saying, "Every Italian house that has anything to do with music has one of these and I have brought you yours." It was a color chromo of the Boldini portrait of Verdi. Of itself it is a thing that any picture-minded person would be appalled at; you can buy one in any music store. Maestro told me how it should be framed and where to hang it. It hung there, directly above the phonograph, as long as I lived at Limonta and now it is on the wall of this room where I work, Verdi looking with his quizzical not-quite-smile across the room at a photograph that caught Maestro in a screaming rage at a rehearsal.

He liked to come to my funny house at Limonta. The piano there was a horror, an ancient thing that I rented from a dealer in Como, because the house if closed in winter was too damp for a good piano. Maestro would sit at that awful piano, which was never properly tuned, and play and sing in his cracked voice. Often he played passages from *Lohengrin*. He knew perfectly well that I had a helpless antipathy to Wagner, except for *Die Meistersinger,* and most of all to *Parsifal* and *Lohengrin.*

"*Che bella musica!*" he would say, almost crooning. "*Dimmi, com'è bella, questa musica!*"

I said nothing.

"Do you know what I am playing?" he would say.

"Yes, Maestro."

"But tell me—what is it I am playing?"

"The second act of *Lohengrin,* Maestro."

"*Ignorante!* And you cannot appreciate it."

He came one day in June, 1951. The house was built on the

side of a hill, so that the front door was upstairs and one went down to the main rooms and the terraces over the lake. Maestro had memorized the stairs as he did all stairs he used frequently. Instead of looking at the steps he counted them. "Fourteen— four—three!" Smiling, he gave me a book that he had brought. My mother had given it to him long ago when she first knew him. It was a curious choice—*In a Persian Garden,* music composed by Liza Lehmann to verses from *The Rubaiyat.* It was Liza Lehmann's own copy. I wonder why my mother chose it and where she bought it. She had written a gauche and charming inscription in Italian; her handwriting was still young and un- formed. She must have been twenty-six years old. I remembered her as she was then; so did he, minutely. It was fascinating to listen as Maestro compared me with her; apparently it gave him pleasure. She spoke Italian better than I, but my handwriting was finer than hers. (All his words.) She was intelligent but I was more intelligent. *She* was beautiful! She had a voice and I had not, but I had a better ear and musical memory; this was hard to believe and would have infuriated her. She was warmer and gayer, but I was more *colta*—how can one put that: educated? evolved?

He had also brought the two most newly-issued of his records. The first was *Vltava.* He stood in front of the gramophone, head bent, his hands gripping the lapels of his coat, sometimes un- consciously conducting. I listened without breaking down. Guido Vanzetti, a dear and gentle friend who had brought Maestro out from Milan, turned away from us and wept. Then we played the new record of *Feste Romane,* an imposing, overwhelming per- formance. At that volume it almost blew the house down. Maestro was pleased. Then—suddenly, he was very very old. He lay down on the couch and dozed. Guido and I went out and strolled up and down on the terrace. After a time Maestro called and pre- tended to be offended because I was a bad hostess and had left him alone. We had coffee. I noticed sharply that his hands had changed. I knew what that meant, I was terribly shaken. Even until the past winter they had remained the great, heavy, fleshy artist's hands they had always been; thick-fingered and full of power. Now they were thin, the look of weight was gone from them.

He was very low in mood at that time. Signora Carla, who had been desperately ill for two years, died a fortnight later. Maestro was desolate. His personal world was shattered, his instincts and habits torn from their roots. He had been married for fifty-four years. By his own fiercely uncompromising lights he had been a devoted husband. In his view a man was married once and once only. There was no such thing as divorce. A widower who remarried evoked his vitriolic abuse. Marriage had nothing to do with the women to whom he was susceptible all his life and who found him irresistible. His legend is full of their echoes and their shadows. He had married to have a home and a family, the master key to the Italian character. He once told me that he had waited until the age of thirty to marry because a man was not serious before then; and that he had chosen a woman ten years younger than himself "so that my life would not be disrupted when I was old, I would certainly die before she did."

When she died he shut himself up in his house in Via Durini and for a time declared that he was finished with music, he would never conduct again. He did not touch his piano or open a score. He wanted to see nobody—a difficult feat in Via Durini where Wally's intense gregariousness and hospitality, and the design of the apartment, all the rooms opening into one another, have always kept streams of friends moving through. I went in to Milan to see him, finding him sunken in gloom and muttering the phrase he used whenever things went wrong—"*Povero Toscanini!*" Translated, this would give exactly the opposite impression from what he meant; he was incapable of self-pity, he was the proudest and surest person I have ever known. He loathed to be disoriented, either in art or in life; and if a situation was less than one to precipitate a total outburst, he vented his frustration or annoyance in that phrase.

By the sixth of August he was rehearsing the orchestra at La Scala for some records that he was to make with them. When I slipped into a dark box he was just beginning the overture to *I Vespri Siciliani*. He was building the crescendo drum-roll that follows the opening pianissimo measures. His baton was furiously stirring the air before him in that motion nobody has ever seen from another; he was intent and excited, he sang and shouted, he whipped the music out of himself and the players as he had done twenty and forty years before. Later at dinner he talked about his programmes for the coming season in New York, at the same time complaining that he was old, he did not feel well, his left leg pained him, he could not balance himself as he had always done, "to bring the big fortissimi up from the ground." He meant what we knew who had always seen him at work, what he did in stupendous climaxes like those in the *Meistersinger* Prelude or the Third Leonore. When about to bring these out of the orchestra he would bend his knees a little, his small feet planted apart and gripping the podium like the paws of a cat; his left fist clenched, his right hand holding the baton at a stiff angle, both hands vibrating with passion; his face contorted, his mouth open, shouting for the blast he wanted; he would bring it up out of the floor to the maximum crash of the tympani and the cymbals. I shall always remember the faces of people sitting near me when they heard and saw those climaxes, open-mouthed faces with tears running down their cheeks.

That autumn of 1951 I began to go to New York for the winters, mostly not to miss Maestro's concerts. His son Walter and Walter's lovely late wife, Cia—a celebrated prima ballerina who danced in the *Orfeo* when my mother made her début with Maestro—came to live with him in the big house at Riverdale, where he was really more content than in Milan. He was sentimental about the house in Milan—"my old house, my beautiful old Italian house"—but there was more to interest and occupy him in New York. There was his orchestra and the routine of rehearsals and programme-making, the long gradual process of putting the bulk of his repertoire on records and approving them for release if he was finally satisfied after many trials and rejections. He was no longer opposed to recording as he had once been, but his standards were uncompromising and his demands of himself fanatical. It was usual by that time that any work he played in concert, if not already recorded, was recorded the day after the concert or, if the live performance had satisfied him, taken off the air. Naturally we were eager that everything be preserved. One week he played the Haydn Symphony No. 104. I adore it. When I began months, even years later, to hope it would appear on a record he almost snarled. I asked him why, the more fool I.

"Because it is a *porcheria!*" he snapped. "One note in the Adagio. One note—*basta!*" It has never been released.

I had become fairly artful at the game of getting out of him performances and incidentally, records, of music that I wanted. He knew it was a game, indeed he made it one, with the utmost mischief. It was fatal to ask him outright to play something, a sure guarantee that he would not play it. Only once did I ask for and get a work, one that he had never played before. That was the Mozart Bassoon Concerto, K. 191. Maestro had rung up to talk. For some reason I mentioned the Bassoon Concerto and Maestro said, "Well, if you know it so well, sing it to me." So I did, to whatever extent it is possible for a non-voice to imitate a bassoon. He was enchanted. He said I sang it in tune (B flat), and I did know it. He amused himself for weeks ringing up and saying, "Sing the *fagotto*." So I asked him if he would play it in a concert and he said, "Why not?"

For years he had left the Mendelssohn Fourth, the Italian Symphony, off his programmes. I began to worry lest he come to the end of his life and not leave it recorded. At that time, the early 1950's, there was only one American recording of it—by an illustrious orchestra with a famous conductor for whom Maestro had no use. I took the record to Limonta and one day when Maestro was there and looking round after lunch for musical games to play, I said, "Maestro, I have such a *porcata* here—the only recording of the Mendelssohn Fourth. Just think, there is no other."

Instantly he demanded to hear it. Within two minutes he was in a shouting rage, shaking his fists, screaming, *"Assassino! Mascalzone!"* I got up to stop the machine. "No, No," he cried. "Leave it alone." He was actually enjoying his own torments and he insisted on listening to the whole thing.

The following winter when he was talking about the programmes he was planning he said, "And that week—yes, that is three weeks—I think I play Mendelssohn."

No cry of joy from me. "How nice," I said, or something equally untypical.

"Mendelssohn *Fifth*," he said. I played right up. "Oh, how wonderful, how heavenly, the Reformation Symphony!" (And it is.) Not a word was said about the Fourth.

So he played the Fifth, a concert I remember like yesterday. And a few weeks later, without a word about it, he played the Fourth. The two exist today on two faces of the same record, one of the treasures of his legacy.

Every writer uses devices, if not outright tricks, to get himself stirred up so that he will start to write. What rouses me and shoots through me a charge of adrenalin strong enough to boot me into action is to play records of Maestro's. I stay in the closed room with the music, the volume at maximum. There is nothing related to writing in the room. I stand in the middle of the floor, concentrating hard. What music I choose is decided by aspects of what I have to do. It will be music by one of the titans, strong in structure, positive, powerfully melodic. As it surrounds me I start to pace up and down the room or sometimes round and round in

a circle; this is unconscious, I think of it only now in describing
the experience. When I must work out something very tough and
seemingly beyond me I need a fugue, a form to which Maestro
himself was not partial. I believe he felt constrained by the rigidity
of the form, which is strange in view of his own exactitude and his
search for absolute precision and fidelity to the score. But that
was the foundation; above it soared his lyric genius, his reiteration
that music is song, that it must breathe; his exhortations to his
orchestra to sing, sing—as he sang, unconsciously and constantly,
while he was conducting. I know in which passages of his recorded
work I can hear him singing in his hoarse, toneless voice. I do not
often deliberately seek these out, that would be sentimentality. It
is enough to know that they are there.

I never told Maestro about this and now I wonder why. He
would not have been displeased. It would not have surprised him
had I said he was inseparable from my work; but then he was inseparable from my life. He was permanence. He was continuity. He
was the person other than my mother whom I had loved always
and who would be spared for me to love the longest. The later
years were when I had outgrown the diffidence of youth and the
impediment of being too shy in his presence to say a word that was
not a predictable bore. He was interested in an astonishing amount
of the minutiae of life, mine or any friend's with whom he was intimate. He would question and cross-question about some happening or encounter, wanting to know every detail. He spent a large
part of his leisure talking on the telephone, mostly during the
night. He slept very little, and then only in snatches. He was one
of the men of extraordinary powers who have proved that they
need only about four hours' sleep a night. He went very late to
bed. When he had guests he liked them to stay late and we usually
left his house, or he ours, long past midnight. After he had retired
to his room he would begin to ring up any of several close friends
with whom he would talk; long talk that might continue the best
part of an hour. His intimates were used to the ringing of their

bedside telephones at one or two o'clock in the morning: Maestro, restless and sleepless, or just waked from a cat-nap, wanting to talk.

His talk ranged over a vast span of time and, naturally, of musical life. His memory was the same precision instrument whether he was using it in the service of his art or for the pleasures of conversation which, in the last years of his life when I was closest to him, inevitably meant a great deal of reminiscence. But even when he was in his late eighties, reminiscence did not mean senile repetition of what he had said before. It did mean clear and astonishingly touching memories of his childhood and youth; of his nine years, from the age of nine, as a pensioner in the Music Conservatory of Parma, a State institution in which the students lived a life of austerity almost suggestive of a reform school. They were the sons of poor or even penniless parents, who were being trained by the State to be professional musicians. The school paid for their tuition and board and the uniforms that they wore. They never had vacations. On Sundays between eleven o'clock and noon, they were permitted visitors, but the mother of little Arturo Toscanini never came to see him.

"Oh!" I said, aching at the thought, "how could she? Why?"

"I don't know," he replied. "She never loved me."

"But that's not possible! You must have been a beautiful child—and surely she was proud of you?" (He received the highest marks all the time he was a student; and a good classical education besides the musical training.)

"Eh!" he said. "I don't know. But she never loved me and I never loved her. I only loved my aunt."

In an Italian woman this indifference to her son seems inconceivable. The suggestion by an Italian biographer that the mother was humiliated by poverty and did not possess a dress she considered presentable, seems unrealistic to me. Poverty is no disgrace in Italy, it has always been the greatest common denominator. The little boy was undaunted by it. The reason why he always had a special affection for the Beethoven Septet in E flat,

Opus 20, was because it was the first score he ever owned. While he was a student he lived on bread and soup, selling his tiny portions of meat to the other boys for coppers which he saved until he had enough to buy the score.

Through the early 1950's his music became other-worldly in its beauty, to me superhuman because his strength was fading, his health frail, he growing very old. The sharp sculptured lines of his head and profile became softer, hazier, as though seen from a distance. His phenomenal heart and circulatory system which all his life had been like a young man's, now from time to time gave reason for alarm. Each season he said was his last, he spoke of retiring, but each season for three years there was a resurgence of his powers that cannot have been other than mystical. On his eighty-sixth birthday, the twenty-fifth of March, 1953, he rehearsed the *Missa Solemnis* of Beethoven from eleven o'clock in the morning until late afternoon. He had not worked with greater dedication and intensity and, I remember, patience, that I could ever recall. To him the *Missa Solemnis* was almost not to be performed, so much closer, he thought, to Beethoven in eternity than to the powers of musicians. It was terrifying to see how he spent himself that day. Yet when he spoke about it he only said, "I cannot understand it myself. The force is no longer in me—I draw it from the music."

In that decade I learned to live with the reality that life is what wise friends of mine have called putting one foot before the other. It was a hard lesson to learn. Always before there had been the sense of propulsive purpose, the urge to be where I had to be because ideas and the characters who personified them came to me that way. I have never travelled for the sake of travelling but I did travel a great deal and I always wound up wondering, "What good is this for my purposes when what I need is Prague?" But Prague was gone and I knew it and tried to stay fixed in the knowledge; and yet I had no peace of it. I wanted to go there and I did not want to go; several times I thought to still the turmoil of uprootedness, to clear away the ragged ends of the unfinished by going there. It was not possible. So I went back and forth between Limonta and New York, vividly grateful for the few but elemental ties, the people who kept me in their lives.

Music was the mainstream and on it there came for the fourth time in my life a voice that gave me whole, total satisfaction, the voice of Leontyne Price. The experience is an acute one, beyond volition, beyond analyzing; wholly personal, not to be sought for but to be possessed by. When I heard her sing the music of Pamina I knew that her voice and her art were part of the keystone of my life and mind. Her instinct for Mozart is preternatural. She is by any measure a great artist, a profound musician with natural gifts that are the mystery in which such quality lives. She has become a treasured friend, a companion in what I know and care most about; a relationship whose outer tegument is warmth and laughter. So much of her art is realized in the music of Verdi and most of all in the *Requiem,* which she sings as nobody else in my lifetime has sung it, that I am always regretting the circumstance that made her too young to have sung with Maestro.

I have never dwelt in memory on his last concert, the fourth of April, 1954. He did not dwell on it. But one should not suppose he did not realize what happened. He knew. He had a moment of dizziness or faintness; this had happened to him several times at home. With it or part of it was a momentary lapse of memory and that too had happened at home. When I saw him on Christmas Day, 1953, he was alone in his studio with his head in his hands, desperately upset because he said he could not remember the words of one of Riccardo's arias in *Un Ballo in Maschera,* which he was about to begin rehearsing for two concert performances in January. Only the words, he said; one aria. Timidly I suggested that the words were hardly the music. He flared up and said that if he did not know by memory every word as well as every note for every voice and instrument in an opera he was not fit to conduct it. He was beside himself. He ordered the rehearsals cancelled. But a few days later all was well. He remembered the words, he remembered everything. The rehearsals were vigorous and sure, the performance one of his best. He had a special sentiment for the opera, one of the first Verdi scores he had conducted in his youth. Perhaps my imagination intensifies this fresh and youthful brilliance all through the recording because of what he said; more probably my imagination has nothing to do with it. It is there.

The forty-five years of my memories of his music have filled my mind so entirely that I believe they literally crowd out that final moment when his right hand faltered and his left hand covered his eyes. I can remember the cold terror at seeing it happen, but none of the sound of the *Tannhäuser* Bacchanale. I can see him dropping his baton and lunging off his podium at the end of the *Meistersinger* Prelude, but what I heard I do not know because I was sensible only of concern for him. I have a lifetime of *Meistersinger* Preludes, all grown into one mighty C major affirmation of immortality.

His last years were eloquent of the Italian nature. Something in this explains the great longevity of Italians, their essential qualities of patience, resignation, a deep resource of endurance. He was calm about the approaching end of his life; fearless because that was himself; sometimes bored and a little fretful. Mostly he was tender and gentle and he held the links of attachment firm about him, his son and his daughters, his old friends. All my life he had been teaching me something fundamental and at the end he taught me not to shrink from the inevitability that was drawing him away. There was no panic in facing his death when there were so many ways in which he would never die.

On Christmas night of 1956 I was with him at Riverdale; a number of us were there as we had been for years on end. I sat beside him at dinner. It was easiest for him to be near someone with whom he felt no sense of effort. He was not well that evening, he was far away and spoke almost not at all. One week later on

New Year's Eve I was there again for the traditional *Capodanno* party, always more a festivity with Italians than Christmas. Maestro was much better. Again I sat beside him and he talked about memories of long ago and counted out the years of friendship that had begun with my mother. At midnight we all rose and circled the table with our glasses of champagne and kissed cheeks and exchanged good wishes. Maestro had not been in such good spirits for a long time. I felt we should leave as early as possible so that he should not be overtired, but it was some time before he was ready for the party to break up. We said our good-nights and left him sitting in his high-backed yellow damask chair. I went to the anteroom which adjoins the coat-room and I heard Maestro speak to me. He had followed me. He held my hands and I kissed him good-night again. He was in a lovely mood, tender and smiling. I looked into his eyes, filmed with that odd milky lustre which was not part of his failing sight; his eyes had always been so. At that moment a certainty came to me that I would never see him again.

I was right. At dawn that day he suffered the first of the cerebral hemorrhages of which he died on the morning of the sixteenth of January. He was eighty-nine years old.

I wrote a novel about hermits, a pretty good one. Often I was asked why I had chosen the subject. Sometimes I was tempted to answer with the truth; but I did not because fiction should be its own exegesis. I am a hermit myself. I am not entirely a hermit any more than I am entirely anything else. The Geminian nature is said to be dual or multiple, and even though that may be nonsense, it is as good a rationale as another. Only two motivations have run undeflected throughout my life, the one since infancy, the other since my first work: music and the enigmatic thralldom of Prague. The former flows through everything I write and must feel before I can write. The latter did the same until an alien force brutally dammed the stream, wrecking the slight bark in which sketches and fragile materials had been tentatively set afloat. I struggled for years with the wreckage. I thought I had a novel to write and I had not. I tried to write what has become this book, parts of which have existed for more than fifteen years. But I could master neither book. I was haunted and hagridden by the monstrosity of that dam. My vision was blocked, my imagination paralyzed; what I needed for fiction I could not devise; what I needed for reality I could not make real. I had to see Prague once again, even though I knew I would see and learn nothing there that I did not already know. I had to exorcise the spell there where it had been cast on me. I could no longer live or try to work under the obstruction of that dam.

By 1965, economic realities and a broadening distension in the world had lightened the monolithic Iron Curtain. It was possible for anybody to go to Prague and I decided I would go. I had no purpose except my own inner necessity; a few days would suffice. I went by road, driving myself. It was the most familiar way to go, it gave me the closest view of the countryside and the villages and the ordinary people, not so many of whom I had known individually, but whose lives and world I had shared for so many years. It was as though I had never been away, in the feel of the land and the streaming rain and the dear ugly language and the ease I felt amongst the people. Somehow the time element of lunch got overlooked on the day I drove from Nürnberg to Prague; in one town it was too early, in another it would be too late. By two o'clock one had to eat somewhere. I was in a village west of Plzeň, the great industrial town with the world-renowned brewery. They told me that the only eating-place was the workmen's buffet, where they eat standing up at high counters. A huge bowl of tasty soup with filling things in it; some chunks of good black bread; a mug of beer. It cost less than ten cents. I was astonished to hear myself speak without hesitation.

In the towns the people looked comfortable. They were presently dressed and stoutly shod, they all wore raincoats of some plastic material in bright colors. There were as many red cheeked, bundled-up children as ever, and as many of the squat hooded perambulators in which the babies are taken out. The people looked as they always had. The villages did not. There was a pall of disrepair and disjointedness over them, most readily understood as the transition from what they used to be to the depersonalization and centrally planned industrialization which has overthrown the rural world and its people and their land-oriented life—even the animals who were part of it. I never saw a goose in the countryside.

I was deeply moved to be there again. By instinct I felt bound to it as I always had; in that sense it struck me in what I must call my heart. Not in the slight, sentimental, unthinking use of the word; but the actual clutch which tells us when we are confronted with belonging to somebody or something. Thereafter, I would see what I knew how to recognize, the effect of what had happened to this place and these people, the slam of brute materialism straight to the brain, to the mind, to the head, whatever you call your power of reason and comprehension. First I would see and feel that something was what it had always been; then I would look again and know that it was not. The double-punch hit me all the time, all day every day. One in the heart, one in the head, one-two, one-two . . .

The first morning I drove up to the hill, naturally by way of the Bridge. Neither then nor at any time did I see or have any sense that I was followed or watched. I was not only let alone; I had the feeling of never having been so alone. There would have been no point in keeping me under surveillance, I had nothing to hide, no motive in being there that could have concerned them; and they were unconcerned. I was relieved to be ignored. The ignoring showed how firmly they are in control of the present, how much they have erased the past, at least in the awareness of those who were not part of it.

I could not have believed that after seventeen years every

inch of the way would remain as familiar as though I had never been away. I drove around the square and turned left up Nerudová, the steep mediaeval street which for six hundred years has been one of the great beauties of Prague. This is the street I have described, with the hand-wrought iron signs hanging overhead from the master artisans' shops, the whimsical signs with the golden whiskers. I had hungered to see this once again and I turned up Nerudová almost literally with a watering mouth.

The signs are gone.

From each house there sticks out a blunt iron rod, its raw end rusting where the sign was lopped off. I stopped the car—not the thing to do on so steep and narrow a street—and sat there staring, too outraged even to weep. I did not even immediately perceive the reason for this act of vandalism. Then as I got the car moving uphill again I knew of course that they had done this with savage intent to obliterate the symbols of private trade. Only then did I pause to peer at the pathetic little shops which had once been the pride of the best craftsmen and tradesmen; my upholsterer had been the proprietor of one, my cabinet-maker of another, a fine fancy baker of another. Now they are faceless and I suppose purposeless, each one part of a *Národný Podnik* (nationalized business) where there is nothing much to buy and nobody to care whether there are clients to serve or anything to supply them. By this time I was angry, and that was my mood as I made the sharp hairpin turn to the right and up to Hradčanské Náměstí, where I had so often ridden with Jan, watching his face as we approached the Hrad.

Desuetude and wilful shabbiness had sullied the way so far, but before the Hrad everything gleamed. At the gates stood armed guards, crack soldiers in the acme of spit and polish; and around them, desertion. In the old days, in the time of President Masaryk and of Edvard Beneš, the people had been encouraged to visit Hradčany, to bring the children and the dog, to walk through its maze of Gothic courtyards, to inspect the state rooms of the castle, to pray in Svatý Vit, the Cathedral; to light tapers in St. George's Church, to show wondering strangers the fairy-tale two-room houses of Zlatá Ulička (The Little Golden Street); to enjoy their common possession of one of the very great architectural treasures of the world.

There was not a soul in sight.

Mr. Novotný was inside, being President of nothingness.

I moved on past the Archbishop's Palace (Beran is a Cardinal now, ending his life in exile in Rome) and into Loretanská, where I parked the car at the bottom of the street. I walked slowly back to the place I had loved better than any other in the world, back to the setting of loveliness and tenderness and horror. I stayed on the north side of the street, across from my house, and stood where Jan had walked the last time I saw him, slowly going up the hill as I watched him from my dark window. I looked at the house, and at those on either side, to my mind as beautiful a row of baroque houses as there is in Europe. It was their tender butter-yellow stucco that had captivated me thirty-five years before and haunted me every day since; the yellow houses in one of which I promised myself I would spend the end of my life.

The houses are grey.

I could not believe it. I had first to make sure that I was not addled by emotion and confused in memory. Yellow?—of course, yellow! Then I realized. I had seen in Italy, where yellow-washed stucco is the commonest building-material, that at regular intervals the stucco must be preserved with a fresh coat of yellow wash which contains a certain quantity of reinforcement for the surface of the stucco. I had kept my own garage and gardener's cottage at Limonta in good repair in just that way, a utilitarian cottage of no significance at all.

And here—where even in the seven years of Hitler the houses were kept in reasonable repair—nothing whatever had been done for seventeen years to preserve them. The golden glow was gone from my dream house, actually as well as in imagination; and from all its neighbors too. They stood there shabby, crumbling, colorless. I could have screamed with pain. But there was worse. I have described the beautiful double casement windows which had been installed in the eighteenth century. Out there across the street I stood and looked in horror. The outer casements, with their graceful frames, had been ripped from every window in the house—from all three stories and the tiny dormers under the roof. Where they had been torn away the raw stucco had crumbled and the weather had wrought its ruin. I could not believe my eyes.

A few steps up the hill the street widens to Loretanské Náměstí, the great open square on two levels. On the lower level faces the church of the Loreta, on the upper the Černinský Palác. I have written all there is to say of my associations with these. On this April morning I had planned to be in the square exactly at noon, because I wanted to know whether the carillon still played St. Mary's Hymn, followed by the great bell striking the hour.

I think I expected them to have silenced the melancholy lovely music which my heart's and my mind's ear will hear until I die. I would not have been surprised at that. I stood alone in the square—I am still haunted by the unnatural desertion of the scene—and as my watch showed twelve o'clock the sounds began.

Cracked? Rusted? Bungled? I do not know. The hymn came forth, out of tune, out of time, the melody garbled, the tone wheezing and feeble. I realized I had never had the curiosity to learn what sort of carillon it was, whether played mechanically or by hand. I supposed the latter. What I heard was desecration. The great bell began the twelve strokes of noon—also sourly out of tune—but suddenly its broken voice was drowned by a roar like the end of the world. I cowered there with my hands covering my ears. A flight of jet fighters had buzzed the square, I later learned, practising the fly-past for part of the coming May Day parade.

When I had pulled myself together I walked slowly to the church. I have prayed in it before and I meant to do so again, though for what except to thank God that Jan had not had to witness these defilements, I do not know. The doors were locked and nailed to the centre one was a weather-beaten piece of cardboard on which was scrawled, "Closed indefinitely for repairs."

So was every other church that I approached closely enough to examine, particularly in the countryside. I do not know what it meant that the famous baroque church of St. Nicholas in Malostranské Náměstí was shrouded in scaffolding, with notices mounted that the church was under restoration; but I would not be surprised one day if it were reopened as a museum.

I have described how the rear side of the house where I lived overlooked a sweeping expanse of park and green hills. Like ancient houses elsewhere, notably in Bergamo, which are built on steep hills that later evolved into streets, the lowest level of my house held the garden that went with my lease. Like every garden in Prague it had a plum tree and a lilac, so old and so tall that its branches hung over the garden wall above the street. In the coldest and wettest spring in years I could not hope for the last time to see and smell the wonderful lilacs of Prague; they would not bloom until late May. But I wanted at least to see the tight dark buds of my lilac if there were any. So I walked down the steep decline of Úvoz and looked up. The lilac had been neglected but I did not linger over its sad condition because I was looking up at the whole rear elevation of the house, with its square tower that held my bedroom and the windows from which we used to lean out to look at Prague in the twilight and listen to the bells.

It was almost a ruin.

Slabs and chunks of the exterior stucco had fallen away, to expose the raw masonry underneath. From this side too every outer casement had been ripped away, leaving the broken walls stained and streaked, the water running from the jagged corners.

What was left of the surface was cracked and crumbling, the color of dry bones.

If all this wrack and ruin had come about because the Communist coup had impoverished the property's owners there would be nothing to say. But the owners, and the owners of all the land and all the buildings in the country had been summarily dispossessed by the first moves of the Red revolution. All land and buildings were seized by the state. There had long been a crucial housing shortage in Prague. The war and the subsequent bureaucracy brought further masses to the capital; it is self-evident that mass housing was an urgent need and mass housing, hideous but functional, has mushroomed all over the city and throughout the country too. I suppose statistics could be cited to show that there was no public money and no labor to waste (they would say) on the repair and maintenance of beautiful old houses. But those in the historic parts of Prague are still the choice places to live, and space in them is assigned to bureaucrats and 'reliable' individuals who are entitled to preference.

Adequate maintenance and repair have been given the historic buildings (all former palaces of the hereditary nobility) which are used as government ministries and for other public purposes. Where it is desirable to scrub the city's face and clean its finger-nails as representative of the Communist image, the face and hands are clean. To my eyes the ruin of lovely once-private houses is sheer sabotage, wanton reprisal against former private property and the traditions both of aristocratic architecture and of the small shopkeeper or artisan who was the basic town-dweller of mediaeval cities like Prague.

I went to hear *The Bartered Bride*. I do not know how many times I have heard it in the National Theatre in Prague, but tens of times; and in many different productions in thirty-five years. They varied according to the stage techniques of their epochs. This work of art is the national opera of a peasant people and their indigenous expressions—their folk music and dancing, their choral singing, their national costume—are its flesh and blood. *Prodaná Nevěsta* has been performed with love and pride on occasions of the deepest national significance, as it was when the theatre reopened for the first time after the Nazis were gone. The opera has a new production again, a couple of years old. I wondered what the difference would be.

The overture began. I was dazzled by the orchestra, especially the strings and woodwinds. They played like the best chamber-music artists; their tone was silky, their execution virtuoso. We have no such opera orchestra. I was a little puzzled by the absence of power and substance where the big climaxes come, but I asked myself no questions then. The chorus was good. The solo artists, except for the mezzo who sang the mother, were crude. The performance had no punch, no drive. The sets were like a couple of cheap postcards. The costumes were caricatures of a lost tradition. Everything possible had been done to obliterate the memory of Sunday best and village festivity, of the handing-down from mother to daughter of headdresses and richly-embroidered silken aprons, the treasured possessions of wealthy peasants owning their own land. The high kid boots are gone. Is this to suggest that the régime has eliminated the mud from country lanes and dooryards? I saw more mud there than I remember from ever before.

My memory bruised by the travesties of scene and costume, I nonetheless gave the fine orchestra and chorus their due and sat back to wait for the polka, the climax of every performance, which always reminded me that the dancers must have been born doing those steps in their native villages.

There was no polka.

To Smetana's music there was danced a bad imitation of early-century Russian-oriented ballet, something you would see in a dull Broadway show due for a quick flop. I was more disgusted than disappointed, for stupidity is intensely disgusting. These people in their determination to manhandle any idea sprung from and evocative of national tradition had thrown away the very elements which in any country, Communist or not, would be a matter for pride if not propaganda.

Of course I am prejudiced. I shall be thought old and inflexible, unrealistic about the world as it is, incapable of evaluating the changes that are here to stay and the differences that have come with the modifications of the outmoded Iron Curtain. As a contemporary note I append that I have seen the widely admired Czechoslovak film, *The Shop on Main Street*. It deserves all the encomia it has received. It is a work of art, a sincere and subtle reevocation of the Nazi years and the degradation of the Slovak Hlinka Guards who were taught by Hitler's S S to hound and violate the Jews. Has anybody pointed out that similar methods were used by Czechoslovaks against their own people after 1948?

The day was sunny and fresh, almost the only day it did not rain, an April day in the open rolling country under the great high sky I love. The state highroad used to pass through the village of Lány. The small walled cemetery was on the right of the road going west from Prague. The state roads have been widened and improved; this one has been deflected before the village in a curve to the left so that the old original road which is much narrower continues on inconspicuously and one would not know the way to the cemetery unless one had been familiar with it. It has been cut off from the stream of notice and accessibility.

It is just the same, a small island of the Old World in every sense, peaceful and tender inside its sheltering walls. On the right towards the far corner, surrounded by a low picket fence, are the graves of the Masaryks, the Founder-President's in the middle, his wife's on his right, his son Jan's on his left. They are beautifully tended and green. Each has a small bronze marker, not over three inches high: the name, the dates of birth and death. There were no such before, it was a tradition indicated by his wish that the grave of T. G. Masaryk was unmarked. But his name was borne by elements of national life throughout the country he created; streets and parks and bridges and institutions and the halls of learning and enlightenment and foundations for the people's welfare. The name lived in speech and habits and tributes. Now it is erased—except from three small plaques in the silence of Lány and from the mind of whoever wants to remember it in his own silence.

It gave me peace to be there. The summing-up came as I had sensed it would. I had known that I could not relinquish Prague until I had seen it once again. And I could not come to what I had long known about Jan until I drew the reality from the earth where he lies. It is better for him that he died when he did. If he had lived longer his life would have been intolerable. I do not know that any help or comfort in this world could have been solace for the loss of his country; I do not know that I or any dedication or devotion could have made his life endurable. At last I could thank God that Jan was at peace, that he had not had to witness from the indignity of exile the degradation of Czechoslovaks who violated their birthright, betrayed their country, and deserted, in Jan's own words, "the lovely Bohemian tradition against cynical and well-organized material dialectics."

There is a design and there is continuity throughout the apparent disparities of life and fate. There is relation amongst the men and women who as I said at the beginning of this book have been the substance of my life, though some were very remote from others. It does all tie together, it does all flow from one source, breaking off into smaller tributaries, then finally flowing together again to form the broad stream from which I look back now. I remember the morning of November the twenty-first, 1952. It was the final rehearsal for Maestro's broadcast concert of the next day; the second act of *Orfeo*. That day there happened what we of music know so well—that the final rehearsal or the dress rehearsal is more perfect, more inspired than the performance, unforgettable though the performance remains. Carnegie Hall was dark and the few of us scattered about in it were close to Maestro. Nobody else, I think, could have listened with the emotions that I felt. Nobody else could have seen what I saw, his beautiful white head gleaming in the single strong light against the memory of the young head and face that had entered the mind of a child forty-three years before—precisely one month short of the very day. He was eighty-five years old. He was transfigured by this music; he was all demon and all god, all fury and all sacrament. It is pagan, yes, but it is the rest of belief and humanity too. It is universal. I heard my mother again, I looked into the world she had opened to me with the music she sang, with the books she gave me that led me to legend and fantasy. I followed where they had drawn me, they and the music that she and Maestro had made my life. I followed again where that music had led me, to Mozart, to his time and his world, to the first book I had to write, to Prague. I listened to that music transported as I have never been before or ever since, overwhelmed by the meaning of what I heard and saw, close in mind to the sense of life and death. This is where I came in, I told myself, and this is where I go out.

It is no accident that the word love, particularly as a noun, has been used sparingly in this book. It is a word that cannot stand over-use, a word to be kept for the silences of life. The love that I have known and the knowledge it has given me are the root and the flower, the reason and the force, the beginning and the end. I am not the one to sum this up, because John Dryden has done it for us all:

> Time and Death shall depart, and say in flying,
> Love has found out a way to live, by dying.

It is spring. My thoughts go to the garden which gave me

delight and consolation for so many years. I think of my roses, the fantastic result of an accident of soil chemistry which made that rocky hillside the medium for great strong shrubs well grafted to yield a Redouté rendering of the world's loveliest flower. Earlier the spring flowers, the spurred aquilegia in its misty colorings, the proud foxglove, the green hillsides sparkling with white and yellow narcissus in the fresh new grass. The thick row of multicolored hyacinths heavy-scented in the bed across the front of the house; later the tall jolly hollyhocks. The rampant vines of solanum with its panicles of china-blue flowers. The dense wistaria roof trained by Giovanni's genius hand to cover the struts of the pergola and give fragrant shade for luncheon over the water. The jasmine climbing and breathing scent all over the house, the perfume of pittasporum in the spring darkness and of oleofragrans in the autumn. Why did I leave it? Sometimes I do not know. Age, probably; I am too old to stretch myself to the care of two places which a solitary person cannot fully use. I thought I might be relieved to find life simplified as most of my generation have simplified it, reduced to one house where one gathers together one's dearest things, music and records and books and pictures and old china and the rest of it; basically to live there, going elsewhere briefly when one felt the need. A good idea; perhaps I thought the time had come for it. And if it were to be one place only, then it must be in my own country. I had come to terms in myself with that too.

But now that I have done it and tried some years of it I am not sure. The cat still prowls. It must be where it is not, it must come and go. I wonder. I long for my trees and my flowers, my fruit and my vegetables, for life in several languages, for the beloved sight of ancient roofs. Can one ever be satisfied? I think not. It is a discontent that I must still put to use.

Index

INDEX

INDEX

INDEX

INDEX

INDEX

INDEX